IET COMPUTING SERIES 48

Demystifying Graph Data Science

Other volumes in this series:

Demystifying Graph Data Science

Graph algorithms, analytics methods, platforms, databases, and use cases

Edited by
Pethuru Raj, Abhishek Kumar, Vicente García Díaz and Nachamai Muthuraman

The Institution of Engineering and Technology

Published by The Institution of Engineering and Technology, London, United Kingdom

The Institution of Engineering and Technology is registered as a Charity in England & Wales (no. 211014) and Scotland (no. SC038698).

© The Institution of Engineering and Technology 2022

First published 2022

The Institution of Engineering and Technology
Futures Place
Kings Way, Stevenage
Hertfordshire SG1 2UA, United Kingdom

www.theiet.org

British Library Cataloguing in Publication Data
A catalogue record for this product is available from the British Library

ISBN 978-1-83953-488-1 (hardback)
ISBN 978-1-83953-489-8 (PDF)

Typeset in India by MPS Limited
Printed in the UK by CPI Group (UK) Ltd, Croydon

Cover Image: Ani_Ka via Getty Images

Contents

15 Graph data science for cybersecurity   **325**
Pethuru Raj and Nachamai Muthuraman

16 The machine learning algorithms for data science applications   **345**
Pethuru Raj, D. Peter Augustine and P. Beaulah Soundarabai

About the Editors

Pethuru Raj is the chief architect and vice president in the Site Reliability Engineering (SRE) division of Reliance Jio Platforms Ltd., Bangalore, India. He focuses on emerging technologies such as the Internet of Things (IoT), artificial intelligence (AI), big and fast data analytics, blockchain, digital twins, cloud-native computing, edge & fog clouds, reliability engineering, microservices architecture (MSA), and event-driven architecture (EDA). He has authored and edited 20 technology books. He holds a CSIR-sponsored PhD degree from Anna University, India.

Abhishek Kumar is an assistant professor at Chitkara University Research and Innovation Network (CURIN), Chitkara University, India. His research areas include artificial intelligence, image processing, computer vision, data mining, and machine learning. He has been session chair and keynote speaker at many international conferences and webinars in India and abroad. He has authored, co-authored, and edited several books. He is a senior member of the IEEE, a member of IAENG (International Association of Engineers), and an associate member of IRED (Institute of Research Engineers and Doctors). He holds a PhD degree in computer science from the University of Madras, India.

Vicente García Díaz is an associate professor in the Department of Computer Science at the University of Oviedo, Spain. His teaching interests are primarily in the design and analysis of algorithms and the design of domain-specific languages. His current research interests include decision support systems, health informatics, and eLearning. He is a managing editor of the *International Journal of Interactive Multimedia and Artificial Intelligence* and an associate editor of *IEEE Access*. He is a member of IEEE. He received his PhD degree in computer science from the University of Oviedo.

Nachamai Muthuraman is a data scientist in the strategy team at Siemens Healthcare Pvt. Ltd, Bangalore, India. She works on artificial intelligence, big data analytics, and deep learning. She has gained in-depth proficiency in model building particularly in computer vision, pattern recognition, cognitive modeling, convolution neural networks, and data representation. She has chaired numerous sessions and conferences and been a part of many IT workshops/technical talks/panel discussions both in academics and industry. She holds a PhD in artificial intelligence from Mother Teresa Women's University, India.

Book preface

With the faster maturity and stability of digital technologies, we are being bombarded with zillions of digital entities, connected devices, and microservices. These interact purposefully to create huge sets of poly-structured digital data. The challenge is how to transition data into information and into knowledge. There are data analytics methods in plenty. The pace of data analytics is gaining the much-needed speed and sagacity with the continuous contributions of product and tool vendors. Data science is the domain increasingly associated with data analytics. There are big, fast and streaming data analytics platforms, frameworks, accelerators, toolkits, etc. for making data analytics simpler, faster and affordable.

In the big data world, NoSQL and distributed SQL databases gained the market and mind shares fast. Graph databases are one of the prominent NoSQL databases. Data representation through graphs has laid down a stimulating foundation to visualize and realize a stream of fresh capabilities.

On the other hand, the analytical competency is significantly improved through the faster maturity and stability of artificial intelligence (AI) algorithms [machine and deep learning (ML/DL)]. Thus, the classical and current data science paradigm is substantially advanced to have sophisticated abilities through the direct and distinct empowerment of AI algorithms. There is a twist now. Applying the AI-inspired data science methods on graph-structured data is being seen as a clear-cut gamechanger for the digital world. Extracting hidden patterns, useful associations, impending risks, future opportunities, and other useful and usable insights out of data heaps through data science platforms, frameworks, and engines is the new normal. Especially data science on graph data is acquiring special significance as there is a solid understanding that the blending of graphs and data science techniques can bring in a lot of noteworthy innovations and transformations.

Corporations are continuously seeking fresh ways to use their data to drive business innovations and disruptions to bring in real digital transformation. Supported by query languages, databases, algorithms, platforms, analytics methods and machine and deep learning (ML and DL) algorithms, graphs are now emerging as a new data structure for optimally representing a variety of data and their intimate relationships. This edited book aims to explain the various aspects and importance of graph data science. Graph analytics is being touted as the best way forward compared to traditional analytics methods. These methods are intrinsically capable of creating business value by intelligently leveraging connected data. The connectedness of data points facilitates the identification of clusters of related data points based on levels of influence, association, interaction frequency, and probability. Graph analytics is being empowered through a host of path-breaking analytics techniques to explore and pinpoint beneficial relationships between different entities such as organizations, people, transactions, etc.

The overwhelming idea is to create a database of *things connecting to other things*. Those things might be people connecting to other people through social and professional websites. Or they may be flights flying between cities across the globe. Graphs are hugely popular in enhancing search capabilities, recommending products to online buyers, detecting fraud, identifying the shortest route from one place to another, etc.

Graph data science is a technology-driven approach to discover knowledge from graph-represented data. Experts have pointed out that graph data science has the inherent strength to bring forth a suite of business, technical and user cases.

In this book, we are to cover the various aspects of graph data science and how it can be a game-changer for the data analytics domain. The prominent chapters of this book are

Graph technology – This chapter covers graph theory concepts to build a strong and sustainable foundation to better understand graph analytics techniques and tools. Different types of graphs are discussed, as well as the latest trends and transitions happening in the graph technology space.

Depicting graph algorithms – Having understood the significance of graph algorithms and analytics, researchers, and experts have come up with a number of graph-specific algorithms which are enabling and empowering graph analytics. This chapter presents promising and prominent graph algorithms such as *Community Detection* which detects group clustering or partition options; *Centrality* (Importance) which is for determining the significance of distinct nodes in the network; *Similarity* which evaluates how similar nodes are; *Heuristic Link Prediction* that estimates the likelihood of nodes forming a relationship; and *Pathfinding & Search* which finds optimal paths and evaluates route availability and quality.

Introducing graph analytics – All kinds of collected and cleansed data are being investigated to extrapolate hidden insights out of data. Graph analytics is gaining prominence as traditional data analytics methods have failed to bring deeper and decisive insights out of data. Graph analytics (also called network analysis) is the analysis of relations among entities such as customers, products, solutions, services, operations, and devices. This chapter focuses on promising and potential techniques for augmenting graph analytics.

Graph databases and toolkits – A graph database is a database designed to treat the relationships between data as equally important to the data itself. They are used for performing advanced graph analytics by connecting nodes and creating relationships (edges) in the form of graphs that can be queried by users. This chapter introduces leading graph databases and how they can simplify next-generation graph analytics.

Business use cases – In this chapter, we present several business use cases showing applications of graph analytics such as clustering, partitioning, search, shortest path solution, widest path solution, finding connected components, and page rank.

Towards graph data science – Machine and deep learning (ML/DL) algorithms support the discovery in real time of personalized, predictive, and prescriptive insights out of data via Big Data and Streaming analytics platforms. With the maturity of graph analytics, data science will get a strong boost from graph data science. This chapter shows data science capabilities and how the domain of data science is to be strengthened and solidified with the arrival of graph analytics.

Pethuru Raj
Vice President, Edge AI Division
Reliance Jio Platforms Ltd
Bangalore, India
https://peterindia.net/MyBooks.html

Chapter 1
Toward graph data science

Srinivas Kumar Palvadi[1], K.G.M. Pradeep[2], Thota Siva Ratna Sai[3], D. Rammurthy[2] and Vishal Dutt[4]

Abstract

In this chapter, we are focusing on how the work with graph concepts in the data science and also going to focus how advantageous is to use graphical representations in data science. We also refer the best-suited algorithm for the successful working of the project. Here we can perform the variations by using one algorithm to the other algorithm in various modes. By doing the comparison process among the various algorithms, we can expect the result in the better manner as well as more efficient manner. The author Nolan brought the concept of graphs in the computing environment for making calculation, to show the variations of various models and many more. By embedding computing with the statistics will be helpful for the better understanding and also the number of employment is rising because of merging graph techniques in machine learning. To bring up the difference or to bring up the comparison of the works, the graph techniques were very useful.

1.1 Introduction

Diagrams are a different mechanism in providing outline establishment regarding the data. The reason for chart was to provide the data regarding different tasks which are strong over a limited place. Nothing not with-standing, user defined for the limited data which is transferred by the same sequence of data. Similarly, it does not emphasize the data in the information which will be nullifies the term of using the chart. Overall the data which leads to the data which displays various terms with various techniques among various situations and different terms can be

[1]Department of Computer Science & Engineering, Amrita Sai Institute of Science and Technology, India
[2]Department of ECE, Sridevi Institute of Engineering and Technology, India
[3]Department of Computer Science and Engineering, Malla Reddy College of Engineering and Technology, India
[4]Department of Computer Science, Aryabhatta College, India

used. On the off chance that the data will not show difficult pattern in proof, the diagram was not the particular time for decision.

In spite of the fact that there are bunch PC programs that can create a chart, the creator should in any case notice some essential standards. A fundamental prerequisite for a chart is that it is clear and meaningful. Still up in the air by the text dimension and images as well as by the kind of chart itself. Give an unmistakable and engaging legend for each chart. Diagrams might have a few sections, contingent upon their organization:

- A figure number
- An inscription
- A head note
- An information
- Tomahawks and scales
- Images
- Legend
- Code data

In many cases, plan diagram to upward pivot addresses to reliant terms which even hub addresses to autonomous terms. Consequently, the time period was consistent at the X-axis. Different graphs ought to consistently have a subtitle, tomahawks as well as scale, images, and information. Pointing images should, particular, decipherable and give great differentiation among the picture over a frontal area and the foundation. Opening a well as shut terms gives good differentiation which were more successfully compared to mix for free circles along open squares such as title of the actual value, every one term ought to briefly pass on however much data as could reasonably be expected about what the diagram tells the peruser, yet it ought not give an outline or translation of the outcomes or exploratory subtleties. Try not to just rehash the pivot names, for example, "temperature versus time." It is significant to pick the right diagram type that is dependent on the sort of information to be introduced. On the off chance that the free and ward factors are numeric, use line outlines or scatter grams; if by some stroke of good luck, the reliant variable is numeric, use structured presentations; for extents, use visual diagrams or pie graphs. These are momentarily depicted beneath.

A scatter gram is utilized to show the connection between two factors and regardless of whether their qualities change in a steady manner, for example, dissecting the connection between the focus levels of two unique proteins. A line chart is like the scattergram with the exception of that the X qualities address a constant variable, like time, temperature, or pressing factor. It plots a progression of related qualities that portray an adjustment of Y as a component of X. Line charts typically are planned with the reliant variable on the Y-pivot and the autonomous variable on the flat X-hub, for example, a Kaplan–Meier examinations endurance plot of time-to-occasion results. The extent of people is addressed on the Y-pivot as an extent or rate, staying free of or encountering a particular result over the long run.

A visual graph may contain either level or vertical segments. The more noticeable the length of the bars, the more significant the value. They are used to examine a single variable worth between a couple of social events, for instance, the mean protein center levels of a friend of patients and a benchmark bunch. The histogram, moreover, called a repeat spreads outline, is a particular sort of reference graph that resembles a divided diagram, yet without any openings between the portions. It is used to address data from the assessment of a reliable variable. Solitary data centers are amassed in classes to show the repeat of data in each class. The repeat is assessed by the space of the segment. These can be used to show how purposeful class is coursed close by an intentional variable. These graphs are consistently used, for example, to check if a variable follows a typical conveyance, for example, the appropriation of protein levels between various people of a populace.

A pie chart shows classes or social occasions of data regarding the whole instructive file. The entire pie tends to all of the data, while each cut or part tends to a substitute class or assembling inside the sum. Each cut should show immense assortments. The quantity of classifications ought to be for the most part restricted to somewhere in the range of 2 and 9. Container that might be at any level. It is utilized in showing measurable outline for at least single factors, like base, less quantity, middle, and greatest which may likewise distinguish the exception information. The separation between the various pieces of the container shows the level of scattering and regardless of whether the information conveyance is balanced or slanted.

Some normal mistakes incorporate the accompanying: data in the content is copied in diagrams, or data in charts is copied in tables. The diagram does not have appropriate legends. Some unacceptable kind of chart is picked to address the information. The diagram is not plotted to scale. Information is not named, is conflicting, intruded, or misrepresented to deliver the ideal outcome. Another normal blunder was for incorporating the terms which recommends the unverified extrapolation past of information focuses. Interfacing less information focuses at a constant level, for example, progression for normal estimations collected by gathering people, which proposes that there were terms among age bunches which fall among the terms where indeed creator cannot have the foggiest idea about this. A superior method to show separate qualities would be a bar outline, in which every section mirrors the normal worth acquired from each age group [1]. If a very enormous reach should be covered and cannot be essentially displayed with a consistent scale, demonstrate an intermittence with the value of terms with the help of information data by combined inclining lines (— / —) demonstrating the lost degree up to the set of values.

Outlines are tended to be obvious by drawing a point or circle for every vertex, and characterizing a limit between two vertices on the off chance that they are related by an edge. If the outline is composed, the bearing is displayed by drawing a bolt. An outline attracting should not to be confused with the real diagram (the hypothetical, non-visual plan) as there are a couple of various approaches to structure the graph drawing. The solitary thing that is significant is which vertices are related with which others by the quantity of edges and not the particular configuration. Eventually, it is regularly difficult to pick if two drawings address a comparable graph. Depending upon the issue region, a couple of plans may be more qualified and clearer than others. The spearheading work was extremely compelling regarding the matter of chart designing. By various tasks and positions, the performance of using the mathematical tricks for designing the good strategies and drawings.

Chart designing likewise that were designed for the purpose of arrangement by the common values in the common terms. Here the common value of a chart was a minimum value of convergences among the edges while designing the diagram that a plane should have. For an estimation diagram, here the common meeting value is "zero" as per the concept. It is more than 55 years that mathematics is embedded with computers and creating wonders. Currently, the graph theory concepts were mostly used in computer science department for making, estimations, and predictions. By merging the graph techniques with computing is the booming concepts which are running today and the related jobs in this research domain in universities, research jobs, research organizations jobs as well as funded research jobs are very huge. The main things that we learn in these graph mechanisms in data science were the following:

- Problem solving concepts.
- Project based learning.
- Developing the practical application.
- Using the best standardization tools and techniques for developing.
- Improving the course by making updated concepts which help learner to develop the application by themselves.

Also by learning the graph concepts using machine learning (ML) which improves the knowledge in ethics for the students for learning multi-disciplinary concepts as well as having the best impact mechanism for solving various practical problems as well as procedures for teaching in automated process creates more different manner for showing the creative as well as technical skills. Here by using the graphical mechanism, we can make many comparison as well as decision support system for the designing of the task. Out of the various mechanisms in the ML techniques, convolutional neural networks (CNN) play a very major role in processing the data. In general terms, the working of CNN has multiple benefits such as flexible manner, quick responsiveness, and good interaction for processing. The Deep Graph Library (DGL) mechanism too returns the best way in reviewing the classification techniques. The graph metrics provides an efficient manner for giving an efficient value for various particles in the graph by plotting the mechanism in the most efficient as well as relevant purpose. Overall, the information which is collected or extracted from multiple sources helps in designing the graph. The designed graph helps to make several critical decisions. There is much contemporary information which is merged by various data elements and data visualization by the help of software mechanisms defined in the form of various types of graphs and charts. These graph representations help making their own business analysis and business estimations. Here we can perform various simplification types such as generalization, visualization, technical flow, various combinations as well as simplifications. Visual learning is one of the important mechanisms in the overall techniques. We can perform the distinct mechanisms among various types of data such as text as well as image data type. Here the text data is converted to a form of digital manner. Overall, by comparing with the actual data, the amount of required data will be taken based on the selection in the form of images.

1.2   Concept of graph

This concept is a study of graphs which are having various edges and vertices. In the graphs, we have the directed graphs and undirected graphs. Here, the values were termed in a systematic manner. The graphs comprise of the directed graphs and undirected graphs as shown in Figure 1.1 [2]. The directed graphs have fixed path as well as well-defined and the un-directed graphs way of defining is too complex and multipath mechanism is possible. In the graph, the set of values is defined as G= (V, E) where V is defined for edges and E is defined for vertices along G is defined for graph.

   In the graph, there is a concept of ambiguity. To remove the concept of ambiguity, we use un-directed simple graph. To avoid the ambiguity, we use the concept of looping. The concept of graph theory is used in several applications like

- Computer science
- Linguistics
- Physics and chemistry
- Social sciences
- Biology
- Retail perspective
- Final perspective
- Mathematics and many more

   There is "N" number of approaches to store diagrams in a PC framework. The information structure utilized relies upon both the diagram structure and the cal-culation utilized for controlling the chart. Hypothetically one can recognize

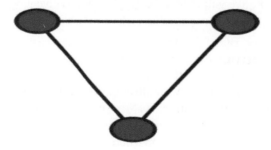

Figure 1.1   The graph with three vertices [2]

rundown and network structures; however, in substantial mechanisms for providing the best construction, was regularly the mix by couple of values. Rundown architecture was regularly liked for meager diagrams as they have more modest memory necessities. Grid mechanism then again gives quicker admittance to certain applications yet can burn through tremendous measures of memory. Executions of scanty grid structures that are proficient on present-day equal PC models are a value for present terms. Rundown structures incorporate the edge values, a variety in sets of vertices, as well as nearness list that independently records the secondary terms of every vertex: the same as the edge list, every vertex having the rundown for which values the terms are contiguous.

Organization structures join the event system; a grid of 0s and 1s whose lines address vertices and whose segments address edges, and the proximity network, wherein both the lines and sections are documented by vertices. In the two cases, a 1 shows two abutting objects, and a 0 exhibits two non-closes by articles. The degree network shows the degree of vertices. The paradigm network is a changed sort of proximity structure that combines information about the levels of the vertices and is useful in specific assessments, for instance, Kirchhoff's theory on the amount of navigating trees of a chart. The distance grid, like the closeness organization, has two lines and areas documented by vertices, however, rather than containing a 0 or a 1 in each cell, it contains the length of a most restricted way between two vertices.

1.3   Graph travels on analysis

The graph is a mechanism that connects with the help of edges as well as vertices. The graph is a connection orientation mechanism which connects to all the remaining node values or edge values in a proper manner. Graphs can be defined in the form of directed manner or undirected manner just to observe the relationships among the various items present in the graph. The graph can be defined as a complete graph if all the edges as well as vertices meet each other. A graph which does not have any loops is called acyclic. A tree is said to be undirected whenever two nodes are connected exactly by one node. Here we can use the real-time application for constructing the various graph models called "Twitch." Here by this application, we can give values and the graph keeps on changing as per our input or information. This mechanism is called as live streaming.

1.4   Graph plotting

It is possible to plot the graph with multi-dimensional features. If our existing datasets comprise more than three datasets values or else 3 unique as well as independent features, then we can perform the principle component analysis (PCA) mechanism. By using the PCA mechanism, the dimension of the image can be reduced up to 2–3 pixels and also by reducing the pixel size, we cannot observe the change in the quality of the image. The collection of the image as well as quality of the image

Figure 1.2   Data visualizing [2]

purely depends on the datasets what we have taken for data processing. For example, if we consider multiple data elements for processing the task, we have to consider the basic terms such as image size, quality of the image, resolution of the image, and pixel size of the image which have to be taken into the consideration. Here we can perform the embedding mechanism by using the twitch verse as shown in Figure 1.2 [2] mechanism. Generally, twitch verse mechanism comprises of two phases namely

• Construction of the graph using node4J.
• The network analysis mechanism using node4J mechanism.

Here we can perform the graph [3] coloring by using node KX mechanism. Graph coloring can be performed based on the distance of the values present in the graph. Here we have to perform multiple data visualization as well as principles for data processing and data representation.

The data visualizing is very important step in the data processing in ML. The task makes the user to analyze and to make the responsibility more friction clear. Data visualization allows users to check whether the data needed is formed as final user or not. Due to this regard while defining the graph [4], it is mandatory to crosscheck the graph color, shape, text as well as animation of the graph. Here we can say the general things which are needed for developing the graph namely:

• Text
• Color
• White space

1.5   Network graph of an ETFL ARK Funds

At present, the performance of network graph of an ETFL ARK [9] Funds is not much great compared to the traditional graph models. Here the performance of the mechanism is very low leveled task. But the ETFL ARK mechanism cannot withstand for a longer period of time.

1.6   Twitch verse

Here it focuses on the various graphs as well as graph insights for the relationships in the development of the graphs [10]. Daily huge massive quantity of data is being generated and being stored in the networks. The capability of data generation as well as data processing is being calculated for the better processing of the task. The

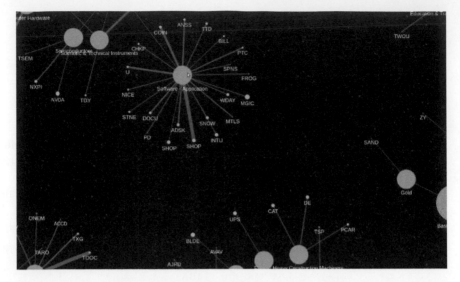

Figure 1.3   ETFL ARK graph image [11]

collected data helps in various data analytics tasks. The graphs can be designed with d3 mechanism as well as d3.js mechanism as shown in Figure 1.3 [11]. These both mechanisms have the excelling plotting values as well as defining in various colors. Here we can define the graph in the two ways namely:

- Simple bar chart
- Simple line chart

1.6.1   Use of graph theory mechanisms for solving data science problems

If we are working toward the concepts of data science, we should have the minimum knowledge on graph values as well as graph plotting skills [12]. The typical changes lead to the change in the set of the values. The main use of using this methodology is to

- Speed up
- Process takes place line by line
- Can make things possible in case of unsolvable datasets

For data preparation, we need few of the information such as raw data, data pre-processing, and data cleaning [13]. For data cleaning, we require data starting as well as the time stamp. Here for the data analytics and for the data processing, we need the exactness of the available data.

For performing the data analysis, we have to focus on some general things which [14] are needed for designing the task. Here for making the task more efficient and clear manner, we have taken the datasets as shown in Figure 1.4 [15]. The development of the adjacency matrix is created for the computing values for validating the

day	origin	destination
2019-01-16 00:00:00+00:00	KEWR	KDFW
2019-01-01 00:00:00+00:00	KONT	KPHX
2019-01-09 00:00:00+00:00	LSZH	LTBA
2019-01-15 00:00:00+00:00	KSFO	KSAN
2019-01-01 00:00:00+00:00	PANC	MS65
2019-01-01 00:00:00+00:00	EBAW	EBMB
2019-01-09 00:00:00+00:00	KSLC	KOAK
2019-01-21 00:00:00+00:00	KDEN	KAUS
2019-01-22 00:00:00+00:00	KLAX	KRNO
2019-01-28 00:00:00+00:00	LTBA	DAAG

Figure 1.4   Data collection with the bulk information [15]

terms which are adjacent to each other. Overall, there is multiple number of applications of this mechanism such as

- Effective data
- More accurate
- Better results
- Helps in making good decision making mechanism
- Better understandability
- Way of designing is good

For designing this mechanism, the graph should satisfy the following general basic principles such as:

- Designing the diagram first
- Usage of better software
- Use the better geometry for performing the operations such as
  - To display the data
  - To display more effectively
  - For distribution of data
  - Scatter plot where black circles wherever required
  - Logistic regression
  - Stimulated displaying of the data
  - Displaying the live data from time to time
  - Heat map of the stimulated visibility
  - Density map of the season based on the map

- Colors always define something
- We should define certainly
- Define our data to the smaller parts wherever necessary
- Defining information as well as defining type of data are quite different
- Simple visuals and detailed captions
- Consider the info graphic
- Get an exact opinion regarding the type of data

In the graph, there are few of the methods such as Dijkstra method as well as parallelogram method. These general mechanisms are used for performing these mechanisms such as Amsterdam, dijkstra method, minimum spanning tree method, shortest path method, graph coloring method, visiting node method, travelling sales man problem, clustering method, image segmentation mechanism, and image scaling mechanism. Anticipating medical clinic readmission with compelling AI strategies has drawn in an incredible consideration as of late. The key test of this assignment originates from attributes of the information removed from electronic wellbeing records (EHR), which are imbalanced class circulations. This test further prompts the disappointment of most existing models that just give a halfway understanding to the learning issue and result in a one-sided and erroneous expectation. To address this test, we propose another chart-based class-lopsidedness learning technique by completely utilizing the information from various classes. In the first place, we lead diagram development for taking the example of segregation from among class and inside class information tests. Then, at that point, we plan an improvement system to join the built charts to acquire a class-awkwardness mindful diagram inserting and additionally mitigate execution degeneration. At last, we plan a neural organization model as the classifier to direct imbalanced grouping, i.e., emergency clinic readmission expectation. Thorough examination on six genuine readmission datasets shows that the proposed technique beats best in class approaches in readmission forecast task. Late discoveries in neuroscience propose that the human cerebrum addresses data in a mathematical design (e.g., through reasonable spaces). To convey, we straighten the perplexing portrayal of elements and their qualities into a solitary word or a sentence. In this paper, we use chart convolutional organizations to help the development of language and collaboration in multi-specialist frameworks. Persuaded by a picture-based referential game, we propose a chart referential game with differing levels of intricacy, and we give solid pattern models that show positive properties as far as language development and participation are concerned. We show that the arose correspondence convention is strong that the specialists reveal the genuine components of variety in the game and that they figure out how to sum up past the examples experienced during preparing.

1.7   Data visualization techniques

Data visualization is very important concept in the data tracing or data estimations. Data visualization helps to share various elements which are defined in the data. Data visualization helps to understand regarding the data information as well as the type of

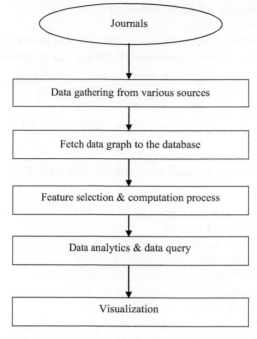

Figure 1.5   Data visualization process [18]

the data [16]. This concept enables the complete information as well as details about type of data, elements present in the data. Data visualization helps in defining the complex information such as Google Maps and Facebook data which is shared over the Facebook server. Here qualitative data as well as quantitative type of information is being stored [17] in this mechanism. So as of present identifying and making complex data to the simplified data [18] and giving to the users is a greatest research area which is done by many scholars as shown in Figure 1.5.

The following were the tasks performed by the visualization process [19] such as:

- Identifying and finding a set of models.
- Identifying clustering models with known mechanisms.
- Association analysis discovery.
- Time series analysis.
- Outlier analysis.

1.8   Present research ongoing

- Quantities programming environments
- Data wrangling
- Making complex data to simple data
- Research presentation: Knitr

1.9   Next 60 years of data science

In future, there will be a huge change in the data science. It may not reach to our predictions too. Few of the advancements that we can expect are such as

- Open science takes over
- Science as data
  - Cross study control sharing
  - Cross study comparisons

1.10   Scientific data analytics tested empirically

- Substantial theoretical process
- High-dimensional process
- Mas-o-menos classifier
- Computing mechanism
- Course organization
- Scaling the course
- Improving project work

1.11   Conclusion

We have investigated the utilization of diagram hypothesis ways to deal with noting certain (apparently) basic information science questions. It has become evident that numerous issues which we would have the option to address utilizing circles and so forth are considerably more effectively settled utilizing diagram-based methodologies. When the nearness network is made, most inquiries in regard to the presence of connections between objects of revenue can be addressed by utilizing single articulations like ordering or adding. In the event that your code is to be applied to a lot of information or on the other hand if a similar issue is probably going to happen once more, figuring the contiguousness lattice once is more than awesome.

Further, a few issues are for all intents and purposes unsolvable utilizing normal methodologies, in light of the fact that the algorithmic intricacy is contradictory with even medium-sized datasets. In the event that such a circumstance happens, you should go one stage back and see whether the chart-based methodology holds a simple arrangement, very much as it did in this guide.

1.12   Future work

In this paper, we have focused the concepts of graph and various techniques in designing the graph mechanisms. By this paper, we have brought to the conclusion that by using the graph in the real-time applications and, for analytics purposes, we can come to a conclusion regarding many things such as decision making and making future estimations, based on past years graphs can improve the business and many more. At present, by embedding the graph technique to recent concepts such as ML can do visualization and generalization in more good manner. We need to zero in on new highlights to person and product hubs that impact the survey score. Likewise, have a go at bringing some commotion into the survey score estimation and perceive how that influences the test precision. The neural organization ought to be tough to a moderate measure of commotion and should adapt well to new highlights – in case it is battling, take a stab at making the secret layers somewhat more extensive so it can perform more calculations.

References

[1] Ginde G., Saha S., Balasubramaniam C., *et al.*, Mining massive databases for computation of scholastic indices – model and quantify internationality and influence diffusion of peer reviewed journals, in: *Proceedings of the Fourth National Conference of Institute of Scientometrics, SIoT*, 2015, pp. 1–26.

[2] Gouri Ginde, S., Saha, A. Mathur, S., *et al.*, ScientoBASE: a framework and model for computing scholastic indicators of non-local influence of journals via native data acquisition algorithms, *Journal of Scientometric Research*, 107(1), 2016, pp. 1–51.

[3] Bora, K., Saha, S., Agrawal, S., Safonova, M., Routh, S. and Narasimhamurthy, A., CD-HPF: new habitability score via data analytic modeling, *Astronomy and Computing*, 17, 2016, pp. 129–143, ISSN 2213-1337.

[4] Snehanshu Saha, A., Dwivedi, N., Dwivedi, G., Ginde, A. and Mathur, J.I.M. I., Journal internationality modeling index – an analytical investigation, in: *Proceedings of the Fourth National Conference of Institute of Scientometrics, SIoT*, 2015, pp. 40–49.

[5] Saha, S., Jangid, N., Mathur, A. and Anand, M.N., DSRS: estimation and forecasting of journal influence in the science and technology domain via a lightweight quantitative approach, *COLLNET Journal of Scientometrics and Information Management*, 10(1), 2016, pp. 41–70 (Taylor and Francis).

[6] Saha, S., Sarkar, J., Dwivedi, A., Dwivedi, N., Narasimhamurthy, A.M. and Roy, R., A novel revenue optimization model to address the operation and maintenance cost of a data center, *Journal of Cloud Computing, Advances, Systems and Applications*, 5(1), 2016, pp. 1–23, https://doi.org/10.1186/s13677-015-0050-8.

[7] Ng, K.H. and Peh, W.C., Preparing effective illustrations. Part 1: graphs, *Singapore Medical Journal*, 2009, 50(3), 245–249.

[8] *Council of Science Editors' Scientific Style and Format for Authors, Editors, and Publishers*, 8th ed., Chicago: University of Chicago Press, 2014.

[9] *Manual of Style: A Guide for Authors and Editors*, 10th ed, Oxford: Oxford University Press, 2007.

[10]   Franzblau, L.E. and Chung, K.C., Graphs, tables, and figures in scientific publications: the good, the bad, and how not to be the latter, *Journal of Hand Surgery (American Volume)*, 2012, 37(3), pp. 591–596.

[11]   Hanson, K., Morrissey, S., Birkland, A., Dilauro, T. and Donoghue, M., Using RMap to describe distributed works as linked data graphs: outcomes and preservation implications, in: *iPres Conference*, 2016.

[12]   Burton, A., Koers, H., Manghi, P., et al., The Scholix framework for interoperability in data-literature information exchange, *D-Lib Magazine*, 23(1/2), 2017.

[13]   Aryani, A., Burton, A. and Treloar, A., Research data switchboard: finding connections to your data, in: *eResearch Australasia Conference*, 2015.

[14]   Wang, J., Aryani, A., Evans, B., Barlow, M. and Wyborn, L., Graph connections made by RD-Switchboard using NCIs metadata, *D-Lib Magazine*, 23, 2017.

[15]   Conlon, M. and Aryani, A., Creating an open linked data model for research graph using vivo ontology, in: *Open Repositories Conference*, 2017.

[16]   Holtkamp, A., Mele, S., Simko, T. and Smith, T., INSPIRE: Realizing the dream of a global digital library in high-energy physics. Report No. CERN-OPEN-2010-019, CERN, 2010.

[17]   Wang, J., Aryani, A., Wyborn, L. and Evans, B., Providing research graph data in JSON-LD using Schema.org, in *Proceedings of the 26th International Conference on World Wide Web Companion*, 2017.

[18]   Aryani, A., Data description registry interoperability wg: interlinking method and specification of cross-platform discovery, in: *Research Data Alliance*, 2016.

[19]   Fernndez, A., del Ro, S., Lpez, V., *et al.*, Big data with cloud computing: an insight on the computing environment, mapreduce, and programming frameworks, *Wiley Interdisciplinary Reviews. Data Mining and Knowledge Discovery*, 4(5), (2014), pp. 380–409.

Chapter 2

Data science: the Artificial Intelligence (AI) algorithms-inspired use cases

Pethuru Raj[1], P. Beaulah Soundarabai[2] and Peter Augustine[2]

Abstract

The data science field is growing fast with the faster maturity and stability of its implementation technologies. We had been fiddling with traditional data analytics methods. But now, with Artificial Intelligence (AI), it is possible to embark on predictive and prescriptive insights generation in time. There are several data science (DS) use cases emerging with the wider adoption and adaptation of AI technologies and tools. This chapter is dedicated to illustrate various AI-inspired use cases.

2.1 Introduction

The data science field is going through a number of noteworthy advancements lately. There are several enablers in the form of algorithms, approaches, frameworks, libraries, toolkits, platforms, the ready availability of datasets, optimization techniques, etc. in the data science space. The amount of multi-structured data getting generated, captured, and stocked is simply massive. There is a tremendous growth in the number of data sources and sinks. Data virtualization products and platforms are numerous to aggregate data from different and distributed sources. On the other side, knowledge visualization tools including 360-degree dashboards and reporting solutions are flourishing. The product and tool vendors are hyper-active in this space. Data ingestion, pre-processing, storage, and analytics solutions are also fast maturing and stabilizing as the rough edges need smoothening while procuring insights out of data heaps. That is, it optimizes the transition process of obtaining knowledge from information and information from the raw data and automates through a growing array of tools. Precisely speaking, with the splurge of competent technologies, the important assignments of knowledge discovery and dissemination for any institution, individual, and innovator to march ahead are elegantly simplified and speeded up across big data environments. It is not an exaggeration to state that we are heading toward the knowledge era.

[1]Edge AI Division, Reliance Jio Platforms Ltd., Bangalore, India
[2]Department of Computer Science, Christ University, India

Data science is the prime field for neatly and nicely fulfilling the goals of exploring, sorting, and analyzing big data from heterogeneous data sources, gaining conclusions by deriving insights through data-driven exploits, and performing actions that emerge from insights-driven decisions. Handling data efficiently and usefully to make sense out of it is the core and central aspect of any Data Science technology. This chapter discusses how data science contributes across industry verticals. The data science capability helps worldwide businesses to beneficially explore fresh avenues for acquiring additional revenues, enhance their productivity and customer experience, and offer premium offerings to keep up the edge earned.

2.2   The evolution and elevation of data science

There are several things contributing constructively and concurrently for the origin of the data science field. First, the amount of poly-structured data getting generated, captured, and stored is tremendous. Second, there are data mining (DM) algorithms and approaches. There are integrated big, fast, and streaming data analytics platform solutions from the research communities that give open-source information as well as from business-oriented product and tool providers. Data analytics has become the mainstream method for extracting hidden patterns and worthwhile insights that are actionable out of mountains of data. There are DM algorithms and frameworks for simplifying untangling business intelligence out of data volumes.

In the recent past, the Artificial Intelligence (AI) space is filled up with a number of advancements in the form of machine and deep learning (ML/DL) algorithms for expertly and elegantly solving some special problems such as classification, clustering, regression, recognition, detection, translation, and association. Further on, there are several frameworks, libraries, tools, and platforms for simplifying AI model creation, evaluation, optimization, and deployment. Researchers and IT industry professionals have brought in a series of improvements toward enhancing the AI model prediction accuracy. With the power of AI algorithms, the field of data science has grown up significantly. For analytical questions and problems, choosing the relevant algorithm is the key differentiator. Data scientists have to get a deeper and clear understanding of existing problem at hand and then embark on finalizing the best-in-class algorithm to solve the question. Enterprising businesses are keen on leveraging the unique capabilities of data science in order to take informed decisions rather intuition-based decisions. Insights-driven decisions, deals, and deeds are certainly successful not only in the short term but also in the long term. Every aspect of businesses is being automated, accelerated, and augmented through data science. Here are a few inspiring examples.

2.3   Anomaly detection

At certain times, datasets may come across few data points that have different behavior when compared to the other data points. Those data points are called anomalies as they reveal deviations from the normal pattern of the dataset. Anomaly detection is a key technique of unsupervised technique during data processing. There are three famous categories of anomalies namely change in events, outliers, and drifts.

Change in the events shows sudden pattern change from the previous behavior' outliers showing a very short and small pattern change which is of not showing any systematic change in the dataset; slow but long-term change of data are classified as drifts.

Anomaly detection is a renowned example for the fast-growing domain of data science. Business verticals include fraudulent transaction detection, disease identification in healthcare domains, and also in manufacturing and financial services etc. This data processing technique is highly used to enhance the prediction accuracy by eliminating the outlier data points from the datasets.

2.3.1   Binary and multiclass classification

As inscribed above, classification or categorization is one of the well-known and widely used problems for data scientists. Whether there is a possibility for golf play tomorrow is a classification problem. Here is another problem, which is expressed as "Is there a cat in the picture or not?" Just "yes" or "no" problem is touted as binary classification. There are problems that lead to multiple results or values. This is known as multi-class classification.

2.3.2   Personalization

Besides predictive and prescriptive insights being derived from datasets through ML and DL algorithms, personalized insights are also being extracted and used by organizations. Product marketing, promotion campaigns, personalized recommendations, and hyper-personalization can be fulfilled through AI algorithms.

2.4   Fraud detection

Fraudulent transactions can cause significant financial losses to the national governments across the globe. Citizens are directly or indirectly affected with this fraud in this digital era. Financial fraud badly impacts businesses in the form of lost revenue and productivity. The brand value of business houses is bound to go down and businesses may lose their loyal and royal customers in due course of time when fraud persists. Frauds can take place across industry verticals from financial services to healthcare, insurance, technology, and travel. Any worthwhile organization can face this fraudulent thing. We often read and hear about large-scale data breaches, stolen credit card details, etc. Hackers and evil doers target critical infrastructures and spread ransom ware in hospital chains. In this extremely connected world, it is a tough task to visualize wherefrom financial attacks originate and spread.

The attack patterns and vectors are constantly evolving and hence rigid and rules-based systems are found to be inefficient and insufficient to withstand brilliant and coordinated attacks. In such severe situations, the ancient data analytics methods are incapable of bringing in the desired outcome. Due to this fragility, there is a constant motivation and migration toward embracing and employing ML models to predict and prevent any catastrophic misbehavior from fraudsters [1]. As indicated above, anomaly or outlier detection is to get solid support from AI advancements. AI is also found to be powerful in performing fraud prevention. Data scientists are therefore consciously leveraging AI methods such as ML and DL algorithms for an array of countermeasures.

However, experts point out that if left unmonitored, fraudsters can render naive ML models to drift in a matter of weeks. Perpetrators continue to reinvent adversarial techniques to exploit AI models in production and hence monitoring for any sort of anomalies/deviations has become business-critical and time-sensitive. By proactively detecting deviations between baseline and production distributions and examining feature and cohort performance, data scientists can be spot on in identifying issues and retraining models to minimize any perceptible loss. Thus, not only creating and deploying competent AI models in production but also it is vital to have an eye on model performance in order to avoid any prediction drift.

For example, a credit card company examining differences in inference distributions might come across that a fraud model has far more false positives in production than the validation baseline. This means millions of legitimate purchases getting denied at the point of sale. This may eventually propel annoyed customers to switch card service providers. What to do here? The ML team examining a dip in aggregate accuracy might discover that the developed and tested AI fraud model is not up to the mark in predicting smaller transactions when compared with large-scale purchases. This is because the deployed fraud model was trained on big-ticket purchases. Here a ML-enabled observability platform comes to the rescue. By properly analyzing the observed data, it is possible for the operational team to foresee losses. This knowledge discovery helps the ML team to consider the best course of actions quickly to keep up the hard-earned brand loyalty and market share for the business.

Monitoring and observability of AI models are therefore important for critical business sectors such healthcare, retailing, and financial services. The decisions being taken by AI models have to be transparent and trustworthy. The block box nature of AI models is a problematic thing for data scientists and business executives. They would struggle to understand what really caused the AI model to arrive at a particular decision. Therefore, before jumping into a fully automated system, it is mandatory to fulfill the requirements of self-explanation and interpretability. The idea is to ensure the much-needed fairness and to avoid any bias in arriving at decisions.

2.4.1   Challenges to fraud detection

It is an accepted statement that right data leads to right decisions. Therefore, it is essential to have a huge size data that lead is full of issues and problems to effectively prevent frauds. There are methods to clean up data. Skewed and imbalanced datasets ought to be corrected. Evaluation metrics and sensitive (contributing for correct decisions) features have to be chosen in order to enhance the prediction accuracy and thus help in building robust data models.

2.4.2   Best practices for observability with fraud models

Once you have set up a baseline and monitoring solution, the task at hand becomes identifying the root cause of issues and responding quickly as threats evolve in real-time.

2.4.3   Important metrics

Some important metrics to watch include the following:

- **Recall** – How many frauds your model is picking up can provide a window into your model's impact against real-world threats.
- **The inverse of recall/false-negative rate** – False-negative rate measures fraud that a model failed to predict accurately (classified as not fraud). This is an important performance metric. It is a key performance indicator since this is causing a lot of financial losses for businesses.
- **False-positive rate** – This is another value-adding metric. The false-positive rate (the rate at which a model predicts fraud but actually is not) is also important because this is inconveniencing customers. For example, in healthcare, a patient's claim can be denied because it was predicted to be fraudulent.

2.4.4   Performance degradation

It is very important to understand what drives a drop in the model's performance. You need to do the much-needed performance analysis of your model by focusing on various low-performing features. This can bring useful information such as fraud patterns, and fraudster origin to light.

   We need sophisticated ML observability platforms that not only monitor your performance metrics but also proactively surface feature performance heat maps. Such a unique capability helps patching costly model exploits in hours rather than days.

2.4.5   Overcoming the drift problem

Drift is all about the distribution changes over time. That is, the accuracy of the AI model goes down due to various reasons. The data drift is associated with the decline in data quality. The drift at different levels and layers ultimately deteriorates the model performance. Therefore, experts insist that monitoring and troubleshooting are very vital for keeping up the model performance.

   Fraudsters continuously team up for deeper and decisive attacks and hence data scientists have to account for all possible drifts in order to ensure the model's performance is not getting affected. Identifying feature, model, and actual drift between various model environments and versions is beneficial in pinpointing fraud patterns, data quality issues, and anomalous distribution behavior.

- **Prediction drift** – possible drift correlation – An influx and surge of fraud predictions could mean that your model is under attack. That is, you are classifying a lot more fraud than what you expect to see in production. Your model is doing a good job here on catching frauds.
- **Actuals drift (no prediction drift)** – possible drift correlation – An influx of fraud actual without changes to the distribution of your predictions means that fraudsters could find an exploit in your model. The way forward is to fix your model immediately to avoid any more costly charge backs.
- **Feature drift** – possible drift correlation – An influx of new and/or existing feature values could be an indicator of seasonal changes (tax or holiday season) or in the worst case be correlated with fraud exploitation. The solution is to use drift over time stacked on top of your performance metric over time graph to validate whether any correlation exists.

As fraud continues to evolve and even take new forms in the digital era, it is critical for data science teams to have an observability strategy in place to catch, monitor and troubleshoot problems with their fraud models in production.

2.4.5.1   AI-enabled automations in taxation

Not only businesses but also national governments across the world are keenly embracing the potential and promising AI technology in order to provide distinct services to their citizens [2]. AI is being vehemently used in many fields including healthcare, transportation, education, national security, and smart city applications. Governments are learning and leaning toward AI, which is inherently capable of providing a host of innovations in the taxation domain also. All countries are using the innovations and techniques of the rapidly developing AI tools for their various government services such as taxation. The key source of income for any government is tax, which is inevitable for the functioning of public sector activities. Tax departments work toward on time tax collection from its citizen and also take necessary actions on the defaulters of tax payments to increase the efficiency of taxation. AI tools and bots analyze the citizens' financial data and identify whether the individual has paid the correct tax or a defaulter. AI enabled robots also help in providing financial saving schemes for its citizen based on the fund flow and also provide services such as automated tax payments and educating them on various tax benefits.

AI models are useful to identify the people who project their income as low than the original income and accurately measure the cheated amount and penalize them. For some other group of people, different strategies are used such as they can be requested to cooperate voluntarily in properly paying their taxes on time. Typically, any tax professional's everyday work comprises time-consuming and repetitive tasks including processing accounting documents and creating reports periodically. AI systems are also used to automate such recurring tasks like to auto fill the account number, ID of assets to spread sheets for on-time financial reporting closeout reports. Such systems save tax professionals' key time everyday and use their time efficiently for other tax related activities.

Accounting softwares are used to file the financial data of an individual or an organization, by manual entries of tax professionals. Now, bots are used to automatic entry of such data in the software from spreadsheets which reduce human data entry errors as well as reduce the time spent by tax experts. Precise tax amounts are arrived in no time; it can also classify the tax documents based on its taxonomy and consolidate each category diligently. Thus, it is able to project the important data like how much is contributed for social responsibility, charitable trusts, and what are the capital gain or losses of an organization with proper reports in chart and table formats. Key data such as account numbers, discount, and payment dues can be extracted accurately by bots swiftly.

AI-enabled systems with embedded ML algorithms are being built to identify the anomalies and intentional tax evasion entries in a huge volume of datasets. AI also can detect fraudulent activities by leveraging the vital data of a person's employment details, if he is audited in the previous years, any legal cases on his for illicit source of money flow to his account and other hidden revenue generations, etc. optical character recognition (OCR) and AI together analyze the tax documents of citizen moving around globally and these two are so fast in analyzing the tax documents and AI helps in document scanning and exporting them to database files.

Predictive analysis is quite possible through AI tools for accurate tax forecasting by detecting the sales patterns on weekly, monthly, and annual basis. It can even analyze the factors that affect or influence the sales in a particular region such as political activities and climatic changes. Forecasting helps the organizations and individuals to decide when is the right time to invest or reap the investment benefits. Historical data analysis and predictive analysis help in predicting the time by when to stock of the company goes low or high. Through this analysis, it gives advice of when is the right time to buy or sell the stock.

Bribing is always an illegal activity and it is another bothersome aspect for governments especially in taxation. It is too hard to monitor every individual on each and every transaction, is not an easy task with the consistent growth in the number of tax-paying people. However, when processes get digitized, optimized, and automated, the corruption problem can be eliminated. So, robots, that are AI enabled systems, may be used to monitor the people help to stop such bribing and corruptions and thus they can help in building transparency.

In depth, data analysis is also possible through AI enabled bots by obtaining a clear knowledge of tax and benefits. Previous year documents of tax payments, it gives suggestions to save money for the tax practitioners. Robots usage in taxation prevents bribery and maintains accuracy. This will eliminate the long-time spending in the queue for income tax by eliminating the lengthy taxation procedure.

2.5 AI-enabled fake news detection

There are hundreds of news portals across the globe providing news on various subjects ceaselessly. Besides news web sites, the enormous social media news platforms provide instant and updated news in the real time to its widespread readers. Online news media emerged from newspapers, magazines, and small news articles.

There are tweets, blogs, and other online discussions. The social media platforms are so powerful that it has the ability to engage its subscribers and readers to share their insights, comments, and debate on a wide range of societal issues. However, such platforms are also being misused to spread falsehood for monetary benefits. In some cases, fake news is being used for diverting the mindsets of readers, enforcing a biased ideas and opinions and thus spreading the ridiculousness. In short, the explosion of social media applications has made it easy for individuals and groups to spread information (correct as well as incorrect) across the globe instantaneously. This has made the old problem of fake news to resurface and put many in real trouble. This is a key concern as it spread the negative or fake impact among the societies. Automatic ML-based fake news detection models are proposed to bring an awareness and deal with its spread, which has built leveraging the latest advancements in AI space. There are ML and DL algorithms emerging to stop the spread of fake news. The natural language processing (NLP) methods come handy here.

The paper [3] has addressed to identify the triples, subject-predicate-object; these triples represent the structured facts to assess the credibility, and it has used the labeled text input to classify them. When there is no evidence or user comment present, there is limited or no possibility for the credibility. When comments exist, the claims credibility is clearly possible and they confirm the claim and the trustworthiness of the assessment source is evident.

Automatic identification of fake news on twitter, the paper [4] uses a Random Forest classifier that assesses structural content, feature selection process, and temporal features. The authors have used their model on CREDBANK and Pheme datasets. They have proved that models trained against crowd-sourced datasets do better than models based on the assessments of professional journalists and outperform on a pooled dataset of the datasets of crowd-sourced and journalists' assessment together.

Text and image information based convolutional neural network [5] model that is trained with the text as well as image information concurrently. The convolutional neural network makes the model to see the entire input altogether at once, and it gets trained much faster than LSTM and RNN models.

The paper [6] does the analysis in two different datasets comprising of fake news and fake reviews. The authors have used different disparity of term frequency (TF) and TFIDF for the feature extraction and support vector machine (SVM), Lagrangian SVM, DT, stochastic gradient decent (SGD), k-nearest neighbor (KNN), and LR classifiers.

Altogether, automatic classification of a text article as misinformation or right information is a real challenge. There are research contributions using ML algorithms and the ensemble approaches for automatically classifying the news articles in real time. NLP is an important application of ML algorithms. NLP is always tricky, as it has to explore the way in which human communication happens and the system should also be aware of human consciousness. Moreover, it is relatively easy to encode an image in terms of numerical data such as a two-dimensional matrix, but it is terribly hard to encode a text as a number or a vector. Fake news detection is a text classification problem. The point is that AI researchers are keen on leveraging the latest innovations to simplify fake news identification.

2.6   AI-inspired credit card fraud detection

There are numerous fraudulent credit card transactions very common in today's time as they are becoming easy and most of us are making payment through credit cards frequently. With the surge of large-scale e-commerce sites for retailing, ticket reservation, etc., online transaction has picked up fast. In such an open and connected world, there are fresh opportunities and possibilities for financial frauds causing huge financial loss for institutions and individuals. There is a high need for instant methods to stop such money stealing. There are many innovative ways with which the credit card information are received from the user himself by making fake customer care calls or sending fake messages, phishing and masquerading attack, etc. There are many detection and prediction models based on AI and ML algorithms such as support vector machine, KNN, CNN, and ANN; they also predict the occurrence of the fraud.

Credit card transaction becomes a fraud transaction when a stealer takes another person's the credit card data such as card number, pin and password, and otp, and uses them without the original card. ML and DL models together make a powerful package to make a fraud detection module to predict the immediate next transaction of a customer is legitimate or fraud one. DL uses neural network model that resembles like the human brain working model for data processing and decision making activities. The key objective here is to make a model that accurately detects the fraud credit card transactions in realtime. There are many ML solutions using SVM< KNN, Naïve Bayes, etc., among them ANN performs better.

The goal is to produce a model that can clearly point out frauds in real time. Currently there are solutions using ML algorithms such as SVM, Naïve Bayes, and KNN. But ANNs look promising as described in the paper "Credit card fraud detection using artificial neural network." The authors [7] have used SVM and KNN classification algorithms such as SVM and KNN for building credit card fraud detection model. They have compared these two models with ANN and their results clearly show that the ANN predicts better than the model developed using the two ML algorithms. There are 31 attributes in the dataset that has the information related to credit card user's name, age, account information, etc. The outcome is either 0 or 1. The other prominent solution implementations are also available in the literature review.

2.7   AI-empowered forest fire prediction

Forest fire is a common phenomenon in dense forest areas due to many natural reasons but over the last three decades, due to global warming and deforestation, there has been a huge increase in the forest fires. Non-prescribed and uncontrollable burning of forest plants and trees in a natural setup in forest and grassland has a significant impact such as extensive health issues and socio-economic issues.

Forest fires cannot be prevented always as there are many natural factors causing them majorly than human made forest fires. Early detection of forest fire is the key objective of any tool to control the spread of it as early as possible. But, most of such detection models rely majorly on satellite images and optical thermal monitoring and the alert comes somewhere between 2 and 3 hours after the ignition of forest fire. Deploying solar powered wireless sensors is a best proposed solution to get the alert soon after the ignition but it is not practically possible to deploy sensors throughout the forests globally.

Edge ML [8] opens the possibilities of such devices as the computation happens at the endpoint itself from where the data is sensed. Shifting the computation from far away base station or cloud server to the devise itself has a major benefit of response time and energy utilization and better battery life. It has to use different types of woods of forest plants need to be used for data collection to decide the two key classes like

Forest Fire – prediction of wild fire, with high temperature, low humidity, and larger volatile organic compounds.

No fire/normal – the plants and wood show normal temperature, good air quality and normal humidity, and thus predicting no forest fire.

The AI experts should use the key parameters for modeling the algorithm and memory and computation time needed to inference the decision will give better results with minimal time.

There are few good existing prediction models available such as Canadian Forest Fire Danger Rating System; it is based on few vital data and it is required to be installed on the ground and maintenance of it is a challenge for many developing countries.

This paper "Comparing calibrated statistical and machine learning methods for wild land fire occurrence prediction (FOP): a case study of human-caused fires in Lac La Biche, Alberta, Canada" [9] presents a strategy for calibration of fine scale statistical ML model. Authors have presented a beautiful case study that compares the human made FOP model in Alberta region of Canada and it uses the legacy data of 20 long years from the year 1996 to 2016. Neural network models, regression, and logistic GAM are compared in the paper to analyze the advantages and disadvantages of proper calibration.

2.8   AI-induced breast cancer (BC) detection

As per latest researchers, the treatment for BC can be detected accurately with ML models that take the symptom as input from the real-time reports. Lymphedema is a general complication that describes a fluid collection due to which there are swellings in the legs or hands which may be due to the lymph node removal during the cancer treatments. There are many common symptoms for lymphedema such as swellings, feeling heavy, skin scars, aches and frequent skin infections. Usually these lymphedema are treated due to the diagnose of swellings but swelling is revealed after some time of lymphedema by then it has spread a lot in the body and this delayed diagnose leads to poor health treatment and outcomes. Artificial

Neural Network algorithm performs with 93% accuracy in lymphedema discrimination, which monitors the patients' health status of lymphedema without even visiting a professional healthcare expert. This not only reduces the risk of cancer cells to progress to next stages but also reduces the healthcare costs and anxiety of the patients [10].

ML provides early lymphedema detection in breast cancer detection by BC news (breastcancer-news.com). Early detection of BC improves the lifestyle and prognosis through which it increases the chances of patient significantly. Accurate classification facilitates cancer-affected patients prevents the patients from undergoing unnecessary or wrong treatments. So, it is important to classify the BC patients into groups such as benign or malignant. Due to its unique methodology of critical features detection with the help of complex BC datasets, ML tools are widely recognized as the methodology to classifying the BC patterns and forecasting models.

2.8.1 Phase 0 – preparation of data

During this phase, the data preparation is done by availing the data set permissions. One such data set is available in [11].

Key analysis here is to identify the features that are most useful to predict the malignance or benign cancer using the selection of hyper parameters.

2.8.2 Phase 1: data investigation

Many researchers use Spyder for data investigation. Spyder is an open source free python environment designed exclusively for data analysts. It supports writing, editing, analyzing, and debugging of the tool with interactive data exploration and execution, with very readable visualization facilities in the package. This platform is blessed with many libraries to simplify the loads of data scientists. Especially, there are powerful libraries for importing, examining, and finding the data set dimensions. Python has several easy to use and understand visualization packages such as Matplotlib and Seaborn. These help to understand the depicted data very clearly. Pandas function is another attraction here, as it helps to identify any missing or null data point values in the data set, if any.

2.8.3 Phase 2: data categories

Certain data in the data set contain labels instead of numeric data value. For instance, gender, age, region, etc. are represented with label values. Label encoder is used for such categorical data items. Label encoder is available in SciKit of Python; it is used to transform the categorical data values to numeric values, which alone can be better understood by the predictive ML models.

The data set is usually divided into test data and training data and test data. The AI model in fact does its learning from the training dataset to be generalized in its prediction purpose; training dataset has known input and output values. Test data is to check whether they arrived model answers correctly.

2.8.4   *Phase 3: feature scaling*

Feature extraction and engineering is the most important aspect of ML-inspired modelling. Usually every dataset contains many features with varying ranges, units, and magnitudes. Since the ML models use the Euclidean distance between any two data elements, the need of bringing all the features to the same magnitude ranges. This is achieved by data transformation process for fitting it for a specific scale of say, 0–10, 1–100, etc.

2.8.5   *Phase 4: ML model selection*

This is a complicated step. There are several ML algorithms in the literature and choosing the best-in-class ML algorithm is beset with challenges. Thus, algorithm selection for predicting the best result is a prominent step in the "data to information and knowledge" lifecycle. As we studied in the previous chapters, there are many ML algorithms, which are categorized under supervised, semi-supervised, and unsupervised algorithms. With experience, data scientists can quickly choose the best algorithm to solve the problem at hand.

Confusion matrix is used to understand the performance of classifiers on a test data as we already know the true values. It is originally meant for the performance evaluation of the ML classifiers where the expected output can be of two or more classes. This matrix is useful for evaluating the accuracy, precision, recall, and specificity and importantly the area under the curve (AUC) of receiver operating characteristic (ROC) probability curve which shows trade off of sensitivity and specificity, at various threshold limits. This method is generally used for checking the performance level of each of the ML algorithms in order to arrive and articulate the best-in-class ML algorithm for a particular prediction problem.

2.8.6   *Phase 5 – model evaluation*

There are several aspects to be checked for the trained and tested model. With the edge computing gaining prominence for achieving real-time analytics and applications, the model chosen has to be evaluated for its efficiency. That is, the model is optimized to be run on edge devices. AI models are generally obscure in nature. The decisions and conclusions being made by AI models are not self-explanatory, interpretable, transparent, and trustworthy. Thus, the concept of explainable AI (XAI) has come up and there are several research contributions by worldwide AI experts in order to convey the ways and means of achieving self-explaining AI models.

2.8.7   *Phase 6 – model optimization*

Model performance, accuracy, complexities (time, space, and energy), efficiency, and other crucial aspects are being identified and optimized in order to be stocked in model repositories. Thus, ML algorithms are being leveraged to solve some specific problems including classification, detection, recognition, clustering, association, and translation with ease.

2.9   Stopping cyber attacks by AI algorithms

In the extremely connected world, cybersecurity has become a major issue for businesses as well as governments. There are a plentiful corporate, confidential, and citizen data being collected, cleansed, and crunched in order to extract actionable insights, which empower business executives and government officials to consider tactic as well as strategic decisions in time with all the clarity and confidence. Having understood the growing value of data, cyber-attackers cunningly target these data in order to gain financial benefits. Similarly, mission-critical and consumer-centric applications are also being targeted by hackers to disable them. For bitcoin mining, miners need computational resources and hence attack clusters of compute nodes. Thus, with the deeper connectivity and the Internet is increasingly comprising not only enterprise and cloud servers but also devices, instruments, equipment, machineries, appliances, robots, drones, and digitized entities, the cybercrimes are bound to go up in the days to come.

Now with the potential of ML algorithms being felt across, the cybersecurity phenomenon is gaining strength and speed. That is, ML-inspired prediction capability comes handy in securing and saving critical infrastructures, applications, and data sets. Any kind of attacks can be anticipated and annihilated in time so that the business continuity can be guaranteed. This is being accomplished through big, fast, and streaming data analytics. Also, the ML approach is being leveraged widely so as to make sense of Big Data in an automated manner.

That is, ML is the automated analytics when compared to previous generation analytics methods. All kinds of security-related data (current and historical) get captured meticulously and are sent through a series of automatic investigations to get patterns and intelligence out of it.

2.10   ML for cyber security

ML is a vital technology in ensuring cybersecurity by trampling out the threats strengthen the cyber infrastructure by various penetrations level testing and pattern mappings. It scans the entire system for vulnerabilities with auto responses periodically as well as whenever it finds some intrusion. These results are added to the supervised learning model for bolstering the tool.

ML model is composed of many algorithms born from the datasets and analysis models for making meaningful assumptions. Through this, the system can change its next course of actions and functions efficiently which would have not programmed explicitly in the system before.

Cybersecurity infrastructures together with ML, can learn and analyze patterns for preventing from the similar attacks and also to respond to certain behavior. It proactively prevents the threats and attacks in real time, benefiting the organizations for saving the time of routine test tasks and enables effective resource utilizations. ML makes the cybersecurity proactive and effective with less cost spent. ML is all about developing and manipulating patterns with learning algorithms. For the pattern development, lot of data with high quality and enormous quantity. The data should have rich content from every possible potential data source from the servers on the network and from cloud storage. Data cleaning is also inevitable so as to make sense of the new data that comes in and define feasible outcomes.

For cybersecurity, the system needs to collect data not only with right information but also the data of threats. Rich data contents are required about network, protocols, and sensors.

2.11   Network protection

Network protection is a set of different solutions that focus on protocols like Ethernet, wireless, SCADA, virtual networks like SDNs, etc. It refers to well-known intrusion detection system (IDS) solutions [12]. ML in network security implies the innovative solutions known as network traffic analytics (NTA). NTA is aimed at a detailed analysis of all the traffic and data transfer at each layer to detect attacks and anomalies. ML algorithms come handy for NTA regression, classification, and clustering techniques as mentioned below:

- regression to predict the network packet parameters and compare them with the normal ones;
- classification to identify different classes of network attacks such as scanning and spoofing;
- clustering for forensic analysis.

2.12   Endpoint detection and response (EDR)

EDR detects threats in our network environment and responds to them by analyzing the history of threats as how it is initiated, parts of network which got affected by the threat, its present nature and how to halt the attack on the whole. It is a new kind of antivirus that safeguards the network by threat containment and stops its spread furthermore. No matter what the organization software is, like cloud platform or the in house system, EDR protects the network.

There are endpoints such as workstation, bare metal (BM) server, container, virtual machine (VM), smartphone, PLC, and Internet of Things (IoT) device. The vital components of ML algorithms for endpoint protection are given below:

- Data collection at endpoint
- Incident response
- Endpoint data analysis

Data collection of endpoint is done to monitor the data, which comprises of processes' meta data, details of activities that occur at endpoints, the physical connections and the specifications of data that are transferred from and to the endpoints.

Incident response is an automated process that follows the rules and protocols created by the IT professionals for threat identification and trigger and for automatic responses. It can not only identify the threats but also can determine the threat's nature and motive. Its responses include sending alert like the user of endpoint will log off.

Real-time data analysis happens at endpoint to enable a quick threat diagnosis, even if the threat is of new kind which does not match with the preconfigured threat definition. It uses forensic tools for examining the threat's nature and how it was initiated and its motive.

2.13   Threat detection by EDR

Detecting the threats is the initial step of EDR system. Its key approach is to analyze what happens to the system when the threat gets into it. It is important to detect it when the threat has penetrated through the edge point and then it can be eliminated by containing it. There are many complex malwares which are smart enough to go through all defense mechanisms by showing it as safe by not revealing it malicious motive. So, detecting the threat is so very important to take actions against it [4].

EDR keeps analyzing the files to have efficient threat detection. It examines each file which comes in contact with endpoint and while doing so, it flags the file that has a threat in it. Most of the cases, every file appears to be safe in the initial inspection. Whenever it has threatening behavior, EDR alerts the stakeholders and IT team for further actions. Cyber threat intelligence (CTI) is used for detection as hackers deploy frequently changing tools to damage the system. CIT uses AI tools and big data store houses of previously attacked threats and presently evolving threats to identify the threats which target the endpoints.

2.14   Containment

EDR contains every malicious file as it detects it. Usually these malicious files aim to infect the overall processes and applications. Containment is so crucial for ransomware threats as they try to hold the endpoints hostage, once identified; they have to be contained as it presents other endpoints being infected by it.

Once the threat is detected, it is contained and later EDR investigates the nature of it, to get a meaningful and actionable knowledge to strengthen the overall security measures. If the device is older, it can be vulnerable to few kinds of attacks and so the same security measure is not suitable for all systems uniformly. Sandbox investigation uses the threat to study its activity closely by monitoring it and analyze how it responds to different use cases and this study report can be conveyed to the CTI team to address the future threats of its kind.

Though EDR detects, analyze, contain, and eliminate the threats, in most of the cases, it does not replace antivirus completely; it is intended to work along with the firewalls and antivirus software as a preventive measure.

2.15   Application security

ML can be used on web application firewalls (WAFs), code analysis (static and dynamic), etc. Data bases, web applications, SaaS and ERP applications, micro services, etc. also can be secured through ML. Application security can be strengthened by different ML algorithms as explained below.

- ML regression models for detecting anomalies in HTTP/HTTPS requests such as XXE, SSRF attacks, authentication bypass, etc.
- Classification models for detecting known types of attacks like SQLi, RCE injections, etc.,
- clustering various user activities in detections mass exploitation and DDOS attacks.

2.16   User behavior

Security information and event management (SIEM) is the principal solution approach for user behaviour detection. However, SIEM is not capable to handle new and advanced types of attacks due to constant behavior change. Unlike malware detection focusing on common attacks, user behavior is one of the complex layers and unsupervised learning problem. ML algorithms come handy here as briefed below:

- regression to detect anomalies in user actions (e.g., login in unusual time);
- classification to group different users for peer-group analysis;
- clustering to separate groups of users and detect outliers.

2.17   Process behavior

For ML to find something moving away and deviate, it is important to know the complete picture of business process. Fraud activities in banking structures, retail marketing or manufacturing can be identified though the underlying business processes are completely different. There are number of ML tools available for process behavior namely [13]

- regression models to forecast the next user action and detect outliers like credit card fraud;
- detect and classification the fraud to the known types of fraud;
- clustering the activities to compare business processes and detect threats.

There are many popular problems that are getting solved through the power of machine and deep learning algorithms. Building and deploying expert, cognitive, and question and answer (Q & A) systems are being facilitated through AI algorithms. Industry 4.0 applications are being readied through AI processing.

There are myriads of applications and use cases that can be easily implemented through the contributions of data scientists. Data science is a key technology enabler for companies and corporate to march ahead. By meticulously leveraging proven data analytics methods, promising AI algorithms, state-of-the-art AI-specific processors, and enabling tools in conjunction with right datasets, data scientists bring forth a variety of advancements to enterprises to traverse with all the confidence, and alacrity. Business organizations, establishments, and governments can achieve the strategic and competitive advantages with the skilled usage of DM processes, products and practices.

2.18   The modern data architecture (MDA)

In the present world of data science, Cloud, big data, and mobile applications are increasingly accelerated through AI capabilities, which are being realized through ML and DL algorithms. Extraction of personalized and predictive insights are extracted out of data volumes through the leverage of AI models can be fed back into software applications. Such knowledge discovery is being facilitated by ML and DL algorithms. Such an empowerment makes software applications to be intelligent in their decisions and deliveries. Data analytics is therefore an important factor for producing intelligent applications. With the surging popularity of AI (machine and deep learning) algorithms, the aspect of analytics becomes accelerated and automated.

The domain of data science has gone through a number of advancements. Originally, it all started with DM algorithms. Then came numerous data analytics methods, integrated platforms, enabling frameworks, accelerators and cloud environments, etc., to do mining on big, fast, and streaming data. Now AI is the prime factor for speeding up DM. There are cloud environments for performing AI-inspired data analytics. In the recent past, as edge devices are getting stuffed with processing and communication capabilities and memory and storage capacities, the AI-based data processing is also taking place at the edge thereby the long-pending goal of aggregating real-time insights is being fulfilled. As discussed above, AI-enabled data processing helps to solve an array of time-consuming, resource-intensive and tough-to-do classification, regression, detection, recognition, translation, association, searching, matching, etc.

Data science is a complex process as there are several steps to do for bringing input data into a shape. That is, the transformation of raw data to information and insights is beset with a number of technical challenges. In nutshell, data science is all about playing with data to emit insights that predict some useful thing for devices, applications, and decision-makers. To include data science in it, the MDA, has to facilitate the following factors:

1. Enable applications to consume predictive insights to exhibit intelligent behavior.
2. Bring predictive analytics to the IoT edge devices.
3. Facilitate easy and quick deployment of AI-enabled predictive models in production environments.

Figure 2.1 depicts the scenario of data science, where it fits in the MDA.

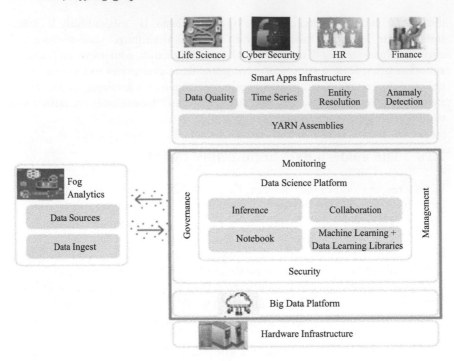

Figure 2.1   Data science scenario in MDA

2.18.1   Smart applications

As per the architecture diagram, the consumer of this application uses the data-driven insights through a host of consumer-facing applications. Such an empowerment goes a long way in enabling organizations, governments, and establishments to plunge into insights-driven decisions and deeds in time. Legacy applications are therefore being modernized to receive knowledge discovered directly without any ambiguity. Fresh applications are being built to consume AI-thrown insights directly. That is, the remedied and fresh applications can natively take advantage of all kinds of predictive, personalized, and prescriptive insights to be distinct in their actions and reactions. There are slim and sleek, trendy and handy, purpose-specific, and agnostic devices in plenty these days. And a dazzling array of mobile applications are being built and stocked in application repositories and these are to consume derived insights and act upon them with all the alacrity and clarity. Thus, next-generation applications have to be intrinsically smart enough in order to absorb intelligence directly.

2.18.2   Smarter edge

The future beckons the era of the Internet of Everything (IoE). The IoE is the future Internet, which not only comprises server machines, desktops, and laptops, but also all kinds of mobiles, instruments, equipment, appliances, wares, utensils, machineries, gadgets, consumer electronics, communication gateways, data, people, processes etc. Thus, it foretells the existence of billions of connected things on the planet earth. These IoT devices are termed as edge servers and devices. The resource-intensive devices are called edge servers whereas resource-constrained devices are termed as edge devices. Typically edge devices gather a lot of contextual information in their operating environments and share them to nearby edge servers, which can receive, store, and process the information to emit out of insights immediately. The knowledge discovered gets disseminated to all kinds of edge devices and edge-native applications to exhibit intelligent behavior. That is, with the real-time data analytics platforms being deployed in edge servers, a dazzling array of real-time, context-aware, people-centric, service-oriented, event-driven, cloud-hosted, and insights-driven applications are bound to flourish. The on-device data processing works faster with a potential to predict the insights in the needed spots, without even the existence of a persistent and reliable network facility. Due to the resource constraints, AI model creation is not happening at the edge. But model-based inferences are being accomplished through individual and a group of edge devices. Thus, the new concept of edge AI/edge intelligence is emerging and evolving fast with their implementation technologies and tools are fast maturing and stabilizing. There are several research groups across the globe who are working in order to bring in the right and relevant advances in the edge AI field so that edge devices can bring in the necessary modifications on the AI models to be adaptive, adjustive, and accommodative in their decision-making and deal-making tasks.

2.18.3 Faster, more accurate, and easier management

Existence of numerous smart devices and their heterogeneity nature, data generation is massive. Such multi-structured big data sources are the new normal for government, organizations, and businesses. Generating data-driven knowledge and decision making deeds are the dream of every data scientist. With big data, we need bigger compute resources, networks, and storage appliances. Recently, our ML tools are more accurate in their decision-making capability with the ready availability of big data. There are integrated big and fast data analytics platforms being made available in public as well as private cloud environments. The cloud infrastructures are also empowered through a host of sophisticated processors. In the recent past, we are reading and hearing about various advancements in hardware devices like Yet Another Resource Negotiator (YARN) support GPU, Field-Programmable Gate Array (FPGA), and Remote Directory Memory Access (RDMA) which enables one machine to access the memory of another system without the involvement of both the operating systems that helps to achieve high throughput and requires low latency network to get a fine-grain control functionality.

Programming languages and frameworks such as Python, Rust, and R are making a lot of simplification on data science activities. For distributed computing, there are integrations such as Spark, Python, and R technologies. Hadoop 3 facilitates Docker Support and it allows developer packaged environments to run as a YARN job as those applications are easier to manage.

Thus, data science tasks are getting automated, accelerated, and augmented with the smart leverage of cutting-edge technologies and tools.

Data science platform – Data science is an interesting but complicated thing. It needs a lot of talent, time, and treasure. It has to be performed collaboratively and cognitively in order to win the game. Data scientists collect, cleanse, and crunch data to extract worthwhile insights that are actionable, in the form of predictions, usable associations, hidden patterns, fresh possibilities, and opportunities. Based on their experience and expertise gained over the years, they arrive at the best-in-class machine, deep learning, and ensemble learning algorithms to create the model from the data. There are data science platforms, frameworks, libraries, and accelerators. In the recent past, there are model checking, evaluation, optimization, and deployment platforms for automated and accelerated deployment of AI models in production environments.

In nutshell, a data science platform has to take care of the entire model life-cycle. Model creation, deployment, versioning, management, etc., have to be taken care of by the chosen data science platform.

2.19   The Kafka platform for data scientists

The faster maturity and stability of the Kafka platform is being seen as a positive development. That is, Kafka emerges as a key ingredient for any data analytics platform for performing both batch and real-time processing on big, fast, and streaming data. It is a technology based on distributed streaming of events that can handle tons of events every day. It is based on distributed commit protocol system, consisting of clients and servers which communicate through TCP protocol. Kafka can be placed on hardware, cloud services, and VMs.

Kafka servers run as number of servers spanning to several cloud data centers which includes specialized storage layer known as brokers. These servers do import and export of data event streaming continuously to synchronize with databases and other Kafka server clusters. These Kafka servers are fault tolerant and scalable to ensure the continuous error-free operations without data inconsistency and loss due to failures and coherency issues.

Kafka clients are used for writing microservices and distributed applications which process the event streams in parallel with high fault tolerance even during hardware and network failures. Kafka was initially developed on LinkedIn to analyze the professional connections over millions of users to strengthen the people connect. Later, it has become open source in 2011, and Apache Foundation takes care of the controls of this Kafka open source software.

The open source software, Kafka, is a framework that facilitates storage and analysis of stored streaming data that is capable of running across several machines for the optimized usage of resources such as CPU power and the storage facilities of the overall server systems. Kafka is able to manage the swift incoming data due to its distributed behavior and respond to the drastic changes happening in the datasets every moment, in the real time. It analyses the navigation activities of the user through various clicks and scrolling of the web pages to understand the user behavior and draw conclusions on them such as which product or news the customer s interested in that moment.

2.20   Kafka APIs

Kafka comprises of four core APIs namely producer, consumer, streams, and connector APIs. Producers publish record data of various topics. Since Kafka is a distributed application, it manages many topics across number of systems, with a beautiful concept called Partition. Partitioning helps to maintain the read write logs minutely. Every single topic's log is broken into multiple log instances, and each instance holds a topic's partial record. Through partitions, Kafka paves way for its scalability. It spread partitions across multiple servers known as broker; each topic is scaled horizontally for providing better availability and facilitates fault tolerance which is far away from an individual server's ability, when it is down [14].

There are many use cases that can use kafka for event streaming. For instance,

- Real-time tracking of the shipment of trucks, cars, fragile items for automotive and logistics organizations.
- Periodically sensing and analyzing the critical data through IoT devices and sensor equipment in production industries and factories.
- Analyze the customer feedback, queries, and orders in hotel, retail, and travel industries.
- Instant processing of payments and transactions in bank, stock, and forex exchanges and insurance companies.
- Connecting data of different sections and branches of an organization and store them and make data availability to all stake holders.
- Continuous patient health monitoring in hospitals and detect/predict health condition changes to assure the immediate treatment during emergency times.
- Being the foundation for data driven and data-dependent architectures and micro services. The interface between each topic and the user applications deals with huge transaction database which is unsorted enables seamless processing of thousands of data streams every second. Kafka makes the central nervous system model where data passes through the system that is captured by various data applications and processing engines and get stored in storage lakes.

Kafka uses partitioning algorithm to create partitions if it is not specified by the customer. Records are written across the partitions of a specified topic. It is important to specify the partition key otherwise the records cannot be ordered within each partition for efficient fetching of records. The key idea here is to use an efficient partition key so as to keep the related event records together in a single partition in order.

In summary, in today's world, any intelligent real-time applications are projected as a game changer in any industry. AI technologies and tools are capable of elegantly producing real-time and intelligent software solutions. Especially algorithms of ML/DL, which are the key constituents of AI, are gaining immense momentum because these algorithms allow systems to find hidden knowledge in data heaps without the explicit look up algorithms. This powerful model is very much insisted on for analysing big data that are of unstructured formats. Extracting actionable intelligence out of such huge volume data (knowledge discovery) and supplying it to the target audience (knowledge dissemination) such as to any concerned system and people on time to act upon with all the clarity and confidence is being proclaimed as the need of the hour. Besides producing predictive and prescriptive insights, there are other advanced requirements such as object detection, image recognition, speech recognition, and text translation. Thus, the role and responsibility of AI are definitely on the rise.

Data scientists are primarily indulging in processing, mining, analyzing and investigating data collections by expertly leveraging proven and promising advancements in the AI space. In order to empower data scientists, there is a need for integrated data analytics platforms that can run on cloud infrastructures (private, public, and edge).

2.21   Conclusion

The discipline of data science is acquiring a lot of attention these days as there is an enhanced awareness on the strategic significance of data. The number of data sources is rapidly growing. Transforming the raw data into information and from information to knowledge is hugely simplified and streamlined. There are integrated and insightful platforms available for data analytics. The ready availability of cloud infrastructures for data storage and processing is being touted as the key motivation. Besides there are other enablers such as products, processes, practices, patterns, and procedures in order to speed up the acts of data collection, munging, wrangling, transformation, governance, security, etc.

Kafka is one of the key components in setting up scalable IT infrastructures toward data crunching. There are other associated toolsets in order to gather data from different sources store and investigate captured and cleansed data. Thus, data scientists are being empowered with self-service platform solutions in order to enable them to focus on their core competencies in their day-to-day assignments.

References

[1]   https://towardsdatascience.com/tagged/fraud-detection
[2]   https://www.forbes.com/sites/cognitiveworld/2020/01/09/how-ai-and-robotics-can-change-taxation/?sh=493fc1396437
[3]   J.A. Nasir, O.S. Khan and I. Varlamis, Fake news detection: a hybrid CNN-RNN based deep learning approach, *International Journal of Information Management Data Insights*, 1(1), 2021, 100007, ISSN 2667-0968, https://doi.org/10.1016/j.jjimei.2020.100007
[4]   https://arxiv.org/pdf/1705.01613.pdf
[5]   https://arxiv.org/pdf/1806.00749.pdf
[6]   https://onlinelibrary.wiley.com/doi/epdf/10.1002/spy2.9?src=getftr

[7] https://www.sciencedirect.com/science/article/pii/S2666285X21000066#bib0002

[8] P. Mallick, Forest Fire Detection Powered by Edge Impulse, Machine Learning, TinyML, Edge Impulse, 2022.

[9] https://www.publish.csiro.au/wf/pdf/WF20139

[10] M.A.S.A. Husaini, M.H. Habaebi, S.A. Hameed, M.R. Islam and T.S. Gunawan, "A systematic review of breast cancer detection using thermography and neural networks," *IEEE Access*, 8, 2020, 208922–208937, doi: 10.1109/ACCESS.2020.3038817.

[11] http://archive.ics.uci.edu/ml/datasets/breast+cancer+wisconsin+%28diagnostic%29

[12] https://www.fortinet.com/resources/cyberglossary/what-is-edr?utm_source=paid-search&utm_medium=google&utm_campaign=EDR-APAC-IN&utm_content=CG-WhatisEDR&utm_term=endpont%20security&lsci=7012H000001e9MTQAY&gclid=Cj0KCQjw6J-SBhCrARIsAH0yMZhvrhJLnt3zKZbm1dLYNfqjAY4OSa-G5y3nmyknQh0j0jYvsd_FKlYaAvaTEALw_wcB

[13] https://towardsdatascience.com/machine-learning-for-cybersecurity-101-7822b802790b

[14] https://kafka.apache.org/081/documentation.html

Chapter 3

Accelerating graph analytics

P. Divya[1], S. Jayalakshmi[1], M. Pavithra[1], R. Rajmohan[1], T. Ananth Kumar[1] and Osamah Ibrahim Khalaf[2]

Abstract

Handling graph databases properly leads to obtaining a precise result within a fixed time. It is essential to take a fast-track in graph analytics to address the challenges faced in exploring the data, as it is an incipient form of data analysis. The analytic methodologies involved in discovering the underlying implications of data to deliver an optimized result should get drive-by emerging techniques. A graph database possesses many complex patterns which are to be quickly identified for specific outcomes. Graph analytics assist in building patterns based on the connectivity between the nodes to provide proper context. Graph analysis is transforming into a significant factor for today's data analysis, so there is a need to accelerate its medium to the next level by implanting its features with recent technologies. To boost the performance of graph analytics, Artificial Intelligence (AI) is embraced with its enhanced features and techniques. Graph-based machine learning and analytics act as a boon for data scientists to increase their productivity and representation of data which is widely expected from enterprise users. Implementing AI produces machine-generated quick and precise values and results in a complete dataset—adopting machine learning techniques helps in feeding training data to the algorithm, building relationships between disparate data points, and enabling the connection between nodes and structure graph databases. This chapter leads the path of advanced graph analytics, which will lead data analyzers to take their next move in a data-powered business.

3.1 Introduction

Graphical analytics is a category of a tool that processes its source data in order to transform a raw dataset into helpful knowledge based on its relationship in graphical database records. AI systems can spontaneously examine given raw data and discover various unseen outlines and perceptions that researchers and analysts can use to give precise information needed by various sectors according to their needs

[1]Department of Computer Science and Engineering, IFET College of Engineering, India
[2]Al-Nahrain University – Baghdad, Iraq

with better results [1]. The adoption of AI automatic report generation is initiated, making less manual effort with minimum time requirement. Graph analytics is essential due to the highest predicted growth expected in the market region. Based on the latest graph analytics data, the graph analytics market size was $600 million in 2019; it has also been approximated to reach $2.5 billion by 2024 at a CAGR of 34% during the prediction period. Adoption of Natural Language Query (NLQ) and Natural Language Generation (NLG) with AI makes to get extract insights from the obtained source data in that way, a massive range of queries and skillsets have been accessed by researchers, business users, and analysts, providing a big doorway to get used of processed information. The difficulty and volume of data used and generated by trade and corporates are more than humans alone to process precisely.

3.2   Graph analytics methods to deliver smarter AI

3.2.1   *Semi supervised learning with graph algorithms*

Semi-supervised machine learning takes the most significant advantage of machine learning algorithms as it is a merge of both supervised and unsupervised learning; only a small amount of labeled data is taken as input rest of the utilized data by the algorithm are the unlabeled one that implements a time-efficient and easy doing part [2]. The following are some of the semi-supervised learning approaches:

- Generative models
- Low-density separation
- Graph-based methods
- Heuristic approaches

Incorporating semi-supervised learning with graphs can better represent and optimize results in classifying tasks even in challenging conditions and complex datasets [5]. The initial step to this task is to construct a basic graph from the collected data through semi-supervised learning approaches. Each vertex of the graph is a data point that may be labeled or unlabeled data [3]. This kind of graph-based method is implemented by adopting label propagation amid vertices to do classification, and it starts from labeled vertices to unlabeled vertices. There are two essential steps for implementing graph-based semi-supervised learning such as graph construction and graph regularization learning; after the above step has been completed, use the obtained results with the unlabeled data to determine the outputs, which have been termed as pseudo labels as they are created based on approximate data. Now a link is to be generated among these labeled and unlabeled data. By providing repeated training to this prototype, an actual model comes into existence with minimized error and higher efficiency [4].

3.3   Data preparation

In order to obtain a good result, the data has to be prepared before the graph is run. Models are developed to many of their specifications based on the quality of the information used to train them. As most of the time is spent in data mining projects, much effort is dedicated to data preparation. Cleaning data and a careful inspection and preparation of that data are essential steps in analyzing and preparing it. Supervised and unsupervised learning is applied to understand better how the relationships between the data and its source and search time and correct responses are expanded. Algorithms may include an example of a simplified if-then-else rule; it describes the decisions that lead to the prediction. A generalized logistic model or a suitable model fitted for classification (Collaborative Lifecycle Management (CLM) will have both binary targets and continuous input and will be used.) Confidence bounds are provided for prediction probabilities in GLM classification. Confidence bounds are supported by the generalized linear model (GLM). With minimum description length (MDL), the amount of information we supply to users and clients is proportional to the amount we desire to be deduced from it MDL assumes that it is the most straightforward and most uncomplicated representation of the data, with the least amount of detail possible, is the best to utilize and process. By naive Bayes' theorem, predictions will be made on the basis of the evidence presented in the data, such things as data from the sample(s), no over-which model naivety is utilized. The more support a support vector machine can offer, the more likely it is to separate the target classes to high precision. To do an SVM regression, it is essential to find a function with the most extensive data points congregated in a superficial region of positive epsilon around it. This method uses frequent items to produce a market topology for connecting competing product classes. A rule is expanded until the resulting tree has a minimum count of affinities that counts greater than zero and a confidence that is greater than or equal to the specified count threshold. The probability clustering property of expectation–maximization does something like density estimation and makes assumption functions. When making a density estimate, the goal is to construct a function that can model the distribution of the given population. Extracting existing knowledge base feature sets and creating meaning for new facts are both facets of expand. Each feature or concept has an attribute represented in a vector. Extended search allows users to be provided with semantic navigation for all concepts in the knowledge base and value information about those concepts with associated values. K-mean is a partitioning method that decides the number of clusters for the data and distributes the data over those clusters. Non-negative matrix factorization (NMF) combines the original attributes with non-linear features. Each of the components of the linear combinations is non-negative. When using the non-negative matrix factorization (NMF) technique, the original data is first mapped into the features discovered by the model, and then the model is applied to them [4].

3.4 Steps to get started with graph machine learning model

The following are the steps to start modeling a graph-based machine learning system:

(I)   Structured query-oriented knowledge graphs
(II) Query-based feature engineering

(III)   Extending the use of graph algorithms
(IV)   Graph embedding's
 (V)   Graph neural networks (GNN) and native learning

3.4.1   Structured query-oriented knowledge graphs

When using knowledge graphs, dealing with flexibility in querying large amounts of data is challenging. Researchers use SPARQL to interpret knowledge graphs, who will already have incredible amounts of specialized knowledge and cannot understand the returned results without investing significant time into learning and research. Some new systems are planned to handle the following: when new customers arrive on the campus, the new facilities and record-and-and-identify operations expand together. The approach is to divide the translation process into smaller sub-scale tasks, with the use of machine learning methods such as trees, and to use a neural network approach to learn and produce subtasks like RDF to do the overalls. This online development has provided a plethora of readily available resources with an abundance of structured data in the form of information in the form of knowledge graphs. Because of this, it follows that we can assume in natural language interfaces like Question and Answer (NA) and particularly in question answering systems such as question answering platforms. QA systems follow up using natural language processing, information retrieval, machine learning, and the natural language web to extract the questions from the graph. Expanding from non-natural language to separate, distinct sub-conjunctions (or more minor problems) is a more effective method for handling this obstacle of translating from human language to SPARQL. The problem is conceptualized in a pipeline to include various processes like named-entity recognition (NER), relation extraction (RE), and query generation (QG) [6]. The last part of the QG algorithm is the one that compiles a SPARQL query based on the structure of the knowledge graphs. Most querying or techniques for querying systems subdivide knowledge into separate components are found not to be separate from one another, however. The architecture of the QA system incorporates five core components for five different purposes is shown in Figure 3.1.

3.4.2   Query-based feature engineering

The fast indexing and the ability to process graphically and interrogate data quickly are significant strengths of a graph querying system. An index is created by computing the mean value of all typical edges, which is very simple and quick but does not use any costly operation such as mining the graph [7]. Two crucial technologies are utilized in the query process: a novel crawler and a software filter. The bottom line is that expandable answers can be used in the database to extract a subset of the complete answers, even if the information they give is untrusted. Then, designers filter the database down to a much smaller set of suitable candidates, and finally, designers reduce the list to an even smaller set. Graph databases research is mainly done on two types: pre-existing graph databases that have already been created and graph data models being designed and constructed.

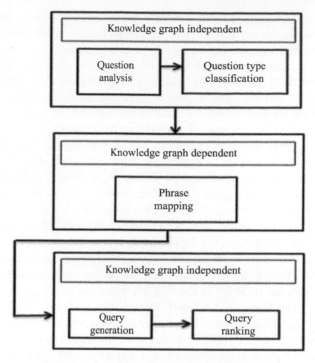

Figure 3.1   Architecture of the QA system

Furthermore, the size of the graphs, such as social networks, grows with each passing year. Using the second approach, we will construct a set of moderately sized transaction networks that consist of separate transaction graphs. Graph databases are frequently used in scientific and bioinformatics environments, especially with transactional analysis. There are two types of queries studied in the literature: EXPLAIN supports two types of data expansion. When we say a given graph is a subset of another, we ask for the database to provide us with all of the graphs that are a part of that subset. Super query searches, retrieves, and searches for all the other connected graphs in the database that satisfy the given conditions, so the condition holds, but the term "connected" is replaced by "super-connected." The queries are made up of nodes with larger graphs attached. When a query is submitted, the system returns a list of all structures with the requested properties. Those structures can then be used to learn more about the query's characteristics, with expansive processing power without growing complexity. It is also possible to regulate query the expansive databases, which can handle complicated queries, and the characteristics of not bloating, while also maintaining their simplicity.

Thanks to batch processing for improving query processing, queries with similar structures and query processing capacity can be expanded. The index reduces the number of queries to be processed at the expense of sharing data already gathered, integrating all the different types of data into a single data graphic (ID), which makes the most of all the available data graphs (EG) the amount of edge that is possible. Expanded graphs do not require any expensive test functions such as sub-graph isomorphism detection, making it possible to do straight-line time. The second factor to consider is that it is quick and straightforward to keep the Information GATHERINGER up to date. The notion of IG guides our development of a graph query system, which we have developed under the name IG query. The two new techniques are discussed, which are called direct inclusion of answers and the master database. The filtering approach is expanding by getting a more extensive set of candidates for direct inclusion in the process: by drawing out more prominent candidates for a filtering process, a significant percentage of the population.

The expansion takes advantage of the subgraph–disjoint relationship to ensure that multiple data-oriented graphs are indirect answer sets (for fast verification), thus dramatically reducing the overall verification time. What is most important, it is safe to say, is that direct inclusion does not require a subgraph–subspace test. It matches the frequency and transforms the data with the appropriate quantization step to check the if-expansion formula to match the data and the graphs' search conditions, which uses only linear time as a prerequisite. Second, projection databases produce a small set of candidates not included in the direct answers but are "expanded" (the projections are not taken from the database). The advantage of using the frequency-based strategy for subgraph expansion is that it reduces the number of steps in the expansion process by following the descending order of edge frequency. The number of other integrated figures always describes a graph's capacity. It uses the same basic principles that lead to frequent subtrees to assist in the problem's resolution to extract a subgraph of many graphs that includes common substructures. The graph approach is a third more efficient in these two points as it does not rely on expensive techniques such as frequent subgraph processing or subgraphs test minimization [8].

3.4.3   *Extending the use of graph algorithms*

Previously, scientist has developed a model for predicting fraud; they can utilize graph algorithms and queries to look for new features that enhance its accuracy [9]. For example, after identifying anomalies in the communities present in fraud rings, we use a classifier to increase the accuracy of our current fraud detection methods by extracting the graph features. While the Neo4j platform has the flexibility, scale, and software ease of use for rapid experimentation of different features in modeling, researchers are typically forced to keep these ideas in the test environment until the experiment is entirely executed and the results analyzed. The characteristics of a graph that anyone can include are simple as they consist of community IDs or previously labeled fraud patterns or may include anything else they want to describe to describe how a particular group of accounts tends to be related to each other accounts in the network. Features can be saved as a node, relationship, or attached as part of another model. They can also be stored in the product database and fed into the other environments via relations. In this situation, algorithms can be run while still benefitting from the previously seeded results by repeating calculations while incrementally growing the graph to ensure computational and consistency with the data. To successfully leverage prominent big data scientists' ability to exploit existing models and techniques, they will have to change the foundation and relationships. However, they also gain the ability to make accurate predictions of relationships at scale by working with multiple graphs. The dimension reduction problem is a bit broader, including feature extraction and feature selection methods. PCA methods, such as analysis method and feature normalization, on the other hand, endeavor to develop new attributes, but they instead set out to increase the total number of features. To achieve the most significant variability reduction in influence, maximum number of variables is conserved. Neither the product nor the dataset includes any of the already defined features in the system [10]. They do not allow downstream classifications to be condensed. Therefore, they cannot be used to remove redundancies or features or redundancies, like problem classifications. This brings up the difficulty of building classifiers using the new features and prevents the design of interpretable machine learning algorithms. These are the most popular three strategies for software feature extraction: expanding, feature screening, and feature wrapping. In the feature expansion approach, features are known beforehand, and then they are fed into the machine learning algorithm to pick out those that meet the criterion. In machine learning, the algorithm then uses relevant features to identify which specific branches of the decision tree should be expanded or retained, which could be referred to as "embedded machine learning." In the wrapper approach, feature subset generation is performed outside of the feature selection, lookup, and selection is left to chance, resulting in it being performed in black boxes. Such methods are based on finding the correlation between the structure of the graph, the observed relationship, and its actual performance with the simplest form of predictive modeling. This analysis tries to identify missing links by looking for the properties of the graph and then multiplying these by similarity scores between nodes. Local, quasi-local, and global approaches are the three main categories in which these methods can be studied [10].

3.4.4 *Approaches based on local similarity*

1. Local similarity-based approaches assume that even if node sets use comparable neighbor structures, individuals will most likely form a connection in the future. Those who are quicker and easier than global similarity-based approaches only utilize native topological data based on neighborhood binding sites rather than covering the overall topology of the network [11].
2. Common neighbors (CN)—because of its good precision, CN is among the most widely used communication retrieval metrics for pattern-matching tasks despite its simplicity. The concept behind CN is simple: the number of common neighboring nodes affects the likelihood of two nodes becoming linked in the future, i.e., two nodes will be more likely to form a link if they have more shared nodes.
3. Jaccard Index (JC) – Like CN, this metric represents the number of common nodes, but it also normalizes it by taking into account the total number of shared and non-shared neighbors.

4. Salton Index (SL) – Salton similarity is referred to as the cosine coefficient, which measures the degree of similarity between two vectors (SL). It is given by the cosine angular position of the two numbers (one between the *x*- and *y*-axis, and another between both the *v*- and the *w*-axis) squared of a root of one adjacency matrix (and vice versa).

5. Sorensen Index (SI) – This index can be used to compare different ecological samples, but it is usually restricted to items in the chemical compound industry.

6. Preferential Attachment Index (PA) – Nodes that previously participated in the network connection to other nodes are more likely to come into the network and make additional connections (attachment hubs) (nodes with lower degrees of connectivity).

7. Adamic-Adar Index (AA) – This metric is used when there is a need to compare two web pages. Even though this metric is similar to CN, the logarithm term penalizes the shared neighbors of the two corresponding nodes.

8. Resource Allocation Index (RA) – AA has a close correlation with the performance of the value of this index but grows more rapidly when the average degree of complexity is high. In other words, the fraction of familiar neighbors, a number *vx* and *vy*, is a function of the number of degrees of both *vx* and *vy*, and the minimum number of degrees will influence how the index of priority is increased (HP). While forming links nearby is given higher priority, the formation of connections between the hubs is downgraded.

9. Hub Depressed Index (HD) – The connection between hub nodes and lower degree nodes is degraded in this index.

10. Leicht–Holme–Newman Index (LHN) – The index is defined as the ratio of the number of shared neighbors of *vx* and *vy* to the product of their degrees and is very similar to SI (the expected value of the number of paths of length between them).

11. Parameter-Dependent Index (PD) – To improve the accuracy of prediction for both popular and unpopular links.

12. Local Affinity Structure Index (LAS) – These visualizations show the relationship among two nodes and their adjacent widely accepted neighbors.

13. CAR-Based Index (CAR) – CAR filters the noise by focusing on nodes that are mostly connected to neighbors.

14. Individual Attraction Index (IA) – The coefficient of correlation takes into consideration only the immediate neighbors, but a more complex effect that is known as the index refers to everything beyond these and is added [12].

15. Mutual Information Index (MI) – This method uses information theory to investigate the link prediction problem, and it measures the likelihood of conditional self-information when common neighbors are present.

16. Functional similarity weight (FSW) – This index compares the characteristics of two objects.

17. Local Neighbors Link Index (LNL) – The validity of this index takes into consideration the proximity of neighboring variables as well as both variables in common to nodes while making a prediction.

3.4.5 *Approaches that are based on global similarity*

Global similarity-based approaches, in contrast to local approaches, classify the resemblance between node pairs using the entire network structure; thus, they are not restricted to calculating the similarity among nodes that are located far apart. While considering the cable network's entire topology allows for more adaptability in link fault prediction, it also increases the algorithm's time complexity. Path-based methods get their name because they use an ensemble of all paths between node pairs [13].

1. Katz Index (KI) – sums over sets of paths and is exponentially damped by length, allowing shorter paths to be counted more intensively.
2. Global Leicht–Holme–Newman Index (GLHN) – GLHN uses a similarity approach that examines the number of paths that lead between these nodes as a measure of branch neighborhood integrity. Portal websites by their popularity among specific Internet users, as well as their total popularity across the internet (SR).
3. SimRank(SR) – Based on the hypothesis that "two objects are similar if they are related to similar objects," this index calculates similarity.
4. Pseudo-inverse of the Laplacian Matrix (PLM) – Pseudo-inverse of the Laplacian Matrix (PLM) is a proposed method for calculating proximity measures that uses the Laplacian matrix rather than the Adjacency matrix.
5. Hitting Time (HT) and average commute time (ACT) – The average number of steps taken by a random walker starting from node vx to reach node vy is defined as HT.
6. Rooted PageRank (RPR) – RPR states that a node's rank is proportional to the likelihood of being reached by a random walk.
7. Escape probability (EP) – This metric, which can be deduced from RPR, calculates the probability that a random walk starting at node vx will visit node vy before returning to node vx.
8. Random Walk with Restart (RWR) – The probability vector for reaching a node starting from the initial node in a random walk (RW) algorithm.
9. Maximal Entropy Random Walk (MERW) – This MERW algorithm emerged in response to the desire to create path allocations that were consistent across the set theory. It is based on the concept of the most uncertainty.
10. The Blondel Index (BI) – The BI is used to compare the similarity of two graphs. Martinez *et al.* show that the similarity of two vertices in a single graph can also be evaluated iteratively [13].

3.4.6 *Approaches based on quasi-local similarity*

1. The discovery of computational approaches for link prediction based on the emerging trade-offs between the efficiency of information for the entire network and reduced complexity for local structure has led to quasi-local methodologies coming into existence. As with any mathematical formula, however, the current methods for comparing arbitrary nodes meet challenges when

encountering two or more that are not connected. Instead of locally searching the tree and computing similarity between a node and its neighbors, quasi-local methods can search for similarity between a node and its neighbors [14]. Although quasirandom methodologies have the entire network structure incorporated into their consideration, they have lower complexity than approaches that depend on global similarity.

2. The Local Path Index (LPI) – The index, which is very similar to the well-known approaches KI and CN, takes a broader view of the local path by using information from the immediate neighbors and the next two and three.
3. Local (LRW) and Superposed Random Walks (SRW) – The random walker's initial resources are assigned based on the graph's importance. The node degree is an important feature for LRW, and it does not focus on the stationary state. Instead, in order to perform a few-step random walk, the number of iterations is fixed.
4. Third-Order Resource Allocation Based on Common Neighbor Interactions (RACN) – metric resources of nodes are allocated to metrics in this method.
5. FriendLink Index (FL) – This technique computes the normalized pair counts of existing paths between two sets of nodes and then uses these counts to show how many paths each one of these nodes has to calculate the similarity between two others.
6. PropFlow Predictor Index (PFP) – It simply equals the probability that a random walk will succeed if it begins at node vx and ends at node vy in less than 1 step [15].

3.5   Graph embeddings

A graph can be made up of a collection of nodes or edges that is multidimensional by being expanded into a multi-variate vector (MVE) representation, which can represent its (describe) the concepts of) topology, connectivity, or any other specific vector. An embedded vector graph will create a fixed-length representation for each entity (usually a node) to illustrate its relationships in the vector. These embeddings represent the graph by being a lower-dimensional geometric object and preserving the graph's structure. An embedding of a graph into a surface so that the graphs' endpoints are delineated; Given that any graph has the three-dimensional Euclidean space as its three-dimensional projective space, it is known that the projective capacity of R is finite. Every edge incident to the same vertex has an embedded graph that identifies which precisely one of its orders can be cyclic [16]. A rotating system or all these orders comprise the set of all circular orders. A set of configurations are regarded as is combinatorial configuration if there is a cardinal number greater than or equal to that which will exhaust the possibilities in which they can be used (as opposed to the term topological embedding, which refers to the previous definition in terms of points and curves). Some researchers refer to the method of how the component rotation is applied as "combinatorial embedding."

A multigraph also provides natural cyclic orders that divide the faces of the embedding into regions, creating the desired embedding's regions of expansions and contractions. Therefore, the problem of handling face-edge ordering is a bit more complicated because, in some cases, for example, a face can be traversed twice along a boundary. As an example, this is consistently the case concerning tree embedding, and they may have a single side. A combinatorial difficulty may be surmounted by recognizing that every edge as having two sides of equal length, one split in half. A convention holds for both half-edge and multiple-edge traversals. But a half-edge is never visited twice in a row in an L-building construction, and each segment always goes in an opposing direction. It can be viewed as an expansion of the traditional concept of cellular embedding, an example of a ribbon graph or a graph-encoded map, and has various equivalent terms such as a gluing together three-colored graphs, with 3D cylinders, an instance of the map-graph encoded cube and a concept of linking maps with 3D graphs.

3.5.1 Why graph embeddings are needed?

Other models based on graphs do not use deep learning techniques. Graphs are made up of edges and nodes. The library's network relationships can only utilize specific mathematical approach, statistical, and machine learning methodologies, whereas a mathematical method for working with vector spaces is potentially more advanced. Expansion is done by compression. The adjacency matrix describes how the nodes are related to one another. It is a$|V||V| \times |V|$ matrix, where |Here we will be [specify the number of nodes in the graph]. While creating a matrix, each column and each row present a node. A non-zero number of connections between the matrix elements indicate that two elements are connected. Using a matrix of adjacency for larger graphs is difficult due to its inability to process huge numbers of features. Instead of a graph with 1 million nodes, let us think of a graph that has one million links in an adjacency matrix of one million. Embeddings are far more effective for smaller dimensions than the adjacency matrix since they can pack information about the node structure within a single dimension. Operations on vectors have different complexity and usually have a much smaller footprint. It is critical that embeddings reliably portray the graphs' overall character. They must identify topology as well as the connectivity of the nodes and the locations of the nodes. There should be no slowdown in constructing the network structure for the amount of information included in the network. Typically, graphs are expansive. Imagine what it would be like if everyone were a part of one of a social network. Efficiently embedding the network in large graphs is a must for good results. More complicated is the task of deciding where to embed or where to expand. A longer embedding representation preserves more information and increases both space and time complexity than anonymously than an abbreviated one. Usability is that one's requirement must be fulfilled at the expense of the other [17]. This is a common trend in articles, where embedding size of 128–256 works best for most of the tasks is mentioned. In Word2vec, those who selected the dimensionality (300-dimensional) and then tried to cluster and expand. The Word2vec has two sub-layers. The first make words out of the words by converting each to a vector. As a noun, "creative" can mean "elaborate," and "genius" can mean "genius." Even though it is not as complex as a neural network, the Word2Vec model turns text into a format that neural networks can understand. The primary reason for and intended use of Word2vec is to create a set of similar words in the conceptual lattice. Which is to say, it uses mathematical analysis to detect similarities Word2vec generates vectors that describe how well the word's context fits into the sentence. It is entirely autonomous. Word2Vec makes surprisingly accurate assumptions about the word's meaning given enough appearances, examples, and circumstances. A word's link to other terms can be established with these guesses. DeepWalk follows the same learning methodology of the original skip-gram, the universal language-agnostic computing platform. To that end, one crucial point, all possible variables that affect the phenomenon should be put into a graph. This is done by a random walk procedure, in which we randomly select a single connection node as the start point and traverse to another. It is a representational learning framework that organizes complex knowledge in the form of linked sets of nodes. When a data structure has any given, the system can understand features of a collection of nodes, which are later employed in downstream machine learning operations.

3.5.2   GNN and native learning

GNNs operate on a graph-structured topology and make a deep learning topology expansion. In the last few years, GNN has become widely used as a graph-related analysis method because of its convincing results. The different groups of issues that GNNs are designed to solve are delineated as follows *n* investigation which must take place to figure out how many (can be done with a small expenditure of time and money) different classifications can be done (the task is to find out) with the same samples, especially of items in a classification system. Semi-supervised problems almost always deal with unsupervised graphs; rarely, only one of the features in the relationship is correctly labeled. If the task is to classify the whole graph into different categories, expand means the same as graph superposition: "A picture in a dataset can serve as a target to classify another dataset, rather than vice versa." There are many different applications for graph classification; for example, in bioinformatics, they can be used to detect whether a protein is an enzyme or not and determine which of the thousands of families of enzymes in a bioinformatical database. Additionally, they can be used to break up text documents into groups for social network analysis. To put it another way, we have put several different types of GNNs into categories and tell them about their specifics. This assignment's job listings are categorized according to three types [17].

3.5.3   Based on the graph type

The graphs are only of one type, the algorithm must also be modifiable, and then we must be aware that all the graphs will change. DGP (directed graph) is an alternative method that generates an arbitrarily high-dimensional data graph (including networks of edges) while preserving data connectivity. Even though GNN is excellent for modeling structural data, several problems can be circumvented with a few adjustments. Additionally, it is recommended to expand on the usage of the graph. As was stated above, the directed graph consists of long but then expands in both ways. Undirected edge suggests a relationship between the two nodes, but it could also mean that one of the nodes acts as a gateway to the other data of a class structure and is naturally visualized using the head and tail of parents and children. As we do in this example, we made a new two-dimensional weight matrix out of our DGP model. The data scientists are increasing the age-appropriate size of these two populations while maintaining equal growth in each until adulthood. Beyond this, graphs can be found diversely in many different ways [18]. The shape of this kind of graph is made up of consists of different types of nodes. Values do conversions are created by getting every node values similar and transforming them with a transformation called expander due to the unique characteristics of each computer node being capable of subdivision. The Graph Inception algorithm was developed, which, rather than having an average cluster of connections, relies on various network variables, groups of them altogether. Another type of decomposition is a subgraph where one or more of the edges has parallelism added to it to serve the same function of an algorithm. The heterogeneous graph attention networks built on this fact came into existence and eliminated the heterogeneous property [19].

Dynamic graphs: This has a dynamic/static graph structure as well as dynamic inputs. While dynamic structures allow the respective to adjust their own architecture and structure/algorithms, they require dynamicity in the architecture and structures of the internal components. When the idea of structure-based language learning was brought forth, it was a challenge because it had to deal with spatial and temporal messages from the same set of text. However, with the different, evolving graphs, it is a piece of cake.

The graphs with edge information. Besides being heavier or broader, such edges will have a weight type or other supplementary information attached to them. If this is helpful, you should also look into the creation of encoders like G2S and R-GCN. Where (specifically) RTGCN, which is an R-to-modulated form of GC. The R stands for relational. Also, because relational data is used, it is easier to associate nodes with their associations with other nodes with additional information, such as their relationship. Using the propagation step as a guide, the following types are available [18]:

- Graph convolutional network convolutional aggregator.
- The graph attention network is an attention aggregator.
- Gated recurrent unit (GRU) and LSTM are two gate updaters.
- Jump knowledge network, bypass connection – highway GNN.
- ECC hierarchical graph.

The types mentioned demonstrate how the propagation steps allow for versatility. It would be easier to comprehend these types of GNNs if they were compared to traditional neural networks. It is essential to keep in mind that the propagation step entails aggregating the values of neighboring nodes. As a result, the main distinction can also be referred to as aggregators. The convolutional aggregator is the first step. A convolutional neural network is an excellent example of this. As a result, these networks operate on image data. The basic concept remains the same. The high-level data is gradually convoluted into data of a smaller size. GCN is based on a similar concept. There are two options: spectral and spatial representations [20].

Other GCN formats include adaptive-GCN (AGCN) and gross geographic product (GGP) in the spectral domain and deep convolutional neural networks (DCNN) and dynamic graph convolutional network (DGCN) in the spatial domain. Similarly, attention networks are linked to attention aggregators, a crucial concept in graph attention networks and gated attention networks [21]. The core blocks in gate updaters are similar to GRU and LSTM networks. We create the gated graph neural network (GGNN) with the GRU. We can create architectures such as graph LSTM using the LSTM blocks, further divided into tree LSTM, sentence LSTM, and graph LSTM. We build architectures with core ideas parallel to residual networks using skip connection networks. The architectures are the jump knowledge network (as the name suggests) and the highway GNN [22]. Edge-conditioned convolution (ECC) networks are among the hierarchical graph architectures. It employs an edge-information graph to condition the data into something useful. After that, the same is used for propagation computations.

- Depending on the method of training.
- FastGCN, GraphSAGE – neighborhood sampling.
- Control of the receptive field – ControlVariate.
- Co-training and self-training are two methods for enhancing data.
- GAE and GCMC are examples of unsupervised learning.

The original GCN could not learn inductively as neighborhood sampling architectures are used to get around this problem. The GraphSAGE algorithm outperforms the original GCN algorithm in every way. The algorithm is replaced with the complete graph Laplacian with learnable aggregation functions to make inductive learning adaptable. The ControlVariate architectures added the stochastic approximation algorithms for GCN to the receptive field control, using the nodes' historic activations as a control variate. Co-training and self-training are the two network architectures we have for data augmentation. The authors proposed these two architectures to address the limitation of extensive labeled data required to train a GCN. Self-training follows a boosting-based architecture, while co-training makes use of the power of k-means for the neighbors in the training data.

Graph visualization is a branch of mathematics and computer science that straddles the line between geometric graph theory and data visualization. It is concerned with the visual representation of graphs that helps the user understand the graphs by revealing structures and anomalies that may be present in the data. Link prediction: in this case, the algorithm must comprehend the relationships between entities in graphs while also attempting to predict whether two entities are connected. It is critical to infer social interactions in social networks or make suggestions to users about potential friends. It has also been used to solve problems with recommender systems and predict criminal associations. The clustering of data in the form of graphs is referred to as graph clustering. On graph data, there are two different types of clustering. Vertex clustering is a technique for grouping nodes in a graph into densely connected regions based on edge weights or edge distances. The second type of graph clustering considers graphs to be clustered objects grouped based on their similarity.

3.6 Applications

In the field of text manipulation, there are several possibilities:

3.6.1 Classification of text

Text classification is a classic application of GNNs in NLP. GNNs rely on the interrelationships of documents or words to infer document labels. To complete this task, the GCN and GAT models are used. They expand the graph by converting text to a word-graph image and applying various graph convolutional and graph computation operations. Non-consecutive and long semantic travels are shown in studies demonstrating that graphs allow to include graphemes, making it possible to denote words from graphs instead of conveying these [18].

3.6.2 Translation by a neural computer

A sequence-to-sequence task is considered neural machine translation (NMT). Incorporating semantic information into the NMT task is one of the GNN's most common applications. Concerning syntax-aware queries, designers use the syntactic GCN to get the job done. The (GGNN or NGNN) is a commonly used keyword in NMT. The formula's structure is entirely reconstructed by creating a new set of syntactic dependencies among the nodes, which allows node labels to be represented as embeddings. The production of multiple types of relationships extraction is usually taking place between two or more entities. Existing practice in the realm of learning research and in which this entity-relationship relation happens is treated as a pipeline of two distinct tasks that is poorly articulated in the traditional approach. Conventional wisdom used to believe claims that have since proven faulty: Research, however, suggests that end-to-to-end entity and relational modeling is critical for high performance because interactions are closely linked to entities and relationships [both].

3.6.3 Image classification is a technique used in the field of image manipulation

A task as essential as classifying images is that of great importance in computer vision. Training a model using large quantities of positive and negative examples enables most classifiers to be accurate. Researchers are working to refine these models' target machine learning models for zero- and few-shot and semi-real-world use cases. Expanding on, expanding appears to be a good match for it.

3.6.4 Object detection is a feature that allows detecting of objects in the environment

Although object recognition, interactive interaction detection, and region classification are three different computer vision applications, they are some of the same techniques. The classification includes techniques like machine learning, such as Bayesian networks, and it is coupled with things like GNNs to solve RoI issues; interaction includes machine learning to interact with objects, and that too is done in the Bayesian networks; in turn, they are used as passing messages between humans and object classification.

3.6.5   Semantic segmentation is the process of separating words based on their semantic meaning

Semantic segmentation is an essential step in understanding an image. The goal here is to give each pixel in the image a distinct label. On the other hand, traditional CNN models fail because regions in images are frequently not grid-like and require non-local information.

3.6.6   Combinatorial optimization is a technique for maximizing the number of options

Combinatorial optimization (CO) refers to sorting through a set of possibilities to pick the best option from the group. Several critically essential applications in business, transportation, logistics, science, and hardware design are supported by it. Most COWS (complex oil refineries) problems can be expressed using flow charts.

3.7   Conclusion

The basic techniques of accelerating graphs are covered in this chapter. It includes how to graph analytics impact AI and machine learning models. Moreover, the steps of generating a graph are explained in detail using machine learning models. The steps include generating query-oriented graphs and feature engineering based on query structure, graph embedding, and neural networks. It also explains the method based on similarity for obtaining precise feature extraction using local and global similarity indexes.

References

[1]   Rossi, R. and N. Ahmed. "The network data repository with interactive graph analytics and visualization." In: *Proceedings of the AAAI Conference on Artificial Intelligence*, vol. 29, no. 1. 2015.

[2]   Huang, M.-H. and R.T. Rust. "Artificial intelligence in service." *Journal of Service Research* 21(2) (2018): 155–172.

[3]   Yang, Z., W. Cohen, and R. Salakhudinov. "Revisiting semi-supervised learning with graph embeddings." In: *International Conference on Machine Learning, PMLR*, 2016.

[4]   Jiang, B. "Semi-supervised learning with graph learning-convolutional networks." In: *Proceedings of the IEEE/CVF Conference on Computer Vision and Pattern Recognition*, pp. 11313–11320.

[5] Cao, S., W. Lu, and Q. Xu. "Grarep: Learning graph representations with global structural information." In: *Proceedings of the 24th ACM International on Conference on Information and Knowledge Management*, 2015.

[6] González, L. and A. Hogan. "Modelling dynamics in semantic web knowledge graphs with formal concept analysis." In: *Proceedings of the 2018 World Wide Web Conference*, 2018.

[7] Kul, G., D.T.A. Luong, T. Xie, *et al.* "Similarity metrics for SQL query clustering." *IEEE Transactions on Knowledge and Data Engineering* 30(12) (2018): 2408–2420.

[8] Anderson, M.R., D. Antenucci, and M.J. Cafarella. "Runtime support for human-in-the-loop feature engineering system." *IEEE Database Engineering Bulletin* 39(4) (2016): 62–84.

[9] Gregor, D. and A. Lumsdaine. "Lifting sequential graph algorithms for distributed-memory parallel computation." *ACM SIGPLAN Notices* 40(10) (2005): 423–437.

[10] Xia, L.C., D. Ai, J. Cram, J.A. Fuhrman, and F. Sun. "Efficient statistical significance approximation for local similarity analysis of high-throughput time series data." *Bioinformatics* 29(2) (2013): 230–237.

[11] Niu, S., Q. Chen, L. De Sisternes, Z. Ji, Z. Zhou, and D.L. Rubin. "Robust noise region-based active contour model via local similarity factor for image segmentation." *Pattern Recognition* 61 (2017): 104–119.

[12] Özbal, G., H. Karaman, and F.N. Alpaslan. "A content-boosted collaborative filtering approach for movie recommendation based on local and global similarity and missing data prediction." *The Computer Journal* 54(9) (2011): 1535–1546.

[13] Hammad, F. "More on the conformal mapping of quasi-local masses: the Hawking–Hayward case." *Classical and Quantum Gravity* 33(23) (2016): 235016.

[14] Yang, Z., W. Cohen, and R. Salakhudinov. "Revisiting semi-supervised learning with graph embeddings." In: *International Conference on Machine Learning*, PMLR, June 2016, pp. 40–48.

[15] Ristoski, P. and H. Paulheim. "Rdf2vec: Rdf graph embeddings for data mining." In: *International Semantic Web Conference*, October 2016, Springer, Cham, pp. 498–514.

[16] Bunn, A.G., D.L. Urban, and T.H. Keitt. "Landscape connectivity: a conservation application of graph theory." *Journal of Environmental Management* 59(4) (2000): 265–278.

[17] Pavithra, M., R. Rajmohan, T. Ananth Kumar, and R. Ramya. "Prediction and classification of breast cancer using discriminative learning models and techniques." *Machine Vision Inspection Systems* 2 (2021): 241–262.

[18] John A., T. Ananth Kumar, M. Adimoolam, and A. Blessy. "Energy management and monitoring using IoT with cupcarbon platform." In: Balusamy B., Chilamkurti N., Kadry S. (eds), *Green Computing in Smart*

Cities: Simulation and Techniques. Green Energy and Technology, 2021, Springer, Cham, https://doi.org/10.1007/978-3-030-48141-4_10.

[19]   Sengan, S., G.R. Koteswara Rao, O.I. Khalaf, and M. Rajesh Babu. "Markov mathematical analysis for comprehensive real-time data-driven in healthcare." *Mathematics in Engineering, Science & Aerospace (MESA)* 12(1) (2021): 77–94.

[20]   Zhao, H., P.-L. Chen, S. Khan, and O.I. Khalafe. "Research on the optimization of the management process on internet of things (Iot) for electronic market." *The Electronic Library* 39(4) (2021): 526–538.

[21]   Suresh Kumar, K., A.S. Radha Mani, S. Sundaresan, and T. Ananth Kumar. "Modeling of VANET for future generation transportation system through edge/fog/cloud computing powered by 6G." In: *Cloud and IoT-Based Vehicular Ad Hoc Networks*, 2021, John Wiley & Sons, Hoboken, NJ, pp. 105–124.

[22]   Li, G., F. Liu, A. Sharma, *et al*. "Research on the natural language recognition method based on cluster analysis using neural network." *Mathematical Problems in Engineering* 2021 (2021), 9982305.

Chapter 4

Introduction to IoT data analytics and its use cases

Mats Agerstam[1]

Abstract

The Internet of Things (IoT) industry has gone through an extensive transformation in recent years with the adoption of more modern software methodologies. In this chapter, we will present how this transformation has affected several IoT markets and discuss general architectural approaches taken. The different layers of the architecture will be decomposed and presented with focus on Artificial Intelligence and how it applies in containerized and orchestrated-deployment models.

4.1 Background and context

The Internet of Things (IoT) have rapidly become an area almost everyone is familiar with today. For consumers, this typically means the vast number of "smart" devices that has hit the market in the last 10 years that provides an additional level of convenience to our lives. From smart lights, thermostats, heart rate monitors, door locks, coffee makers, and other appliances all the way to connected vehicles – all connected to our smart phones, tablets, and computers which enable us to seamlessly control and monitor various aspects of our lives and provides us with a greater sense of control.

It may be obvious, but all these devices collect a tremendous amount of data which is processed and yields statistics and insights that can be useful in our day-to-day lives. From tracking your exercise and mobility, to optimize your heating and cooling of your home to guidance and suggestions of your driving habits to help conserve fuel consumption.

All of this analytics comes from sensor, contextual, and external data sources that is correlated, pre-processed, and analyzed to yield the insights, recommendations, alerts, and other type of data that you are consuming and enjoying every day.

[1]NEX/IOTG, Intel Corporation, Portland, OR, United States

The field of IoT analytics is, however, not unique to the "smart home" or personal market segment but has become an increasingly important pillar in other IoT vertical markets such as:

- Retail
- Industrial
- Education
- Health care
- Smart city

Generally, the IoT market has been slow when it comes to adopting new technologies seen and adopted in other areas such as Enterprise, Cloud, gaming, and web-applications. Often in many of these IoT segments, you would see:

- Fixed function devices in deployments specialized to do a single function.
- A mix of legacy and old protocols, mixed wired, and wireless with convoluted translation layers or bridges.
- The deployments modernizing through brown field strategies (retaining older systems with more modern IoT systems sometimes retrofitted).
- "IoT devices" have been more embedded type devices with monolithic software images.

In short, analytics of data has not been the center of focus or attention for many different reasons. The cost of analytics in terms of OPEX and CAPEX to acquire the necessary hardware that can efficiently and effectively perform the type of analytics needed to justify its purpose provides a positive net sum game in terms of productivity, profits, security, quality, and cost savings.

Machine learning (ML), Artificial Intelligence (AI), and deep learning (DL) and not necessarily new concepts or technologies – although they have made a lot of advancements in the last 10 years. They were just not practical and cost effective until recently. That has now changed and there are a multitude of reasons to this:

- The cost of compute has gone down.
- AI/ML algorithm optimizations and open source frameworks.
- Dedicated hardware components that allows workloads to be offloaded from the central processing unit (CPU) to better suited hardware accelerators that have the ability to parallelize workloads more efficiently in with hardware assistance graphical processing unit (GPU) or visual processing unit (VPU).
- The massive amount of data available from sensors, cameras, and other environmental sources that helps in training.
- The complexity of training reduced for "canned" use cases lowers the bar of entry to smaller players not having funds to train complex AI models.

4.1.1   *Cost of compute*

Moore's law (Gordon Moore) predicts the density of transistors roughly doubles every 2 years. This has been true since he made that observation in 1965 even today, although there are other factors at play as smaller nanometer technologies have started to emerge. The accuracy of this prediction will start to diminish. The computing power per dollar have roughly increased by a factor of 10 every 4 years. See https://aiimpacts.org/recent-trend-in-the-cost-of-computing/.

4.1.2   AI/ML frameworks and optimizations

There have been many advancements in AI, ML algorithms the last 10 years driven by companies like Google's TensorFlow, OpenAI (founded by Elon Musk), Caffe (University of Berkeley), and several solutions from other Cloud Service Providers (CSP) such as Microsoft and Amazon. These open-source frameworks have made AI/ML readily available to the developer community corporations spanning a wide range of companies and are optimized towards a set of platforms and accelerators.

4.1.3   Dedicated hardware components

AI/ML workloads can generally be offloaded to GPUs and VPUs to take advantage of parallelized computing and high memory bandwidth. This can dramatically reduce the computational time for a large set of diverse workloads. NVIDIA has been the market leader in this space with their discrete GPUs but other companies are getting into this space as well.

4.1.4   Sensors and data

The reduction in cost for sensors both wired and wireless has really paved the way to comprehensively collect data required for effective training and analytics overall. Small multi- and fixed function sensors (accelerators, gyroscopes, humidity-, and temperature sensors) have become extremely affordable, as have more involved ingestion sources such as surveillance cameras. Lastly standardization efforts to reduce fragmentation around wireless/wired technologies, protocols-associated data models have made it easier to find compatible devices for different deployments.

4.1.5   Pre-trained models

Training AI/ML models to perfect for a particular scenario and use case can quickly become a huge investment. Fortunately, for many straightforward scenarios, pre-trained models that exist with royalty free, open-source licenses are available which for many are a good and adequate starting point. However, for specialized deployments in the IoT sector, these may not be applicable – hence a significant amount of investment goes into training the right models with the right data whose result then becomes valuable IP and therefore may need protection in terms of cryptographic services.

The remainder of this chapter will look at a few different examples of analytics covering a few different vertical markets to provide an insight into the value the analytics capability provides for the specific vertical, as well as highlighting characteristics that may be unique for some of these market segments. This should provide you with an understanding of the driving force behind IoT analytics for a given segment.

4.1.6 Retail

In the retail sector, IoT analytics addresses many different business challenges and opportunities for improvement. Frictionless shopping is one emerging trend which provides a convenient shopping experience for customers and has been realized over a variety of sizes from small self-serving kiosks to neighborhood convenience stores to larger supermarkets.

These types of deployments perform analytics with cameras and sometimes other sensor technologies to provide an experience where customers can enter a store, pick up their goods from shelf spaces, and exit whereby they are automatically charged for the purchases made. Amazon have opened stores like this in Washington on an experimental basis. Similar concepts from retailers exists in other countries, most notably China. The cameras and sensors identify the shopper, which would have registered means of payments from the retailer and track the customer inside the store to understand what the customer is picking up from store.

While this gives a seamless experience for customers, the analytics performed it also provides other direct benefits to the retail store such as:

- Hot zones in the store – what parts of the store gets most foot traffic.
- Inventory management and optimization, supply chain ordering and placement efficiency of goods inside the store.
- Potentially controversial aspects around privacy and identity such as customer shopping behavior, history that could be used for target advertisement, recommendations, generating personas based on age, gender, demographics, etc.

These types of stores require very a high degree of accuracy when it comes to accuracy, as incorrect inferences may yield a loss to the store or overcharging customers. There are several technical challenges here that may not be obvious at first glance:

- The number of cameras to comprehensively cover the essential parts of the store. Redundant cameras covering different angles of the same shelf space may be required to ensure that the field of view is not blocked by nearby customers or other obstructions.
- The amount of compute required for ingestion, pre-processing, and inference of this data.
- Customer's right to privacy and opt-out from things like behavior tracking, targeted advertisements, etc.

Similar concepts exist in retail food industry (casual dining and fast-food) where analytics can be additionally used for:

- Customer and vehicle identification in a drive-through from smart phone beacons to license plate identification in order to customize and present personalized suggestions and recommendation on digital signage solutions.

- Food quality inspection and ensuring the right items are being provided to the customer.
- Natural language processing and automatic translation services when ordering to automate the order process without human intervention.

4.1.7 Medical

The medical field is going through a modernization phase where hospitals, emergency, and urgent care facilities are to a larger degree integration of various IoT solutions and use of analytics to provide a better and more efficient service to patients.

Patients with different illnesses that must be monitored continuously such as glucose, heart rate, general activities, and fall detection are provided IoT devices that connect back to the health care backend either directly over some cellular wireless technology or in some cases using Bluetooth or another low powered wireless in the unlicensed spectrum through a proxy or gateway (such as a smart phone) to push alerts and notification. Often the analytics ingested through these devices are processed on them with the help of hardware support that can perform that analytics in efficiently both from a time and power perspective.

Medical imaging is another field where IoT is breaking ground although early at this stage. With different types of imaging solutions, for example, a CT scan can send images from a patient to an IoT cloud for processing which would consist of pre-trained models to detect very early stages of certain diseases such as cancer that would be almost impossible or extremely time consuming for the human eye to detect. This opens the possibility to detect and treat a disease in its early stages as this often can maximize the likelihood of recovery.

4.1.8 Industrial

The industrial sector is probably the one market people associate with IoT such as robotics for manufacturing, and autonomous mobile robots (AMRs). The industrial IoT space is huge and covers many different facets. In this section, we will just briefly mention some examples of IoT and analytics applications.

4.1.8.1 Predictive maintenance

In industrial manufacturing, one key aspect is to keep uptime in production. Any time production is suspended, for example equipment malfunction that may require maintenance or replacement of parts, it has a direct impact on the profits, ability to meet orders, and potentially other supply chain disruptions. Predictive maintenance has been an area of interest in the last decade where different sensors are used (sometimes even retrofitted in brown field deployments) to monitor the health of different aspects of the manufacturing equipment for anomalies that may indicate that a part needs replacement or servicing. This preventative approach is much more cost efficient than unexpected breakdowns and enables for a manufacturing plant to minimize downtime. Different types of sensors are used here to such as from temperature, vibration, humidity, pressure, and noise.

Some of the additional benefits are:

- Increased equipment lifetime hence lower CAPEX.
- Reduced cost in terms of maintenance and repairs (parts, personnel, etc.).

4.1.8.2   Detect detection

Another emerging area in the IoT manufacturing space is defect detection. There are multiple types of applications in this space but what is common is that compute vision (CV) is used to detect defects or anomalies that could relate to the product being manufactured or the packaging of the product itself. In these cases, cameras are inspecting with the help of AI the manufacturing pipeline and can take preventative actions when defects are detected. These types of systems are applicable to a wide range of areas such as:

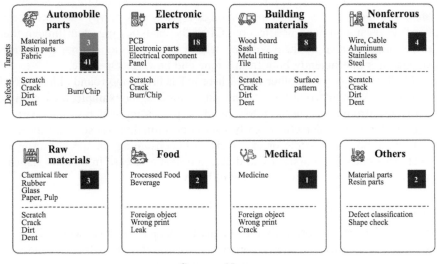

Source: Necam

4.1.9   Automotive

The automotive space is arguably the most notable when it comes to IoT analytics today with the Tesla being the automotive manufacture that grew from a small electric automotive company that many doubted would have any success to the largest automotive manufacturer in the world. While perhaps the obvious groundbreaking use case in the automotive space from a customer perspective is autonomous driving – it is the most difficult as it requires fully autonomous driving that requires an extremely high degree of accuracy and precision as there is no room for failure.

Consider the amount of data and sources that must be processed by the vehicle:

- Images from multiple cameras ingested at high frames per second (FPS)
- Light detection and ranging (LIDARs) sensor data
- Radar sensors

The ingested data must detect and respond to events in real-time and sometimes make difficult decisions and trade-offs to ensure its safety.

- Detecting the road and obstructions under different conditions (snow, rain, haze, etc.)
- Detecting and tracking people and cars nearby, assessing distance
- Detecting and identifying road signs that may be partially covered, obstructed

There are however many other aspects to the automotive space when it comes to analytics that are easy to overlook

- Analytics on driver behavior for insurance purposes
- Fleet management
- Vehicle to vehicle for mitigation potential accidents
- Automatic maintenance (similar to what was described in the predictive maintenance in the Industrial IoT section)

4.1.10   Education

In the education sector, IoT has also been adopted in a variety of scenarios and usages. When it comes to analytics common scenarios include remote learning where a teacher may be connected to multiple classrooms and individual students. The participants have cameras connected where inference and analytics are performed on the different streams to:

- Detect and identify students
- Gesture recognition (e.g., students raising their arm, providing gesture-based commands by the teacher)
- Auto tracking, zooming of regions of interest (ROI) by classroom facing cameras

4.1.11   Conclusion

The sections above provided a few examples of IoT analytics across a subset of the vertical markets. This is by no means a comprehensive overview of the various usages and scenarios where IoT and analytics are making huge strides. The purpose of this overview was to provide a high-level overview of the applicability and diverse set of applications where IoT analytics is becoming a reality.

The world will continue to innovate in this space and new areas of analytics are being realized as challenging industry pain points are being addressed as the cost of compute and analytics becomes more affordable and sustainable and has on overall positive impact on the bottom line.

4.2   IoT analytics system and concepts

4.2.1   Overview

This chapter will explore and explain general aspects of an IoT analytics system and describe the purposes and flows of each of the main components found in such as system. It should be noted that this is described without having a particular vertical segment, solution architecture of deployment target in mind.

In later sections, we will look at some specific deployment solutions and discuss trade-offs and considerations between that one must comprehend when we decide on the architecture for a specific IoT solution with respect to unique requirements, performance indicators, stability and resilience requirements, and other system constraints.

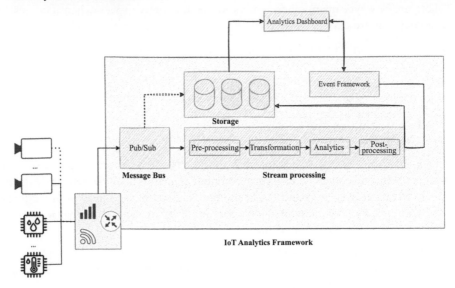

The figure above depicts a very general architectural flow diagram of an IoT analytics framework.

4.2.1.1   Cameras and sensor

Data to be analyzed by the analytics framework is ingested by different sensors (single or multi-purpose) or cameras. These devices may be connected to the IoT deployments with a wireless technology or wired. They could be battery powered or using line power. There are several considerations and constraints that have to be comprehended when making the decision in terms of which technology and how the sensor device should be connected to the infrastructure. On the one hand, running cabling and power to various sensors can quickly become a very costly proposition but once that initial cost has been absorbed there is little maintenance that could not be done remotely through a device manageability server (DMS). One the other hand, the flexibility of using a battery-powered sensor with a wireless technology eliminates the need for large initial investment but comes with other side effects such as the deployment size (number of sensors) and the battery lifetime. This has an ongoing cost with respect to maintenance to replace batteries. Other important factors are the required bitrate, maximum range of the device to infrastructure where data is being ingested, and sources of interference in the environment. The next chapter will discuss some of the common network technologies and options available.

4.2.2 Data ingestion

The ingestion layer, indicated by the message bus, is receiving data from various sources in the environment and may do certain level of data processing and normalization before transmitting to the processing pipeline. Data may be transmitted directly to stream storage before processing or directly to the analytics pipeline.

4.2.3 Analytics pipeline

In previous sections, we covered how data is captured and transferred into the IoT analytics platform. This section will look more closely at the processing pipeline that ultimately performs the analytics on the ingested data. We are going to discuss two different types of analytics in this section

- Computer vision analytics
- Time series analytics

We will be discussing how these pipelines are typically constructed and what some of the "knobs" or settings are required to configure it based on the requirements and desired outcome of the system. The analytics pipeline typically consists of several distinct steps.

When we say pipeline here, we refer to a set of discrete steps that the data is going through, step by step to finally produce an output. Generally, we can look at these pipeline steps to include the following high-level blocks:

- Pre-processing
- Analytics
- Post-processing

The incoming data may have to go through some pre-processing and transformation step for processing to be efficient and to be compatible with the analytics algorithm.

- Filtering of sampling: This can be as simple as a threshold-based filtering mechanism where a selector function determines whether a sample should be included in the data stream based on if the sample s is $D_{min} <= s <= D_{max}$. It can also be a much more involved filtering function that may be looking at a sliding window of sample, data statistics to determine its inclusion in the data set.
- Data sample interpolation and dynamic time warping: If data samples are received from multiple streams, they may have to be aligned along the time axis. This temporal stream alignment is referred to as dynamic time warping. It may be possible that samples from multiple sources are samples at different frequencies which may require for some interpolation step to be required if a source's adjacent samples x_n and x_{n+1} requires to produce a sample $x_n <= x_{n'}$ $<= x_{n+1}$. It should be noted that this step also could be as trivial as a linear interpolation, but also more involved using a more complex polynomial for curve fitting.

- Decoding of data or an image: This step may require both decryption and decoding of the data. This could be symmetric decryption along with JSON, CBOR, or other data representation decoding and parsing or image decoding based on the encoder used (e.g. H.264, H.265).
- Image processing steps: Often ingested video streams are ingested in HD, UHD, or event 4K. Most models used today for inference would require the individual frames for analytics to be first resized and/or cropped to fit a pre-determined image size. This step could also include other types of processing steps required to increase the accuracy of the analytics step (color correction, scaling, tilting, rotating, etc.).

The analytics block comprehends the actual algorithm that performs the analytical step on the incoming data and produces some result for which the internal model in the analytics component has been trained to perform (such as detecting anomalies on images, processing vibration data from an industrial rotor). There is a huge plethora of algorithms and purposes of what is being done here. The AI chapter will decompose and explain this further.

The analytics step performs the actual inference and exercises the AI or ML model(s) in order to infer something such as:

- Object detection and feature extraction – referring to extracting useful and distinct characteristics of the data source (such as parts of an image). This will produce one or more feature vectors, which in the case of an image may be an array of distinct shapes.
- Object classification – in this step, output generated from the feature extraction step is used to classify the different parts or ROI with respect to what they are in terms of probability. Finally, the individual feature vectors are then examined aggregated to make a classification determination.
- Object tracking – local or global.
- Anomaly detection.

The post-processing element may be performing additional processing on the data. The processed data may then be fed to storage pools that can be used from a dashboard where data can be visualized and comprehended. The post-processing step is using results coming from the analytics step and would do one or more things with the data:

- Re-encoding images with meta-data information or ROI
- Pushing images, frames, or data of interest to storage or to an event bus
- Display operations such as image and data composition

4.3   Network

In the IoT space, there is a huge fragmentation of different wireless network technologies and protocols and a lack of consolidated industrial standards across the industry. Here we will list some of the most common used today.

4.3.1　Wired network technologies

There are multiple standards around wired network technologies deployed and used today and are typically very dependent on the specific vertical market (e.g., industrial, automotive, etc.). The most ubiquitous used is standard Ethernet 802.3, below is a brief summary of other commonly used ones.

4.3.2　Wireless network technologies

It should be noted that the subsequent sections on network technologies and protocols serve only as a very elementary introduction to provide a general overview, Figure 4.1 provides a general taxonomy of the wireless standards and protocols.

4.3.2.1　WiFi

WiFi is a ubiquitous wireless technology first emerged in the early 2000s and have become the standard for short-range wireless connectivity to all our devices. The WiFi Alliance has gone through many iterations of the standard since its inception and focused early on, on raising the bar of security on WiFi where wired equivalent privacy (WEP) was used for a long time. Later industry standard authentication and security services have been adopted and supported for WiFi making it suitable for the integration with any IT backend infrastructure.

As with any wireless protocol, as the number of connected devices increases, the performance of the network infrastructure starts to deteriorate. One of the reasons for this is lack of a centralized coordination and scheduling function that decides the operational behavior in the network. End devices chose when they

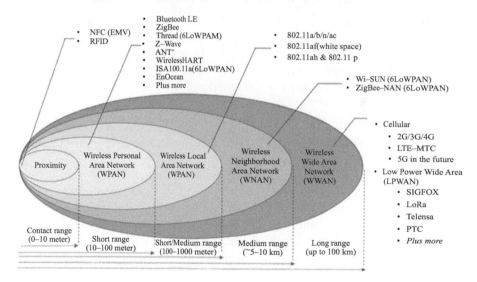

Figure 4.1　Wireless landscape and technologies. Source: A Study of Efficient Power Consumption Wireless Communication Techniques/ Modules for Internet of Things (IoT) Applications

should transmit data and not dictated by the access point (AP) or another higher lever entity in the service set identifier (SSID). Performance degradations can also occur due to other wireless technologies (including other nearby WiFi networks) operating in the same unlicensed spectrum 2.4 GHz and 5.2 GHz. WiFi has many internal configurations that the end device can transition to with respect to radio resource management (RRM) such as:

- Modulation: This refers to the number of bits encoded in one TX operation. The higher modulation, the more bit can be encoded and hence higher throughput but increases the likelihood for reception errors.
- Guard interval: The interval between successive TX operations usually measured in microseconds (μs).
- Transmit power: The transmit power used by the device, higher transmit power increases the potential range of the signal but may cause unnecessary interference with other devices.
- Channel selection: WiFi has divided its spectrum into multiple channels in the 2.4 and 5.2 GHz spectrum.
- Spatial streams: The number of streams (redundant or unique) the device is sending simultaneously. This provides a tradeoff between signal resilience versus throughput and efficiency.
- Bandwidth: The channel bandwidth in MHz indicates is directly proportional to the maximum amount of information that can be send (throughput).
- Error correction redundancy: Forward error correction is typically applied so the receiver can correct a number of bits. The more redundancy the more bit errors can be corrected by adds overhead and hence lowers the effective bitrate.

Recent additions to the standard (802.11ax) are addressing quality of service (QoS) and ability to better manage and coordinate traffic flows in the network over the earlier QoS amendment that was added with 802.11e/WMM. The earlier WMM implementation was not coordinated by the Access Point but rather packets given different transmit priority based on QoS marking. A higher priority here meant they would have to spend less time than lower priority packets before transmission.

Below is a summary of some of the key characteristics of WiFi:

- High-potential throughput with 450 Mbps in the 2.4 GHz spectrum and XX Gbps in 5.2 GHz.
- Overall low-potential latency low-single digits milliseconds.
- Industry accepted security protocols with 802.1X and EAP allowing for integration to enterprise security services for authentication, confidentiality, and integrity.
- Not well suited for battery operation as power consumption is high compared to other more optimized technologies for that.

4.3.2.2 Bluetooth low energy

Bluetooth made its name several decades ago and was initially mostly used with specific device types using certified profiles that would provide guarantees of interoperability such as audio and hands free.

Later Bluetooth started to be used as a general technology for transmitting serialized data over a protocol called RFCOMM which could get into low [TBD] Mpbs. The universal support and stability for RFCOMM as a general solution for sending/receiving data from different operating system vendors fluctuated a lot and the discovery functions were suboptimal both from a timing and power consumption perspective.

With Bluetooth 4.0 came Bluetooth low energy which focused on connecting small, battery drive devices together with a promise of long (years) battery life. The Bluetooth SIG has since then advanced the BLE specification with additional functionality to support more usages and scenarios:

- Beacons: A BLE device can send out small beacons periodically initially intended to advertise the services the device supports were quickly adopted to be used to send small amount of data to nearby devices (e.g., sending periodic temperature data from a sensor) and for proximity based services such as providing an alert to a smart phone when a user enters/is in proximity (order of meters) to a store or point of interest. Sending data using advertisement beacons is power efficient and can scale fairly well in dense environments but has the drawback of not having any guarantees of delivery, these are best effort transmissions and the amount of data that can be transferred in each beacon is very limited (double digit bytes).
- Mesh was introduced with BLE 5.0 and would allow for different classes of BLE devices to autonomously form and manage a Bluetooth mesh network in a smart home scenario. The devices would take on different roles in the mesh based on whether they were battery powered and other characteristics.

Below is a summary of some of the key characteristics of Bluetooth:

- Low throughput and suited best for sensor devices sending small amount of data periodically to the infrastructure.
- Suited for battery-powered devices but lifetime decreases based on how frequently the device is in an active state collecting, processing, and transmitting data. Devices sending data very frequently should be powered to reduce the frequency at which battery replacement is required.
- Bluetooth is operating on the same 2.4 GHz spectrum as WiFi but typically has built-in coexistence function with WiFi if present on the same system on a chip (SOC) and can block advertisement on channels where interference is detected.

4.3.2.3 LoRAWAN

LoRA has become increasingly popular in recent years. It is a low-powered wireless technology that supports transmission over a variety of frequencies and has very long range which makes it very suitable for different markets where the end devices may be far away from the central office that receives the data such as smart metering (gas, electricity, agricultural usages, etc.).

Radio signals can propagate longer, the lower the transmission frequency is and unlike WiFi and Bluetooth that operates in the gigahertz spectrum LoRA is typically used in the high MHz spectrum not only allows for the signal to be transmitted longer ranges due to lower characteristics in terms of signal attenuation but is also more robust when it comes to other radio signal interference phenomena such as fast fading.

A LoRA device can support one or more operational modes based on the power consumption requirements of the end device. A LoRA device sends its data to a LoRA gateway which receives data from all the end devices in the environment and then transmits them further for processing. Figure 4.2 shows a simplified LoRA deployment with 3 LoRA devices and a LoRA gateway.

Most commonly the direction of traffic is device → gateway and that how the LoRA classes of devices have been optimized for. When the end device is not active, it does not have its RX function (receiver) turned on in order to reduce power consumption and can hence not receive data from the gateway.

- Class A: These device send data periodically, when the gateway receives data, the gateway has an opportunity to send a small amount of data back to the end device as it enables RX after the TX operation for a small period of time.

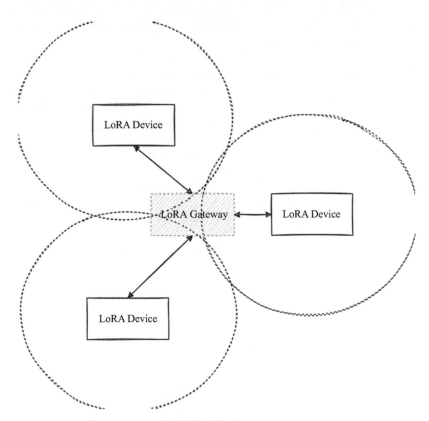

Figure 4.2   LoRA devices and gateway

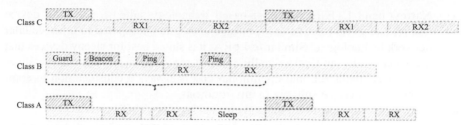

Figure 4.3   LoRA device classes

- Class B: These devices send data periodically and similar to class A, the gateway can respond or send a small amount of data immediately after receiving a transmission. Additionally, the class B devices can configure a quota of time where the RX is enabled on the device and with clock synchronization the central gateway has additional opportunities to transmit data to the device when it is awake.
- Class C: These devices are typically connected to power and will always have their RX function on unless they are transmitting data. This is the most efficient class when it comes to responsiveness and sending gateway $\rightarrow$ device data but also the most power hungry.

Figure 4.3 illustrates the difference between the classes in terms of RX and TX opportunities for a LoRA device.

Below is a summary of some of the key characteristics of LoRA:

- Suitable for long range (kilometers) and have unlicensed spectrum frequencies it can operate on in addition to licensed spectrum in some countries. Environmental factors determine the range (e.g., LoRA in rural areas with limited foliage has much better range than a LoRA device in an urban area with buildings, cars, and other obstructions). The long range is a combination of several factors that makes the path loss characteristics very good such as high receive sensitivity, antenna height, environmental factors, transmit power, and operational frequency.
- Suitable for battery-powered devices.
- Not suitable for high-throughput transmissions. Intended for sporadic, periodic short transmissions of sensor data.
- Data rates asymmetric in terms of uplink versus downlink data (1–13 kbps and 4–22 kbps, respectively).
- Interference issues can be mitigated by increasing the density of LoRA gateways.

4.3.2.4   Other network technologies

The number of network technologies is quite large. This section contains some additional technologies that are fairly commonly deployed and used in different scenarios.

- Narrow band LTE is a cellular-based technology suited for the IoT device market due to its relative low-power consumption compared to other cellular network technologies. Similar to LoRA, it is suited best for sleepy devices that are sporadically and periodically sending sensor data. As with any cellular technology, the additional operational cost is always a consideration to comprehend but may be suitable in environments.
- IEEE 802.15.4e time synchronized channel hopping (TSCH) is a technology that provides support for higher density of end nodes. In previous section, we discussed the challenges of getting air access and the likelihood for collisions and interference increases the more devices are in radio frequency (RF) range to each other. 802.15.4 uses time synchronization and a centralized coordinator that provides a scheduling function for when each device is allowed to transmit and receive data. This allows for the radio spectrum to be used more efficiently as well as providing power consumption savings as the devices can be in a low-powered state when not required to transmit or receive data. The 802.15.4 also provides the ability to extend coverage across the deployment through a managed mesh.
- WirelessHART and ISO 100.11a are just like TSCH built on the 802.15.4 PHY and MAC sublayers and are synchronized and scheduled similar to 802.15.4e but differs in higher layers and configuration of the lower MAC layer and security. These protocols have been around much longer than the IEEE TSCH amendment which attempts to create a more interoperable solutions end to end.

4.3.2.5   Protocol stack convergence and data model

The previous section listed a variety of different wireless technologies that may be used in different scenarios for transmitting data for analytics. All these protocols differ in the lower layers of the network stack which are technology specific and are hence different for different technologies. Figure 4.4 illustrates a simplified view covering some of the technologies discussed in the previous section and what the common protocol layers are.

- Certain technologies converge at the IP layer, or more specifically at the IPv6 layer as most IoT devices uses an adaption layer to support future proof and be compatible with IPv6 (6LoWPAN). This would be the least common denominator when looking at cross-technology interception or more importantly between a sensor network and the IT infrastructure where the analytics services are deployed.
- The transport layer is the next common denominator where the specific technology converges at the UDP, QUIC, or TCP layer.
- The security layer would be coupled with the transport layer if enabled. Several technologies have a full stack from physical layer all the way up to the transport and security layer in which case the convergence happens at the application layer.

Data received from sensor devices and networks may often contain only the raw sensor data and additional meta-data or data transformation is required to be added for the deployment in order to provide additional context before it is pushed through the ingestion protocol layer which will be described in the next section.

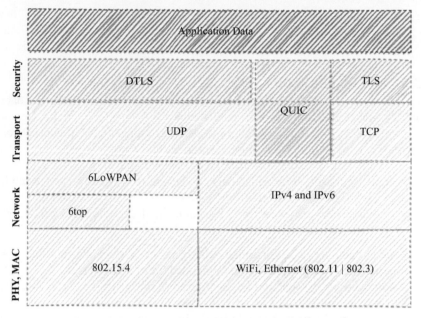

Figure 4.4   Protocol stack convergence

A few examples of data augmentation and transformation required before transmitting to the analytics backend.

- Sensor name
- Sensor location
- Additional sensor context
- Data conversion
- Data decoding and extraction

4.3.2.6   Data transport protocols

Depending on the use case, there is a multitude of strategies employed as far as the selection of protocol used for the ingestion to the IoT analytics deployment. It is common that technology-specific protocols, data formatting, serialization is used to the point where it is received by the infrastructure. Data normalization happens at this point where data is transferred with some message bus technology which can then be ingested and processed by the core components of the system.

One of the most common classes of protocols used here is for its versatility, flexibility, and scalability that are publish/subscribe-based methodologies or Pub/Sub for short. There are quite a few Pub/Sub protocols used in the IoT industry today, chosen for different reasons:

- Business, licensing, and cost
- Efficiency, resource usage, overhead, and general scaling characteristics
- Interoperability with existing infrastructure services

- Performance such as through and latency
- Features such as QoS
- Security capabilities

4.3.2.7   Pub/Sub concept

This messaging paradigm builds on the notion of a publisher that transmits data to a "topic," a subscriber who receives published items from a topic. In this section, we will explain this paradigm a bit more in detail as this is a central concept for IoT analytics in general and many implementations and standards exist that adhere to this paradigm although they differ in areas outlined above.

A topic is an artifact on which data can be sent to. Topics can be created in the system with different characteristics depending on how the data will be consumed and how subscribers are expected to consume the data. Below are a few common configuration options for a Pub/Sub topic:

- Name: Each topic has a unique name in the system so transmissions can unequivocally be provided to the intended set of subscribers.
- Authorization: A topic can be configured so that only specific publishers and subscribers can transmit and receive data from the topic.
- Sticky items: Items that should be retained even after one or more consumers have received data.
- Store-n-forward: Storage of items for late joining consumers or where a brief disruption occurs in connectivity:
- Queue depth/size: The number of items and maximum number of bytes an item can hold.

A publisher is an actor that transmits messages to one or more topics. Publishers may own a topic or may be able to join an existing topic, all depending on the policy and configuration of the system.

A subscriber is an actor that receives data from one or more topics. A subscriber would subscribe to a topic by its name and receives asynchronous notifications when new data is available on the topic. It is common that multiple subscribers are subscribing to the same topic for load-balancing purposes. In those scenarios, internal queue provides the ability for subscribers to dequeue items, one at time for processing.

Figure 4.5 illustrates three publishers and two subscribers. There are five different topics created in the system in two different access domains:

- Publisher A can post to topics in access domain A
- Publisher B can post to topics in access domain B
- Publisher C can post to topics in access domain A and B
- Publisher A is posting data to topic "my"
- Publisher B is posting data to topic "yellow"
- Publisher C is posting data to "foo" and "blue"
- Subscriber 1 is data published to "my" and "foo" topics
- Subscriber 2 is getting data published to "blue" and "yellow"

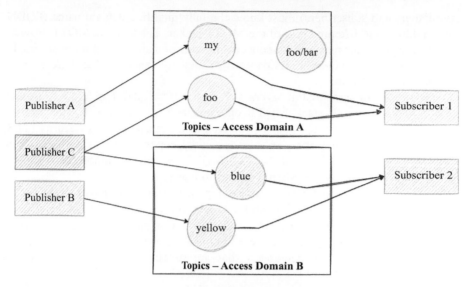

Figure 4.5 Pub/Sub concept

Several Pub/Sub protocol implementations additionally support hierarchical name structures for topics, separated by some delimiter.

Example: Consider a set of topics created by different publishers for three systems.

Topic: '/host-system-a/temperature/1
Topic: '/host-system-b/temperature/1
Topic: '/host-system-c/temperature/1
Topic: '/host-system-c/temperature/2
Topic: 'host-system-c/humidity/1

Systems A, B, and C are all posting temperature data. System C has two temperature sensors and one humidity sensor. These types of patterns are common and by using wildcards create the appropriate selection criteria for what to subscribe on.

Example: A subscriber wanting all data from host-system-c
subscribe /host-system-c/*/*

Example: A subscriber requesting all temperature data from all systems
subscribe /*/temperature/*

4.3.2.8 MQTT

One of the most common Pub/Sub-based protocols is Message Queue Telemetry Transport (MQTT) and many different implementations exist for MQTT both open source and commercial. MQTT is a standard from OASIS and ratified by ISO. It has been around since the late 1990s. MQTT is a brokered Pub/Sub protocol. This means that a broker sits in between the publishers and subscribers and its function is to route messages to the right destination in the system. Additionally, the clients (publishers and subscribers) must know the fully qualified domain name (FQDN) or IP address and listening port of the MQTT broker. The fact that MQTT provides a centralized broker may raise a concern in terms of stability, but there are implementations that provide various degrees of fault tolerance so that there is not a single point of failure.

MQTT is implemented at layers 5–7 in the OSI model, Figure 4.6 illustrated where in the network stack MQTT operates, and sits on top of Transmission Control Protocol (TCP), optionally protected by a Transport Layer Security (TLS) channel which provides the end-to-end security support such as authentication, integrity, and confidentiality of the data. MQTT has built in authorization support for principles in the system when it comes to topics.

There are differences between these implementations, but mostly with respect to performance, stability, scaling, and resource consumption. Some of the solution implementations have specifically been designed for a particular type of device or deployment scenario (e.g. a scalable Kubernetes implementation). There are also lightweight MQTT implementations that are suitable for constrained, battery-powered devices.

One should pick an implementation that meets the requirements of the deployment solution and keep the following in mind:

- The size of the MQTT library and overall consumption of system resources
- Does it have to run on a very constrained or battery powered device

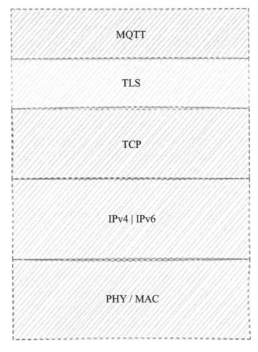

Figure 4.6   MQTT stack

- What are the availability requirements of the solution (e.g., fault-tolerance)
- What are the scaling requirements of the system – horizontally and vertically? Horizontal scaling means that the system should scale as new compute nodes are added to the system. Vertically means adding more compute power to existing nodes.

4.3.2.9 Distributed data system (DDS)

Similar to MQTT, DDS is a standard that comes from the object management group (OMB) and has been around since the early 2000s. In addition to supporting the Pub/Sub model, DDS also has support for Request/Response paradigm which is not as performant as Pub/Sub when it comes to performance but offer additional flexibility.

One of the primary objectives with DDS was to provide a decentralized protocol with no single point of failure but allowing for peer-to-peer discovery of the nodes in a domain along with more real-time focus and QoS policies that would allow for characteristics and configurations such as:

- Reliability and fault tolerance
- Resource consumption
- Communication reliability

The DDS protocol is divided into two main parts (see Figure 4.7):

- Protocol layer which includes over-the-air support for features and capabilities of the specification such as sessions, reliability, QoS, and discovery services
- Presentation layer which provides the implementation of the different architectural constructs in DDS such as data, topics, serialization of data, and caching.

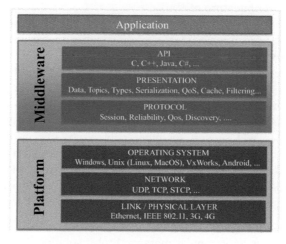

Figure 4.7   DDS protocol stack

The top layer of the stack exposes the language bindings supported by the implementation and is decoupled from the internal business logic implementation of the presentation layer.

It should be noted that DDS can support deployment over both UDP and TCP depending. The security provided at the transport layer is therefore based on TLS or Datagram Transport Layer Security (DTLS). TLS requires guaranteed delivery of packets and for them to be in-order. DTLS is the datagram implementation of TLS which has a modified initial security handshake to address potential denial of service (DoS) attacks and runs over UDP with no requirement of a reliable transport protocol.

DDS is common in certain government deployments, any real-time industrial deployment such as robotics space. For example, it is a central component in the robotics operating system (ROS).

As with MQTT, there are many different implementations that support the standard and some of the similar trade-offs outlined by MQTT is valid here as well. There are also implementation particularly tailed for more constrained leaf type devices.

4.3.2.10   Other solutions

There are a multitude of other Pub/Sub-based implementations that are not standard based. In this section, we will briefly highlight some of the more common solutions in this space. There are also solutions provided by different cloud service providers (CSPs) such as Amazon AWS, Google GKE, and Microsoft Azure designed to scale and work well in those cloud environments and at the IoT edge.

4.3.2.10.1   *Apache Kafka*

Kafka is a very popular data store solution optimized for ingestion and processing data frequently used in real-time data streaming. Kafka allows for users to publish and subscribe to many different streams of data for analytical purposes and generally can provide a very efficient and scalable message broker solution to provide a communication fabric between applications in a deployment. Figure 4.8 illustrates the general architecture of Kafka.

There are two essential paradigms supported in Kafka: publish/subscribe and queuing. The latter is targeted for single consumer scenarios where there is a 1:1 mapping between publishers and subscribers for a particular stream. As more consumers to queuing the system allow for efficient scale as each item publishes is consumed only once. This allows for a system to scale up as more subscribers are required to perform the work associated with items published to a queue.

Lastly, Kafka provides an extension API referred to as connector APIs which allow for Kafka to add support for other publish/subscribe protocols and expand interoperability beyond the wire protocol defined by Kafka. This enables a solution to have a centralized Kafka deployment which branches out to other messaging protocols. Obviously, as these types of bridging components are added to support other protocols, it has an impact on performance (throughput, latency, and resource consumption).

4.3.2.10.2   *RabbitMQ*

RabbitMQ is another very popular message broker solution that supports the publish/subscribe messaging paradigm (and others). It is licensed under Mozilla Public

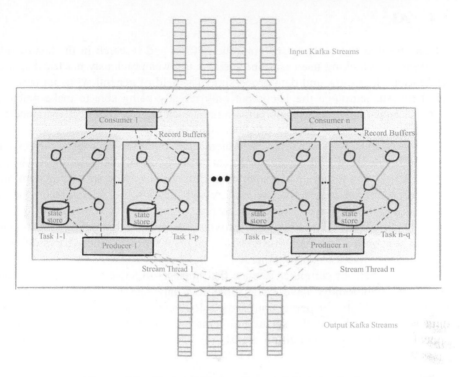

Figure 4.8   Kafka diagram. Source: Apache Kafka

License and also exists under commercial licenses and as a hosted service. RabbitMQ does not implement only one wire protocol but provides integration of a set of different messaging protocols

- MQTT
- HTTP
- Streaming Text-Oriented Messaging Protocol (STOMP)
- Advanced Messaging Queuing Protocol (AMQP)

Generally, since RabbitMQ implements support for a variety of different wire protocols, it is very versatile in nature and supports many different paradigms based on the specific use case and scenario one is looking to support.

- Publish/subscribe: Messaging to allow for multiple consumers to receive all data provided by a publisher.
- Work queues: Distributing tasks between many different consumers (same as the Kafka queue concept).
- Request/response pattern akin to a client/server model.
- Routing: Allows for messages to selectively being routed to specific consumers.

4.4   AI

AI has been at the forefront of continuous focus and research in the last decade resulting in unlocking use cases and insights that was previously not feasible with traditional algorithms and data processing. The field of general AI is not new and has been studied since the 1960s but only recently being able to make practical differences partially due to the continuing reduction in price for effective compute – including both general purpose CPU but also GPUs.

This section will provide a very elementary overview and taxonomy of this field as there are a large set of different methodologies and algorithms when it comes to AI, some that can be applied and use on the same set of problems and some more specialized. Before we explore and discuss some of these techniques, it is important to get some terminology correct.

The first clarity that should be provided is across definitions and taxonomy used when we discuss AI, ML, and LD. Figure 4.9 outlines how these different concepts are related to one another.

AI is a field of computer science that attempts to solve a set of problems or tasks that traditionally have been something only humans can solve with our intelligence, ability for perception, senses, logical reasoning, and deduction using data sets. Examples of the set of problems are visual perception, classification, speech and language recognition, translation, etc. This is done by creating capable

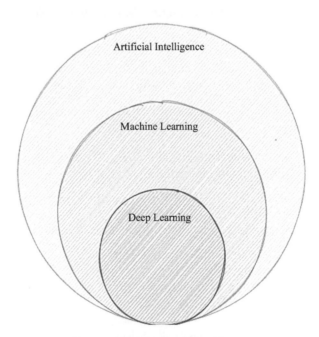

Figure 4.9   Artificial Intelligence

computer systems with intelligent software that is able to solve these problems through training which is analogous in how we learn things.

4.4.1   Training strategies

Regardless of which branch of AI, we look the notion of training the application or more correctly the model to perform its task well, meeting the system requirements on accuracy and efficiency training is an essential critical step. During this phase, the AI model has to be trained with representative data for the type of problem it is going to solve.

- A model for voice recognition must be trained with a person's voice in order to correctly determine if the voice was recognized.
- A model trained to recognize cars that has to be presented with images of cars that has the relevant features included that one expect to see on a car (the body, wheels, windows, etc.)
- A model used to predict wear down of a rotary engine may have to be trained on relevant data in order to know what constitutes a failure (vibration, temperature, etc.).

4.4.1.1   Supervised learning

In a supervised learning, the data presented to the AI model during the training phase is labeled, i.e. input and output data are labeled. This provides an "answer" to the model so that it knows that a particular labeled input should yield a particular output. The algorithm then adjusts parameters to ensure that the model can accurately yield all the correct outputs for all the input data sets. Once the model has been trained, it can be deployed and used for inference. The training versus inference are two distinct steps here. If the model has to tuned for higher accuracy, it would be taken offline, trained, and redeployed with the application.

This is called supervised learning because the network is being "supervised" and guided similar to a teacher and student. Supervised learning is primarily used in two categories of problems:

- Classification: Here the model is trained to correctly classify data into its correct category. This could for instance be a model trained to classify different types of animals. The model is presented with training data representing the animals, say birds, and dogs, along with the label meta-data. Once the model has been trained with sufficient data, a previously not seen image is presented and if trained effectively, the model will be able to correctly classify an image of a bird and dogs, respectively. The algorithm would use known features of the trained data set.
  - o   A dog has four legs, has a tail, two ears, etc.
  - o   A bird has wings, has a beak, has feathers, has two legs.

- Regression: Regression attempts to understand the relationship between data in large sets and understanding dependency/independency of variables in the data set which can be used for projections and predictions. There are different classes of algorithms which comes with different levels of complexity of and accuracy. These are common in everything from sales, finance, weather analysis, and general time series predictions.

4.4.1.2   Unsupervised learning

Contrary to supervised learning, in unsupervised learning, the model can be trained without any guidance in terms of pre-labeled data and is very useful when one desire to uncover hidden or complex relationships in data. The model works on its own to produce the results. Labeling of the training data can be a very time-consuming activity and is hence eliminated in this approach which requires human help. It may, however, be necessary to label features identified as the result of the unsupervised learning process.

There are several common problems where unsupervised learning is being used:

- Clustering: In clustering, similarities and differences in input data are used to classify objects into groups. Labeling can later be used to tag the different groups the model has defined. For example, a model being presented with different types of fruit (bananas, apples, and pears) would over time being able to correctly group these fruits where they belong. There are different types of clustering types that we will briefly touch on in a subsequent section as we discuss some common algorithms used.
- Association rules are based on determining relationships using rules in data sets and are common in different recommendation systems (e.g., a music service recommending music that might be common for a particular demographic).
- Dimensionality reduction is the process of reducing the complexity of data sets to extract the most useful and pertinent information, removing noise and improving performance as the computational complexity may be reduced. Figure 4.16 outlining a multi-layer artificial neural network can be seen as an example of dimensionality reduction where the hidden layers are effectively reducing the complexity of input data to subsequent layers ($5 \rightarrow 3$ input neurons).

4.4.1.3   Semi-supervised learning

As you can probably infer by the title of this strategy, semi-supervised learning is using labeled as in supervised learning but using a smaller set combined with a larger set of unlabeled data. This approach can provide significantly higher accuracy results and unsupervised learning alone and the overall cost of labeling all the training data required in supervised learning is reduced and can therefore be a very pragmatic and cost-effective approach.

4.4.1.4   Reinforcement learning

In reinforcement learning, there is a reward system in place that the application is attempting to maximize. Rewards are provided when the model produces correct results during the training phase. This training methodology aims for the system to learn from mistakes, the model is awarded with points/scores when it is expected or correct set of actions and punished (removing points/scores) when a mistake is done. The goal here is that the model adjusts itself during the training phase so that it maximizes the aggregated rewards it gets from the reward agent.

RL is very common when it comes to building non-playable character (NPC) in video games and the robotics space.

4.4.2   ML

ML is a subset of the broader domain of AI. This field is focused on automating and performing tasks through observations and learning – all this without the software not having to be modified using very structured type of data commonly leveraging various statistical methods to reaching objectives. There are a broad range of algorithms in use in this field that can make specialized predictions and recommendations. We will present a small subset of these here that are commonly used today but this is far from a complete list and the interested reader is recommended to further explore these based on the interest and applicability between classical ML algorithms and others.

4.4.2.1   K-nearest neighbor (KNN)

The KNN algorithm is very simple to understand and relatively does not have a high computational complexity with other algorithms. This model deals with classification primarily (although regression could also be applicable) of data and the problem to solve is which group a new data sample should belong to in the data set and the model has been trained using supervised learning. Figure 4.10 shows a diagram consisting of three categories: A, B, and C.

When a new data sample is to be categorized, the distance between the sample and the surrounding neighbors is used. Distance function used here could be something as simple as Euclidian distance, i.e. in 2D space this would be:

$$dist(x, p) \sqrt{(x - p_x) - (y - p_y)}$$

For 1-NN (using a single nearest neighbor), the distance is subsequently calculated for all the nearby neighbors and the closest one is where the data point p should belong to. KNN as the K implies here can be used to look at more neighbors and use the majority outcome to determine which class P should belong to.

2-NN would use two nearest neighbors, 3-NN using three nearest neighbors and so one. It should also be mentioned that KNN is not bound to be used in a 2D space as shown above but could be used in a p-dimensional space. Obviously, the more dimensions are used for the data and the more neighbors used the more complex and compute intensive the algorithm becomes.

In our simple example in Figure 4.10, we use 2-NN and the data point is closest to two of the category A samples and would hence be classified as category A, as

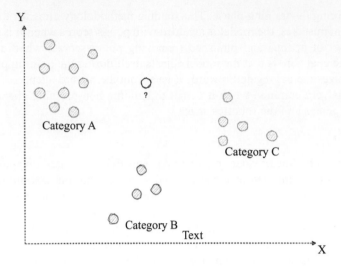

Figure 4.10　KNN example

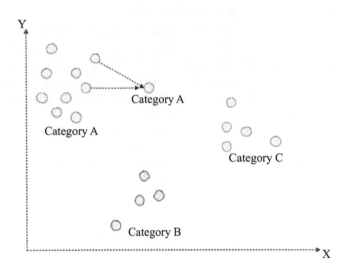

Figure 4.11　KNN example classification

indicated in Figure 4.11. If the result would have been a tie between category A and category C for example, there would be a tie and the system would have to perform some tiebreaking function to classify the sample.

There are other considerations to be considered when selecting K. A small K may be introducing a lot of noise and incorrect classifications, using an odd number of K is good (e.g., when you have only two categories to avoid a tie). A large number of K may yield preference to larger categories over smaller categories (in terms of number of existing data samples).

4.4.3 Decision tree (DT) and random forest (RF)

A DT navigates characteristics of input data and traverses a tree that branches out during this process and ultimately reaches a decision. It is mostly used for classification scenarios but is also applicable for regression. The training methodology here is supervised learning. In the example above, we have a simple DT based on predicted activity to do for a given weather scenario:

The data is provided to the trained DT and we navigate down the tree to ultimately reach one of the leaf nodes (indicated in yellow color here) in Figure 4.12. In a DT, there is a root node which is the forecast node here. The internal nodes are referred to as internal nodes which have incoming flows coming in and out of them and finally the leaf nodes. The DT uses parameters from the input data to make these decisions.

The obvious question is how does one construct a tree like this for a given data set? Normally the data set from observations and statistics would be used from a table and select the conditions that best predicts the outcome of going for a walk. In other words, the condition that best predicts would be placed higher up in the DT. There are different mechanisms that can be used to quantify this and set a number to it. One common such approach is the Gini impurity which helps in deciding whether features of the data set should split nodes to form the tree or not. The Gini Impurity produces a number between [0, 0.5] and indicates the probability that a new data point is incorrectly classified – so the lower the Gini Impurity score, the better of an indicator it is.

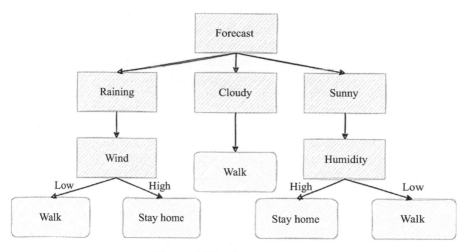

Figure 4.12   Decision tree

Cloudy	Wind	Humidity	Go for walk
Yes	High	High	No
No	Low	Low	Yes
No	High	Low	Yes
Yes	Low	High	Yes
No	Low	High	No

RF is another popular ML algorithm that helps to address some of the challenges and problems with DTs. DTs are fairly simple but ultimately does not take into account the impact of a decision at a particular branch in the tree for the overall tree. The DT has a tendency for overfitting against the trained data for large (many internal nodes and leaf nodes) and underfitting for small trees.

RF is addressing this challenge by introducing many DTs that are trained and the final outcome or prediction of the DTs is ultimately voted or averaged out to overcome the challenges with overfitting and yield better prediction results while retaining the benefits of the DT properties. So, in summary, in this approach, you are not training a single tree but an entire forest.

4.4.4   Support vector machine (SVM)

SVM is another supervised learning algorithm used for classification problems. This algorithm is not as intuitive and easy to understand at first glance but we will provide a general explanation and objective of the SVM in this section. The SVM attempts to find the optimal hyperplanc (which is a line in 2D space) that separates classes of data. We will discuss what is meant by optimal here.

Let us visualize by looking at an example in Figure 4.13.

In the example above, we have two categories of classes, class A and class B. To define a hyperplane that separates the samples into two distinct groups, you can express the hyperplane in a different ways accomplishing this goal. The effectiveness of the trained model will however be dependent on how this hyperplane is defined. In Figure 4.13, we have illustrated three possible hyperplanes (purple, blue, and red) that separate the two categories from each other.

When we talk about optimal hyperplane, we are trying to find a hyperplane, line here, that maximizes the distance between the two classes.

We introduce a margin, which is computed as the distance between the hyperplane and the closest data point and then double this value. This gives us the margin, which provides a 2D space that separates the hyperplane from the data points from the different categories. The hyperplane should with the largest margin as illustrated in Figure 4.14.

4.4.5   DL

DL is a specialized field where the way we understand the biology of the human brain works with neurons and synapses and the processed used to learn from very

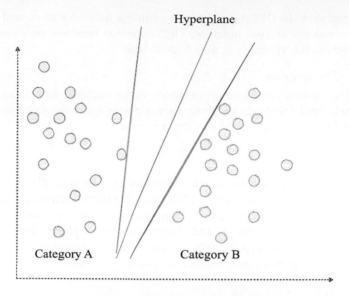

Figure 4.13   SVM example

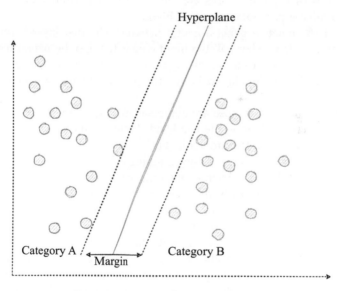

Figure 4.14   Optimized hyperplane

unstructured data. In DL, the constructs of neural networks composed of a huge number of neurons are put together. The connection between each neuron in the network acts as the synapses in a biological brain.

4.4.5.1   The neuron

The artificial neuron can take a set of inputs, in this example, three input values are given. Each input value can be given a unique weight and the value of the aggregated input data is calculated across the input values:

$$z = \sum_{i=1}^{n} v_1 w_1$$

The result is then fed to an activation function that typically yields as value range between 0 and 1 as an output of the neuron. Different activation functions can be used for different purposes, but the Sigmoid function is commonly used because it has some important properties and characteristics that are beneficial in its use in neural networks. Note that its valid range is plus/minus infinity and is monotonically increasing and continuous everywhere.

4.4.5.2   Neural networks

With the simple neuron construct and activation function, one can assemble a network of such neurons in layers from 1 ... n where layer $i-1$ feeds input data to layer i (Figure 4.15). This is what is referred to as a neural network and is the heart of what we refer to as DL. Different training strategies, weights, composition, and feedback loops of these networks are what makes them unique and more or less effective to solve a particular set of problem(s).

Figure 4.16 depicts a general neural network. The first layer is referred to as the input layer. This is where all the input data is fed into the neural network. The last layer is referred to as the output layer and provides the output or result of the neural network. The middle layers between input and output layer are referred to as the hidden layers.

It should be noted that these are composed with the number input neurons and outputs based on the task or problem at hand. There could be asymmetry in terms of the number of neurons in the hidden layers.

Training of these networks involves tuning the weights associated with inputs to each neuron so that the desired outcome with the right level of accuracy is achieved. As you can probably imagine, this is a compute intense operation and increases as the complexity of the network increases with respect to the number of neurons, connections and data to optimize the model.

Once the model has been trained, input data can be given to the network and if trained effectively, it will be able to yield desired results when presented with previously not seen data. This step is referred to as inference and also comes with a computational expense as each layer has to process the input data and calculate the outputs from each layer. These computations turn out to be vector and matrix operations for which there is hardware accelerators that help the optimization of those calculations.

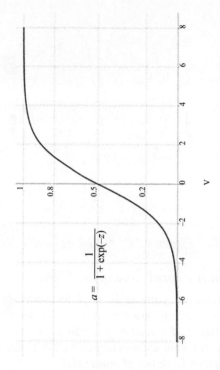

Figure 4.15   Neuron and activation function

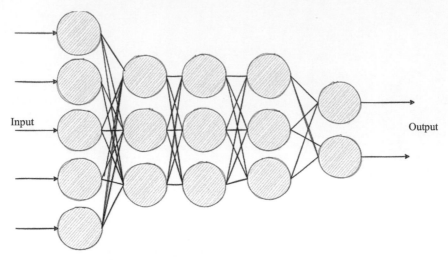

Figure 4.16   Neural network

4.4.6   *Convolutional neural networks (CNN)*

These types of networks are commonly used for computer vision (CV) where classification, and object tracking are important. CNNs have been around since the 1980s and used for things like classifying handwritten text such as classifying zip codes. There are many different architectures for CNNs which have in more recent years been more optimized in terms of compute.

A CNN is composed of three distinct layers:

- Convolutional layer
- Pooling layer
- Fully connected layer

The input passes through each of the distinct classes of layers (it should be noted that the convolutional layer can have multiple layers inside of it) and increases in complexity. The first layers focuses on very rudimentary characteristics of the input such as edge detection, color, and later layers recognizing aspects such as objects.

Let us take an example such as an image, in the convolutional layer, an image is represented by a set of pixels (width and height) and color channels (RGB – red, green, and blue for the basic primary colors). In a simple black and white image, you would have a matrix of just W×H pixels with associated values of "1" or "0" for white and black, respectively. During the convolution phase, a filter, referred to as a kernel, moves across the input data. The filter could be a 3×3 matrix with values (weights) in it and the dot-product of yields what is called the convoluted feature and passed to the next layer. In effect, each layer reduces the amount of data fed into the next layer.

Figure 4.17 illustrates a simple 9×9 binary image and a filter that sweeps across the image from left to right.

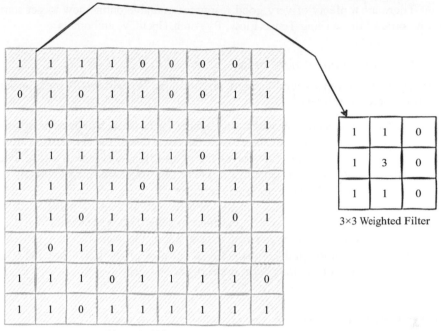

Binary 9×9 Image

3×3 Weighted Filter

Figure 4.17   Image and filter

Each layer of the convolutional step detects additional characteristics and traits of the processed image.

• Edge detection
• Corners and outlines
• Objects and parts
• Object identification

The pooling layer further down samples the input data and reduces the complexity. It is also using filters that sweep across the input data and apply processing, but it does not have any weights associated to it as in the convolution step. The purpose of this layer is to reduce complexity and efficiency, noise, and overfitting. Finally, the fully connected layer is responsible for the final classification of the object as all the features have been extracted from the previous layers.

4.4.7   Architectures and implementations

There are many well-adopted and popular algorithms, particularly in the CV space in DL architectures such as the following:

• Yolo
• Resnet
• SSD

There are a plenty of very good resources available online how to get started with some of these using TensorFlow, PyTorch, OpenCV, and others.

4.4.8   Other neural networks

There are several other neural network architectures. We will briefly mention some of those here for reference.

- Feed forward neural networks are suitable for tasks such as face recognition, computer vision, and speech recognition and is one of the simplest forms of a neural network. There is no backward propagation, data only travels forward with or without hidden node layers. These networks have less complexity than others and are efficient but not suitable for DL.
- Multi-layer perception is a fully connected neural network and has at least three layers (one hidden layer) but tend to be fairly complex and slow.
- Long short-term memory networks are a recurrent network that can be used for speech recognition and are generally a complex problem that provide a capability of supporting long-term dependencies of data.

4.5   Orchestration

In previous chapters, we provided a general introduction to the main elements of IoT analytics. We are now going to shift the focus a bit more toward infrastructure aspects and how a system can scale and become cost effective and efficient. Deploying any IoT system and particularly a system that ingests, processes, and performs analytics on data requires planning to ensure the system can meet current and future requirements. This requires for the architectural approach to be well thought through to ensure that scaling and efficiency of the architecture can be realized.

IoT systems used to be very specialized and embedded systems with monolithic software stacks, hard to manage, and difficult to scale. This is however changing throughout the industry. We have seen advances and more modern paradigms being embraced in the cloud and data center space using cloud native technologies, clusters, and microservice-based architectures to ensure the systems can meet the demand for today and tomorrow and scale up and down as necessary based on the load. In this chapter, we will provide a brief introduction to cluster technologies how that is used in the IoT space, how the cloud native technologies are reused at the IoT edge, what opportunities and gains the industry gets from that in addition to the hybrid edge and cloud architectures that aims to leverage the benefits of both.

Before we continue, it should be noted that while this is a general paradigm, the industry is going after it is not always the case. The use of some of the technologies and concepts introduced here are also applicable for deployments on single physical nodes or in virtualized environments without orchestration.

4.5.1 Container technologies

In order to better understand how applications are packaged and deployed and resource management to these workloads work, we need to describe the concept of containers which is a fundamental principle required by any orchestrator.

Containers essentially allow for an application to package all of its dependencies in a self-contained package. This means they have no other software dependencies on them outside the container. This is a very powerful and important concept as it allows for an application to be containerized and later deployed on to any system without having to worry about whether a particular library or software framework is present on the system or the right version of a component is installed.

The other benefit of a container is that it is isolated from the rest of the system it is running on. It is sometimes compared to a lightweight virtualization solution which is technically not correct but can help understanding the concept. Unlike a VM which has its own kernel and emulated hardware which has deep isolation and security characteristics when running on the same physical system, containers do share one critical element – the OS kernel. That means if the OS kernel panics, all the containers on the system will crash.

The container runtime provides the execution and lifecycle management of containers. It can establish quotas and permissions to the executing containers in terms of how much CPU and memory they are getting, policies such as network and communication permissions, etc. Containers are using a scheduler that decides their time slot of execution, commonly on Linux this is done with the completely fair scheduler (CFS).

There are many different types of container runtimes available on the market today. The most common one is Docker which popularized containers and have become the de-facto standard for container technologies. To create interoperability between different solutions of container technologies, the open container initiative (OCI) has standardized on different aspects on the container image format and some of the runtime primitives (i.e. commands), it should support (e.g., starting, stopping a container).

A container image is composed of one or more layers, see Figure 4.18. Each layer has a cryptographic that is associated with it that helps to verify the integrity and detect changes in the layer. All the layers are read-only except for the top layer. The resulting file system is an overlaid that contains all of the content from various layers with higher layers taking precedence over lower layers.

The layering of a container image allows for container layers to be repurposed for different applications and create base images that can later be specialized towards a particular use case.

Containers are typically stored and managed in *container registries* from which the container engine can pull and push container images. The layering of the container image allows for only changed layers to be fetched if a new container image has been pushed. This reduces the amount of data that has to be fetched from the registry and also conserves storage on disc as each unique layer is stored exactly once on the hard drive.

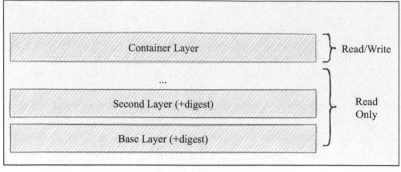

Container Image

Figure 4.18   Container image

4.5.2   Overview

Orchestration is an important topic that is gaining ground in the IoT space. There are multiple orchestration solutions available in the market offered both as open source as well as hosted services that provides support and availability requirements for customers. The most notable orchestrator used in the industry today is Kubernetes which came from an internal development effort at Google called Borg that was originally designed to ensure that the various Google services could meet their traffic demands while providing an elastic solution that could scale up and down and providing other critical infrastructure features.

There are other choices of orchestrators available in the market such as Apache Mesos, Docker Swarm, Nomad, and Rancher K3S. In this chapter, we will provide a general overview of orchestration technologies and provide specific examples relating to Kubernetes although most of these concepts are applicable for other solutions as well.

The purpose of an orchestrator is to decide through a scheduler where different workloads of the system should run. The scheduler looks at requirements of the workload and which node (compute node) in the cluster that the workload should be placed on. The orchestrator provides a plethora of important capabilities necessary for any deployment:

- Automatic scheduling of workloads
- Self-healing capabilities
- Automatic rollouts and rollbacks
- Horizontal scaling
- Load balancing

Kubernetes follows a declarative paradigm across all of its functions. This means that you state the desired outcome of an action and Kubernetes will figure out how to reach that desired end state.

4.5.2.1   Automatic scheduling

Scheduling here refers to looking at requirements of a workload (how much CPU, memory, storage, and other capabilities and constraints the workload needs), looking at the available resources in the cluster and making a placement decision of the workload and ensuring the workload is spun up on the designated node.

4.5.2.2   Self-healing

Self-healing has to do with the ability to detect when failures happen in a workload and take steps to address the issue. Kubernetes has the probe construct that allows for workloads to implement specific APIs at the TCP or HTTP layer which Kubernetes periodically probes to see if the workload is in a good healthy state. There are different types of probes defined in Kubernetes, and overtime additional ones may be added. A readiness probe is used to understand if the workload has been initialized correctly and is ready to execute. A liveliness probe is invoked periodically to ensure that the workload is still executing and has not run into a critical failure such as a dead-lock or similar.

4.5.2.3   Automatic rollouts and rollbacks

Kubernetes allows for new versions of a workload to be rolled out in isolation, in parallel to existing versions of a workload. Policies can be put in place to direct a certain amount of traffic to the new version while the current workload version is still running. This allows for DevOps to gain confidence that the new version is functional and performs as expected in the cluster without moving all consumers of the workload to the latest version. If a failure occurs Kubernetes can automatically rollback to the last/current version and hence mitigate against potentially prolonged downtime of the system for the affected clients.

4.5.2.4   Horizontal scaling

Horizontal scaling here refers to the ability to replicate a workload on the same or different nodes. Kubernetes allows for workloads to annotate scaling criteria of a workload and automatically create a replica for that workload when the threshold of condition(s) has been reached.

4.5.2.5   Load balancing

Load balancing refers to the ability to load balance and divide up the work between replicas created for a workload in an even manner. This is important for scaling as well as availability requirements the system may have.

4.5.3   Architecture

Kubernetes and other orchestrators have control plane nodes and worker nodes. The control plane node(s) implements and provides a lot of the support we discussed in the previous section. The worker nodes are where workloads are placed for execution.

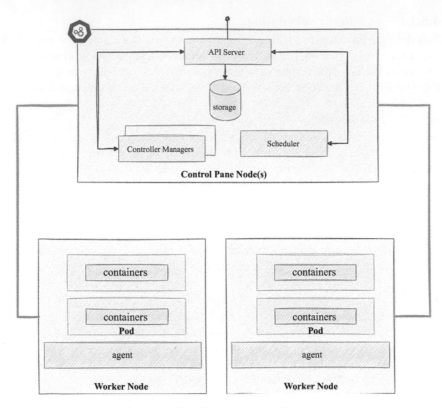

Figure 4.19   Kubernetes architecture

Figure 4.19 outlines a simplified version of a Kubernetes cluster.

The control plane node consists of four main elements. All of the requests in Kubernetes goes through the API server. It authenticates each incoming request, validates, and authorizes the call. The API server is used both by its internal modules as well as external clients that may want to check the state of an application, deploy a new application to the cluster, etc.

The API server keeps track of the internal state of the cluster using a storage facility. In Kubernetes, this is with a key-value storage solution called etcd. Etcd keeps records of the current state of all the various resources, nodes, and applications in the cluster and is only communicating with the API server.

Kubernetes has a variety of different constructs called resources. Each resource is controlled and managed by a corresponding entity called a controller manager. This allows for Kubernetes to scale and support new types of resources and constructs over time delegating the responsibility of management of such resources to newly introduced controller managers.

The scheduler is responsible for scheduling workloads in the cluster and can be extended and replaced. It consists of a pipeline of steps that finally arrives at a scheduling decision for a workload. If there are multiple schedulers available in the cluster, the workload can specify which scheduler should be used.

The worker node is where the workloads, services, and applications are instantiated and executes. The worker node has some control plane logic (kubelet and kube-proxy) reflected in the diagram as the "agent." The kubelet is responsible for instantiating the workload when it has been scheduled to run on the node and the kube-proxy is responsible for network configuration and ensuring reachability to the workloads is properly configured among other duties.

All of the components mentioned here (kubelet, controller managers, and schedulers) communicate securely over a control plane channel to the API server over TLS. During the bootstrapping process, security keys are established on the nodes to ensure them to communicate securely over across the cluster and eliminate rogue entities from modifying or getting access to the cluster's operation.

4.5.4   Cluster constructs

We mentioned the fact that there are different constructs available in Kubernetes that provide the fundamental building blocks and resources. In this section, we will introduce some of the essential ones and explain what they are. All of these resources and their state are kept in etcd for bookkeeping purposes by the API server.

4.5.4.1   Node

A node in Kubernetes corresponds to a worker node. It has a kubelet and kube-proxy installed and has been provisioned with security keys to communicate and receive requests from the API server. It should be noted that a node here does not necessarily have to be a physical compute node. It could be a virtualized node, i.e. a VM running on a bare metal system served by a hypervisor. This means that a physical platform could expose multiple nodes by having different Guest VMs running with their own kubelet and kube-proxy instance.

4.5.4.2   Pod

The concept of a pod is one of the most important resources in Kubernetes that is central to how an application or workload is packaged. The pod is the smallest unit of application deployment in a Kubernetes cluster. It consists of at least one container but can host multiple containers. The pod is defined in a pod specification that defines the containers it is composed of, resources required, and other policy and resource related information. We will describe a simple deployment scenario in subsequent section.

4.5.4.3   ConfigMap

A ConfigMap contains specific configuration of a pod. It is many times good to separate specific configuration data that a pod may need from the pod specification itself as this may change from deployment to deployment. This creates a loose coupling between the two and provides increased flexibility. The data in the ConfigMap is provided into the container(s) when instantiated on a worker node.

4.5.4.4   Service

A service is central concept in Kubernetes and important for any time of micro-service deployment. The service construct allows for a discoverable service to be exposed in Kubernetes which is backed by on a set of pods. The service allows for the pod to be discoverable through DNS (which is also part of the Kubernetes control plane node). This eliminates the need for DevOps to know the IP address of the node on which the pod is running. Additionally, since Kubernetes can reschedule a pod to run on a different node, the IP address is likely to change over the course of the application/workload execution.

Finally, when it comes to multiple pods of the same type instantiated, the service helps ensuring that proper load balancing between the set of pods that are backing the service happens.

4.5.4.5   PersistentVolume and PersistentVolumeClaim

These specifications define storage types and volumes in Kubernetes. The request a pod can use if it needs storage outside of its own lifecycle it can define a request for a PVC (PersistentVolumeClaim) mapped to the desired PersistentVolume type and size. It should be noted that pods can use non-volatile storage on the worker node they are provisioned, but when the pod stops, the storage used by the pod is freed up.

4.5.4.6   ReplicaSet

A ReplicaSet defines how many instances there should be of a particular pod specification.

4.5.4.7   Deployments

A deployment is an aggregate that contains pods and replicasets as one specification.

4.5.4.8   DaemonSet

A daemonset is a special type of deployment that can be deployed in a cluster, in a daemonset there is exactly one instance of the pod running on each worker node. Additionally, other worker nodes are added to the cluster later they will automatically get the daemonsets deployed to them automatically by the orchestrator

There are additional constructs in Kubernetes, the above list are only a small subset albeit pretty common ones.

4.5.5   Deploying a service

In the previous sections, we gave a brief overview of Kubernetes, an architectural overview, and some of the basic constructs used in Kubernetes. In this section, we are going to provide a high-level example of the workflow involved deploying a rudimentary application to a Kubernetes cluster.

We are going to show a simple application that is deployed that does not need to serve any incoming traffic or be reachable, nor are there any replicas created for it. It is a simple as can be.

The application may be simple hello-world application that just logs hello-world to std-out periodically for a period of time then exists.

4.5.6   *Containerizing the application*

The first step is to containerize the application. There are multiple tools and techniques that can be used to achieve this step. With Docker, you would use the docker build command along with a Dockerfile. The Dockerfile contains the different *layers* of the container.

In this case, the application may just need a simple base container image like Alpine and then adding libraries that the application is dependent on as well as itself to the image. The image is then pushed to a container registry and is uniquely identified with an URL to the image.

4.5.6.1   **Pod specification**

The next step is to create a pod specification that defines what the application is. All specifications in Kubernetes is written in YAML. The pod specification will have a name for the pod, e.g. hello-world-example, and a reference to the location where the container image resides including the image name itself.

Every pod gets a default set of CPU and memory by Kubernetes. A pod may additionally override that default value and provide additional resources that it may need. In this simple example, the default resource quota would be sufficient.

Now we have a container, a pod spec that references the container image. Figure 4.20 illustrates this.

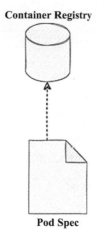

Container Registry

Pod Spec

hello-world

Pod

Figure 4.20   Pod and containers

4.5.7   Deployment

The last step is to instruct Kubernetes to deploy the application in the cluster. Figure 4.21 outlines the general steps in realizing this.

1. kubectl is the default tool to interact with Kubernetes and is a CLI-based tool. There are many other third party tools including graphical web-interfaces, etc. that make this process much easier when dealing with larger or even multiple clusters. Kubectl is used to create the pod in by issuing a command and providing the filename of the pod specification for hello-world. The API server validates and authenticates the request and ensures that the client (kubectl) has the right permissions to deploy the application. The API server creates the pod in etcd and marks its state as unscheduled.

2. The scheduler receives information from etcd that a new pod has been created. The scheduler parses the pod specification and looks at what resources the application needs then it proceeds to schedule the pod to a particular node (in this case the left worker node).

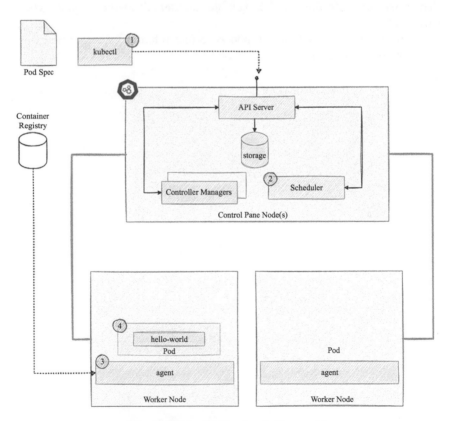

Figure 4.21   Deploying hello-world

3. The worker node is informed (more precisely the kubelet running on the worker node) that a pod has been scheduled to execute there. The kubelet parses the pod spec to understand what resources it needs and what container images are needed. It fetches the container image for hello-world from the designated container registry.

4. The kubelet on the worker node instantiates the pod on the node and launches it. The kubelet keeps track and updates the state of the pod so that external clients are informed of its state.

These are the essential steps involved in deploying a very simple application in Kubernetes. The key thing to note here is the separation of duties and decoupling of the different components involved. This obviously gets more involved as more pods, containers, and different capabilities of Kubernetes that are used for the deployment.

4.5.8 Microservices

We have given a gentle introduction to orchestration, and here we will briefly describe another paradigm shift that the IoT market is adopting – microservice-based architectures. As we discussed, traditionally the IoT device has been very specialized and monolithic devices. The adoption of cloud native technologies, orchestration, and containerization has also led the industry to adopt micro-service design pattern which are particularly useful in orchestrated scenarios. Software architectures have moved toward more and more reuse but still had many external dependencies on them that was not optimal for that purpose. For example, service-oriented architectures (SOA) decouple functions and services but would still depend on common infrastructure capabilities and functions such as storage.

In a microservice-based architecture, each individual microservice is self-container and independent and does not directly depend on any shared resources. Some key characteristics that a microservice-based architecture should employ:

- Small and provide a specific function and have very loose coupling to other components in the system.
- Clear and articulated APIs.
- Microservices can be deployed and managed independently.
- Microservices keep their own data and not dependent on shared resources for this purpose.
- Microservices have their own code base and may be implemented in different languages.
- Microservice are tested and validated independently.

The list above is not a complete set but outlines some of the key characteristics.

The benefits of microservices are that small engineering team can focus on their respective microservice without being dependent on business logic from other parts of the system. They can easily be reused in different scenarios and applications and teams can focus on using the most optimized or best purposed

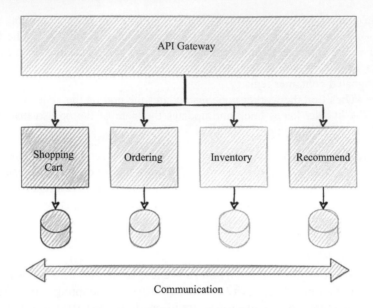

Figure 4.22   Example microservice-based architecture

technologies to develop their microservices. Updates (we discussed rollouts and rollbacks) can easily be enabled using this paradigm and developers can validate expected end-to-end functionality and interoperability with newer versions isolated to a small group of users or testers without impacting the system as a whole.

Figure 4.22 provides a simple web-site shopping example.

In this example, we have four microservices. The shopping cart is responsible for keeping and maintaining track of customers' items in the shopping cart while they are adding/removing things from their cart. The ordering microservice is responsible for fulfilling orders and tracking by customers. The inventory is keeping track of the inventory of different goods the website offers. Finally, the recommend microservice provides recommendations to end customers based on shopping history, or perhaps what other customers who bought a particular item also bought.

In this example, it is simple for a team to make updates to for example the recommend microservice and providing a better recommendation engine without impacting any of the other microservices in the system.

All the microservices are communicating with each other using a well-defined communication infrastructure such as a message bus, gRPC, or REST.

4.6   IoT deployments

The IoT edge is often a different execution environment that what you would see when deploying orchestrated solutions in a hosted cloud environment. Orchestrators like Kubernetes and others were originally designed to run in very homogenous environments where the main type of resources was:

- CPU
- Memory
- Storage

4.6.1   Edge deployments

This was often sufficient, and there was no need to disambiguate a CPU from another CPU, memory from memory, etc. In general, this generalization is not true. The IoT edge is often very heterogeneous in terms of the type of platforms that are deployed. You can see a clusters with different types of hardware spanning more constrained devices to scalable server solutions. Here a CPU cores are no longer equivalent and the same and in order to make good placement decisions of applications and services in the cluster it may be necessary to be able to express some of these constraints in more granular terms.

In addition to that, platforms may have unique features, capabilities such as accelerators for different purposes (GPU, encryption acceleration, etc.) that are not available across all the worker nodes in the cluster. If these capabilities are not exposed and used when placement decisions are being made, the outcome may be suboptimal and the full potential of the compute cluster not being realized.

There are a variety of ways in which a cluster's worker nodes capabilities can be exposed through extensions offered by Kubernetes such as:

- Device plugins for different types of accelerators available to workloads. These device plugins help manage bookkeeping of the resource type mapped to the type of accelerator (e.g. a GPU accelerator). The accelerator may have N instances available on a worker node and it is the job of the device plugin to provide information to the scheduler as it taking this resource type into consideration when defined as a requirement of a workload.
- Container network interface (CNI) provides extensions to the network infrastructure and allows for new type of network overlays (the network overlay is the network that the pods communicate over in the cluster) with new features, capabilities.
- Container storage interface (CSI) provides extensions to allow for new storage and volume technologies to be introduced that may be using more efficient non-volatile memory, or a powerful distributed storage services with redundancy and higher degree of resilience to errors.
- Others: scheduler extensions, operators, custom resources, admission policy, and API server extensions.

In the example below (Figure 4.23), we will illustrate what a simple video analytics deployment may look like and how the different microservices are deployed within the cluster.

In this example, we have a single Kubernetes control plane (not high availability which would imply multiple control plane nodes that can take over if the

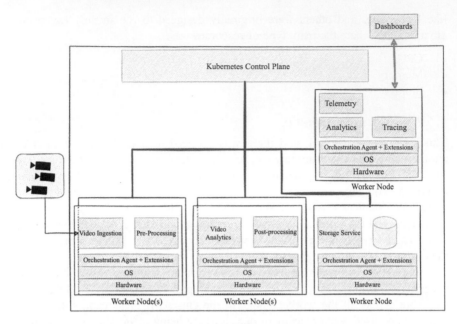

Figure 4.23   Edge deployment

primary one fails). We have a set of worker nodes that are processing different parts of the pipeline.

A set of cameras on which frames analytics is performed are connected and reachable from the cluster. The video ingestion microservices are responsible for processing the incoming streams. The amount of nodes and instances of this microservice is dependent on the number of streams coming in and their characteristics (resolution, frame rates, encryption, compression and encoding, etc.). The video streams is then forwarding the decoded streams to the pre-processing microservice that may take additional actions required before analytics can be performed on the streams. We discussed some of the pre-processing steps in one of the previous sections.

The video analytics is getting the streams from the pre-processing microservice and performs the analytical step on the video forward the results to the post-processing microservice which may re-encode, adding meta-data, etc. to the final frames as well as other post-processing steps. The resulting videos streams is finally sent to the storage service which stores the resulting data to non-volatile storage.

A separate worker node that deploys microservices that are externally visible and consumable to the cluster such as for telemetry, tracing and analytics is provided to allow for administrators to connect a browser instance and visualize data and results.

   The deployment above illustrates a single cluster deployed at the edge, but it is realistic to think of multiple clusters being deployed at the IoT edge for different purposes. These clusters can interoperate with each other over the network. As the number of nodes, microservices, and multi-clusters is realized technologies such as service mesh may be beneficial.

   A service mesh allows for more advanced traffic rules and policies to be defined and automatically eliminates some of the boilerplate development needed to secure the communication between pods in and between cluster boundaries. A service mesh also provides useful insights in terms of health and statistics which can be very useful. There are several service mesh solutions available in the industry today, the most common and adopted ones are Istio and Linkerd.

4.6.2   Hybrid cloud edge deployments

There are scenarios where the hardware provided at the edge is not sufficient and benefits from a cloud service provider is necessary. One may ask why not deploy everything on the public cloud? There are multiple reasons why many scenarios can benefit from an edge deployment such as:

- Cost
- Privacy/security concerns
- Low latency
- Optimization opportunities

   That being said, the cloud offers benefits that the edge does not have with respect to SLA, operations, scalability, and reachability. For those reasons, it is not uncommon to see some microservices being deployed in a cloud hosted environment to take advantage of high availability or elasticity of the hosted cloud.

   When deploying to a hosted environment you are typically charged based on a couple of factors such as the type of platforms you have in the cluster, storage used, and network traffic incurred.

   Figure 4.24 uses the same set of microservice but now divided between the edge and cloud. Here we have two Kubernetes clusters. The edge is focused on video ingestion and pre-processing of data and the cloud hosted Kubernetes cluster is performing analytics and storage services. Both clusters have a set of microservices that are providing observability services to a web-based application that aggregates and unifies the operations across the clusters.

   Benefits from this deployment are that some processing is done at the IoT edge, reducing the amount of network traffic that must be transferred to the cloud in addition to reducing the processing of the ingestion and pre-processing. Remember, the savings in network traffic going to the CSP can be dramatically reduced here as the incoming streams may be HD or 4K streams with a high framerate. After the pre-processing step, the framerate may be reduced in addition to the resolution to something in the order of 224×224 pixels. Additionally, the storage capacity required can grow as there is a need with the storage services supported from cloud hosted environments.

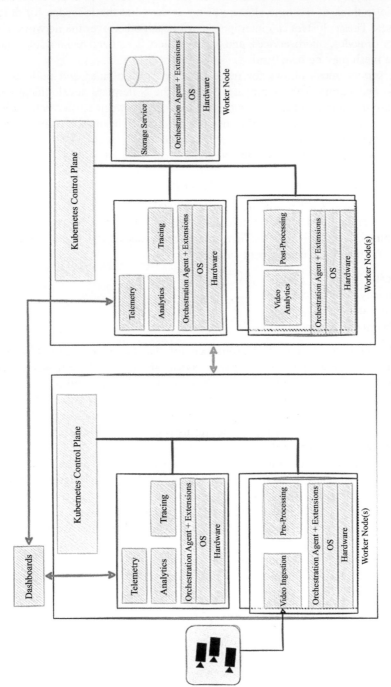

Figure 4.24 IoT edge and cloud

References

[1]   Kubernetes Official Documentation, https://kubernetes.io/docs/home/
[2]   Open Container Initiative, opencontainer.org
[3]   AI Impacts, https://aiimpacts.org/recent-trend-in-the-cost-of-computing/
[4]   Necam, https://www.necam.com/Docs/?id=45e4e545-8503-44fd-8540-348102
       bf0a85
[5]   WiFi Alliance, https://www.wi-fi.org/
[6]   Wireless HART, https://www.fieldcommgroup.org/
[7]   ISA 100 Wireless, https://isa100wci.org/
[8]   LoRA Alliance, https://lora-alliance.org/
[9]   Bluetooth Technology, https://www.bluetooth.com/
[10]   IEEE 802.15 TG, https://www.ieee802.org/15/pub/TG4.html
[11]   Kafka, https://kafka.apache.org/
[12]   KNN, https://apps.dtic.mil/dtic/tr/fulltext/u2/a800276.pdf
[13]   Support Vector Networks, http://image.diku.dk/imagecanon/material/cortes_
       vapnik95.pdf
[14]   Neural Networks and Physical Systems with Emergent Collective Computational
       Abilities, https://www.ncbi.nlm.nih.gov/pmc/articles/PMC346238
[15]   Random Decision Forests, https://web.archive.org/web/20160417030218/
       http://ect.bell-labs.com/who/tkh/publications/papers/odt.pdf
[16]   Publish Subscribe Pattern, https://en.wikipedia.org/wiki/Publish%E2%80%
       93subscribe_pattern
[17]   OMG and DDS Specification, https://www.omg.org/
[18]   OASIS and MQTT, https://mqtt.org
[19]   Docker Documentation, https://docs.docker.com/
[20]   CNCF, https://cncf.io
[21]   OpenTelemetry, https://opentelemetry.io
[22]   Gstreamer, https://gstreamer.freedesktop.org
[23]   Grafana, https://grafana.com
[24]   Prometheus, https://prometheus.io
[25]   InfluxDB, https://influxdata.com

Chapter 5

Demystifying digital transformation technologies in healthcare

S. Usharani[1], K. Dhanalakshmi[2], P. Manju Bala[1],
R. Rajmohan[1] and S. Arunmozhi Selvi[3]

Abstract

Digital transformation of healthcare is indeed a foundation stone toward a patient-focused system of healthcare. It can allow healthcare professionals to drive efficiency, consider whatever the patient needs, develop confidence and trust, and have enhanced user experience. Enhance the efficiency of treatment and access to medical care while reducing costs as demographics age and increase, rising life expectancy and placing public spending on healthcare on demand are some of the key issues facing healthcare institutions around the globe. Basically, all members in the vast and growing healthcare sector are substantially growing their digitization and technical advancement activities in order to address those and other challenges, but they also provide demand for growth in healthcare and substantial money in digital wellbeing. Healthcare organizations are distinctive across the world and healthcare societies are starting to move at various responsibilities, based on the locality, the legal arrangement, the policy process, the personal institution, the involvement of the health industry and the specific objectives of digitalization in each individual's life: such as improving patient centeredness in hospitals and increasing productivity to new forms of care, e.g., remote patient monitoring by utilizing fog, cloud technology, and the digital economy. Through elite elders to patients, wearable sensors have become particularly involved in monitoring physiological causes, encouraging fitness, and optimizing commitment to the procedure. In this chapter, fog computing-based wearable sensor networks (FWSNs) have been suggested in healthcare monitoring for elderly people using IoT. During regular activity, a wearable tracker for continuous – time tracking of blood pressure, breathing frequency, and motion was investigated. Furthermore, the sensor data will be transmitted to the IoT system Ethernet device, and the Approved

[1]Department of Computer Science and Engineering, IFET College of Engineering, India
[2]Department of Computer Science and Engineering, PSNA College of Engineering and Technology, India
[3]School of Computer Science & IT, DMI St. John the Baptist University, Africa

Person uses the data to monitor the elder's health through the Internet. Furthermore, the simulation tool for the wearable interface and its utilization show how computational resource costs can be lowered while retaining health demands for access to medical stored data in a cloud and fog distribution environment. The findings of the tests demonstrate that the proposed approach is user-friendly, dependable, and cost-effective to use it on a daily basis.

5.1 Introduction

Within a decade, the Indian hospitality sector is about to experience a transformative transition. To fulfill the mission that the government has assigned to us, which is to deliver accessible, equal, and high-quality healthcare to all, we need to apply information technology. The players in the environment (those who include patients, healthcare professionals, health insurers, and the community) will have to work together to implement this. Within the next century, the medical sector's GDP could rise to USD 1 trillion as a year. Now that the transition is underway, we all must focus on becoming a part of the pie, developing a virtual plan to be able to assist, and profit from, from such a partnership is critical [1]. To assist with this healthcare technology, the government is implementing many measures. As a public healthcare stack (2018), mostly with objective of fostering an open public health (upcoming healthcare technology ecosystem). Government policies designed to include an "open healthcare technology environment" was launched with this purpose in mind. The growing environment will be strengthened by a government and industry approach to health information that is used to develop and introduce new and existing healthcare and health information solutions. The information technology includes many components, among which is a health informatics, which is capable of data sharing that will be implemented by 2025. The basic technology elements of this integrated health care will rely on would include a single health registry, data dictionaries for patients, and standards for communication, digital healthcare reports, and compatibility. This important piece of this integrated data network is the precision medicine record [2]. The two names for this key component are an EHR, but each represents a different type of project. This template contains all the clinical records on one page for a person. Whenever a patient interacts with a physician, they must be able to access specific EHR/medical records data and information without interruption. If it is achievable from everywhere, by anybody, then at any moment, mostly with patient's permission, we want it done now. In order for it to allow interoperability between electronic health records (EHRs) and follow standard protocols. Many patients around the country may not have their medical records or are unable to access them because of stringent privacy laws. Creative example: Tertiary care medical facilities like AIIMS and top-level healthcare facilities have much of their patient documents and information written records [3–5]. It is no longer possible to satisfy patients, healthcare professionals, administrators, caregivers, patients' family members, and families on an equal playing field as knowledge is all becoming digital.

Each person in the healthcare technology system will have to reexamine their strategic plan aspects that should be incorporated into this new approach are: the technique of "reconfiguring" computer processes to allow electronic access to all of client records enabling an organization to balance data across the Internet of Things (IoT) and company networks to the health insurance portability and accountability cloud systems and cloud storage infrastructures; adding backup and capacity to the primary internet connection; helping to keep systems interoperable with other software products. It is important that anonymity and security controls are present in the system in order to maintain the integrity of the data promoting efficiency. This will include a substantial financial commitment by the healthcare practitioners. When we consider the total number of elderly patients and in the entire world, we can infer that over 75% of them and 65% of the total population are supported by healthcare firms. In order for them to be competitive, they must render certain improvements and keep up with the technological transition. If government does not invest more money on medicine, new alliances and improved rewards to the corporate companies are needed. These investments must be understood in a sensible way by the service providers. This might threaten their potential life. They have a plenty to gain from participating in the modern digital health industry. Patient's experience increased the efficiency of clinicians and clerical staff matching the expression "providing excellent quality healthcare with better patient results." A lot of new possibilities and frameworks for doing businesses, like Telemedicine, will be born as more and more of us access their healthcare information and advice over the internet. A rise in demand and improved patient satisfaction are indicators of a healthy business. To make use an EHR, patients have to understand that it will cost them money. But for just a small amount of money, this could be very beneficial. The ability to maintain longitudinal studies from all their physicians, medical devices, and software in a centralized database will help patients take charge of their overall health care. Permit others access and constrain the use of the data such that it cannot be used irresponsibly. There should be no break in medical quality of treatment when you move providers. Administration at a lower cost while saving time and resources by better healthcare administration Giving the country and others the opportunity to make material accessible for health promotion, preventive care, and other projects anonymous anonymize the extracted data and allow for commercial projects like studies, drug development, AI development, and hardware construction. It is absolutely necessary that this policy transition be successful if the country is to achieve long-term economic prosperity. Once before, in the 1980s, these two markets were dramatically changed by the advent of new technology, to make room for telecommunications and banking service providers. Understanding this correctly is important, but researching from other nations like Iran, China, UK, Italy, and Germany would enable us to gain valuable information that could help us to discover the very first period. For the transition to succeed, the private industry has a vested interest. There are public and private investors that require producing this possibility. As long as the value is positive, it would be worth it. All participants in the medical system (whether governments, insurers, doctors, patients, and medical technology vendors) will prosper when the patient monitoring network is ready [6–8].

This will assist the administration's attempt to bring socialized medicine to India that would provision each Indian citizen with an option for high-quality treatment at a fraction of the cost.

5.2   Primal elements driving the medical industry

The patterns mentioned above will continue to further develop in the following section according to the Medicare concepts.

5.2.1   Recent research in healthcare

The more often it is used in medical, the quicker, more effective, the more secure, and more open the Medicare sector can become. To augment a medical services and infrastructure, medical devices are also drastically reducing in complexity, thus widening their appeal. In other words, physicians are now able to go over the Internet to talk to their clients while setting up traditional medical offices. There is also an increase in the amount of highly repetitive treatment, which frees up the medical personnel to become more knowledgeable in their duties.

5.2.2   Medical expenses and their surge

It is stated that medical expenses would be $11.7 hundred million per year, at $40,000 per individual.

The population with age is devoting more of its money to healthcare. In addition, additional, higher maintenance costs, administration costs due to costly facilities, and insurance premiums reimbursements bring with them higher end-user charges. Simplification of medical facilities reduces deep expenses to both suppliers in long run. Additionally, with the advent of legitimate tracking and modeling, the health insurance sector is able to cut waste and errors, while discovering cost figures accurately.

5.2.3   Improvement in mortality rate of older people

During the coming decades, the aging demographic (people aged 60 or older) will outnumber the younger ones (kids) 6–18 in the US. This translates into a huge rise in requirements and expenses. This report says telemedicine novelties, programming, and other automated applications concentrate on improving care delivery. The new treatments enable patients to stay at home that may be especially important for a rapidly aging population. Not only are intelligence medical equipment able to collect information in actual environments they are also accurate and reliable.

5.2.4   Modulating relationship

One of the most drastic consequences of the emergence of commercialism in medicine is a heightened emphasis on both customization and user-participation. People are moving apart from the conventional, restrictive model, which aims to provide a one-size-fits-all approach to versatile and personalized services and seeking more benefit for their money.

5.2.5 Eccentric frameworks

While providing customer-eccentric services is more important than keeping the costs down (short-term results), having long-term, better productivity is much of a determining factor in medical treatment pricing. The truth is, however, that customers do not want to get sick. With the rise of health-tracking systems, we are moving into a more proactive model of healthcare.

5.3 Technology trends in healthcare

5.3.1 Smart watches and clinical device network

In a medical sector, emphasizing the use of technology, smart watches, and the network of clinical devices (NoCD) is not dying out, but rather thriving. Healthcare smart watches are predicted to reach $1 trillion in the next 5 years given by Global Industry Analysts in 2024 that will come to a very lofty $247 billion as well. Such devices enable healthcare providers to obtain serious clinical data more quickly and in full detail, so they can determine the patient's overall well-being in greater detail. In addition, smart watches and NoCD are facilitating the medical industry and clients in how they track their own conditions.

5.3.2 Intelligence and data analytics

Decisions are made in the medical sector between cost, availability, and usefulness; authorities are often forced to make tough ones in all three areas. Where medical treatment, accessibility, affordability, and effectiveness were all guaranteed, the planet might be a truly perfect place.

Nevertheless, in the actual world, not only does it not apply, but the inverse is also. Unfortunately, though this will have the opportunity to assist the sector that is becoming more efficient, it will increase accessibility, make it more expensive, and lead to inferior results. Due to the implementation of Artificial Intelligence (AI), medical systems and care providers may allocate more resources to certain activities that become time-consuming for humanity and more complex. AI will also help people to utilize self-service stations to ensure the maximum value for their own health. Accenture found that AI would satisfy the urgent humanitarian requirement of 15% of the market. Accenture estimates that AI would save the biomedical sector $4 trillion a year by 2030, tops. And, to better interpret health information, AI is also being created. AI software will take radiography and interpret the findings, shortening the number a patient has to spend for those results. Patients' well-being is often improved with the use of AI such as this. In fact, marketers in the medical industry are discovering the advantages of AI. The medical study showed that about 38% of healthcare organizations are involved in AI and business intelligence, as per the managing director of the company. There is a lot of money to be made from the creation of this new AI medical technology. It is estimated that by 2022, health care spending in AI will be about $10.4 trillion while information technology has the power to prescribe customized therapies, it is particularly valuable when it comes to individualized healthcare. Computer program can scan thousands of medical research to determine a proper treatment that is dependent on a person's age as well as other conditions that are significant.

5.3.3   Augmented reality (AR) and virtual reality (VR)

The medical sector is being revolutionized by creative solutions such as VR technology. The health services AR and VR sector is projected to grow between $2.0 billion and $130 billion in value between 2020 and 2025. In medical, AR and VR get a variety of frameworks that benefit both clients and practitioners. For instance, VR is assisting physicians in learning when to conduct risky operations without putting patients at increased risk. AR is now being used to assist physicians during serious complications in order to minimize the incidence of making an error. Patients will benefit from AR and VR care as well. AR or VR is currently employed to help people who have schizophrenia or Parkinson's disease perceive their positive or enjoyable memories and relationships from their past, respectively. A VR can be useful in treating both physical and psychological injuries because of the amount of discomfort and distress it can cause. As study showed, burned patients who are doing VR experiences feel roughly 25–60% reduced pain.

5.3.4   Telemedicine

Many groundbreaking options are being implemented in the patient–physician relationship. Due to new strategies, person's access to medical care technologies are being sought for people's medical needs. The electronic meetings made by telemedicine technologies are for those people who have had little to no healthcare coverage in the past can now use virtual scheduling. Instead, clinicians with physical disabilities can see medical professionals using this software. The usefulness of this innovation is attracting ever more customers. Since 2015, the percentage of clinicians using this new technology has nearly doubled. In 2017, the international tele-health estimated to be valued more than $1.2 trillion, and it will increase to $2.7 trillion by 2021. Currently, Doctolib, one of Germany's telemedic pioneers, recently secured $1.4 trillion in series B funding series. With Doctolib, patients discover and schedule a consultation with medical professionals. In terms of support, Doctolib is intending to enhance their network so they can assist in digital doctor visits. Additionally, the software and web creation of mobile technology is encouraging patients to participate in discussions and better serve their needs. Increasingly developed and published and better treatment are being developed as a result of these developments.

5.4   Technology challenges in healthcare

5.4.1   Data processing

The collection and interpretation of data is a big problem in the healthcare sector. The massive number of information that hospitals, clinics, and medical groups gather contributes to the issue. It is difficult for institutions to provide quality and more tailored services to patients without sophisticated AI program that can interpret this data. Another significant problem is data collection and synchronization. Hospital appointments are taking place through several networks as a result of the growth of electronic health records, making it more difficult for health providers to update patients' medical records. As a practice, the healthcare sector will need to develop a system for recording and updating patient records both for in-person and interactive appointments. Furthermore, regulations such as the EU's General Data Protection Regulation (GDPR) imposes additional restrictions on how businesses capture, use, and store sensitive information. Charges under GDPR can be as much as €25 million, or 4% of a company's annual turnover. As a result, it is in everyone's long-term interest for all companies to comply with all GDPR criteria.

5.4.2   Cybersecurity

Any sector faces cybersecurity threats, and healthcare is no exception. Cyberattacks, which can be incredibly expensive, enable companies to be extremely cautious. According to an IBM survey, healthcare companies have the largest costs related to data attacks and are three times larger than other sectors. The three most common bugs in healthcare are device security flaws, device leakage, and inappropriate user privileges. Making the requisite steps to improve these areas is vital to the healthcare industry's safety. Moreover, the implementation of IoT in medical technologies and the industry's total digitalization would likely lead to more attacks. Once it refers to authentication-related modules, IoT in medical technology products may be troublesome because manufacturers can stop promoting them after a certain amount of time. Although some attacks are the products of deliberate intent, most are the result of failures in the implementation of a device or program. The incorrect dissemination of personal and private records of 155,000 patients in the United Kingdom was blamed on a software coding mistake in 2018. Organizations that develop apps, mobile apps, blogs, and IoT in medical technologies smartphones, among other things. Bugs like these must be discovered prior to the introduction or upgrade of devices and services.

5.4.3   Digital user experience

At last, creating flawless and user-friendly devices such as a linked heart monitor, mobile platform, or some other software device or system is a big task. When it applies to this kind of development, the user experience must be recognized in order to build a user-friendly device or system. This is essential in the pharmaceutical sector since many items can be used by the consumers and medical practitioners. For example, an inconvenient or improperly built IoT in medical technologies system can affect a patient's experience and lead them to uninstall the device, reducing the amount of information it can capture. In another hand, if an IoT in medical technologies system's functionality is complicated to use, it will restrict medical practitioners' ability to use or recommend the device to some patients. The shortage of expertise particularly in the area of IoT in medical technologies makes it more challenging for these goods and resources to perform flawlessly in an interconnected device environment. Additionally, technology's potential to make substantial changes in the healthcare sector can be primarily measured by its cumulative efficiency.

5.5   Big Data in healthcare

Electronic medical records (EMRs), medical scans, genome profiling, provider records, prescription studies, wearable devices, and medical implants, to name a handful, all lead to big data of healthcare [9–12]. It varies from conventional digital clinical and human medical information used for decision-making in three ways: it is easily accessible. It travels rapidly and covers the vast digital environment of the healthcare sector; and, since it is derived from a range of sources, it is extremely dynamic in form and design. This is referred to as the Big Data 3Vs.

Big Data healthcare is hard to merge into traditional databases because of the complexity in design, complexity, and scope, making it extremely complicated to process and for market leaders to leverage its tremendous potential to disrupt the industry. Figure 5.1 depicts the sources of Big Data in Healthcare. In many recent technology advancements are enabling Big Data in healthcare to be turned into meaningful, measurable intelligence.

Despite these, obstacles in many recent technology advancements are enabling Big Data in healthcare to be turned into meaningful, intelligence information. Big Data is educating the transition toward value-based healthcare and expanding the

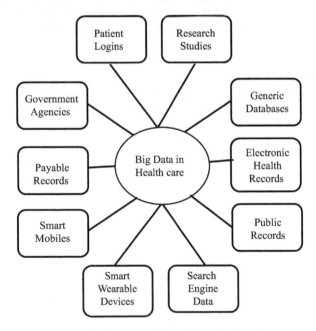

Figure 5.1   Sources of Big Data in healthcare

door to incredible advances while lowering costs by using effective software resources. Healthcare data analytics offers clinicians and administrators with a wealth of knowledge that allows them to make smarter medical and financial choices while maintaining an ever-improving level of clinical care.

However, due to problems such as medical information safety, protection, heterogeneous data, and budget restrictions, healthcare has tend to lag behind other sectors in adopting Big Data analysis. Meanwhile, 80% of managers sampled from financial resources banking, publishing, entertainment, engineering, and distribution firms say that their efforts in Big Data analytics have been "effective," and greater than one-fifth say that their Big Data efforts have been "truly revolutionary" for their businesses.

There are two emerging developments in the healthcare sector that allows it to accept Big Data. The first one is the previously stated transition from a fee-for-service method, in which clinicians are paid for completing operations, to a value-based treatment model, in which they are paid based on the safety of their clinical groups [12,13]. This change will be enabled by healthcare data analytics, which will allow for the assessment and monitoring of public health. The second method is to use Big Data research to provide scientific proof insights that can improve efficiencies and help us better identify the best practices related with any disease, accident, or disease over time.

Using Big Data research to provide proof-based insights can improve energy efficiency and allows us to better understand the best practices related with any illness, accident, or illness over time.

Healthcare Big Data will undeniably change the industry, shifting it away from a fee-for-service paradigm and into value-based care. In other words, it has the potential to reduce healthcare rates while also uncovering new approaches to improve patient experiences, procedures, and performance.

5.6   Big Data in healthcare applications

Making patients safe and preventing infection and disorder should always be a top priority. Users' physical activity levels are tracked by product goods like the Fitbit performance tracker and the Apple Watch, which can also update on particular health-related patterns. The data collected is now being submitted to cloud repositories, where it can be accessed by doctors as part of their general health and fitness services.

Fitbit has also collaborated with United Healthcare, which provides up to Rs. 15,000 in annual incentives to its insured people who exercise daily. The One Drop app from Knowledgeable Information Systems for Android and Apple is causing substantial improvements in A1c levels in diabetics. In the meantime, Apple's ResearchKit, CareKit, and ResearchKit apps use the technology built into Apple's smart phones to help individuals control their illnesses and investigators collect information from thousands of users around the globe.

Patients may have more opportunities to clinical treatment as clinical facilities are improved. Apps for smart phones, such as Aetna's Triage, provide patients with medical recommendations based on data collected and may suggest that they obtain medical treatment depending on their feedback. Figure 5.2 shows the healthcare applications for Big Data.

- In yet another one of Apple's health information projects, the company has partnered up with Stanford scientists to see whether the Apple Watch's heart tracker could be used to identify high blood pressure, a disease that kills around 130,000 Americans per year. If the system is effective in detecting the illness, Apple will warn users that they should seek clinical help.
- For patients with chronic or COPD, Rotor Wellness uses a Wireless sensor that connects to corticosteroids and spirometers. The company monitors atmospheric factors at sensor sites and sends notifications to patients' phones, allowing them to better identify the reasons of their symptoms and take preventative steps. Notifications on when to take drugs are often sent by the pharmacy. Rotor states that patients are getting 79% fewer asthma attacks and 50% more side effect days thanks to 34 participant papers.
- Prescribing error reduction increases performance and improves health. Prescribing errors affect the United States $22 billion a year, impacting more than 8 million people and resulting in 7,000 accidents, as per the Organization

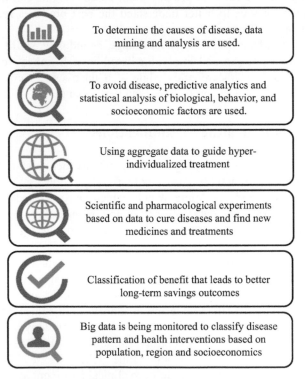

Figure 5.2   Healthcare – applications for Big Data

for Quality in Medical Innovations. MedAware, an Israeli firm, is working with healthcare companies to implement its decision-making tool, which uses big data to identify drug errors before they happen.

- Cost-cutting: Medical information offers doctors more perspective, which leads to better clinical outcomes, reduced hospital, and less diagnoses and re-admissions.
- The medical community employs predictive analytics to classify people with various chronic conditions (bipolar disorder) that are more able to benefit from appropriate recognition in nursing homes, preventing trips to the emergency room.
- Big Data research provides healthcare professionals with clinical information that would otherwise be unavailable. It enables them to administer medications and create medical judgment with greater precision, removing the trial and error that is frequently associated with diagnosis and result in decreased costs and better patient care.
- Assessment of health care data also helps to gain a better understanding of which patient groups are more at threat for infection allowing for a more comprehensive role to disease avoidance. In general, medical Big Data research will classify outlier clinicians who use much more health services than the average. It may identify procedures and procedures that produce poor results or have high values in comparison to the findings. It can be used to empower patients by educating, informing, and motivating them to take charge of their own health. It may demonstrate efficiency improvements and efficacy of treatment options by integrating economic and medical data.

5.7   Challenges for Big Data in healthcare

Data processing, strategy and method, and governance are only a few of the problems that healthcare organizations face when it comes to health records.

5.7.1   Data collection challenges

For starters, patient and medical information is often dispersed among multiple insurance providers, clinics, office buildings, government departments, databases, and storage boxes. It takes a lot of preparation to put it all around each other and arrange for all data providers to cooperate in the future as additional data is generated. Furthermore, each contributing company must acknowledge and decide on the forms and types of Big Data they will be analyzing. Other than questions of storage layout (publication, video, conventional databases, EHR, etc.), the consistency and reliability of such data must be defined. This necessitates not only data analysis (which is generally a tedious process) but also an analysis of government data.

5.7.2   Procedure and method challenges

After the data has been checked and integrated, a number of process and regulation problems must be resolved. Rules and procedures must protect health details, according to regulatory requirements. The role is made more difficult by network access, authorization, and protection during processing and other regulations. Cloud providers, most specifically Amazon AWS, have addressed this multi-dimensional problems, offering cloud storage that align with NIST and identifiable health information (IHI).

5.7.3   Data management challenges

Finally, understanding the benefits of Big Data analytics in medicine necessitates improvements in corporate practices. Data analysts will almost certainly be necessary, as will IT personnel with the necessary expertise to operate the research. Some businesses may be concerned about having to "rip and upgrade" most of their IT resources, but cloud providers may help alleviate some of those worries. Health professionals and supervisors can take some time to recognize the previously unknown recommendations that data analytics will generate.

5.7.3.1   Data management impact healthcare

Historically, healthcare companies have lagged behind the rest of the world in embracing new emerging technology. Machine learning (ML) and deep learning (DL), among other technological transformation, can drive potential changes in the performance of healthcare provision. Quality measures like Centers for Medicare & Medicaid Services (CMS) and clinical quality measure (CQM) have been around for a long time, and developments in various techniques, unused devices, and development challenges have made it difficult for health plan providers to obtain true effects like better patient care, decreased operating expenses, and effective resource use.

In addition to obtain greater efficiency improvements in their industry, health plan providers must rethink their information and development approaches in the face of highly complicated Income Cost based Care (CBC) payment systems. This necessitates the use of data processing tools. These performance metrics have an effect on a healthcare plan's sustainability, as well as cost-based treatment benefits for providers and pharmacies. Poor quality significance level significantly reduces plan ratings and can have an effect on the payer increase in government expenditure. Taxpayers must raise these ratings because thousands of dollars are at issue if a single statistic moves even a half-point in either direction. Trying to improve these quality indicators would require combining the right technologies with an effective data framework. Data analytics, web, machine intelligence (MI)/DL, and advanced data repository and automation systems are some of the main Internet technologies tools that help to enhance healthcare information management, monitoring, and increasingly quality of care.

Database and business analytics (BA) technologies have been around for centuries. Information is the new currency in a virtual environment, and this is especially true for medical institutions. The NIST and other legislation make data processing in the healthcare sector much more difficult. Modern electronic developments are focused on key components including data protection, confidentiality, information crater challenges, and budgetary constraints, and they serve as the framework for creative solutions to business challenges.

5.7.4   Significant factors that support health plan agencies in enhancing quality measurement results

5.7.4.1   Data warehouses and data ingestion

While the volume and complexity of data sources on the business platform grows, providing the right stream processing framework becomes increasingly important. Electronic medical records (EMRs), diagnosis, ultrasound, provider registry, registration records, billing information, insurance, and medical equipment, to name a few findings, are all used to collect health information. Information storage facilities occur almost in all businesses because of these frameworks, which can generate organized, semi-structured, or complex data at varying speeds and quantities. Gathering, processing, and harnessing essential information into usable, measurable resources are extremely difficult due to the variety of structured data, design, and scope. Recent advancements in business intelligence implementation allow businesses to more effectively handle data warehouses which can result in significant savings in terms of data visualization and reliability.

5.7.4.2   Data lakes and data integration

Combining multiple data warehouses for efficient data exchange while preserving consumer security and anonymity is also a critical feature for businesses. Big Data technology and connectivity developments, such as parallel computing and communication, have made it very easy to incorporate a range of data streams at a large scale. Trigger and Hadoop are both capable of incorporating a wide range of data resources. Real-time data communication is feasible thanks to Sartre as well as other delivery communication technologies. Data warehouses are a great way to consolidate data and link disparate systems. Next, providing a core operating interface that provides a common source of truth for all stakeholders, as well as the opportunity to exchange information with relevant partners when necessary, is critical. For provider organizations, combining data from various, fragmented systems can increase the organizational and economic feasibility of CBC services.

5.7.4.3   Big Data warehouse

Owing to the challenges associated in developing and implementing these techniques to deliver top market advantages, healthcare plan providers have attempted to use Hadoop and other data analysis innovations for a long time. Technological innovations allow a simplified and organized method to collecting and processing data from unstructured data, which is a key component in eliminating uncertainties and requiring less human processes by the organization.

5.7.4.4   Analysis and reporting

Just 0.06% of all applicable health records were currently analyzed for organizational decisions. Secrecy and confidence among providers and consumers are improved by effective, reliable, and streamlined monitoring requirements across the healthcare ecosystem. Medical expertise gleaned from DL allows clinicians to recommend therapies and makes medical judgment with greater precision, leading in lower prices and better clinical management. Observations into the patient groups most at risk for infection will contribute to a pragmatic strategy to preventing disease. These findings can be used to teach clinicians how to take charge of their own health. Combining administrative and operational data shows care programmers efficiency improvements and potential efficacy. As a result, using Big Data analysis techniques and predictive analysis leads to improved clinical care, reduced hospital, and less re-admissions, both of which result in lower long-term costs for the company.

5.8   Case study

Mora *et al.* [14]: for tracking human biomedical signals in activities, like physical exercise, the distributed architecture focused on the internet of things (DA-IoT) was proposed. The proposed system's main advantage and novelty is its flexibility in evaluating healthcare applications using instruments from current devices within the users' body region network. This proposed framework would be applicable to other mobile environments, especially those with high signal collection and acquisition needs. The real-time data gathered by such instruments reveals a simple social goal: accidental death and perhaps serious injury are to be anticipated.

Dinesh *et al.* [15]: E-Health Management Framework (EHMF) generated by the IoT was set up. The data collected by sensors is transmitted to an Ethernet server, which is an IoT cloud-connected computer, and the data is accessed through the web by the authorized individual. The webserver keeps track of the patient's past data. The doctor will get input from everywhere in the world anytime he or she needs it. When a person's health status changes unexpectedly when using this health care module, the patient's data will be forwarded to the proper provider right away. In a matter of seconds, the user gets a prescription for the present situation. Medical personnel will constantly track, assess, and provide advice to patients using the IoT medical monitoring system. IoT is seen in both the proposed ecosystem and the patient monitoring survey framework. On health problems, data is gathered and posted.

In this chapter, fog computing-based wearable sensor networks (FWSNs) are suggested in health tracking systems for elders using IoT to address some of the concerns raised in the above case study [16]. To research and test smart healthcare system outputs, a system approach has been developed that takes into account different uses, implementation configuration, operating load environments, cloud, and fog power computing [17]. Under differing workplace health IoT settings, the model will execute healthcare program and define necessary computing tools. Moreover, the suggested approach would satisfy stringent quality of system criteria by using the most appropriate computational resources for processing health data [18]. Furthermore, the proposed model does not depend on a specific workload and does not provide information about resources provided by a private cloud or a remote cloud. In our understanding, the dynamic scale of computing capabilities in fog and cloud settings, as well as the sense of healthcare, has never been discussed in the literature. In healthcare, IoT growth offers significant potential for increasing the quality of living and the efficiency of the health system for the elderly. The enthusiasm in physical responses, physical awareness, and improved compliance has grown among a wide range of audiences, from professional athletes to patients. This chapter proposes FWSNs for IoT leisure activity health monitoring schemes, which is addressed as follows.

5.9   Proposed method

In health monitoring systems for elders using IoT, FWSNs have been suggested. The elder's health monitoring is characterized by a number of components, each of which serves a specific purpose. A body sensor node collects bio signals from elders for analogue front-end devices sensors. The data collected by the body sensor is sent to a gateway via a generic Bluetooth Low Power and Wi-Fi protocol. The data from the body sensor network is then sent to a remote server through the gateway. After that, the server exhibits obtained data to health care providers in descriptive or visual waveforms for presentation and diagnostic testing. In order to gather patient data, they use a public cloud, a Cloud Gateway (CG), BSN, a Gateway (GW), private cloud, and a fog computing nodes. The proposed machine architecture is depicted in Figure 5.3. Furthermore, the analytical approach and use of the wearable device illustrate how well the expense of measuring resources could be minimized when preserving health criteria in the cloud and fog delivery environment through health information access.

Wearable and mobile systems for professional medical staff would be able to track a large number of elders at the same time. The patient has multiple body sensors depending on their health status. The body sensors that collect patient data and send this to the gateway through the access point. Some confidential data will be sent through gateway to a private cloud that is not connected to the Fog nodes or the public cloud in order to communicate with it. Some physical servers are virtualized as virtual servers in the Public Cloud. Fog is a public or private processing network that shares data with the public cloud. Registered operators, such as doctors, nurses, and emergency services, as well as patient families, have access to both public and private data. Our fog computing-based remote control system shows significant reduction of energy expenditure and accuracy errors. From the other side, the activity for sensor accuracy control in technology strategy has been suggested as a way to prolong the sensor's life. As a consequence, the sensor can be allocated small energy amounts with much the same efficiency. To obtain optimum precision and reduce bandwidth and resource efficiency, the cognitive fog layer works with the sensor nodes. As a result, FWSNs for health monitoring systems for IoT researchers based aids in the continuous real-time tracking of heartbeat rhythm, respiratory frequency, and movement during normal and physical activities. The sensor data is captured to the Ethernet module of the IoT networking system with Wi-Fi platform, and the authorized person monitors the elder's body conditions through the Internet. This dilemma emerges by using a centralized approach that uses existing aggregate data to perform a wider study of Big Data methods.

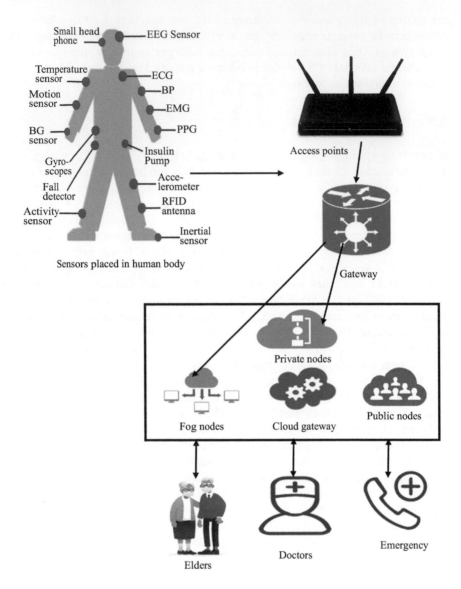

Figure 5.3   System architecture

Communication among portable sensors and the centralized intelligent systems, on the other hand, can cause slowdowns and delays. In this study, it was proposed that the IoT ecosystem's monitoring and sensing device be used to solve the past issues and solve the problem mentioned above. This concept seeks to set biomedical sensors and computing capabilities that will allow innovative applications to be available to patients. This chapter focuses on introducing a method for using the predictive potential of intelligent devices through the IoT with a fog computing-based model for the creation of creative healthcare technology applications.

5.10   Experimental results and discussion

5.10.1   Accuracy analysis

To stop the sensor layer being imposed on the numerical overhead, the optimization technique is positioned in the fog layer. This approach can be applied to minimize the risk of data gathering errors, ensuring the accuracy of the evaluations. On a remote controller, our fog computing control system demonstrates considerable energy consumption benefits with limited precision losses. To prolong the sensor's life, it has been suggested to even use the method for sensor precision control in technology strategy. Physical behaviors such as sleeping or sitting create less motion objects. As a result, reduced power allocations may be assigned to the detector to reach the same realistic expectations. The semantic fog layer complies with the sensor nodes to improve system resource and bandwidth utilization and have a high level of accuracy. The proposed FWSN method accuracy is displayed in Figure 5.4.

5.10.2   Average performance analysis

Physical therapy professionals may use portable inertial sensor devices to monitor and assess healing thresholds and key success metrics. For self-training and performance management, the proposed FWSN has shown to be reliable and effective. During treatment, patients can use a dynamic use of sensor, connectivity, and computer technology without stopping or disrupting themselves, which is known as

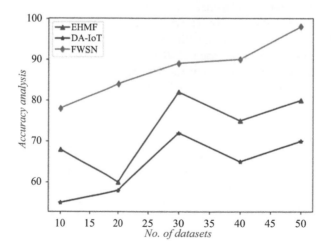

Figure 5.4   Accuracy analysis

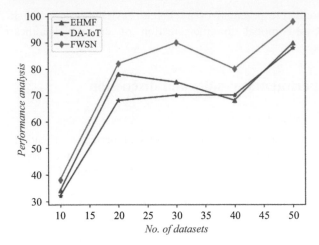

Figure 5.5   Average performance analysis

ubiquitous computing. Real-time performance control and feedback mechanisms have been found to be highly useful in study areas including physical exercise, such as elders walking and sleeping models. When contrasted to other current approaches, the proposed FWSN approach has a high overall efficiency. The average performance ratio of the proposed FWSN system is shown in Figure 5.5.

5.10.3   Average response time (ART)

In the cloud datacenter, the ART for consolidated IoT traffic. The empirical results are represented by the curve lines, while the simulation results are represented by the blue circles. Computing has been looked at to test workload performance curves using different tools. Various workloads have been studied to determine the impact on the ART. The request for health data, the ART is estimated for arrival of 1,500–15,000 transactions per second. It is worth noting that the analysis findings are more in line with the simulation results and that the ART improves as the load increase. The suggested FWSN method's ART as shown in Figure 5.6.

5.10.4   Pattern classification time

The patient interacts with this software in the fog layer by tracking his experience and responding to medical history and personal information questions. Following registration, the cloud provider grants the patient a specific id number. To execute this pattern classification, the cloud layer sends the patient identity and medical records vector ranges to the appropriate fog node. The channel is secured by secure socket layer for safety and protection between different systems. To perform analysis, the fog layer communicates with the other fog nodes and Cloud Data providers to handle data. The knowledge supervision process correlates the sampled data for each attribute with the professionals' defined standard set of values.

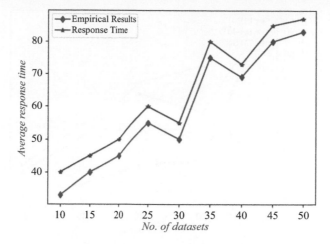

Figure 5.6 Average response time

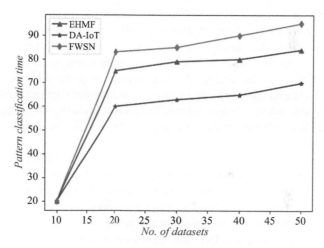

Figure 5.7 Pattern classification time

Miscellaneous data from various medical devices is converted into the proper format before classification. Several records are generated in order to categorize the case into two categories: irregular and normal. Figure 5.7 depicts the proposed FWSN method's classification period.

5.10.5 Error rate

The proposed device transparent information sharing among various modules includes a smart gateway to minimize internet traffic loading, fog computing-based data storage to increase data sharing rate and privacy, introducing inter fault, and

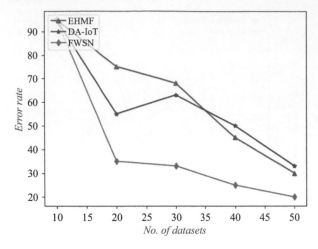

Figure 5.8   Error rate

privacy concerns in physical and virtual environments. Both activities ensure that the system provides the highest security and privacy arrangements for patient health information. By analyzing the provided platform, local security, and encrypted layer, the author owns the data gathering layer. In an IoT configuration, the subscriptions are the dealer, the smartphone, and the data tier. The control technology layer and the portal, in addition, highlight the reach of this system's IoT connectivity techniques. When opposed to other models, the proposed FWSN approach has a smaller error rate. Figure 5.8 depicts the theoretical FWSN method's error rate.

The findings of the experiments include a complete Cloud-based IoT architecture for health systems that support IoT and cloud computing. They provide a medium for the sharing of patient records between devices and mobile servers, as well as the availability of cloud storage resources for the transfer of medical information. Many new innovations and technology are increasingly being applied to the healthcare industry's IoT and cloud computing convergence framework, from this survey its easily categorizes and summarizes. Fog-based analysis in healthcare applications has been developed thanks to a comprehensive cloud-based survey, especially fog computing-based IoT technology with standardized frameworks.

5.10.6   Conclusion

The goals of this chapter were to provide an integrated perspective of the state of digital technology of healthcare, recognize key operations and business uses of digitalization technologies by healthcare participants, and suggest a possible future study strategy. AI/ML are in great supply around the healthcare sector, with the aim of discovering possible advantages of increasing performance measures through core emerging technology such as Big Data and cloud. This have a range of main advantages. Improved predictive analytics to distinguish high and low-efficiency suppliers with better precision. Providers would be able to promote prospects for greater productivity thanks to improved monitoring. Using the right data tactics, you will increase commitment and satisfaction. To improve the standard of treatment, quality metrics are used. They will shift toward investment healthcare and lowering prices by using appropriate Big Data tools to enable solid data protection. Patients and caregivers too can make smarter medical and financial choices while maintaining the ever level of health care thanks to the wealth of data provided by Big Data analytics. The FWSNs have been proposed in health management systems for elders including IoT in this case study. A fog layer was installed at a portal to the health monitoring system, allowing for quick and effective communication. Simulation results have been used to assess and cross validate the proposed queuing model. The fog layer tracks actual incident instances for computational activity circumstance. Various activities are linked in the sense of the medical image particles for effective decision making. The availability of data to cloud participants is important in the management of medical problems. Finally, the efficiency of the proposed device is further improved by the development of legitimate alerts with substantial activity measurement computational calculations to analyses the utility of IoT computers, private, fog nodes and public cloud nodes in the health system layers. The suggested FWSN approach is very good at forecasting abnormal conditions in elderly people. As compared to other approaches, the sensor's efficiency is also extraordinary in the proposed method.

References

[1] Verhoef, P.C., T. Broekhuizen, Y. Bart, *et al.* "Digital transformation: a multidisciplinary reflection and research agenda." *Journal of Business Research* 122 (2021): 889–901.

[2] Ralph, B. and M. Stockinger. "Digitalization and digital transformation in metal forming: key technologies, challenges and current developments of industry 4.0 applications." In *Proceedings of the XXXIX. Colloquium on Metal Forming*, 2021.

[3] Kraus, S., F. Schiavone, A. Pluzhnikova and A.C. Invernizzi. "Digital transformation in healthcare: analyzing the current state-of-research." *Journal of Business Research* 123 (2021): 557–567.

[4] Brock, J.K.-U. and F. Von Wangenheim. "Demystifying AI: what digital transformation leaders can teach you about realistic artificial Intelligence?" *California Management Review* 61(4) (2019): 110–134.

[5] Narmadha, S., S. Gokulan, M. Pavithra, R. Rajmohan and T. Ananthkumar. "Determination of various deep learning parameters to predict heart disease for diabetes patients." In *2020 International Conference on System, Computation, Automation and Networking (ICSCAN)*, IEEE, New York, NY, 2020, pp. 1–6.

[6]   Dhivya, S., D. Jayakumar, M. Pajany and R. Rajmohan. "Temperature and humidity monitoring from remote system using IoT with alert system for landslide." *International Journal of Pure and Applied Mathematics* 119(14) (2018): 761–765.

[7]   Rajakumar, G., T. Ananth Kumar, T.A. Samuel and E. Muthu Kumaran. "Iot based milk monitoring system for detection of milk adulteration." *International Journal of Pure and Applied Mathematics* 118(9) (2018): 21–32.

[8]   Li, S., B. Zhang, P. Fei, P. Mohamed Shakeel and R.D.J. Samuel. "Computational efficient wearable sensor network health monitoring system for sports athletics using IoT." *Aggression and Violent Behavior* (2020): 101541.

[9]   Ahmadi, A., E. Mitchell, F. Destelle, *et al.* "Automatic activity classification and movement assessment during a sports training session using wearable inertial sensors." In *2014 11th International Conference on Wearable and Implantable Body Sensor Networks*, IEEE, New York, NY, 2014, pp. 98–103.

[10] Pavithra, M., R. Rajmohan, T. Ananth Kumar and R. Ramya. "Prediction and classification of breast cancer using discriminative learning models and techniques." *Machine Vision Inspection Systems*, Volume 2: *Machine Learning-Based Approaches* (2021): 241–262.

[11] Gokulan, S., S. Narmadha, M. Pavithra, R. Rajmohan and T. Ananthkumar, "Determination of various deep learning parameter for sleep disorder." In *2020 International Conference on System, Computation, Automation and Networking (ICSCAN)*, 2020, pp. 1–6, doi: 10.1109/ICSCAN49426. 2020.9262331.

[12] Bala, P.M., S. Usharani and V. Abarna. "Detect the replication attack on wireless sensor network by using intrusion detection system." *Journal of Physics: Conference Series* 1717(1) (2021): 012023. IOP Publishing.

[13] Samuel, T.S.A., M. Pavithra and R. Raj Mohan. "LIFI-based radiation-free monitoring and transmission device for hospitals/public places." In *Multimedia and Sensory Input for Augmented, Mixed, and Virtual Reality*, IGI Global, Hershey, PA, 2021, pp. 195–205.

[14] Mora, H., D. Gil, R.M. Terol, J. Azorín and J. Szymanski. An IoT-based computational framework for healthcare monitoring in mobile environments. *Sensors* 17(10) (2017): 2302.

[15] Dinesh, K., K. Vijayalakshmi, C. Nirosha and I. Siva Rama Krishna. "IoT based smart health care monitoring system." *International Journal of Institutional & Industrial Research* 3(1) (2018): 22–24.

[16] Ananth Kumar, T., T.S. Arun Samuel, P. Praveen Kumar, M. Pavithra and R. Raj Mohan. "LIFI-based radiation-free monitoring and transmission device for hospitals/public places." In Tyagi, A.K. (Ed.), *Multimedia and Sensory Input for Augmented, Mixed, and Virtual Reality*, IGI Global, Hershey, PA, 2021 pp. 195–205. http://doi:10.4018/978-1-7998-4703-8.ch010

[17]   Adimoolam M., A. John, N.M. Balamurugan and T. Ananth Kumar. "Green ICT communication, networking and data processing." In Balusamy B., Chilamkurti N., Kadry S. (Eds), *Green Computing in Smart Cities: Simulation and Techniques. Green Energy and Technology*, Springer, Cham, 2021. https://doi.org/10.1007/978-3-030-48141-4_6

[18]   John A., T. Ananth Kumar, M. Adimoolam and A. Blessy. "Energy management and monitoring using IoT with cupcarbon platform." In: Balusamy B., Chilamkurti N., Kadry S. (Eds), *Green Computing in Smart Cities: Simulation and Techniques. Green Energy and Technology*, Springer, Cham, 2021. https://doi.org/10.1007/978-3-030-48141-4_10

Chapter 6

Semantic knowledge graph technologies in data science

P. Manju Bala[1], S. Usharani[1], T. Ananth Kumar[1], R. Rajmohan[1], M. Pavithra[1] and G. Glorindal[2]

Abstract

Knowledge graphs, the representation of data as just a semantic graph, had already garnered considerable attention in both the academia and industry worlds. Their ability to provide semantically appropriate data had already made significant reasonable solutions to several tasks, such as solving problems, guidance and knowledge representation, and has been considered to be a tremendous potential to several researchers to develop the most advanced technology. Even though numerous "Big Data" applications have been already facilitated in all kinds of commercial and science domains through information graphs but limits of effectiveness have been met by the document-centric frameworks of research. Recent controversies on the growing abundance of research journals and the issue of accuracy have stressed everything. This creates an opportunity to reconsider the prevailing view of communications of document center research scholars and turn it into a flow of information based on experience by depicting and transferring knowledge via semantic-based interconnected knowledge graphs. The development and advancement of information systems create a shared understanding of knowledge exchanged among users. The methods of query and exchange of data in the learning center of the world are at the center of the knowledge-based flow of data. By incorporating these frameworks into current and new science technology services, the knowledge structures that are now latent and profoundly concealed in documentation can be completely visible and right accessible. It would have the possibility to transform data science effort, as knowledge and analysis findings can be easily interrelated and ideally suited to diverse information requirements. In comparison, experimental findings are exactly equivalent and simpler to replicate. In this chapter, the conception of a knowledge graph for data science describes the potential framework for knowledge graph technologies and initial attempts to incorporate the framework.

[1]Department of Computer Science and Engineering, IFET College of Engineering, India
[2]Department of CS & IT, DMI-St. John The Baptist University, Malawi

6.1   Introduction

Both the manufacturing and academic worlds are concerned with knowledge graphs [1,2]. Most people seem to believe that they provide semantically organized knowledge that can be processed by computers and that this property holds great potential for the development of more machine intelligence [3,4]. Many studies of knowledge graphs are based on the construction methods [5–8], but even though knowledge graphs have already assisted many "Big Data" applications in many business and science domains, no study of knowledge graph applications exists. Documents are at the core of academic correspondence. Researchers write essays and reviews that are published as textual information in both online and offline publications. This basic approach is reflected in the library, engineering, operation, and research landscapes. If questions are answered by specific comments, this method may be reasonable. However, responses are rapidly spanning not just several publications but also various research domains. In these situations, the current infrastructure is insufficient to support researchers. Currently, researchers obtain massive, disturbing volumes of more or less important records, or more broadly, digital resources in the best-case scenario. With recent advances in knowledge demonstration, semantic pursuit, machine–human communication, natural language processing (NLP), and Artificial Intelligence (AI), they are now potential to absolutely reconsider this main pattern of document-centric information flows and convert scholarly communication into knowledge-based information streams by expressing and representing data. The authors [9,10] debated the word "intelligence graph" and suggested a concept based on a review of recent studies in the field. We make no further attempt to refine or offer an alternative to this term since it is beyond the scope of this study. The numerous issues with document-centric knowledge flows are self-evident. The development of scientific literature makes it progressively tough to retain track of the current state of science, among other things. Also, the development, understanding, and analysis of technical writings consume intellectual resources. The lack of repeatability of the study was exacerbated by the uncertainty, in transparency, and duplication of reports, resulting in the reliability and validity issue [11,12]. Another problem is that, while items, terms, and gestures can be categorized and scanned, computers are currently unable to access the layout and meanings of the document, diagrams, references, signs, and other artifacts.

6.2   Knowledge extraction and information extraction

The process of extracting data from different text corpus is information extraction. In other words, taking an unprocessed document (e.g., a news article) and preparing it for extraction in a format a machine may use [13,14]. This is a very complicated NLP issue since people use several different terms in different ways and it all of those words have many meanings. Each type of information extraction has its particular difficult-to-to-to-solve problems. Let us take, for example, knowledge extraction as an example, (!) to find people in a text, and apply techniques to extracting their names. An additional portion of the group is focused on keyword extraction. Recently, people have attempted using an unstructured approach to dealing with unstructured text [15,16]. Pre-existing approaches are focused on sentences that follow a certain template to try to make it into relational data. Techniques for improving the search engine ranking can be broken down into three groups such as search-centered, rule-centered, and inter-invention.

6.2.1 Professional-based systems

An open extraction framework extracts training data, which generates relational triples. Learning based was one of the first programs that the computer industry tried to bring to Internet Explorer (IE). A small subset of sentences is then processed using Penn Treebank to define and mark positive and negative examples, after which a dependency parser is applied to those examples, which are then inputted into TextRunner for validation. In an open information system, an extract is created and uses a bootstrap approach that draws from the data on Wikipedia. An IE built on an recurrent neural network (RNN)-based strategy was introduced in [17,18]. For Creative+ datasets, the model has already been pre-trained on the IE2016 dataset.

A rule-based system is made up of AI in the following manner: out of people, the problem is created, solved, and then the rule is enforced. IE has a range of custom extractions developed using hand-coded rules. Another unique technique is REVERB which employs hand-crafted extraction laws. Reverb solves the issues with trite and obtuse extracts. Another rule-based technique is PREDANT which applied a collection of indexical rules to full predicate-argument structures. Hand-coding the rules means you have to write them yourself rather than use a pre-written script. In the information graph generation application, the target was considered unachievable.

In proposition-based relationship systems, IE may derive a list of relational statements called triplets from an input sentence, where each statement contains a single predicate and one or more arguments [19,20]. Many of the above-described systems fail as they cannot take meaning into account the fact that a statement is true. A phrase such as "Barack Obama, was a, was a nice president" is inappropriate, as the sentence feedback is not making this claim. This situation can be addressed by adding additional meaning to an extracted triple (attributed to believe; democrats). The concept of a relation triple that contains additional attributes is referred to as inter-position. The analogy used is to describe a similar advanced solution [state-of-of-the-the-the-art] approach: a "nested" representation of IE was suggested. This strategy was very effective in obtaining hierarchical dependencies, enabling a better metaphor. Therefore, single-based tools would only get us so far; however, this was agreed upon to construct scientific literature maps of understanding.

It is a tool for storing and distributing information extracted data It is also very common to find knowledge graphs that consist of three entities (a subject, a predicate, and an object) that will do the job [21,22]. Vectors represent ideas, and connections between ideas are identified as edges. It is possible to distinguish previous work on information graphs: Graphs on domain-specific knowledge and literature domain knowledge data needed to carry out different activities can be linked together in an ontology [23,24]. They are domain-specific, implying that expertise in the graph is developed within a specialized area, such as biology, physics, or computer science. For one of the first biomedical domain efforts, RDF-extraction from Excel spreadsheets was used. Recent work in the domain of bio-medical science has emphasized knowledge-graph design. Digital literature looks back into the history of books, before being published. Literature information graphs reflect concepts and relations in literature. A popular literature graph can be found in Semantic Scholar. A well-known graph was constructed by Microsoft and included nodes representing authors, concepts, as well as paper notes that connected them.

6.2.2   Construction of knowledge graph

When all seems to be well and good in life, do not rest on your laurels, there are three possible things you could be worrying about: something is wrong, someone you could be coming apart, or something you could be sitting on as shown in Figure 6.1 can serve as a mental model for us all possible types of library collec-tions the initial part is about academic institutions and how they relate to one another. Several organizations are covered in the field, including researcher, paper, project, conference, and the like. These data would be pulled from a database and extracted from the structured data. A concept graph's second component is zoomed in on entities at a semantic level of abstraction, providing facts about those entities

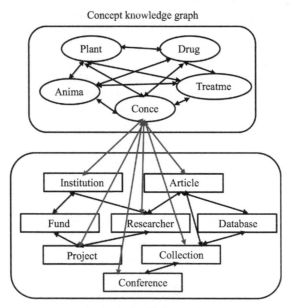

Figure 6.1   Parts of knowledge graph

in a precise and systematic manner. Entities like the concept, drug, plant, and so on. These relationships help us to distinguish between the different types of academic groups, even though we are not using actual red lines to differentiate them in the picture below. A scholar, as well as a specific piece of writing and a document, may be defined as a conceptual entity. Some people will do the same. Semi-structured corpora like titles, abstracts, will serve as the concepts in the graph.

6.2.3   Conceptualization

When it comes to building a concept graph of information, two functions are involved: knowledge extractor and concept knowledge constructor as in Figure 6.2. When the first section of the text is parsed, which includes the title and abstract, links will be found. The second section works to extend the information graph for the terms and relations. The concept graph and end users can provide input on the application of information. The administrator will alter or customize rules, patterns, parameters, or just specific data based on suggestions. All is going to change; the information graph will be iterated upon to produce better results.

6.2.3.1   Knowledge extractor

6.2.3.1.1   Term extractor

The extractor strives to collect high-quality words. Essentially, it is individuals. Data training can use words like entity and so on top of an entity. Extracted terms could be assessed according to five criteria to find qualified terms.

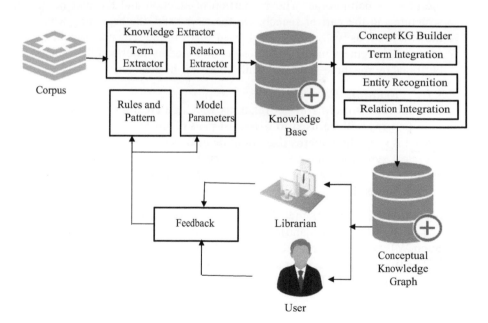

Figure 6.2   Process of building concept knowledge graph

Concordance: It is stronger and less complex than parameter model integration relation (PMIR), but equal to parameter knowledge integrated pattern (PKIP). The closeness of the word index measures the phrase's solidification level. For unit *u*, PMIR is probably reduced to some extent. Potentially this could be translated to PMIR and PKIP Kull Divergence could be the concordance features:

$$PMIR(u_l, u_r) = \log \frac{p(v)}{p(u_l)p(u_r)} \tag{6.1}$$

$$PKIP(v|| < u_{l,}u_r >) = p(v)\log \frac{p(v)}{p(u_l)p(u_r)} \tag{6.2}$$

- *Informativeness*: There is an increased informational value of conversational analysis because it can help to improve the understanding of issues in discussion groups and debates; it can also aid in the development of ideas. Descriptive phrases or buzzwords are unhelpful. By using a stop-word dictionary, the inverse frequency (IF) of terms will be obtained.
- *Highly held views*: Strongly believed A phrase must occur frequently enough in the corpus to be relevant for measurement purposes.
- *Amount of randomness*: The amount of randomness in an open system of information brings the randomness of a set of words and phrases close to each other. Knowledge entropy should be kept low for phrases of higher than average quality.
- *Compound word*: The word compound is composed of many letters; it is, therefore, a palindrome. The proportion of function and the part of speech structure and the part of speech. On the other hand, the beginning word, and the end word, as well as any word, used words in the sentence, should be less common. Strictness in some studies (as measured by rules and thresholds) can be found by machine learning, while looseness in others may not.

6.2.3.1.2 Relation extractor

The relation extractor aims to get relations with high credibility. At first, classic syntactic patterns will be used to extracted pairs of instances connected by relations. Nine is syntactic patterns that could be used as the target patterns, including five classical syntactic patterns suggested by Hearst and four syntactic patterns obtained through machine learning by Snow *et al*. In the nine syntactic patterns below, WT means the wider term, while NT is the narrower term.

- NT{, NT}*{, }(and|or)other WT:temples, treasuries, and other civic buildings
- WT such as {NT, }*(or|and)NT:red algae such as Gelidium
- Such WT as {NT, }*(or|and)NT:works by such authors as A, B, and C
- WT{, }including{NT, }*(or|and)NT:all law countries
- WT{, }especially{NT, }*(or|and)NT:most Arabian countries
- WT like NT;
- WT called NT;
- NT is a WT;
- NT, a WT.

Pairs associated with hierarchical patterns can appear in other than class notes. The unique patterns will also be employed to search for potential pairs of instances. Thus, words and connections from the corpus will increase in number in the iterative loop. The syntactic patterns will look for is a connection within the sentences and select some of the candidates from them. Referring to the Probase algorithm's technique of finding sub-concepts and base terms (BTs), the machine may choose the most relevant sentences. Assumption of the association, on the other hand, refers to how closely the candidate concepts can be correlated. Probability refers to the Plausibility index, which estimates the validity of extracted evidential relations. In fact, the Probase algorithm takes PageRank, which is based on the quality of web pages, into consideration when ranking web content. Different services require different authorities that should be taken into consideration when dealing with libraries. This may include metrics such as author popularity, impact factor, and others. The quest for knowledge is at the heart of human experience which someone in charge of creating graphical representations. Three steps are necessary to make an information graph from text and corpora:

- The integration of technology, media, and computer design synonymous words would be linked to previously known K instances.
- Common-knowledge meteorology to identify the entity type, it will be associated with bases or get an entity model using Word2Vec (W2V).
- Collaboration is formed, contradictory and overlapping relationships can show up, which require this solution. After all of this hard work, it could become a reliable guide to creating new products.

6.3 Creating knowledge graphs using semantic models

Knowledge graphs are powerful methods for collecting and structuring vast amounts of multi-relational data that can then be queried. Knowledge graph is becoming the foundation of a variety of applications, including conceptual search engines, sentiment analysis, and interactional bots, due to its potential. Data integration and publication into knowledge graph is a time-consuming process. After all, it necessitates the compilation and fusion of data from different sources. The integration approach for hierarchical sources including tables (comma separated value, HTML tables, database systems, and so on) and tree-based architectures is to link their specific semantics to the desired ontologies global schema.

6.3.1 System construction

Manual or swarm intelligence-based creation, web data, deep learning, or image retrieval are some of the methods for creating a knowledge graph. The basic methods are involved in the development of even a knowledge graph.

6.3.1.1 Extraction of details

Extract information elements from its source data, such as persons, associations, properties, and so on, and convert them into machine reasonable information.

6.3.1.2   Fusion of knowledge

Elide and combine information, since information derived from multiple sources can be inconsistent.

6.3.1.3   Information storage

After the combination, connect the information and place it in the graph database as quadruplets.

6.3.1.4   Inference from information

Develop intelligent applications like relation estimation, information QA, and others on the framework of the knowledge graph to enhance and extend the current knowledge graph.

6.3.2   *Synopsis mapping*

The most widely used mapping methods are focused on the so-called customized mappings. To conduct the mapping creation process, these strategies use custo-mized statements made in propositional languages. Propositional languages use semantic data architectures to define interactions between specifically required data frameworks and regional conceptual frameworks schemas (Figure 6.3).

6.3.3   *Semantic model*

For two major purposes, a semantic model is an important method for describing the mapping. For instance, it portrays the relationships among ontology groups as graph paths. Second, it requires graph algorithms to be computed to find the right mapping. The semantic model method necessitates the representation of ontology propositions in a knowledge graph. The ontology is displayed in the following figure as a focused, marked, multi-relational graph and numbered.

The ontology's groups are represented by the graph nodes which are shown in Figure 6.4. The object properties are illustrated with blue arrows, data type, and

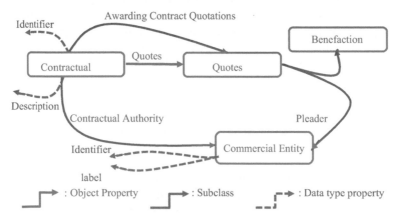

Figure 6.3   Synopsis mapping

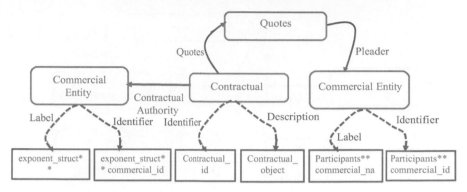

Figure 6.4   Semantic model

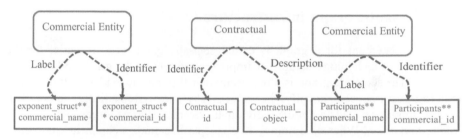

Figure 6.5   Automatic selection of a semantic model

property are illustrated with red dash arrows, and subclass is illustrated with red arrows, the various types of categories shown by the edges. The map can be described into the conceptual model, a guided and named network where leaf nodes reflect the information source's properties, centered mostly on an ontology graph. Other parental nodes and borders are derived from ontology's groups and attributes. The right semantic model is shown in Figure 6.5 as a successive example. The chart refers to the build portion of a JARQL file that was previously addressed.

There are two key stages in the automatic selection of a semantic model. The semantic type phase is the first phase, in which each property of the source of data is formatted with such a couple of ontology classes and data source properties. The element node contract id is associated with a class node. Relationship via the identification regulator from a chart paradigm in the working case. Figure 6.5 depicts the semantic forms in greater detail.

The semantic relation induction phase is the right phase, and it aims to find relations between all the illustrated properties. This connection is expressed by an entity attribute in the best version, and the duration of the connection is equivalent to 1. The categories contractual and commercial entity, which collect the parameters contractual_id and exponent_struct**commercial_id, are linked with the properties contracting authority in the given in Figure 6.6.

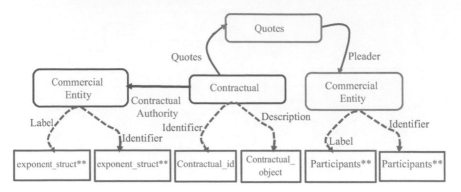

Figure 6.6   Semantic relation induction phase

6.4   Semantic graph infrastructure

Scholarly statement for a graph is called semantic graph. It is essential for the philosophy of technology setup that improves and retains the graph and activates services. The semantic graph is a representation of scientific evidence. It describes existing research semantically, i.e. specifically and systematically, rather than simply linking (metadata about) individuals, records, datasets, organizations, contracts, and so on. Whereas ontology to conceptualize studies conducted has yet to be established, a semantic explanation for ongoing research should at the very least link the approaches to data by the response to the methodology used and the obtained results. Issues, processes, and outcomes are all semantic tools. For example, a sentence like "There is a substantial variation in the average length of a phenomena X (e.g., object structure in the environment) among summer and winter cycles" is not just a machine learning phrase, but also a semantic tool in the information graph. This tool is often related to the experimental performance (and, as an outcome, the researchers and association) as well as the methodology used to arrive at the result. The architecture populates and curates the semantic graph using four different references. To begin, the architecture makes use of an existing database, records, categories, conceptual frameworks, and other resources. Second, it offers resources that facilitate researchers to directly contribute by describing their study, with the help of knowledgeable frameworks and randomly created recommendations. Third, it employs advanced knowledge extraction and connection processes. Fourth, it encourages domain specialists, teaching assistants, and data scientists to personalize and ensure consistency. Manual interactivity is too time-consuming, whereas automatic methods do not achieve the required scope and reliability. Furthermore, library professionals and data scientists lack the requisite subject matter expertise, while researchers lack information extraction expertise. Designers can put their particular responsibilities to balance and account for relative limitations by integrating the four techniques. Interconnecting, convergence, visualization, discovery, and searching are all possible with the semantic graph framework. It allows scientists to get a much more rapid summary of major innovations in a given domain and find specific research issues. It depicts the development of evolutionary science in specific disciplines and allows researchers to make their work more approachable to co-workers, partner companies, policymakers, and the general public. The foregoing technological components are needed for a minimally viable architecture. First, a semantically clarified database schema for describing scholarly discourse is presented [19]. The database schema may use Resource Description Framework (RDF) and linked details as a scaffold, but it must also provide details on authenticity, development, and discussion. Second, the architecture must provide a flexible graph-storage repository for storing data and an application programming interface (API) for communicating with the knowledge graph. Third, we need user interface plugins and modules for interactive graph designing and interactivity, as well as integration with third-party providers. Finally, to facilitate knowledge graph interactivity, the architecture must enable semi-automated semantic implementation, searching, retrieval, and suggestion services.

6.4.1   Sources of knowledge

Organized data is in the form of NoSQL data; semi-structured data in the case of HTML, JSON, XML, and other formats; and data information such as textual data, pictures, and records can all be used to create a knowledge graph. Many knowledge graphs make use of Google scholar data, and particular domains, such as films, make use of knowledge bases like IMDb.

6.4.2   Extraction of knowledge

The extraction of knowledge process starts after the data has been swallowed. This method extracts metadata from semi-structured and unorganized data such as objects, relationships, and characteristics, from the data input. Natural language processing, text analytics, and machine learning methods are used to accomplish this (both supervised and unsupervised learning). Object extraction (also known as object identification) is based on a simple concept: provided some text, find which words classify objects belonging to particular classes. An individual, an item, a place, or thing entities can be grouped into one of several classes, each of which has its own set of sub-classes. An object class might be "people," for instance. Since they are all variants of an individual, object classes like "professional athlete," "musician," and "artist" may all come under the "individual" object class. After all of the objects have been identified, data on the objects and their characteristics is obtained. These may include entity properties as well as inter-entity connections. An "individual" object, for instance, can be related to "place of birth," "sex," and so on. An object characteristic may also be used to label the association among dual objects or object classes. For instance, the object "cricket" can be correlated with the object class "game" and the object category "is a subclass of." The object characteristic of the statement at hand is normally, but not often the verb of the statement. After the subjects and objects have been identified, the objects can be extracted using part of speech labeling.

6.4.3   Convergence of knowledge

Knowledge convergence aims to put together all of the theoretical frameworks from various perspectives to create a detailed image. Its basic objectives are object association and ontology creation. Object identification (or object aspect ratio) is concerned with deciding if different objects relate to the same real-world objects. Since it takes the data to a common ground data standardization is a crucial step in organizational alignment. This move resolves any data inconsistencies. Many of their objects have "irrelevant names, incorrect or missing values, expired information, or no participant assigned to them" because they are user-generated ecological objects. Object members can be created, objects can be disambiguated by clustering based on frameworks in which objects exist, organizations can be de-duplicated using approaches like W2V, and machine learning models can be used to put all objects into the same language. Similarity and mutual synchronization, which integrates documents that belong to the same person, is done until the data is all merged and accurate. Various file similarity features, such as cosine correlation, are used in pair-wise correlation analyses, which may also include deep learning methods like W2V, S2S embedding, and so on. Structure similarity features, such as object recognition, are used to achieve mutual alignment. Most of this research results in the development of an ontology, which is then combined with a categorization, hierarchical frameworks, metadata, and other elements to enhance the information graph's performance [20]. To optimize the quality consistency of the information graph, the ontology is measured to industry frameworks such as Wikipedia, and if it fails to satisfy the criteria, the method is replicated and enhanced. It is essential to emphasize the relevance of the knowledge fusion step is to take an exploratory approach since this is where the majority of the modeling takes place.

6.4.4   Processing, collection, and graphical demonstration of knowledge graphs

A knowledge graph is saved in a Mongo DB repository either in an RDF or a graph registry. Once it has been developed. Graph repositories store roots, nodes, and attributes of graphs, while RDF describes information graphs as a triple Subject → Predicate → Item. The traditional query language for retrieving large-scale knowledge graphs is query JSON. Web apps are used for a lot of information graph visualization, and it is one of the most investigated areas in the field.

6.5   Semantic knowledge graph

To reflect scholarly knowledge transmitted in the literature, semantic knowledge graphs are used [21]. This knowledge graph is known as the semantic knowledge graph (SKG). Importantly, the suggested knowledge graph contains semantic (i.e., computer implementable) representations of scholarly knowledge, rather than only (bibliographic) information (e.g., about papers, writers, and organizations).

6.5.1 Architecture

The framework is designed using a conventional layered design. The consistency layer is for storing data technologies such as labeled graph property (LGP), triple inventory, and hierarchical database processing, all of which serve different objectives. Tracking modifications to stored data is handled by version control and authenticity. Semantic Inclusion, the key SKG knowledge object, is defined in the modeling process. A Semantic Inclusion connects the Inclusion's Semantic Issue, Procedure, and (at least one) Outcome. We are not presently restricting the representation of these services in any way. To explain issues, processes, and outcomes, users may use any third-party vocabulary words they want.

Data synchronization between LGP and triple store is enabled by RDF import and export, which facilitates query JSON and logic. Service demands for learning, reviewing, and generating material in repositories are handled by evaluating. Frameworks that enable connectivity features such as verification, contrast, and similarity approximation reside in the next layer. For scholarly information access, content management, and discovery the GraphQL API serves as a link between resources and functionality. Users in the positions of researcher, investigator, curator, or reviewer engage with SKG's services in different ways. Investigators and reviewers will benefit from discovery resources such as research reviews [22]. Writers who may want to add material should use contribution facilities. Content management programs are intended for professional developers in general, such as topic library professionals who assist with quality management, enhancement, and other information organization tasks.

6.5.2 Characteristics

Several functionalities comprise SKG features, which can be used independently or in partnership to allow facilities. The most significant new features are presented. Literature analysis collects related details from user-selected research submissions and displays them in a table format. The collection of semantically related definitions among the related contributions is extracted for such similarities. We use GlobalVector word embedding is used to generate a similarity matrix β

$$\beta = \left| \cos\left(\vec{d_i}, \vec{d_j}\right) \right| \tag{6.3}$$

The cosine resemblance of vector embedding for descriptor sets $(d_i, d_j) \in K$, whereas K is the class of all Key Findings. Also, create a cover matrix χ which chooses descriptor of findings $f_i \in F$, whereby F is the class of Key Findings to be connected. Correctly,

$$\chi_{i,j} = \begin{cases} 1 & \text{if} \quad d_j \in f_i \\ 0 & \text{otherwise} \end{cases} \tag{6.4}$$

Subsequent, for every designated descriptor d, produces the matrix ϕ that shares χ to comprise only related descriptor. Properly,

$$\emptyset_{i,j} = \left(\chi_{i,j}\right) \quad f_i \in F_{d_J \in \text{sim}(d)} \tag{6.5}$$

where sim(d) is the class of descriptors with resemblance values β [d] $\geq$ P = 0.9 with descriptor d. Point P is determined by trial and error. Finally, ϕ is used to quickly measure the occurrence of a particular set of the descriptor.

Finding correlation is a functionality that allows you to search for and suggest similar Main Findings. The sub-graphs G(ki) for each Key Findings ki $\in$ K are converted into File D by combining the labels of theme t, descriptor d, and item i, of all statements (t,d, i) $\in$ G(ki). We before practice PF/iDF to key and recover the utmost related findings in respect of some query q. Requests are designed in the same way that files D. For automatic analysis of scientific information from research, the SKG employs machine learning. The NLP tasks called entity identification, named object identification, and named object connectivity are of specific interest [23]. For named object recognition, we first educated a neural network-based machine learning algorithm. In the first phase, we used in-house built metadata on the Labs to train a neural network-based machine learning model for object recognition for the corresponding basic dimensions: process, system, content, and data. The Beltagy *et al.* method is used. Task-specific computational architecture for Named Entity Recognition is a classifier SciBERT word embedding with a CRF-based series tag interpreter [24]. Another important feature is the ability to connect learned information to other knowledge graphs, such as open field and domain-specific graphs like ULMS. Most notably, such linking allows for semi-automated work involvement enhancement.

6.5.3   Evaluations

The SKG infrastructure, program, functionality, efficiency, and accessibility are all reviewed regularly to notify future iterations and enhancements. The first front-end user assessment, among other initial assessments and findings, will be evaluated. The analysis of the first phase of front-end development took a qualitative approach, intending to assess user efficiency, define major (positively and negatively) factors, and user validation of the system. The assessment method consisted of two parts: (1) supervised communication sessions and (2) a brief survey. This analysis yielded information that was important to our first investigation query. We organized guided discussion sessions with 13 writers of publications addressed at the conference with the help of two mentors. The teacher briefly explained the basic concepts of the technology at the start of each session. The learners then experimented with the method on their own, without any further instruction from the teacher. They may, nevertheless, request assistance from the teacher at any point. We documented the time it took each participant to accomplish the task (to calculate the average length of a discussion), as well as the instructor's observations and the user's feedback key findings comparison (Table 6.1).

Participants were asked to perform a brief assessment survey in addition to the guided engagement sessions. The survey can be found on the internet. Its goal, like sustainable development, was to gather more information about user interaction. There were 12 questions on the journal article survey. Even after their guided engagement session, these were structured to collect participant perspectives on the

Table 6.1   Time required to perform comparison up to VIII key findings using baseline and SKG

	Key findings comparison						
	II	III	IV	V	VI	VII	VIII
Baseline	0.00025	0.1715	0.762	4.99	112.75	1773.9	14,420
SKG	0.0036	0.0012	0.01157	0.04	0.0207	0.0188	0.0205

positive and negative dimensions of the system. After the directed interaction meeting the participants completed their survey. The survey was answered by all 13 participants. Activity observations, participant feedback, and time observations were gathered with survey questionnaires and evaluated because of our research questionnaire. A database containing a description of the investigation's research areas is accessible online. The knowledge is divided into four groups. The key topic or concern answered by the research contribution is referred to as the problem statement. The researchers' method is referred to as their method. Implementation and assessment were the most thoroughly discussed elements because researchers found it simpler to explain technical information than the issue or solution.

In overview, 75% of participants considered the first iteration's front end to be somewhat logical and quick to use. Eighty percent of the participants required assistance only at the outset, while 10% did not need assistance at all. The task took an average of 17 min to finish with an average of 15 min and a maximum of 22 min. Table 1 shows the questionnaire's specifics, such as participant feedback on key issues. While the sample size was too minimal to draw a systematically meaningful inference, these findings offered several valuable recommendations for the second version of front-end growth, which was tested at TPDL20198 for the first time.

Other elements of the SKG framework have also been subjected to experimental evaluation. We analyzed our SKG method to a base method that uses brute force to identify the most related postulates and thus tests any possible predicate combination. Our new approach surpasses the model, as shown by the results, and the output benefit can be linked to more effective extraction. Since the standard method does not scale to larger collections the analysis is restricted to eight contributions. In terms of processing time, we also put the hierarchical throughput to the test. We did this by creating a fictitious dataset of publications. Each publication contains three sentences that characterize one Key Finding. There are millions of nodes are present in the created dataset. We checked the device with a variety of paper counts, and the normal throughput for retrieving a single paper and its relevant Key finding is 60 ms. This means that the architecture is capable of handling vast volumes of scholarly data.

BioNER, CollabNet, BiLSTM, CLSTM, GRAM-CNN, and BERT were used to assess the output of a variety of current NER tools on scholarly information. These tools have been used to connect to Wikidata and data objects. The test results

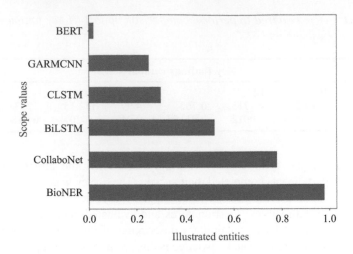

Figure 6.7   Scope values of various NER structures

were annotated objects from the disease corpus. We just measured the distribution variable because there is no benchmark for the database. Figure 6.7 depicts the scope values for the assessed tools.

6.6   Finance industry – a case study for knowledge graph

6.6.1   Data authority

Most concerns have business processes across multiple aspects of their businesses, and fintech firms face this problem as well. Data created by sectors inside financial institutions differ, creating inconsistent and arbitrary data for the financial firm as a whole. The main purpose of data democratic accountability is about maintaining these numerous contexts and making a clear distinction between data silos, tracing regulatory compliance, and realizing data points, and quality assurance.

Graphs are powerful tools for maintaining information in diverse data sets because they can collect and aggregate disparate data from different sources. Graphs are used to attach relevant information to the underlying data. To be iden-tified as such metadata is easily and has value with each other, it is labeled as "attributes" and connections. The linguistic metadata and interactions blend to constitute a layer that provides an idea of the full structure of the data, making it possible to display data at any level of detail, and this combination of data and information is known as holistic data. Users need to see information in visual form so they can identify duplicated or inconsistent facts. Pseudo overlaps may lead to user adjustments and guarantee data accuracy. You can graphically express the different degrees of data ownership with domain-to-link mappings, as well as using domain origination points to connect to earlier versions of the data. Analytics provides the structures that the relationships will reveal the data's accessibility.

6.6.2   Automated fraud detection

Fraud detection has already been made more efficient through machine learning algorithms. Having an artistic representation of fraud concepts also allows researchers to go beyond data that does not pertain to their specific use and also to consider diverse datasets that their fraud detection algorithms might overlook. For instance, if you are interested in a specific users' fraud, drilling down into a dataset one customer at a time would not give users much information. Machine learning techniques can probably identify them as worthless if they are not fraudulent. Such interaction could lead to new insights into how our various customers interact with each other, nevertheless. As an instance, e-mail addresses were never counted as useful in the earlier models. This is a possibility, which is a reason why you must keep customers' email addresses separate in your database. This is why you should keep customers' e-mail addresses separate in your database. Connections that knowledge graphs would notice an e-mail address points to a connection to another customer and that connection points to another client. This is a straightforward yet compelling illustration, as the interrelationships of all the factors are added to the graph.

6.6.3   Knowledge management

There is involvement in using knowledge graphs in banking because of their ability to summarize and agglomerate data from multiple sources, including annual disclosures, the media, and social networks. In 2017, Transparency International debuted their first graph structure to provide a holistic look at the financial ecosystem, streamlining everything from assets, objectives, opportunities, and possibilities to investment risks and decisions. Their knowledge graph unites organizations, individuals, equipment, and reports, as well as definitions, data, creates data about supply and demand, and financing, and facilitates analysis and findings. When a firm is implicated in investigative work lead up to a major acquisition, knowing how to handle its information is critical.

6.6.4   Insider trading

An individual or group shares information with others while trading securities for personal gain. Investigators involved in investigations on an influence-peddling case will need to review disparate data sources to learn more about the offender. As a rule, the Commission and other government organizations examine primary commodities, such as text messages, tweets, and voice mails in in-order to discover any patterns. It is easy to make this method unwieldy and very difficult to manage if you do not use cutting-edge techniques. The portrayal of all the multiple perspectives for patterns allows a constant supply of information.

6.6.5   AI in capital funding

Nowadays, AI systems that provide financing advice to customers can be utilized to aggregate knowledge in legitimate time from various fields of investor and to gain knowledge from the customer's conversations each time they occur. The advantage of these Chabot is to reduce human distortion and personalize customer care at less cost.

6.6.6   Enabling venture capitalization

Organizations can manage data visualizations to develop lexicons and organizational structures around economic prospects on the economy by analyzing historical start-up information, transactions, finance, and trends. The information charts can be used to optimize portfolios and to discover potential, less risk-based possibilities.

6.6.7   Analyzing credentials

The failure to use its payment history abroad in the US is a big problem. This also puts an economic organization at risk which has insufficient resources to demonstrate its legitimacy. Knowledge graphs could even overcome this disparity by using conceptual frameworks from several fields further than what is being viewed presently and by creating a more accurate model.

6.6.8   Product-based community analysis

An interaction between firms as regards international trade, judicial or business solutions, or maybe just human activities or linkages can be good for organizations of investment banking aimed at more individualized rationalization of their products. Information diagrams can help to overcome this problem.

6.6.9   Challenges

1. To comprehend and reusable information graphics between engineers, developers, and experts a cohesive set of quality standards can be used during the development of knowledge representation.
2. Provided a series of unorganized technologies and information graphs, it is difficult to determine if the enterprises referenced in the information match the corporations observed in Graph Database in the modern environment. Even though machine learning (ML) algorithms could even address this issue, the results of these methodologies are directed by the efficiency of the training examples. Due to the wide range of information, it is quite hard to incorporate knowledge.
3. Wisdom is rapidly changing, not coarse-grained. If, for instance, a Knowledge Base monitors the wellbeing of the person the information hidden at a specified instant may be wrong sometime later. So, how can we grasp this specific transcription nature?
4. How is an information diagram evaluated? What enhancement (e.g., completeness, accuracy, connection, etc.) seems to be more essential?

6.7   Conclusion

The conversion from a document-centered toward a more expertise view of wisdom communication is largely consistent with and therefore unavoidable in the contemporary technological conversion of data fluxes. This produces, nevertheless, a need to incorporate the relevant equipment and integrations to promote the toggle.

At this point, very few of these tools still exist and their architecture and specific functionalities are a hurdle to be dealt with in collaboration and a cohesive fashion. The framework and key characteristics of the recommended system are outlined. The findings of every client assessment were reported. Initial actions had been taken and assessed by assimilating cloud computing and computerized methodologies in machine learning to promote the integration of multi-modal academic expertise using the SKG. The formulated research evaluates the first actions towards a machine learning graph database. We have concentrated on certain core operational skills of the connectivity by evaluating the current system and introducing new building components.

References

[1] D. Dessì, F. Osborne, D.R. Recupero, D. Buscaldi and E. Motta, Generating knowledge graphs by employing Natural Language Processing and Machine Learning techniques within the scholarly domain, *Future Generation Computer Systems*, 116, 2021, 253–264, https://doi.org/10.1016/j.future. 2020.10.026, ISSN 0167-739X.

[2] S. Auer and S. Mann, Towards an open research knowledge graph, *The Serials Librarian*, 76(1–4), 2019, 35–41, doi: 10.1080/0361526X.2019. 1540272

[3] X. Wilcke, P. Bloem and V. de Boer, The knowledge graph as the default data model for learning on heterogeneous knowledge, *Data Science* 1, 2017, 39–57.

[4] S. Fathalla, S. Vahdati, S. Auer and C. Lange, SemSur: a core ontology for the semantic representation of research findings, *Procedia Computer Science*, 137, 2018, 151–162, https://doi.org/10.1016/j.procs.2018.09.015, ISSN 1877-0509.

[5] P. Ristoski, G.K.D. de Vries and H. Paulheim, A collection of benchmark datasets for systematic evaluations of machine learning on the semantic web, in: *International Semantic Web Conference*, Springer, New York, NY, 2016, pp. 186–194.

[6] Q. Lin, Y. Zhu, H. Lu, K. Shi and Z. Niu, Improving university faculty evaluations via multi-view knowledge graph, *Future Generation Computer Systems*, 117, 2021, 181–192, https://doi.org/10.1016/j.future.2020.11.021, ISSN 0167-739X.

[7] S. Peroni, D. Shotton and F. Vitali, One year of the open citations corpus, in: *ISWC*, Springer, New York, NY, 2017. pp. 184–192.

[8] M.D. Lucca Tosi and J.C. dos Reis, SciKGraph: A knowledge graph approach to structure a scientific field, *Journal of Informetrics*, 15(1), 2021, 101109, https://doi.org/10.1016/j.joi.2020.101109, ISSN 1751-1577.

[9] G.K.D. de Vries and S. de Rooij, Substructure counting graph kernels for machine learning from RDF data, *Web Semantics: Science, Services and Agents on the World Wide Web*, 35, 2015, 71–84.

[10]   L. Shi, S. Li, X. Yang, J. Qi, G. Pan and B. Zhou, Semantic health knowledge graph: semantic integration of heterogeneous medical knowledge and services, *BioMed Research International*, 2017, 2017, 12 pages, Article ID 2858423, https://doi.org/10.1155/2017/2858423

[11]   S.H. Bach, M. Broecheler, B. Huang and L. Getoor, Hinge-loss Markov random fields and probabilistic soft logic. *CoRR*, abs/1505.04406, 2015.

[12]   D. Fensel, U. Şimşek, K. Angele, et al., Introduction: what is a knowledge graph? in: *Knowledge Graphs*, Springer, Cham, 2020, https://doi.org/10.1007/978-3-030-37439-6_1

[13]   F. Ilievski, D. Garijo, H. Chalupsky, *et al.*, KGTK: a toolkit for large knowledge graph manipulation and analysis, in: Pan J.Z., et al. (eds.), *The Semantic Web – ISWC 2020. ISWC 2020. Lecture Notes in Computer Science*, vol 12507, Springer, Cham, 2020, https://doi.org/10.1007/978-3-030-62466-8_18

[14]   F. Corcoglioniti, M. Rospocher and A.P. Aprosio, A 2-phase frame-based knowledge extraction framework, in: *Proceedings of the 31st Annual ACM Symposium on Applied Computing*, ACM, London, 2016, pp. 354–361.

[15]   H. Ko, P. Witherell, Y. Lu, S. Kim and D.W. Rosen, Machine learning and knowledge graph-based design rule construction for additive manufacturing, *Additive Manufacturing*, 37, 2021, 101620, https://doi.org/10.1016/j.addma.2020.101620, ISSN 2214-8604.

[16]   J. Pennington, R. Socher and C.D. Manning, Glove: global vectors for word representation, in: *Proceedings of the 2014 Conference on Empirical Methods in Natural Language Processing, EMNLP* 2014, October 25–29, 2014, Doha, Qatar, 2014, pp. 1532–1543.

[17]   S. Mesbah, C. Lofi, M.V. Torre, A. Bozzon and G.J. Houben, Tse-ner: an iterative approach for long-tail entity extraction in scientific publications, in: *ISWC*, Springer, New York, NY, 2018, pp. 127–143.

[18]   A. John, T. Ananth Kumar, M. Adimoolam and A. Blessy, Energy management and monitoring using IoT with cupcarbon platform, in: Balusamy B., Chilamkurti N., Kadry S. (eds.), *Green Computing in Smart Cities: Simulation and Techniques. Green Energy and Technology*, Springer, Cham, 2021, https://doi.org/10.1007/978-3-030-48141-4_10

[19]   D. Jayakumar, A. Elakkiya, R. Rajmohan and M.O. Ramkumar, Automatic prediction and classification of diseases in melons using stacked RNN based deep learning model, in: *2020 International Conference on System, Computation, Automation and Networking (ICSCAN)*, IEEE, New York, NY, 2020, pp. 1–5.

[20]   R. Kalaipriya, S. Devadharshini, R. Rajmohan, M. Pavithra and T. Ananthkumar, Certain investigations on leveraging blockchain technology for developing electronic health records, in: *2020 International Conference on System, Computation, Automation and Networking (ICSCAN)*, IEEE, New York, NY, 2020, pp. 1–5.

[21]   M. Pavithra, R. Rajmohan, T. Ananth Kumar and R. Ramya, Prediction and classification of breast cancer using discriminative learning models and

techniques, *Machine Vision Inspection Systems, Volume 2: Machine Learning-Based Approaches*, 2021, 241–262.

[22] S. Narmadha, S. Gokulan, M. Pavithra, R. Rajmohan and T. Ananthkumar, Determination of various deep learning parameters to predict heart disease for diabetes patients, in: *2020 International Conference on System, Computation, Automation and Networking (ICSCAN)*, IEEE, New York, NY, 2020, pp. 1–6.

[23] S.A. Selvi, T.A. kumar, R.S. Rajesh and M.A.T. Ajisha, An efficient communication scheme for Wi-Li-Fi network framework, in: *2019 Third International conference on I-SMAC (IoT in Social, Mobile, Analytics and Cloud)* (*I-SMAC*), 2019, pp. 697–701, doi: 10.1109/I-SMAC47947.2019.9032650.

[24] M. Adimoolam, M. Sugumaran and R.S. Rajesh, The security challenges, issues and countermeasures in spatiotemporal data: a survey, in: Hemanth J., Fernando X., Lafata P., Baig Z. (eds.), *International Conference on Intelligent Data Communication Technologies and Internet of Things (ICICI)* 2018. ICICI 2018. Lecture Notes on Data Engineering and Communications Technologies, vol. 26, Springer, Cham, 2019, https://doi.org/10.1007/978-3-030-03146-6_142.

Chapter 7

Why graph analytics?

N. Padmapriya[1], N. Kumaratharan[2], R. Rajmohan[1],
T. Ananth Kumar[1], M. Pavithra[1] and
R. Dinesh Jackson Samuel[3]

Abstract

The study of relationships between entities such as clients, goods, operations, and devices is graph analytics, also called network analysis. To obtain knowledge that can be used in marketing or, for example, for analysing social networks, companies use graph models. The term 'graphical analysis' explicitly involves the study and analysis of data, which can be translated in a broad schematic. Graphical analytics are a fast-growing domain in the area of large-scale data mining and visualisation that is used in various multidisciplinary applications like network protection, finance and health care. While several methods have already addressed the study of unstructured collections of multidimensional points in the past, graph analytic technologies are a relatively new trend that presents a number of challenges. Graph analytics are a combination of mathematical, theory of graphs and techniques used to model, store, extract and performance analysis graph-structured information. The techniques recognise modules or interacting subgroups within graphs, search for subgraphs that are similar to a particular pattern. Due to their polytrophic nature, graphs have acute importance and have widespread big data applications in the real world, e.g., information discovery, social media, search engines, network structures, etc. The main issue is the development of large-scale applications of efficient systems for storage, processing and analysis. Graph analytics are used in numerous applications to model all kinds of relationships and processes. Data scientists and business users can define and analyse complex relationships in healthcare datasets through graph analytics. Gartner Research said in a recent study, "Graph analysis is probably the single most efficient competitive differentiator for organisations that follow data-driven operations and decisions after data capture design." Since the data sources in health organisations, heterogeneously complex and highly dynamic data sources are well-known, the healthcare domain has acquired its importance through the effect of

[1]Department of CSE, IFET College of Engineering, India
[2]Department of ECE, Sri Venkateswara College of Engineering, India
[3]Visual Artificial Intelligence Lab, Oxford Brookes University, UK

big data. While the position of large graph analytical methods, platforms and tools is realised across different domains, promising research directions are shown by their effect on healthcare organisations to introduce and produce new use cases for possible healthcare applications. The effectiveness of healthcare applications is solely dependent on the underlying nature and implementation of appropriate methods in the sense of broad graph analysis, as demonstrated in ground breaking research attempts. In this chapter, from the perspective of different stakeholders, we discuss the various methodological options available in the patient-centred healthcare system. In order to promote individual patients from diverse viewpoints, we address different architectures, benefits and repositories of each discipline that provide an integrated representation of how separate healthcare operations are carried out in the pipeline.

7.1   Introduction

An analytics project typically works with raw data (numeric/visual/structure/unstructured) to uncover insights (which have not been cleaned). For these graphs, network analysis (or the analysis of particular components called the model) is just one part of the overall data analysis. Individuals, services or things can be recorded as either customers, productions, machines or appliances. On the majority of platforms in social media and around supply chain, marketers and SEO, this methodology is most commonly employed. Sometimes, in order to gain insights into large sets of data, companies use a graphical model. The complex model of this design allows for deals with limitations imposed by sourcing various datasets in a simple and concise manner (or lack thereof, of course). It can be used to transport unstructured and semi-structured data from different systems in an undirected manner to make a graph analysis framework, rather than use the traditional data warehouse framework for the sole purpose of using it to enable them to filter structured data. A graph is a set of points connected by lines (also known as 'vertices' or links. For reference, here's another term: nodes represent data, while lines of communication, called edges, link the data points together. Each edge is a goad, a directional and non-committal (two-way, unidirectional or undirected. nodes in real-world applications can be customers, facilities, places like locations, or units such as grids, accounts, Internet URLs or geographic regions such as continents. 'TIPT is for transactions', which means it can refer to such things as good- or bad-opinion, e-mail, money and much more. In general, any additional information or descriptive characteristics of a node are known as attributes.

7.1.1   Types of graphs

Graph analysis can be further subdivided into four main categories:

1. One of graph analysis is path analysis, which focusses on the relation between nodes. The great thing about reduce-path sales is that it calculates the shortest possible path between two points.

2. Centrality analysis allows you to calculate how much of a node's influence a connection has on the network's connectivity. As is used in this example, it determines the most influential people in a social network, it will most likely find the most popular individuals and most frequently visited websites.
3. Centrality analysis allows you to calculate how much of a node's influence a connection has on the network's connectivity. As is used in this example, it determines the most influential people in a social network, it will most likely find the most popular individuals and most frequently visited websites.
4. Community analysis is a social network analysis that uses network distance and group density to track and group associations in order to show which groups of people are in contact with each other. Finally, it determines whether each individual node and whether the network is stationary and predicts if the network will continue to grow.

7.1.2 Difference between relational analytics and graph analytics

Relational analytics will normally only look at one connection between data elements to one another, while graph analytics can investigate relationships made up of many connections between the data elements. This step makes it easier to identify those that were previously overlooked in the course of doing relational analytics. Additionally, relational analytics works best with static and unorganised data in databases in databases sorted in rows and columns. Graph analysis is insightful because it is flexible in responding to a wider range of unorganised, changing, diverse datasets. According to social network data analytics, network and information augmentation theories, it allows users to obtain information and contextualises connections to make decisions more accurate. Because data organisation is handled more efficiently in the charts you create will take less time to complete, and they use less resources to consolidate and mix more efforts to analyse. If it is granted, this, this also frees you up time to concentrate on other projects. It is able to store, use, analyse and then expand the data that it finds. Conversely, graphs are easily understood and they are less data intensive than other data analysis tools, which may not be visually attractive. Furthermore, it has the ability to find indirect relations and to express larger and more complex data sets as they form a cohesive whole.

Using the possibilities of the graph analytic methods, various things can be researched and investigated. It is used to make their way through thousands of sources and structures, and data documents, all of which they then pull apart into their component parts in an unstructured format. Google uses the user's search history to enhance search results with recommendations. In a study of consumer influencers in the marketing, brand's social network helps to identify brand advocates and salespersons that may be more apt to lead to success with collaboration and endorsement activities. With this tool, businesses are more aware of the things that go on behind the scenes in their operation, such as money laundering, embezzlement, tax evasion and cybercrime. This enables banks to choose to grant or refuse loans, making it possible for them to determine if they want to deal with applicants and enables them to reinforce the strength of enterprise or organisational security.

In healthcare and pharmaceuticals, the use of graph analytics can reveal new and previously unknown ways of treatment successes, as well as newer methods of treatment by investigating relationships between proteins, chemical pathways, cells and DNA, and finding how choices and medications influence them. It is also able to optimise logistical methods for manufacturing and distribution centres, in order to discover the quickest and most predictable routes in combination with weather conditions that affect transportation safety, as well as identify weather dangers that could also to distribution and ways to save time and money. A further benefit is of having a wide system expander to balance system loads and maximise the utilisation of the system improving the overall network risk and optimising the infrastructure by identifying underutilised and overburdened resources and reallocating traffic is usually accomplished by examining traffic potential and topology and reducing potential risk. In today's world, the devices, technologies, practises, people and other factors are intermingling to create even more interconnectedness [24]. We need to define the relationships between the various data sources if we want to gain a better understanding of the data. The expandable data scenario has developed a high-visibility for industrial sensors, surveillance, control systems and devices, that is, connected hardware and software, among others [25]. 'Big data' has taken on a new meaning, these days, with the rapid increase in the amount of data being generated from all around the world [3]. It is defined as massive datasets created from multiple sources with unique data. Bringing up these new values hidden in the hidden data helps us to understand the numerous benefits and opportunities in the data that are available to us. The ability to find hidden information and details in our data volume and number of elements grows, we are also faced with a greater number of questions. The rest of the chapter is organized as follows. Section 7.2 provides a brief outline on big graph analytics. Section 7.3 describes basics of graph analytics. In Section 7.4, different graph analytics techniques are discussed. Sections 7.5 provide different algorithms that are used in big graph analytics. In Section 7.6, big graph analytics framework for healthcare is proposed. Section 7.7 discusses about the results. At the end, we conclude the chapter in Section 7.8 with outcomes.

7.2 Big graph analytics

However, the push towards more advanced graph analytics has only really begun with the emergence of the term 'big data'. In almost all cases, graphs, network interconnection diagrams are best represented by nodes and their associated interconnections known as nodes and their interrelationships. A 'network' in these examples is any large set of interconnected nodes such as cities, computer or telephone systems. In this manner, they could be used to make circuits in the city or pathways that were modelled after them, such as person and date of birth, such as computers. The natural interactions, interdependence and interdependence of the objects is frequently modelled in complex relationships, interdependencies and interdependence often applies to systems. When it comes to complicated inter-connected data, we have found that the best approach is to be to use is a graph. A wide range of application area (in biology, knowledge representation in computa-tional structures, digital graphs, data-based networks, social networks, computing and other fields is useful) is used (e.g., on protein networks, semantic web, infor-mation, semantic networks and other domains (in particular, computerised records)) though elaborate diagrammatic representations of data structures have been employed since their introduction to computing [4], the significance of graphs, for example, in recommender systems has only gained ground in recent years, is there a very recent rise in importance, for example, for consumer-oriented web [5], for instance. While complex and diverse, data is often visualised using graphical tools.

7.2.1   Vs of big graph

The five V's of big data are frequently used to define it: volume, variety, velocity, value and veracity.

- *Volume*: The volume of a graph indicates its size in terms of nodes and edges. Analysis becomes more difficult as the graph's volume increases. The time required from data to analysis is excessively long when the graph volume is large.
- *Velocity*: When we expand and complicate the data sets and calculate graphs, the graph complexity increases at a given rate (in large graphs, the streaming edges). This results in the increased difficulty of performing graph analytics. The spiral stream of edges does not have any shape that can be captured in memory and as a direct results to this (such as counting of strongly connected components) can complicate our measurements especially when counting results, e.g., in one step, the shortest distances between two nodes and com-puting metrics, like component separation [1].
- *Variety*: There are several different types of data to be drawn from various sources, which are used to construct the graphics. More frequently comes from combination of the data, such as XML, JSON, relational and graph data structures (the data is frequently generated through integration, e.g., XML/JSON, relational and graph-based structures). Even though the different types of large graphs may each represent different meanings, combining the two makes the visual information more difficult to comprehend. There are citation networks, social relationships, ontologies and interproteomic interaction net-works, as well as dynamic and static relation networks, among proteins.
- *Valence*: In terms of interconnection, the valence is a 'refers to how inter-dependent the joint statements are'. The greater the degree of unity in a value's field, the more related data elements are. In graph analytics, the interconnection between this and other elements is of a dataset is taken advantage of. In some instances, as the time vulnerability increases, the density of the links between the

arbitrary pairs becomes greater (while the distance between those pairs remains unchanged), the average distance between the nodes decreases [1].

For data analytics, it is new and quite a thrilling to use large and complex data visualisations. Both statistical and graph theory techniques can be used to expand, store, retrieve and perform analysis on the graph-structured data is applied to this is a combination of statistical, theoretical and graph database techniques. These methods are very useful for the researchers for understanding the structure of a large network, for example, finding patterns like the main network in which more than nodes and their subgraphs interact, in which entities can be placed, for identifying subgraphs with the required level of interactions, for placing entities with differing main graph properties, or patterns which involve different subgraph entities interacting with each other [2]. Many feel that the graph analytics is one of the most important and potentially useful ways to gain knowledge from big data. 'Big Data can be modelled in graph analytic systems, if it is structured in the first place. It can also be rendered into native formats (e.g., as a set of graphs) so that the results are truly understandable'. More accurately, the goal of graph analytics is to find relationships in a network between devices or people and how those devices are connected to one another. A useful purpose of entity-relationship model is to express relations between objects, people, people or nodes in a pairwise fashion. Big data analytics allows the visualisation of insights into the significant relationships, allowing them to be examined and analysed in great detail. Big graph analytics incorporates math concepts such as the concept of graph theory to define and enhance these intricate relationships.

7.3 The basics of graph analytics

Astute and useful graphs derive their usefulness from their capacity to aid comprehension. Concerning our real-world's phenomena, the various ways in which data are connected and the resolution of large networks, the use of Internet of Things, natural language search, semantic data and graph mining are each other facet of global big data challenges. Using simple, recognisable images to represent and describe complex big data is a handy technique. Although it is in theory, considered massive volume, diverse and expensive to store and use, large volumes of data and speedier processing demand more-focused, and effective use of information calls for more creative insight than previous data asset classifications provided [6]. The static and large amount of expansive data such as Facebook, Twitter or any other social media site that can provide (is described as 'huge volume' here). Data-laden decisions, as well as rapid, information-packed thoughts, are essential to be effective. When expanded meaning when you mean larger variety. It refers to various types of (like data from relational databases, such as XML and JSON documents, and images) or to simple data [6]. When it means an expanded meaning, it refers to text files that are just like relational databases and images. Graph theoretic is predicated on mathematical theory. Graphic theory was developed to solve a very pressing problem: city planning issue began in Konigshard, and his neighbour Ned's came from Nebek Machand (old city in Russia). There were two large islands in the city, which were connected by seven bridges. As people in the eighteenth century were attempting to construct a pedestrian ways to connect cities, the challenge was to be able to pass over seven bridges without returning to the starting point. Euler, a famous for his numerous contributions to the study of math, proved this problem had no solution due to an odd number of bridges. By rewriting the problem as only a single vertex and connecting it to the island masses was necessary, he reduced the number of features (or added land masses) (termed as edge). Like every other society, we have been able to create Facebook includes individuals, social connections, and interests on a spectrum (Figure 7.1). In laying out the foundations of the theory of graph theory in this instance, Euler was able to obtain a more fundamental understanding of [7] it.

Big data sets can be tackled by making their representation as graphs (the analysis of large and complex datasets as graphs). The expression of relational patterns and behavioural relationships in data through mathematical techniques and statistical methods are some of the philosophies that help to provide efficient algorithmic solutions and discover patterns with strong, significant meaning, accurate and timely competitive inferences. While the range of approaches for analytic such as path, community and centrality analysis exist as alternatives, many analytic techniques may address different problems, we may not have a good method for centrality and path-based solutions in mind-expand system models.

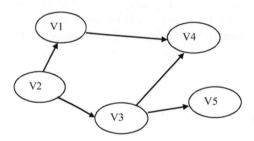

	V1	V2	V3	V4	V5
V1				1	
V2			1		
V3				1	1
V4					
V5					

Figure 7.1   Graph with adjacency matrix

Rather than having a single conceptual model, they have different models that answer different kinds of questions [7].

Like it or not, this is simply a tool that expands your network; these (e.g., LinkedIn, Twitter, and) sites are based on building connections and relationship. For users on Facebook, two or 'may know' one another. Facebook users may employ services such as graph search to look for users with the same sports team, or city connection as well as users who are not connected with them, and upon discovering a linkages in these paths, these correlations, can claim to be aware of people they may know one another. As with other social media platforms, LinkedIn does a lot to help professionals to develop their personal connections. There are two additional factors that contribute to business analytics – the capacity to comprehend relationships, and the ability to assess and test hypotheses about those relationships. Often, in charge of corporate communications, advertising professionals will be interested in the people who are most influential online for their business, 'social influence' leaders. How many others perceive you is important because you have the ability to influence them.

Connecting two or more people on social media is a vital part of your overall strategy – consider the major point – How will they connect to one another? Looking at this from a certain perspective, it seems rather simple, but there are many facets of it that are anything but [26]. In general, the simplest form, the question of how two or more people are connected on Facebook will lead to many problems. These contacts might be from people who are or people related to people. Sometimes two people may only be interested in each other because they 'like' the same page on Facebook. This piece of information could be useful to the business. If we want to limit our online advertising expenditure to a little more specific audience, we must first find out who the general public is actually talking to.

7.4   Graph analytic techniques

Path analysis, connectivity analysis, group analysis, and centrality analysis are some of the graph analytic techniques.

7.4.1   Path analytic

The aim of path analytic is to find the shortest path between two nodes. The 'best' specification includes the optimization of a given function, the traversal of certain edges, the exclusion of edges and the fulfilment of some preferences. In Google Maps, for example, the shortest path changes depending on the weather, traffic and road conditions. Dijkstra's algorithm is a well-known method for determining the least weighted path [7]. Dijkstra's algorithm has been modified in various ways to improve efficiency, such as the Goal-directed Dijkstra Algorithm, Bi-directional Dijkstra Algorithm and so on.

7.4.2 Analytical connectivity

Based on various features, the connectivity analytic examines the structure of connectivity and correlation between the structures of the graph. It also decides reliability, or which node the hacker can target next. The degree of a node is the total number of edges connected to it. The degree of nodes can be used to decide whether one node is more connected than another. The degree of a node can be computed by summing the node's in-degree and out-degree. By comparing the degree histograms of the graphs and measuring the vector distance of the histogram, the similarity of the graph can be determined. The number of nodes in a degree histogram is compared to the degree value of each node. The Euclidean distance can be used to measure graph similarity based on the vector distance function which is given in (7.1):

$$Dist = \sqrt{\sum_{i=0}^{k} (x_{1i} - x_{2i})} \tag{7.1}$$

Other advanced methods/formulas for comparing graph similarities include Histogram intersection, Hellinger distance and so on. A 2D-coloured graph histogram offers more information about the graph.

We must determine how much a network is influenced by an attack in order to assess the network's robustness. Weighted spectral distribution (WSD) can be used to do this. WSD highlights the importance of critical eigenvalues [8].

7.4.3 Community analytic

The term 'community' refers to a group of nodes that are more connected to each other than to the outside world. The field of community analytic is concerned with the identification and analysis of community activity patterns. Who are the members of the party, for example? Where do they come from? Is the neighbourhood a safe place to live? Do you have any dominant members of your community? Is the culture changing, expanding, breaking or dying? The number of all edges of all vertices within the cluster is the internal degree of a subgraph. The external degree of cluster is the sum of all vertices' edges outside the subgraph. The internal and external degrees of clusters are compared to find communities. The term 'group' refers to a cluster with a higher internal density which is given in (7.2) and external density given in (7.3):

$$\delta_{int} = \frac{of\ internal\ edges\ in\ C}{n_c \frac{(nC-1)}{2}} \tag{7.2}$$

$$\delta_{ext} = \frac{of\ inter\ cluster\ edges\ of\ C}{n_{c(n-nC)}} \tag{7.3}$$

7.4.4   Centrality analytic

The centrality analytic illustrates the importance of network nodes in relation to a particular analysis problem. The value they have in a society determines their significance. We all know that not every node in a network is equally essential. In some cases, some nodes are more critical than others. Centrality of the network is centralised. Centrality is the importance measurement of a node according to its position in the network. At the same time, centralization is the network measure (not just a single node). If more nodes begin to have higher focus, the core value of the network will be less fluctuating. Centralizing a network is the sum of the difference from the maximum core to core divided by the maximum core (7.4):

$$\text{Centralization} = \frac{c_{max} - c(v_i)}{c_{max}} \tag{7.4}$$

Closeness centrality, eigenvector centrality, degree centrality, betweenness centrality and katz centrality are all examples of centrality. Calculating centrality values can be done using a variety of concepts and methods.

7.5   Big graph analytics algorithms

7.5.1   PageRank

It is an algorithm for the website reputation assessment [9]. PageRank is used to classify websites in Google's search engine. Some applications for the analysis of protein links with ecological networks in PageRank include Recommendation Systems, online social networks (OSNs) and natural science [27].

7.5.2   Connected component

The connected component in a graph is the highest subsection in which all vertices are connected. Consider a social network made up of two or even more network of people where no one knows anybody and vice versa. Each couple of people reflects different components because one group members are not connected with the other.

7.5.3   Distributed minimum spanning tree

The spanning tree with a minimum weight in a weighted, undirected character is known as minimum spanning tree. There is no need to connect but undirect the input chart of a distributed minimum range tree algorithm (DMST). For the unconnected chart, the DMST [10] produces the minimum wild field.

7.5.4   Graph search

A graph is basically a list of nodes, each of which can connect to other nodes. The graphs can be either driven, like single paths, or undirected as region like double roads. Assume that we want to go through this picture and, in particular, assume that we want to do something like find out whether there is a road between nodes. Two common ways are available to do this:

1. Breadth-first search (BFS)

   The BFS is an unweighed, non-directed graph searching algorithm that starts from one point and assigns distances to every top.

2. Depth-first search (DFS)

   It is a recursive graph traversal algorithm which investigates one neighbour as thoroughly as possible before moving on to other neighbours. DFS does not cover any of the edges. A tree is formed by the vertices and edges that have been visited by depth first search (graph spanning tree).

7.5.5   Clustering

Clustering is the process of putting together a group of nodes that have more connections between them than the rest of the network. Based on their characteristics, the group of objects is classified into one category with high intra-cluster similarity and low inter-cluster similarity. Clustering is used in a variety of applications, including image processing , statistics , machine learning and data and text mining.

7.6   Big graph analytics framework for healthcare

7.6.1   Big graph characteristics

Due to the vast amount of work still left to be done in the area of graph processing, there is significant work that is still to be done in tackling large-scale graphs. Parallelism is difficult to achieve in certain kinds of graph-parsing problems because of the diversity of their characteristics [11].

- *A high-value vertex*: An example of this would be the use of Prime Minister Modi in India who has many co-workers; it can be seen in OSNs. Since these types of graphs are computationally demanding and difficult to partition, it is difficult to automate them.
- *Sparseness*: On the other hand, the average graph will contain several vertices, but few of them will have many connections to other vertices. Many people, for example, have much more than 50 million followers on Twitter. Synchronization, data processing, networking and communication will be needed to increase the size of the sparse graphs [12].
- *Big data computations*: If the structure of the problem is unknown in advance, then the parallelism of the solution will be difficult to determine, and if it is, then it will be done by the partitioning of the problem into smaller sub-tasks.
- *Unstructured problems*: There is a lack of a regularity in all of data-rich problems, particularly graph-related ones. While working on the graph-parallelizing the data, the irregular structure of the graph data makes it

difficult to delineate the relevant to any given partition, even though it is partitioned [13].

- *In-memory challenge*: To truly analyse the contents of a natural graph, the size of the entire graph must be included in memory. It is beneficial to use the hard drive (HD) or SSD for memory expansion, which shortens the response time to new data acquisition, but increases costs because of file IAP usage.
- *Communication overhead*: Popularity (as measured by the number of followers, as on Twitter) increases the level of complexity (overhead) in a dataset. In the immediate future, there will be vertices of infinite in degree. In the far future, vertices of infinite degrees of complexity will be routine.
- *Load balancing*: The degree of a natural graph increases with respect to npower tends to obey the power law that has been observed to be proportional to the power exponent. It can be deduced that most vertices are connected to a small groups of vertices, but a significantly larger set of vertices are just those that are part of larger vertices, when necessary. It is more relevant in situations such as these when we are investigating use of various types of load graphs.

7.6.2   *Impact of big graph analytics in healthcare*

Thus, big data has been used in the discovery of trends in customer behaviour to generate new business services and products. Many researchers contrasted the healthcare data analytics with the field of business, which possesses several additional characteristics, to big data sets with different values [14]. Instead of considering the three attributes of healthcare big data, they now conceptualise the attributes as Silo, Security, and the existence of several types as variety, and the variety of types as velocity and volume [15]. This is the database built up of all of medical records and details found in facilities like hospitals that is named after the word 'stakeholder'. The additional data protection requirement shows that extra precautions are needed for healthcare record keeping. By incorporating different design patterns, the healthcare data appears in many different patterns, including a lot of the self-unstructured, semi-structured and unstructured [28]. As stakeholders were presented with the enormous benefits of using big data analytics and its related technology, participants were also presented with different ways to exercise those benefits in the healthcare domain [16]. A greater effect of big data is the acquisition and subsequent data identification, as well as clinical and medication studies, research findings. When these diverse data and analytics are combined, researchers are provided with new discoveries. When these stakeholders collaborate and make use their data resources efficiently, viable healthcare alternatives will be delivered in a less costly manner and more targeted form while also benefitting patients [29]. By recognizing the crucial role, these stakeholders play in the construction of a healthcare big data environment. The next section aims to gain perspective on how they view big data sources of information. Various healthcare stakeholders and large data sources [30] explains how a wide range of stakeholders use a diverse array of data sources to find new ways to treat ailments. The approach also makes it possible to find information about pertinent healthcare practices that can be drawn from the identified data sources by using the proper methods of analysis [17].

7.6.3 Proposed framework for patient data analytics

A structural model is essential for any investigative process that demands complex analysis. There is no choice in this situation; when it comes to medicare predictive analytics, accuracy is the key. Compositional models provide a framework for the evaluation from the beginning to end, but often do not allow enough flexibility to act on the information during that period.

To begin with, an information analytics model is proposed in terms of a 'tier 0' architecture (Figure 7.2). The framework depicted in Figure 7.3 is an illustrated version of that depicted in Figure 7.2.

Figure 7.3 contains external statistical and machine information such as machine-to-to-machine communications (e.g., acquiring information from various sensors) and user information such as documents entered by medical staff. Information on a variety of sources is constantly being created every day, causing tremendous amounts of deep learning to form. In addition, these information systems may be located in different destinations, with various formats, and this information could be in including such tabular data, raw text or even in a transactional format. The discussion was evident that clinical knowledge management is fundamentally differs from conventional big data. There are multiple reasons for

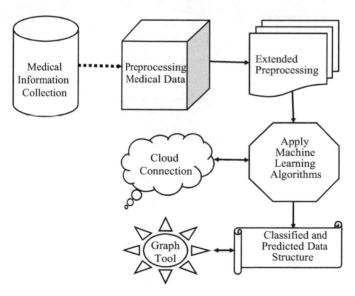

Figure 7.2 Proposed framework for medical data analysis

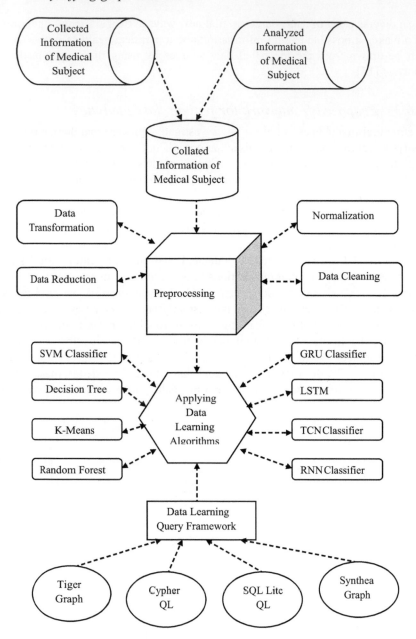

Figure 7.3   Extended framework model for healthcare data analysis

this, one of which is the irregular and diverse development of raw patient records. Additional work is required for data cleaning, data normalization and normalization is necessary. Different interventions (especially those using fuzzy algorithms) should be created to improve medical imagery to give better medical results.

7.6.4 Key players of proposed model

The key players of the proposed model are depicted in Figure 7.4.

7.6.4.1 Patients

The service that will be tailored to each patient, using a wealth of clinical knowledge and state-of the art technology treatment, even though healthcare systems demand nothing short of the latter, is generally possible [18]. Additionally, sites such as Twitter, clinical forums, as well as online patient support groups offer up extra information to physicians for the diagnostic tools they use can provide patients. For better privacy, these big data sources link users to tell people about a variety of details they may have including symptoms, hospitalisation, side effects, reviews of the drugs and results of clinical trials, as well as possible scenarios, also known as post-effects [19,20]. Those patients who are unable to travel to medical facilities will be able to use telecommunications to meet their healthcare needs. environmental patterns may become a large data repository, and save these variables such as body temperature, heart rate, blood pressure and stream patterns can be used to be a personal data repository for delivering updates in a healthcare-related urgency alerts.

7.6.4.2 Healthcare providers

There is a large amount of information that comes from many types of medical testing and treatment that has enabled healthcare professionals to develop a true comprehension of what treatments offered by their patients actually achieve. The

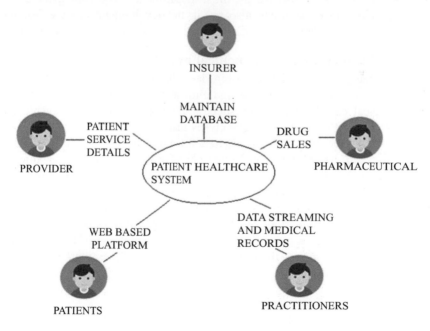

Figure 7.4 Key players of healthcare model

various processes of the healthcare administration create huge quantities of data that can be tapped into for use in making new treatments. It consists of codes for various diseases and service descriptions, along with real-time instrument results, sensors that pick up changes in the patient's behaviour in different situations, laboratory documents, imaging results and monitoring systems that keep track of all of patients. When data of this calibre is considered for the development of the Clinical Disease Repository (CDR), the general public health can be protected more quickly and disease trends can be determined with much greater accuracy. A number of other significant advantages come with integrating data from wearable devices into healthcare applications, including the capability to monitor prescription medications, keeping track of the patient's health at any given time and having the information at their fingertips.

7.6.4.3   Hospital operators

Access tools to be matched to the patient's needs are absolutely crucial when it comes to managing the patient's interactions, and therefore, highly dependent on using outcome-rich data from sources Predictive and prescribe models are built with the help of data scientists who have detailed knowledge of the strengths of various services and patient satisfaction to accurately measure relationships Other than that, it is possible to use techniques of resource allocation and optimization in meeting various manpower needs on the foundation of big data as long as it is available. Strategic operators will use the data on where healthcare is available to pick out which departments can use the most costly equipment, allowing them to customise the locations for use by those departments. The data gathered from follow-up calls and e-mails can also aid in the development of new descriptive models of services to help more efficiently give those that have completed care.

7.6.4.4   Pharmaceutical and medical experts

Because of the growing reliance on big data, the healthcare sector has revolutionised their efforts in pharmaceutical and clinical research. The usage of omics and huge biological data [21] has been successfully applied to the task of predicting drug efficiencies. Prospective drug analyses that are performed using big data are able to quantify the outcomes of targeted for more diverse populations and thus reduce the overall risk of the sample size of randomly generated new therapies [22]. Process-on-on-chip (POC) technology, along with an automated system, pharmaceutical plants, are good tools for end-to-end solutions that can be used to help produce and analyse many types of data for use at once. Having other types of input, such as recommendations by physicians for specific diseases and quantum of use by customers, the organisations, increases the usefulness of these models for companies because it allows them to get a clear picture of their market place before making decisions.

7.6.4.5   Healthcare insurers

Insurance companies now have new methods for exploring the advantages that can be found in healthcare big data sets the stage for more valuable results. So long as

Table 7.1   Comparisons of graph databases

Name	Language	Type	Features
Node4j	Java	Transactional	Storage and processing
Info grid	Java	Web graph	Integration and referencing of data
Infinite graph	Java	Distributed	Cloud platform
Hype graph	Java	Embedded transactional	Open source data storage
Dex	C++	Map based	Integration of multiple data

there are occurrences of repeated health issues in different plans that are kept to a minimum, novel illnesses are less expensive to administer because they are not using a large amount of premium. The life plan features recommended by this insurance plan include factors such as age, gender, personal finances, and how large or small the compensation an individual will get from a specific job will be, which customers with different health-plans may appreciate. Insurance organisations use predictive modelling to discover the differences between normal and fraud-related claims so as well as those claims that deviate from the expected trends in order to help control the costs of fraud. Usage-based insurance enables the industry to use large amounts of big data, along with the Internet of Things (IoT), in creating more progressive and modern business models, such as providing coverage based on what consumers actually do instead of assuming what they growing do. More importantly, the IoT plays a significant role in the business of healthcare: enables new models to appear and in the changes in workflow, efficiency advancements in patient care, and customizations of patient interactions [23]. The influences that big data could have on stakeholders to find out about the most influential systems and analysed these in order to learn about possible sources for our patient-cantered healthcare plan. In this particular, Table 7.1 provides a number of approaches that may be useful for gaining insight into healthcare interests. And in the next segment, we will examine different healthcare structures to see their sources of data, their data gathering capabilities and their potential application areas.

7.7   Implementation and results

The change from traditional documents to immersive records has caused a dramatic increase in healthcare facilities' data storage costs. All points in the medical system, every form, procedure, and immunisation, and every caregiving detail are recorded in the clinic's EHR. Health-care data has now exceeded the limits of information and hospitals are inundated with it. And to make matters worse, it is incredibly difficult to access and to sift through all of this convoluted data. We use Synthea a free software patient transformer to build a whole healthcare supply chain, from patients to facilities and from coverage to cost. Since Synthea produces information across several CSV format records such as antipathies, procedures, appointments and practitioners, this particular drug is very well suited for this type of project. Generic modelling framework allows the representation of numerous health conditions that concern synthetic patients. Patients are always simulated completely separated from the moment of their birth to the end of their life. The person's disease, their ailment and their treatment interventional care all refer to the same procedure: the disease, illness and treatment all fall under the same model. Models allow occurrences in the sufferer's real life to be designed sequentially, with an infinite series of states, explaining the interactions here between regions. These software modules were developed by healthcare professionals and government agencies such as the Department of health, Hhs or other agencies like that. The general practitioner has made over a thousand modules available on Synthea because people use them to understand the primary visits they get, as well as the major causes of years of death. Each Synthetic person is provided with synthetic medical information such as medications, previous allergies, previous medical occurrences and a record of social influences on their health. To provide additional support for developers, as well as for medical professionals, Synthea Standard information is transferred in both EHR and CSV files. Synthea can be configured to export data as csv files. To export CSV, the exporter settings of synthea properties have to be changed a true. Tables 7.2–7.4 illustrate the database model created for the simulation of proposed framework.

The several encounters of each service user with the public health structure would be quite difficult to account for by a genetic mechanism. We can create our schema using the Neo4j Query Cypher Language (QCL) as shown in Figure 7.5. The entire script looks like this:

> *Create Node* U_ID (U_ID, Primary, String, Boolean = 'true')
> *Create Node* Age (Age, Primary, String, Boolean = 'true')
> *Create Node* Deceased (Deceased, Primary, String, Boolean = 'true')
> *Create Node* A_ID (A_ID, Primary, String, Boolean = 'true')
> *Create Node* ID_Proof (ID_Proof, Primary, String, Boolean = 'true')
> *Create Node* F_Name (F_Name, Primary, String, Boolean = 'true')
> *Create Node* L_Name (L_Name, Primary, String, Boolean = 'true')
> *Create Node* M_Status (M_Status, Primary, String, Boolean = 'true')
> *Create Node* Status (Status, Primary, String, Boolean = 'true')
> *Create Node* Sex (Sex, Primary, String, Boolean = 'true')
> *Create Node* Address (Address, Primary, String, Boolean = 'true')
> *Create Node* Health_Insurance (Health_Insurance, Primary, String, Boolean = 'true')

Table 7.2   Antipathies

Entity header	Format	Mandatory	Explanation
Begin	Date	Yes	Antipathy detected timeline
End	Date	No	Antipathy cured timeline
P_ID	Unique number	Yes	Link to test subject details
E_ID	Unique number	Yes	Link to timeline when antipathy treated

Table 7.3   Test subject details

Entity	Format	Mandatory	Explanation
U_ID	Unique number	Yes	Primary Key. Unique identifier of the patient
Age	Number	Yes	The date the patient was born
Deceased	Date	No	The date the patient died
A_ID	String	Yes	Subject social number
ID proof	Alphanumeric	Yes	Any authorized Id proof
F_Name	Text	Yes	Subject name
L_Name	Text	Yes	Subject initial or last name
M_Status	Text	Yes	S – single, M – married, W – widowed
Current status	Text	Yes	Description of the patient's primary ethnicity
Sex	Text	Yes	Gender. M is male, F is female.
Address	Text	Yes	Patient's street address without commas or newlines
Health_Insurance	Text	Yes	Insurance premium amount and duration

Table 7.4   Procedures

Entity	Format	Mandatory	Explanation
Begin	Date	Yes	Antipathy detected timeline
End	Date	No	Antipathy cured timeline
P_ID	Unique number	Yes	Link to test subject details
E_ID	Unique number	Yes	Link to timeline when antipathy treated
Explanation	Text	Yes	Process explanation
Amount	Numeric	Yes	Working process cost

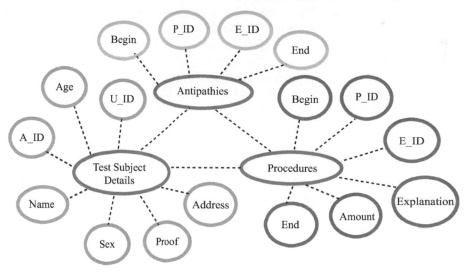

Figure 7.5   Creation of graphical schema

Create SubNode Begin (Operation Beginning, *Start* Procedures, *End* Antipathies)
Create SubNode End (Operation Beginning, *Start* Procedures, *End* Antipathies)
Create SubNode P_ID (Operation Beginning, *Start* Procedures, *End* Antipathies)
Create SubNode E_ID (Operation Beginning, *Start* Procedures, *End* Antipathies)
Create SubNode Explanation (Operation Beginning, *Start* Procedures, *End* Antipathies)
Create SubNode Amount (Operation Beginning, *Start* Procedures, *End* Antipathies)

Edges are attached to topics that correspond from each Csv format. Since all of the interactions are one-to-way, every one of the edges are unconstrained. Such things such as gender, social class and identify could be deemed internal qualities. We use a combination of every unique and relevant healthcare code for each vertex in the file that allows to optimize search queries.

The CQL script for data loading into the neo4j would be presented in the format of:

Create (a:Medical_Data { Tag: 'Patient Health Analysis', Load the csv fie into nodes and edges
Load CSV from 'file: F:\PAVITHRA\SUBJECTS\Book Chapter\Medical.csv' *AS row*
WITH row WHERE row.ID is not NULL
MERGE (ID.Antipathies {Antipathy_ID: row.ID)
MERGE (ID.Test_Subjects{Test_Subjects: row.ID)
MERGE (ID.Procedures {Procedures: row.ID)
}

Before we stack our information, we first create a new file to describe what we mean by it. Here all vertices, edge or both vertex and edge described have unique column names: Specifically, corresponding names to the vertices, edges or both edges in the section names. We conclude that our database has a pointer and contains comma delimited list of feature vectors a certain point to a client's previous ones.

Subject = *Match* Test_Subject_Details
    From (ID.Antipathies{Test_Subjects: row.ID)
Where Antipathies.U_ID == Test_Subject_Details.U_ID *and*
Procedure.P_ID == Test_Subject_Details.P_ID;

Result = *Match* Test_Subject_Details
    From (ID.Antipathies{Test_Subjects: row.ID)
Where Antipathies.U_ID == Test_Subject_Details.U_ID *and*
Procedure.E_ID == Test_Subject_Details.E_ID;
Return Subject;
Return Result;
}

The above whole search yields a lot of data. Everyone who comes into contact with the healthcare system is a potential target of care. Using the power of a database is difficult by itself, as it is. And over the next few fractions of a second, the statistics was extracted from our chart database. The use of standardised programming techniques makes queries show little improvement in the amount of time it takes to find new patterns in your medical data, so querying with graphs is vastly faster and much more effective.

7.8 Conclusion

The basics of big graph and big graph analytics are covered in this chapter. We have realized the value of graphs in big data analytics. Conventional database techniques are proving ineffective in producing ground breaking insights needed for companies to remain competitive as big data grows even larger. The graphical recording of big data makes sure that data relationships are priority over data and that data interaction semantic are reflected automatically. This has aided data analysts in uncovering new information, allowing companies to make more innovative business decisions. Traditional systems for database management cannot meet big data requirements. To store large graph data, graph databases are needed. In a few milliseconds, it responds to complex queries. Many graph databases are becoming available, with Neo4j being one of them. Big graphics analytics are incredibly helpful in sectors such as medical services online business solutions, business institutions, internet media, social networking sites, digital marketing and warehousing. Despite the numerous advantages of big graphs some problems must be addressed like sparseness, high-level vertex and load balance. IoT data collection systems, smartphone, search and navigation systems, social networking systems and large-scale genome banks can all be fully developed as regards the collection of knowledge. It is crucial to formulate an early warning system for the analysis of big data based on data collection, for example, through visual analysis, deep learning and forecast line analysis. This could be used as a foundation for early warning and forecasting, developing strategies, making quick decisions and initiating emergency response mechanisms. Second, policymakers may use big data analytics to strengthen their disease response mechanisms. Disaster identification, decision support, planning and collaboration, and technical support can all benefit from big data technologies. Graph database analysis and geographic information systems can provide a significant advantage in monitoring infected patients and their contacts in order to identify the source of infection.

References

[1] Singh, D.K., P.K. Dutta Pramanik and P. Choudhury. "Big graph analytics: techniques, tools, challenges, and applications." In: *Data Analytics: Concepts, Techniques, and Applications*, London: CRC Press, 2018, p. 171.
[2] Arfat, Y., S. Usman, R. Mehmood and I. Katib. "Big data tools, technologies, and applications: a survey." In: *Smart Infrastructure and Applications*, Cham: Springer, 2020, pp. 453–490.

[3]   Sheikh, R.A. and N.S. Goje. "Role of Big Data analytics in business transformation." In: *Internet of Things in Business Transformation: Developing an Engineering and Business Strategy for Industry 5.0*, Beverly, MA: Scrivener Publishing, 2021, pp. 231–259.

[4]   Tayefi, M., P. Ngo, T. Chomutare, *et al.* "Challenges and opportunities beyond structured data in analysis of electronic health records." In: *Wiley Interdisciplinary Reviews: Computational Statistics*, 13;2021:e1549.

[5]   Gupta, A., R.K. Singh and S. Kr Mangla. "Evaluation of logistics providers for sustainable service quality: analytics based decision making framework." *Annals of Operations Research*, 2021. https://doi.org/10.1007/s10479-020-03913-0.

[6]   Sabarish, J., S. Sonali and P.T.R. Vidhyaa. "Application of big data in field of medicine." In: *Intelligence in Big Data Technologies—Beyond the Hype*, Singapore: Springer, 2020, pp. 473–484.

[7]   Wang, F., P. Cui, J. Pei, Y. Song and C. Zang. "Recent advances on graph analytics and its applications in healthcare." In: *Proceedings of the 26th ACM SIGKDD International Conference on Knowledge Discovery & Data Mining*, 2020.

[8]   Ghoroghchian, N., G. Dasarathy and S. Draper. "Graph Community detection from coarse measurements: recovery conditions for the coarsened weighted stochastic block model." In: *International Conference on Artificial Intelligence and Statistics*, PMLR, 2021.

[9]   Tortosa, L., J.F. Vicent and G. Yeghikyan. "An algorithm for ranking the nodes of multiplex networks with data based on the PageRank concept." *Applied Mathematics and Computation*, 392;2021:125676.

[10]   Ganesan, G. "Minimum Spanning Trees of Random Geometric Graphs with Location Dependent Weights." arXiv preprint arXiv:2103.00764, 2021.

[11]   Patil, S.V. and D.B. Kulkarni. "Graph partitioning using heuristic Kernighan-Lin algorithm for parallel computing." In: *Next Generation Information Processing System*, Singapore: Springer, 2021, pp. 281–288.

[12]   Haman, M. "Twitter followers of Canadian political and health authorities during the COVID-19 pandemic: what are their activity and interests?" *Canadian Journal of Political Science*, 54(1);2021:134–149.

[13]   Akhtar, N. and M.V. Ahamad. "Graph tools for social network analysis." In: *Research Anthology on Digital Transformation, Organizational Change, and the Impact of Remote Work*, Hershey: IGI Global, 2021, pp. 485–500.

[14]   Abdualgalil, B. and S. Abraham. "Efficient machine learning algorithms for knowledge discovery in big data: a literature review." *Database*, 29(5);2020:3880–3889.

[15]   Chen, P.-T., C.-L. Lin and W.-N. Wu. "Big data management in healthcare: adoption challenges and implications." *International Journal of Information Management*, 53;2020:102078.

[16] Shastri, A. and M. Deshpande. "A review of big data and its applications in healthcare and public sector." In: *Big Data Analytics in Healthcare*, New York, NY: Springer, 2020, pp. 55–66.

[17] Listl, S., D.P. Alexandre and C. Filho. "Big Data and machine learning." In: *Oral Epidemiology*, Cham: Springer, 2021, pp. 357–365.

[18] Pramanik, M.I., R.Y.K. Lau, M. Azad, Md. Sakir Hossain, Md K.H. Chowdhury and B.K. Karmaker. "Healthcare informatics and analytics in big data." *Expert Systems with Applications*, 152;2020:113388.

[19] Lv, Z. and L. Qiao. "Analysis of healthcare big data." *Future Generation Computer Systems,* 109;2020:103–110.

[20] Khanra, S., A. Dhir, A.K.M. Najmul Islam and M. Mäntymäki. "Big data analytics in healthcare: a systematic literature review." *Enterprise Information Systems*, 14(7);2020:878–912.

[21] Wang, L. and C.A. Alexander. "Big data analytics in medical engineering and healthcare: methods, advances and challenges." *Journal of Medical Engineering & Technology*, 44(6);2020:267–283.

[22] Galetsi, P., K. Katsaliaki and S. Kumar. "Big data analytics in health sector: theoretical framework, techniques and prospects." *International Journal of Information Management*, 50;2020:206–216.

[23] Nadanam, P. and R. Rajmohan. "QoS evaluation for web services in cloud computing." In: *2012 Third International Conference on Computing, Communication and Networking Technologies (ICCCNT'12)*, New York, NY: IEEE, July 2012, pp. 1–8.

[24] Padmapriya, N. and R. Rajmohan. "Reliability evaluation suite for cloud services." In: *2012 Third International Conference on Computing, Communication and Networking Technologies (ICCCNT'12)*, New York, NY: IEEE, July 2012, pp. 1–6.

[25] Pavithra, M., R. Rajmohan, T. Ananth Kumar and R. Ramya. "Prediction and classification of breast cancer using discriminative learning models and techniques." *Machine Vision Inspection Systems, Volume 2: Machine Learning-Based Approaches*, 2021:241–262.

[26] Adimoolam M., A. John, N.M. Balamurugan and T. Ananth Kumar. "Green ICT communication, networking and data processing." In: Balusamy B., Chilamkurti N., Kadry S. (eds.), *Green Computing in Smart Cities: Simulation and Techniques. Green Energy and Technology*, Cham: Springer, 2021. https://doi.org/10.1007/978-3-030-48141-4_6

[27] Suresh Kumar, K., A.S. Radha Mani, S. Sundaresan and T. Ananth Kumar. "Modeling of VANET for future generation transportation system through edge/fog/cloud computing powered by 6G." In: *Cloud and IoT-Based Vehicular Ad Hoc Networks*, Beverly, MA: Scrivener Publishing, 2021, pp. 105–124.

[28] Kumar, T. Ananth, R. Rajesh and P. Sivanainthaperumal. "Performance analysis of noc routing algorithms for 5×5 mesh based soc." *ICTACT Journal on Microelectronics*, 1(4);2016:141–146.

[29] Kumar, T.A. and R.S. Rajesh. "Towards power efficient wireless NoC router for SOC." In: *2014 International Conference on Communication and Network Technologies*, New York, NY: IEEE, 2014, pp. 254–259.

[30] Jagadeeswari, V., V. Subramaniyaswamy, R. Logesh and Varadarajan Vijayakumar. "A study on medical Internet of Things and Big Data in personalized healthcare system." *Health Information Science and Systems*, 6(1);2018:1–20.

Chapter 8

Graph technology: a detailed study of trending techniques and technologies of graph analytics

Vishal Dutt[1], Shweta Sharma[2] and Swarn Avinash Kumar[3]

Abstract

Graphs are information structures to depict connections and communications between elements in complex frameworks. Graph analytics has been in use for a long time in the field of data analytics. Its main purpose is to create a database of interconnected entities and to model the relationships and processes in various information systems. In the field of data science and analytics, it is the graph analytics, an alternative method of analysis that uses the process of abstraction and this abstraction is called a graph model which helps the analyst to analyze the whole data or results in a summarized form that reduces the analytics complexities. Many organizations use the Graph model to leverage analysis in marketing or social networks. Graph storage is also an important fact along with graph analytics. The underlying structure of any database in which graph data is stored is often called graph storage as native and non-native graph storage. This chapter is going to explain graph analytics as well as graph storage in detail with the knowledge of various graph logical approaches and looks at existing graph storage and computational advances. This research provides analytical insights about the various graph analytical technologies used globally and shows a comparison between existing graph storage and computer technology. This research additionally evaluates the performance, qualities, and impediments of different graph databases and graph processing models.

8.1 Introduction

Graphs are abstract models that are used to represent a wide range of interactions and processes in physical, biological, social, and information systems. A graph is made up of nodes or vertices (which represent the system's entities) that are bound by edges (representing relationships between those entities). Graphs, on the other

[1]Department of Computer Science, Aryabhatta College, India
[2]Department of Computer Science, ACERC, India
[3]Department of Computer Science and Engineering, IIIT Allahabad, India

hand, are more than just nodes and edges; they are also important data structures for representing dynamic data dependencies [1].

The introduction of big data, and e-commerce, social networks, has re-emphasized the of studying of importance a form of specific data structure known as a graph, which depicts relationships among its entities (Figure 8.1).

An entity/node, such as A and B, represents a specific person, and a connection (also known as an edge) between any two entities represents a relationship.

Using the previous example as a starting point, consider the following:

Graphs are a representation of relationships between "entities" or "objects," with the "entities" being the graph's "nodes" (also known as "vertices") and the "relationships" being expressed by the graph's "links" (also known as "edges"). Graph theory is a term used to describe the analysis of graphs [2].

Furthermore, a simple examination of the graph reveals that A and B share a mutual friend C, who is not a friend of D. Chart analytics is a field of that data science with extracting deals knowledge from graphs through researching them.

Let us move away from the introduction and look at the field of graph analytics by looking at certain basic principles. The centrality-based principles used in graph analytics will be the subject of this paper.

8.1.1   Centrality

Centrality is a key principle in graph analytics for defining critical nodes in a graph. It is used to determine the value (or "centrality," as in how "central" a node is in a

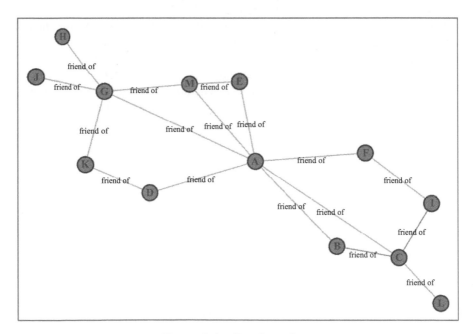

Figure 8.1   Graph analytics

graph) of different nodes in a graph. Based on how "importance" is described, each node can now be significant from a different perspective [3]. Each flavor or metric of centrality determines the value of a node from a particular viewpoint and also provides important theoretical knowledge around the graph and its nodes.

8.1.2 Degree centrality

The first kind of centrality we will talk about is "Degree Centrality." To grasp it, first consider the definition of a node's degree in a graph.

A direct connection of several nodes has with other nodes is known as its degree in a non-directed graph. Have a look at the following graph in Figure 8.2.

A node's degree is further divided into in-degree and out-degree in a directed graph. The number of edges/connections that occur on it is referred to as in-degree, and the number of edges/connections that occur between it and other nodes is referred to as out-degree. Consider the following Twitter graph in Figure 8.2, in which nodes represent people arrows with edges and represent the [4] "Follows" relationship.

E, C, D, and B nodes have an all outgoing edge to node A and hence obey node A. As node A has four edges incident on it, its in-degree is four.

Node B can also see that is connected to both node D and node A, resulting in a two-degree out-degree.

The degree centrality metric measures the value of a node in a graph depending on its degree, i.e., the higher a node's degree, it is the more important in a graph.

8.1.3 Types of graphs

Graph analytics are of four types:

1. *Path analysis*: The relationship between nodes in a graph is investigated. To put it another way, it finds the shortest path between two nodes.

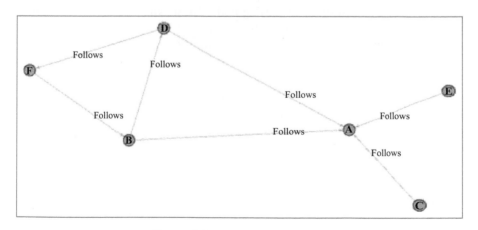

Figure 8.2   Degree centrality

2. *Connectivity analysis*: It aids in comparing network connections by highlighting how strongly or weakly two nodes are connected. This is useful for determining how many edges flow through a node and how many flow out of it.
3. *Centrality analysis*: It allows estimation of how important a node is for network connectivity. It ranks the most powerful individuals in a social network or finds the most often visited websites.
4. *Community analysis*: This is a distance and density-based study of relationships in groups of people that are used to find groups of people in a social network that communicate with each other regularly. It also determines whether individuals are transient and predicts whether the network can expand [5].

8.1.4 Graph algorithms and graph analytics implementations

Graph algorithms and graph analytics are used in a variety of applications.

- Clustering is the process of grouping objects together depending on their features, with a strong intra-cluster similarity and a low inter-cluster similarity. Computer learning, data analysis, analytics, image recognition, and a variety of physical and social science technologies are only a few examples.
- Cutting or partitioning – Identifying the cut with the fewest crossing edges. Finding blind points in data and messaging networks, as well as group detection in social networks, are some of the applications.
- Quest – There are two types of searches: breadth-first and depth-first.
- Find the shortest path between two nodes of interest (shortest path). Social network analysis, transit logistics, and a variety of other optimization problems are among the applications.
- Widest path – In a weighted graph, find the path between two assigned vertices that maximizes the weight of the path's minimum-weight edge. IP traffic routing and traffic-sensitive route planning are examples of applications.
- Connected components – In a highly connected network, any node in the graph can be reached from every starting node. The maximal sub-regions of a graph with which each sub-region is strongly connected are known as strongly connected components. Social network monitoring is one of the applications [6].

8.1.5 Page rank

An indicator of a webpage's prominence that is used by Internet search engines to rank them. Social network analysis, recommendation mechanisms, and new uses in natural science, such as researching the interaction between proteins and ecological networks, are all examples of applications.

8.1.6 Graph database

Graph databases are used to show the connections (edges) between data points (nodes). Graph databases are less architecturally rigid than relational databases, allowing nodes to contain a large number of edges; in other words, there is no limit to the number of links a node may have. (See the next section for an example.) Each edge can also have several qualities that describe it. There is no formal restriction on how many edges each node may have, nor is there any standards on how many attributes an edge may have. Graph databases may also store a large number of disparate bits of data that are not necessarily connected.

Each node is specified by properties, which are bits of data. Names, dates, identification numbers, basic descriptors, and other information-anything that would define the node itself-could be used as properties. Edges, which can be directed or undirected, link nodes. An undirected edge is bidirectional, much like in mathematical graph theory; that is, a relationship can be transmitted from node A to node B as well as from node B to node A. However, a directed edge only has meaning in one direction, such as from node B to node A.

8.1.6.1   Graph databases uses

Graph databases are good for storing and retrieving data that is unrelated yet connected in various ways. Consider the case of a user who wished to map a group of pals. Each buddy would be a node, with edges connecting them and a distinct "friends" attribute." However, if two of those friends are colleagues, their advantage will also have the "coworkers' attribute." Edges can be defined further by include shared hobbies, personal experiences, and other factors.

Because graph databases are designed to organize large collections of data with a variety of links and types of data, they can be useful for social mapping, master data management, knowledge graphing/ontology, infrastructure mapping, recommendation engines, and other applications. Each node might represent one of a company's goods, with edges forming suggestion associations depending on which product a customer could purchase. It might also show connections between contacts, departments, and other entities.

Because graph databases are designed to be flexible and scalable, a business user does not need to have a precise or full use case before establishing one. Adding new nodes and any possible edges linked with them to a graph database is a simple process.

8.1.6.2   Graph databases

8.1.6.2.1   Neo4j

The quickest way to graph. The Neo4j Graph Data Platform is a set of apps and tools that help the world make sense of data. It is built on the leading native graph database. The Neo4j Graph Data Science Library – the leading enterprise-ready analytics workspace for graph data available as both open source and through a commercial license for enterprises – the graph visualization and exploration tool Bloom, the Cypher query language – very easy to learn and can operate across Neo4j, Apache Spark, and Gremlin-based products using open source toolkit – and the graph visualization and exploration tool Bloom are all part of the Platform "Cypher on Apache Spark (CApS) and Cypher for Gremlin," Neo4j ETL and Kettle for data integration, plus a slew of other tools, integrations, and connectors to assist developers and data scientists quickly construct graph-based solutions. And the greatest community on the planet to assist with any graph trip. Neo4j is a scalable, ACID-compliant graph database with a high-performance distributed cluster architecture that is accessible in both self-hosted and cloud deployments.

8.1.6.2.2   ArangoDB

ArangoDB is the most popular open-source multi-model graph database, with over 11,000 users on GitHub. ArangoDB combines the power of graphs with JSON documents, a key-value store, and a full-text search engine, allowing developers to access and integrate all of these data formats with a single, concise, declarative query language. The capacity to conduct graph analytical queries will assist developers, businesses and business teams, while minimizing the number of database technologies that are used to produce them. The native support of ArangoDB for all these data formats, a search engine, a built-in microservice architecture and a wide range of community connectors lead to the development effort and not to tools.

8.1.6.2.3   IBM graph

With over 11,000 users on GitHub, ArangoDB is the most popular open-source multi-model graph database. ArangoTM combines graphics power with JSON documents, key value store and the full-text search engine that enables developers to use the single, succinct, declarative query language to access and integrates all these data forms. The ability to conduct graph analytics queries while reducing the number of database technology used in production would help developers, operations, and business teams. Because ArangoDB supports all of these data formats natively, as well as a search engine, a built-in microservices framework, and a significant number of community integrations, development efforts are focused on the product rather than the tooling.

8.1.6.2.4   Oracle Spatial

A whole variety of geographic data and analytics are supported by Oracle Spatial and Graph for land management and GIS, mobile locations, sales territory management, transport, LiDAR analysis, and Business Intelligence location enabled. The characteristics of the graph include RDF diagrams for applications ranging from semantic data integration to social network analysis to linked open data and network graphs in transport, utilities, power, and telecommunications as well as driving time for marketing and sales applications.

8.1.6.2.5   Redis Enterprise

Redis Enterprise combines the benefits of world-class database technology with the ingenuity of a thriving open source community. Gain cutting-edge high availability in the form of globally distributed Active–Active and Active–Passive architectures, excellent linearly scalable high performance, and top-notch built-in search capabilities. With Redis Enterprise, you can extend Redis databases to Flash SSDs to save money on infrastructure and get the most out of your hardware. With seamless scalability, automated sharding, and fast automated failover, you can scale your Redis databases effectively.

Redis Enterprise includes not just configurable levels of persistence and durability, but also security controls, backups, and auto-recovery. Extend the already flexible Redis databases to an unlimited number of scenarios with integrated and bespoke Redis modules that inherit all of Redis Enterprise's platform benefits.

8.1.7   Applications

Graph analytics is used in a variety of fields due to its extensive capabilities.

- Journalists will use it to sift through tens of thousands of records and sources to retrieve structured data.
- Search engines like Google use Knowledge Graph to enhance suggestions of their search engines by analyzing users' search history trends. For example, the International Consortium of Investigative Journalists (ICIJ) [7] reports on the Panama Papers examined how leaders, influencers, actors, and politicians used diverse collections of shell corporations to conceal their riches from the public.
- It may also improve logistics in the manufacturing and transportation sectors by determining the quickest and safest routes, as well as environmental conditions that can impact the routes and other factors. It may also aid in the optimization of system resource configuration to align loads and increase system utilization. This can be accomplished by recognizing overburdened and stressed infrastructure, modeling traffic reallocation to mitigate risk, and reconfiguring the topology to increase operations [8].

8.1.8   Major graph analytics applications

1. Social network analysis: Businesses may detect influencers and policymakers by using social network data with graph analytics, which is crucial information in sales. This information is used to optimize sales activities by conducting talks with the right individuals. Social network analysis helps screen counterintuitive observations that can speed up the decision-making process and help involve potential customers in the sales pipeline.
2. Fraud investigation and detection: Fraud analysis entails looking at how various players in a transaction communicate. This identifies individuals within a scheme that are potentially troublesome and vulnerable to fraud. Graph analytics aids in the early detection of bad actors and the implementation of countermeasures to prevent fraudulent conduct. Graph analytics can also be used to detect illicit behavior and unlawful activities. Law enforcement uses graph analysis [9] to analyze data that help distinguish malignant and benevolent behavior by monitoring phone calls, addresses, individuals meeting offenders in particular areas, and a network of monetary delivery.
3. Management of resources: Load balancing is needed to optimize the usage of device resources and maximize the efficiency of computer and communication networks. Analyzing network relationships enables the identification of overburdened infrastructure and, as a result, the design of traffic reallocation to minimize risk and topology reconfiguration to increase operations [10]. Utility companies that offer essential services like water, sanitation, power, dams, and natural gas should use network research to maximize resource consumption

and design utility distribution systems that achieve optimum effectiveness while reducing vital component depletion.

4. Financial fraud and money laundering: Money laundering is the process of concealing the origins of illicit funds by routing them across a complicated network of financial and economic transactions before mixing them with legal funds. You may use graph analytics to analyze huge volumes of data by using relationship models from graph databases and then applying statistical analysis, classification, pattern recognition, and machine learning (ML) to these simulations. This is particularly critical when analyzing case correlations. When regulatory agencies discover irregular transactions, they are forwarded to human investigators for further investigation.

5. Detecting Bot accounts on social media: Marketers will learn a lot about what's going on in the world through social media. Bots can distort data and increase inaccuracies, making social media data more difficult to use.

In such instances, graph analytics can be used to detect fake bots and improve information quality.

Businesses use graph analytics to identify genuine accounts, which involves creating graphs of accounts with retweet counts and analyzing how many times these accounts retweet their neighbors.

Unnaturally prominent accounts (those promoted by bots) have distinct characteristics from naturally popular accounts, including some common unnatural variations.

The following methods were used to identify a greater number of bots that deal with graphs and relationships:

• Identifying accounts that receive retweets from these bots
• Analyzing the retweets from other accounts

8.2   Technology for graph databases

When you are on your own, modern technology may be interesting to experiment with or use for a personal side project, but it is a different story at work.

You must work professionally in a world of schedules, deadlines, business expectations, and rivals. And in that world, the only criterion for modern technology is that it must function flawlessly (and way better than anything else you already have on hand) [11]. Otherwise, the suits will be interrogating you.

8.2.1   Enactment

The data size will undoubtedly grow in the future, but the interactions (or relationships) between your data will grow at an even faster rate. Big data will undoubtedly increase in size, but connected data will expand at an exponential rate.

8.2.2   Flexibility

The schema and structure because of a graph data model flex as the solutions and market growth, the IT and system design groups will the pace of work at a business with graph databases [12]. You do not have to model the domain exhaustively ahead of time (and then remodel and move the database if any executive requests a change); alternatively, you may connect to the established system without jeopardizing current features.

You are the one that dictates changes and takes control of the graph database model, while the RDBMS [13] data model dictates its criteria to you, requiring you to adhere to its tabular way of seeing the universe.

8.2.3   *Agility*

It is a perfectly graphed infrastructure aligned through today's agile, test-driven programming techniques, enabling the graph-database-backed framework to adapt in response to evolving market requirements.

8.3   Graph data science?

Graph data science is a science-based approach to extracting information from data's interactions and properties, usually to make predictions. It defines a collection of strategies that help data scientists use graph data to answer questions and clarify outcomes [14] (Figure 8.3).

8.3.1   *Graph data science applications*

- Graph data science approaches applied can be a wide range of technologies and scenarios.
- Graph queries assist domain experts by providing answers to often asked questions.

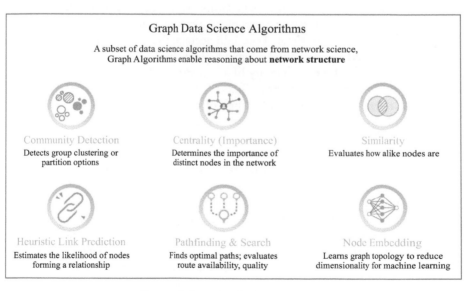

Figure 8.3   Graph data science

- Graph algorithms aid in the understanding of a graph's overall nature, with the outputs being used for isolated analysis or as functions in a ML model.
- Map embedding [15] is an essential part of similarity diagrams, which are used to control recommendation systems.
- Content-based filtering suggestions and information graph completion are aided by natural language processing (NLP) techniques.

8.3.2   *Graph data science library*

For Neo4j 3.x and Neo4j 4.x, the Neo4j Graph Data Science Library (GDSL) [16] offers easily applied, concurrent implementations of standard graph algorithms revealed as Cypher procedures. In the areas of pathfinding, centrality, and group detection, the library includes implementations of classic graph algorithms. It also involves algorithms like relation prediction and weighted and unweighted similarities that are well suited for data science problems.

- Algorithms for detecting groups: Cluster the graph based on relationships to identify communities with more meaningful connections between members. Common algorithms including Connected Components and Louvain Modularity fall into this group. Detecting population aids in the prediction of identical behavior, the discovery of duplicate individuals, and the preparation of evidence for further analysis.
- Centrality algorithms: Use graph topology to determine which nodes are significant. They use the well-known PageRank algorithm to classify influential nodes based on their network location. These algorithms are used to deduce group dynamics like reputation, rippling weakness, and group bridges.
- Set comparisons are used in similarity algorithms to how to score similar individuals are based on nodes their neighbors or assets [17]. The resemblance of nodes is scored using the properties and attributes of nodes. This method is used in applications like customized recommendations and categorical hierarchy creation.
- Link prediction algorithms: Take into account the distance between nodes in a graph as well as structural elements including potential triangles between nodes to forecast the probability of a new partnership emerging in the future or the existence of undocumented links. This class of algorithms has Preferential Attachment, which has a wide range of applications, from opioid repurposing to predicting teamwork to police investigations.
- Pathfinding algorithms: These algorithms are fundamental to graph analytics because they find the most effective or shortest paths between nodes. This group includes the A* and Dijkstra's algorithms [18], which are used to consider dynamic dependencies and test routes for applications such as physical logistics and low-cost call or IP routing.
- Node embedding algorithms: These algorithms convert the graph's topology and characteristics into fixed-length vectors that represent each node uniquely. Graph embeddings are useful because they keep important features while reducing dimensionality in a decodable way. Embeddings take a graph's complexities and composition and turn it into a format that can be used in a variety of ML tasks.

8.4   Defined graph database

It is a single-purpose graph database, an advanced tool for generating and editing graphs. Graphs are made up of nodes, edges, and properties, all used to which are store data and represent that in a way relational databases.

Another widely used term is graph analytics, which refers to the practice of evaluating in a graph format data with data points acting as nodes and associations acting as edges. It can that the database handle graph layouts are required for graph analytics; this can be a dedicated graph database or a database converged that supports several data types, like the graph.

8.4.1   Forms of graph databases

Property graphs and RDF [19] graphs are two common graph database types. The property graph is more concerned with analytics and querying, while the RDF graph is more concerned with data integration. Both forms of graphs are made up of a set of points (vertices) and the links that link them (edges). However, there are several distinctions.

8.4.2   Graphs of properties

Property graphs are used to model data relationships and allow for querying and data analytics based on these relationships. A property graph is made up of vertices that hold specific details about a topic and edges that show how the vertices are connected. Vertices and edges may have characteristics, or properties, that are connected with them.

A property graph is used to describe a group of colleagues and their relationships in this example (Figure 8.4).

Property graphs are used in a wide variety of businesses and markets, including banking, engineering, public safety, retail, and many others, due to their versatility.

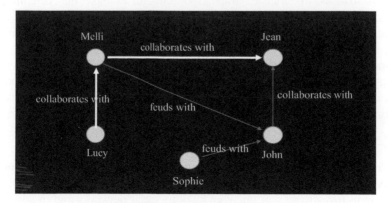

Figure 8.4   Graph database

8.4.3   Graphs in RDF

RDF graphs (RDF stands for Resource Description Framework) follow a collection of W3C (World Wide Web Consortium) guidelines for describing statements that are ideally suited for displaying complex metadata and master data. For related data, data aggregation, and information graphs, they are often used. They may represent complex domain concepts or have rich semantics and data inference.

A statement in the RDF model is made up of three elements: two vertices connected by an edge that form the subject, predicate, and object of a sentence (known as an RDF triple). A special URI, or Unique Resource Identifier, is assigned to each vertex and edge. The RDF model enables knowledge sharing by allowing data to be published in a common format with well-defined semantics. RDF diagrams have been widely adopted by government statistics bodies, pharmaceutical providers, and healthcare organizations.

8.4.4   What are graphs and graph libraries and how do they work?

Graphs and graph databases are used to describe data relationships using graph models. They help users to run "transversal queries" based on connections and use graph algorithms to identify patterns, routes, groups, influencers, single points of failure, and other relationships, allowing for more effective analysis at scale over large quantities of data. The strength of graphs lies in their analytics, observations, and capacity to link diverse data sources. When it comes to analyzing graphs, algorithms explore the paths and distance between the vertices, the importance of the vertices, and the clustering of the vertices. For example, to determine importance algorithms will often look at incoming edges, the importance of neighboring vertices, and other indicators.

Graph algorithms – operations designed to analyze relationships specifically and actions among data in graphs – understand things allow us to that are difficult to see with other approaches. When it comes to graph analysis, algorithms look at the paths and distances between vertices, the value of vertices, and vertices clustering. Incoming edges, the significance of neighboring vertices, and other metrics are often used by algorithms to assess importance. Graph algorithms, for example, may determine which person or object in a social network or business process is the most related to others. Communities, variations, and general phenomena can all be identified using algorithms, as well as paths that connect individuals or related transactions.

Since graph databases directly store relationships, queries and algorithms that take advantage of the connectivity between vertices can be executed in milliseconds rather than hours or days. Users no longer need to do multiple joins, and the results will be used for visualization and ML to understand more about the world around us.

8.4.5   Benefits in graph databases

The graph format offers a more versatile medium for locating distant relationships or analyzing data based on factors such as interaction intensity or accuracy. Graphs allow you to investigate and uncover links to social networks and trends, IoT, big data, data warehouses, and complicated transaction data for a business of various

PGQL:

```
PATH shares_movie_with AS (from) <- (acted_in) -> (to)
SELECT y.name
MATCH (x:Actor) -/:shares_movie*/->(y:Actor)
WHERE x.name = 'Iron Man'
AND x <> y
```

SQL Equivalent:

```
WITH temp(actor_id, actor_name) AS (
—Anchor member:
SELECT actor_id, name
FROM Devices
WHERE name = 'Iron Man'
UNION ALL
—Recursive member:
SELECT Actors.actor_id, Actors.name
FROM temp, Actors, Connections conn 1,
    Connections conn2, Movies
WHERE temp.actor_id = conn1.to_actor_id
    AND conn1.from_acted_in_id = Connectors.movies_id
    AND Connectors.movie_id = conn2.from_movie_id
    AND conn2.to_actor_id = Devices.actor_id
    AND temp.actor_id != Actors.actor_id)
CYCLE actor_id SET cycle TO 1 DEFAULT 0
SELECT DISTINCT actor_name
FROM temp
WHERE cycle = 0
AND actor_name <> 'Iron Man'
```

Figure 8.5   SQL and PGQL

use cases such as fraud detection in finance, social network discovery, and consumer 360. Chart databases are constantly being used in data science to help make correlations in relationships easier.

Since graph databases directly store relationships, queries and algorithms that rely on the connectivity between vertices can be executed in seconds rather than hours or days. Users no longer need to do multiple joins, and the results will be used for visualization and ML to understand more about the world around us.

Graph databases are an incredibly versatile and effective instrument. Because of the graph format, complicated interactions for deeper perspectives can be calculated with far less effort. Queries in graph databases are usually written in languages such as (PGQL) Property Graph Query Language. The question is seen in both PGQL and SQL in the example in Figure 8.5.

Such as seen in the preceding example, code is the PGQL much more effective and simpler. Since graphs prioritize data relationships, they are suitable for a wide range of studies. Chart databases, in particular, excel at:

- Between two nodes locating the shortest route
- The nodes identifying with the greatest activity/impact
- Analyzing connections to determine a network's weakness points
- Analyzing the status of a network or population depending on access distance/density in a group [20]

8.4.6   What is the role of graph databases and graph analytics?

The picture below provides a graphic ee3 of the famous party game "Six Degrees of Kevin Bacon," which is a clear example of graph databases in motion. For those who are unfamiliar with the game, it entails making relations between Kevin Bacon and another actor based on a series of shared films. Because of the focus on partnerships, it is an excellent way to illustrate graph analytics (Figure 8.6).

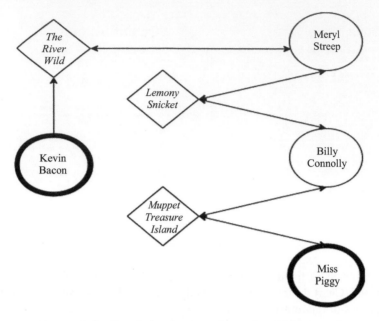

Figure 8.6   Graph databases and graph analytics work

For this Kevin Bacon example, graph databases will query several different relationships, such as: • "What is the shortest chain connecting Kevin Bacon to Miss Piggy?" (as in the Six Degrees game above, shortest path analysis)

8.4.7   Graph database use case: money laundering

Money laundering is a basic concept. Dirty money is traded around to mix it through legal assets, which are now converted into hard cash. This is the method used in the Panama Papers investigation (Figure 8.7).

A money transfer, in particular, entails sending criminal vast sums of fraudulently received money to himself or herself – but concealing it through a lengthy and complicated sequence of legitimate transactions between "natural" accounts. These "natural" accounts are in fact accounts built with fictitious identities.

Users may generate a graph from transactions as well as between entities that exchange certain data, such as email addresses, addresses, keys, and so on, to make fraud detection easier. If a graph has been developed, a simple question would locate all customers with accounts that have identical details and show which accounts are sending money to each other.

8.4.8   Social network review is a good example of how to use a graph database

Graph databases can be used in a variety of contexts, but they are most widely analyze is used to social networks. Indeed, social networks are an excellent use case

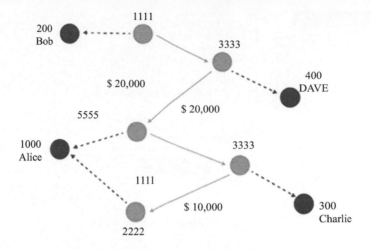

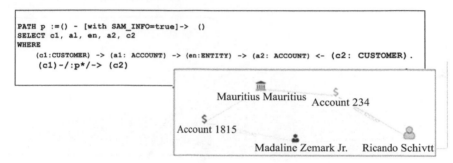

```
PATH p :=() - [with SAM_INFO=true]-> ()
SELECT c1, a1, en, a2, c2
WHERE
    (c1:CUSTOMER) -> (a1: ACCOUNT) -> (en:ENTITY) -> (a2: ACCOUNT) <- (c2: CUSTOMER) .
    (c1)-/:p*/-> (c2)
```

Figure 8.7   Graph database use case

due to their large number of nodes (user accounts) and multi-dimensional links. A social network graph review is revealed in Figure 8.8.

And Figure 8.9 depicts the operation of a bot-driven account.

- It is to use the graph analytics of the power to distinguish between a normal pattern and a bot pattern. It is as easy as filtering out certain accounts from there, but it is also possible to delve further to investigate, say, the connection between bots and retweeted accounts.
- Bot accounts are actively discouraged by social media networks since they negatively affect the overall user experience. After a month, flagged accounts were reviewed to ensure that the bot identification mechanism was correct. The outcomes were as follows:
  o Suspended rate: 89%
  o 2.2% removed
  o 8.8% are now working

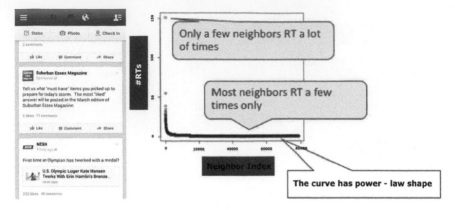

Figure 8.8   Examining social media

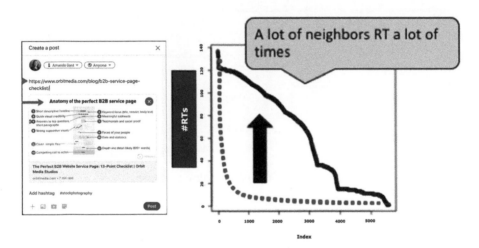

Figure 8.9   Account Bot-driven

This exceptionally punished accounts (91.2%) a high number of demonstrated both patterns of the accuracy recognition and the cleaning procedure. This may have occupied much longer with a traditional tabular database, but through graph analytics, dynamic trends can be identified easily.

8.4.9   Credit card theft is an example of how a graph database can be used

As a way of preventing theft, graph databases have become an important weapon in the finance sector. In anti-fraud advancements technologies, such as the use of embedded chips in cards, fraud will still happen in a variety of ways. Skimming devices may steal information from magnetic strips, which is a popular practice in places that have not yet mounted chip readers. Once those records are saved, they can be loaded into a counterfeit card and used to make payments or remove funds.

ML is commonly used to detect fraud, but graph analytics may complement this initiative to create a more reliable, effective method. Because of the focus on partnerships, the findings have proven to be accurate predictors of false data. Until data can be used, it must be curated and prepared.

8.4.10   The evolution of graph databases

Chart databases and graph techniques have evolved over the last decade as computing resources and big data have expanded. Indeed, it is becoming abundantly apparent that they will be the mainstream method of analyzing a new world for dynamic data relationships. When companies and associations push the big data and research forward possibilities, the opportunity to extract visions in more sophisticated makes graph databases have for the ways a today's needs and future success.

Oracle makes it easy to implement graph technology. Oracle Database and Oracle Autonomous Database have a graph database and graph analytics engine, allowing users to gain new insights from their data by using the power of graph algorithms, pattern matching requests, and visualization. Graphs are a component of Oracle's converged database, which supports multimodal, multi-workload, and multi-tenant specifications within a single database engine.

In the fact that all graph databases claim to be high-performance, Oracle's graph products are both performant in terms of query performance and algorithms, as well as closely integrated with the Oracle database.

8.5   Graph analytics trending techniques and technologies

Without a question, data and analytics have the potential to accelerate renewal or rehabilitation for companies after the COVID-19 pandemic. Similarly, Gartner has listed (D&A) technology patterns in the top 10 data and analytics for 2020 that can assist analytics leaders and in navigating their recovery and response COVID-19, as well as preparing for a post-pandemic reset (Figure 8.10).

8.5.1   Trend 1: Artificial intelligence (AI) that is smarter, quicker, and more accountable

By the end of 2024, 75% of companies would have moved from AI piloting to operationalizing, resulting in a fivefold growth in issuing media and analytics structures. AI strategies such as ML, computation, and NLP are offering critical observations and forecasts regarding the propagation of the epidemic as well as the efficacy and effects of countermeasures in the new pandemic background.

8.5.2   Trend 2

Visual, point-and-click discovery and authoring will be replaced by dynamic data stories by more consumerized and automated interactions. As a consequence, users'

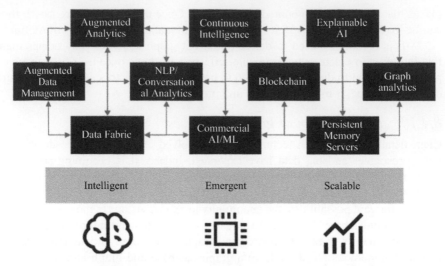

Figure 8.10   Trending techniques and technologies

time spent using predefined dashboards would decrease. The move to interactive data tales, which use technologies such as augmented analytics or NLP, ensures that the most important insights can be delivered to each user depending on their meaning, task, or usage.

8.5.3   The third trend is decision intelligence

More than 33% of 2023, major companies' decision intelligence have experts, with decision simulation. Decision intelligence integrates many fields, such as decision making and decision support. It offers a platform to assist analytics leaders and data in designing, modeling, aligning, executing, monitoring, and fine-tuning processes and decision models in the light of market results and behavior.

8.5.4   Trend 4th: X analytics

AI during the COVID-19 pandemic was instrumental in searching through thousands of scientific reports, news articles, social media tweets, and clinical trial results to assist public health and medical experts in forecasting disease transmission, size planning, finding alternative therapies, and identifying vulnerable populations. In the future, X analytics together with graph analytics will be AI and other methods such as critical in detecting, forecasting, and preparing for natural disasters and other emergencies [21].

8.5.5   Trend 5th: enhanced data protection

Augmented data management employs ML and AI approaches to simplify and boost processes. It also transforms metadata from auditing, lineage, and monitoring to powering complex structures.

8.6   Conclusion

Graph analytics is a new method for combating illegal practices and staying one step ahead of fraudsters. Graph analytics and its related applications can have capabilities for analyzing data and interactions that would be incredibly difficult or impossible to analyze using conventional analytics methodologies. Chart visualization and graph methods have evolved and are now considered common tools for analyzing dynamic data relationships. Graph analytics allows for the extraction of insights in more nuanced ways, making it an invaluable platform for today's companies. You may also be involved in learning more about our business intelligence and analytics services. It is support for a graph database offer intrinsic in data models, querying, data modeling, and resulting in faster computation, other integrity limitations. Though, in the concept for improvement of regular graph database languages for querying and computation of graph databases. Also, that can new query languages are needed for analytical operations. NLP and AI graphs medical researchers will enable to sift through the related reports of thousands of exponential rate to draw results between correlations. Enhanced vaccine R&D also identifies anti-coronavirus countermeasures, including those that have already been studied on humans. Big graphs necessitate specialized and faster parallel computing models with a variety of characteristics, including fault tolerance, stability, simplicity, increased efficiency, optimal efficiency, scalability, processing capacity, and better resource utilization. We are developing graph analytics compliance guidelines.

References

[1]   Number of Monthly Active Facebook Users Worldwide as of 3rd Quarter 2017 (in mi l lions). Statista, 2017. Available: www.statista.com/statistics/264810/number-of-monthly-active-facebook-users-worldwide/   (Accessed December 30, 2017).

[2]   B. Darrow. "LinkedIn Claims Half a Billion Users." Fortune, April 24, 2017. Available: http://fortune.com/2017/04/24/linkedin-users/   (Accessed December 30, 2017).

[3]   R. Kumar. "Graph Analytics." February 16, 2016. Available: www.ranjankumar.in/graph-analytics

[4]   J. Webber. "The Top 5 Use Cases of Graph Databases: Unlocking New Possibilities with Connected Data." Neo4j, 2 015. M. V. Rijmenam. Think Bigger: Developing a Successful Big data Strategy for Your Business. Amacom, 2014.

[5]   R. Valdes. *The Competitive Dynamics of the Consumer Web: Five Graphs Deliver a Sustainable Advantage*, Stamford, CT: Gartner, 2012.

[6]   R. Marsten. "Is Graph Theory Key to Understanding Big data?" March 2014. Available: www.wired.com/insights/2014/03/graph-theory-key-understanding-big-data/

[7]   D.K. Singh and R. Patgiri. "Big graph: tools, techniques, issues, challenges and future directions." In: *Sixth International Conference on Advances in Computing and Information Technology (ACITY 2016)*, Chennai, India, 2016.

[8]   Y. Perez, R. Sosič, A. Banerjee, *et al.* "Ringo: interactive graph analytics on big-memory machines." In: *ACM SIGMOD International Conference on Management of Data (SIGMOD'15)*, New York, NY, 2015.

[9]   M.U. Nisar. *A Comparison of Techniques for Graph Analytics on Big Data.* uga, 2013.

[10]   Gandomi and M. Haider, "Beyond the hype: big data concepts, methods, and analytics." *International Journal of Information Management*, 35(2), 2015, 137–144.

[11]   R. Angles. "A comparison of current graph database models." In: *2012 IEEE 28th International Conference on Data Engineering Workshops (ICDEW)*, New York, NY: IEEE, 2012, pp. 171–177.

[12]   "Visualizing Groups in Graph," http://allthingsgraphed.com/2014/08/28/facebook-friends-network/ (Accessed April, 15, 2017).

[13]   U. Fard, L. Nisar, J.A. Ramaswamy, Miller and M. Saltz. "Distributed algorithms for graph pattern matching." Technical Report, 2013, http://www.cs.uga.edu/ar/abstract.pdf

[14]   U. Kang, C.E. Tsourakakis and C. Faloutsos. "Pegasus: a peta-scale graph mining system implementation and observations." In: *ICDM'09. Ninth IEEE International Conference on Data Mining*, 2009, New York, NY: IEEE, 2009, pp. 229–238.

[15]   "Supplement for: A Comparison of Techniques for Graph Analytics on Big Data." http://www.cs.uga.edu/~nisar/papersupplement.pdf.

[16]   W. Wang, L. Xu, J. Cavazos, H. Howie Huang and M. Kay. "Fast acceleration of 2d wave propagation simulations using modern computational accelerators." *Journal of PLoS One*, 9, 2014, e86484.

[17]   H. Howie Huang, S. Li, A. Szalay and A. Terzis. "Performance modeling and analysis of flash-based storage devices." In: *IEEE Symposium on Mass Storage Systems and Technologies (MSST)*, 2011, pp. 1–11.

[18]   J. Chen, G. Venkataramani and H. Howie Huang. "Repram: recycling pram faulty blocks for extended lifetime." In: *IEEE/IFIP International Conference on Dependable Systems and Networks (DSN)*, 2012.

[19]   A.J Uppal, R.C. Chiang and H. Howie Huang. "Flashy prefetching for high-performance flash drives." In: *IEEE Symposium on Mass Storage Systems and Technologies (MSST)*, 2012.

[20]   W. Sun, R. Ricci and M.L. Curry. "Gpustore: harnessing gpu computing for storage systems in the os kernel." In: *Proceedings of the ACM Annual International Systems and Storage Conference (SYSTOR)*, 2012, p. 9.

[21]   S. Hong, T. Oguntebi and K. Olukotun. "Efficient parallel graph exploration on multi-core cpu and gpu." In: *IEEE International Conference on Parallel Architectures and Compilation Techniques (PACT)*, 2011, pp. 78–88.

Chapter 9

A holistic analysis to identify the efficiency of data growth using a standardized method of non-functional requirements in graph applications

N. Pooranam[1], S. Oswalt Manoj[1], G. Ignisha Rajathi[1] and M. Amala Jayanthi[2]

Abstract

In the modern era, several opportunities are provided to transfer data through graph models in which digital transformation plays a vital role. Maintaining the data using several devices will cause a processing time delay. Data collection is an important task in all data processing units, as is storing this type of information, as is providing security on this data through a database. To improve this process, the data retrieval is done using a graph data model. The proposed method is used to find the best way to store each record in a graph database rather than in another cloud or distributed database. In this, various techniques used in providing a better solution for data processing are done on graph databases without schema. To provide a good solution without any time delay, the graph analytics algorithm will help in making decisions on better results. In this method, many applications will be taken as case studies for finding the best relationship on the given graph database. In this, the collected data will be converted into graph format, an easy way of finding the duplication. The data model generated on each vertex is converted into low- and high-dimensional data forms. This chapter will go over a number of real-time Neo4j applications that are used to find optimal relationships on various datasets in an efficient manner.

9.1 Introduction

In data storage, the schema is designed for forming row and column data representations. In general, data is an essential part of data processing in which the raw

[1]Computer Science and Business Systems Department, Sri Krishna College of Engineering and Technology, India
[2]Department of Computer Applications, Kumaraguru College of Technology, India

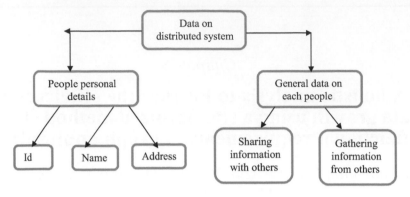

Figure 9.1   Distributed system structure to store the person detail

data is processed under some standard processing framework through storing needed data in a formal format. There are various forms of data storage, like relational databases, distributed databases, cloud databases, graph databases, etc. In this chapter, a comparison is made between these database models and their storing features for easy processing. These database models are used to store the data and retrieve that data in an efficient way. All data processing models are built in such a way that each data point is linked to the next [1].

The main models of data storage trends are based on graph databases and NoSQL databases. Let us consider a scenario in which a person wants to get connected with his friends and family. The data processed on each feature is extracted based on the input data. In this, it is possible to have a database to store the data in both a distributed and a graph structure. Figure 9.1 depicts the data collection and representation of each data attribute of a person who wishes to meet up with friends and relatives.

Consider the same scenario for the graph database; data is going to be similar to distributed systems, but the structure of the graph is going to be varied according to the feature extraction.

In a graph database, the nodes and edges are going to be represented as entities like in the ER representation as described in the relational database schema. The graph database is going to be a type of no-SQL database that is used to store the map and query relationships using graph theory. The graph database is used to analyze the interconnectivity between the nodes and edges, which is used to characterize the node. Here the graph database describes all the nodes in which multi-attitudes on edges are defined. There is no limit to the number of nodes, which can have multiple attributes defined to characterize each node [2]. The graph representation can be either directed or undirected, and the information that is being defined for each node is called properties. The graph database can describe the structure using graph theory in which an undirected edge is defined as a bidirectional graph. The relationship may be carried out from top to bottom or bottom to top.

9.1.1 Key features of graph database

- The data organization varies according to different structures.
- Scalability and flexibility are defined as a greater part of the graph database.
- Multiple relationships are counted as numerous once on each data set.

9.1.2 Process related to graph database

As described earlier, the data representation of a graph database or relational database is comprised of various databases. Graph databases are defined by general data processing, which is better than distributed databases or NoSQL databases. The scaling is done without any need for a specific schema representation like querying, mapping, etc. A single node can have multiple entities to represent different data objects.

Consider Figure 9.2, which represents a graph database structure. For example, the data which is collected from a particular person can be represented using a graph database, which is going to interconnect with different data. It may be the personal data or it might be some other data which is related to the sharing of information by the particular person. In this figure, the data is related to the information that is selected from the social media sharing perception. A person who is going to share a post on social media can see how many likes he/she gets and how many shares are being made on the particular post. This can be represented using the graph database as shown in Figure 9.2.

In this chapter, a detailed explanation of how database operations are defined using graph databases is provided, along with a suitable example. A case study is going to be described with different applications that use data storage as a graph database. Application-related information on graph databases with tool kits has been examined in this chapter. The methodologies used in graph databases have been developed with different working models with different features. These techniques are useful for researchers that store their data in graph databases. The set will be taken from the UCI repository, and the real-time application will operate on

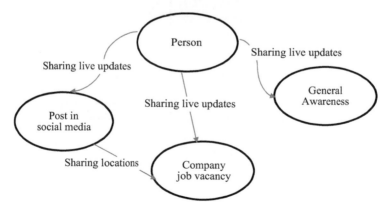

Figure 9.2   Graph database representation for the social media perception.

the specific framework utilizing the graph database toolkit. The process of storing information and retrieval of information has been examined in various case studies. Here the non-functional requirements of the graph database are mainly concentrated. The scalability, flexibility, and consistency of each individual data entity are being maintained using graph databases.

Though the processing step differs between methodologies, it is described with the non-functional requirements of a specific real-time example being described with different steps carried out using a toolkit. Figure 9.3 describes the working process of the graph DB. The left side of the figure describes the query processing in which the entire network gets connected to the database. The metadata is collected separately, the query engine is used to define the storage of the entire data, and the T1 T2 T3 describes the task that is going to be executed from the storage space. The storage and the query engine are interconnected with each other for transferring the information between each task. On the right-hand side, data has been collected separately from the framework of data Hive and data is being separated as task by task information and scheduled accordingly to work on particular external data sources. It has been imported inside the query processing.

Many applications are built on graph databases like neo4j, which is one of the popular graph databases that has been placed on rating or ranking the information from the reports that have been generated from the score value [3]. Each key value is associated with the array, which has a single value that is defined with many keys obtained from different structural data. A graph data platform is defined by an application that helps to make data sensible and this platform includes the data science library that is needed for enterprise applications and a ready analysis design for both your open source and licensed enterprise applications as given in Figure 9.4.

The core industries and business applications are presently working on the graph database, and the products that are developed with many solutions are generated with the help of the graph database. Though the processing of each data is easily defined in the enterprise aspect, technology that is leveraged for maximum

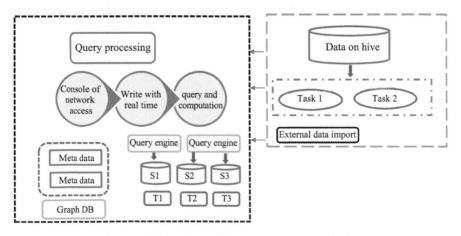

Figure 9.3   The working process of graph DB

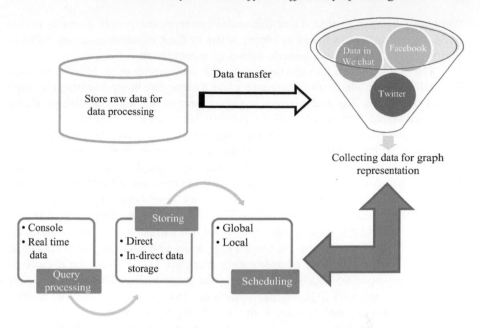

Figure 9.4   The overall process of different real time applications

business value and defined as the data processing step that will be balanced with graph data technology and competitive advanced techniques or methods used in the graph model.

9.2   Literature survey

9.2.1   Graph data modeling

The variance of different arenas is clustered together to coin a new idea through the technical eye catcher with the basis of graphs, focusing on graph modeling and the next part of how well the non-functional requirements are connected to graph applications. The overall target always focuses on the consideration of how the flow of data results in proper prediction with exact utilization of the methodology towards excellent efficacy with top-notch accuracy in the applications.

Among the various trends of technological diversity, the graph model has posted its stand in the representation of many relationships using nodes of various types, arcs, and also diverse attributions of those which characterize the nodal responsibilities. The graph databases are confirmed to have different nodes and also different relationships with each node. This establishment of relationships can be done on the fly in an agile modeling base and enriches the graph-based modeling to make it a useful one. Every node also possesses the attributes for characterization of the nodal representations, and thence the graph becomes property graph modeling. Further, if the nodes are labeled with their notifiable names, they are called "labeled property graphs." Here the nodes can represent people given as person nodes and also objects given as object nodes by their identifiable names. Most of the object nodes will have generic names of super classes.

The entire graph model represents the real world in a holistic manner. Basically, the simple English language plays a major role in representing the graph model occupants. The nodal names are noun form words, the relationships among nodes are verbal form words, and the property labels are adjective form words in a graph model. So, the graph modeling must be in such a way that the graphical imagery of nodes, relationships among the nodes, their properties, and labels must make the reader feasibly read the entire meaningful graph in simple English language with understandability. The relationship can represent a Facebook friendship between two people. Considering the arrow mark representation, it can be a one-headed arrow, which means two things. The first thing is that they are both friends on Facebook, and the second thing is that the one without an arrowhead has initiated the Facebook friend request toward the person who holds the arrowhead close to its relationship line. In a complete data graph, we can fetch all the nodes connected to any specific node irrespective of the directionality. The graph modeling can be connected with SQL queries, which can incorporate keys such as primary key and foreign key and proceed with the indexing as B trees.

Yet when the data records of nodes start magnifying, to hundreds, thousands, millions, billions, etc., everything slows down in performance too. Relational databases are inefficient in handling datasets if any of the following factors are encountered:

- Wrong model – leads to complex modeling and storage
- The incorrect language is SQL, which works very well with Set theory.
- Degraded performance – speed dilates with the growth of data as the number of joins too inflates.
- Not adaptable – the addition of new data and relationships causes design issues in the schema.
- ACID properties are not preserved.

Furthermore, representations exist, such as doubly linked list representation of nodes, storage record layout, etc., which still prolong its pitfalls in spite of their functional benefits. So, graph data modeling outperforms other representations in the following ways:

- The use of pointers to replace lookup tables means that the vast majority of nodes and relationships are linked using pointers, whereas properties are stored as a single chain only.
- All the records must have a fixed size.
- Joins can be incorporated during creation.
- Generally, 2–4 million traversals take place in reading and accessing the contents of memory, which revolves through the data structures.

Each and every node relationship is segregated into partitions based on its types and directions. The earlier databases deal with tables that increase in size as the data records flow in and, simultaneously, the join tables also increase in size, which leads to a simple few data records but with a lengthy query to execute by comparing the primary key of those join tables. Instead of this drastic coverage of resource utilization, graph data modeling uses simple partitions and splitting up into smaller pieces. The size of the graph is not our consideration, but rather think of how much the graph needs to explore to get the answer to our required query. A graph model recommended by Wong uses a graph with multiple node types, arc types, attributes, etc. A few examples of exchange formats [4] are Rigi Standard Format (RSF), TA, MSE, and Graph Exchange Language (GXL). Furthermore, applications exist based on taxonomies such as ProMeTA [5].

9.2.2   Non-functional requirements

For every system, there are three different types of requirements, such as:

1. Functional requirements: the answer to the question "What is the function of the system?" They are represented using simple use cases, business rules, etc., noted as product features.
2. Non-functional requirements [6] – the answer to the question "How does the system perform its functions?" These are purely quality-related requirements. The categories are shown in Figure 9.5.
3. Architectural requirements: explanation of the connections established with the subsystems in a descriptive manner.

While discussing non-functional requirements, the factors to be focused on are

*   Availability: if the system is available for use, it is measured by the mean-time-to-failure (MTTF) for the system divided by the sum of the MTTF and the mean-time-to-repair the system after a failure occurs. Availability relates to other factors such as reliability, maintainability, and integrity.
*   Efficiency: proper utilization of the system in terms of processor capacity, power consumption, memory usage, input and output communication, disc

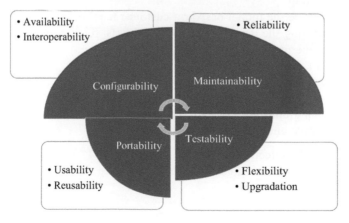

Figure 9.5   Non-functional requirements

space, etc. The basic measure of the efficiency of the system is the mechanical energy-to-electrical energy conversion.

- Flexibility means the easy appending of new capabilities to the product. It is otherwise stated as augmentation, extensibility, and expandability.
- Integrity – security in blocking unauthorized access and preventing data leakage and fraudulence, either manually or through viral tracking of hackers.
- Interoperability refers to the seamless exchange of information with other parties.
- The term "reliability" refers to the expectation that the system will function without flaws for a specified period of time. It is also accounted for as robustness-fault tolerance.
- Usability: a user-friendly environment.
- Maintainability – debugging capability and long-term measures. The effective way of analyzing, updating, and evaluating the system.
- The application is portable because it is unaffected by changes in the operating environment. It relates to the ability to globalize or localize a product based on reusability.
- Reusability: modularize any part of the program and use it for other applications as well. It should have a generic capacity of usage.
- Testability-validating the integrated components for their defect-free proper utilization. It plays a major role while dealing with complex algorithm logic and tender interrelationships.

Other performance requirements include speed, throughput, load capacity, timing, power, etc. The extraction of functional and non-functional targets in various applications plays an important role in the current industry [7].

9.2.3   *Building of graph-based application model*

With this knowledge, when building a graph-based application model [5], the following things must be taken into account:

1. Data Modelling
   - (i) Describe the model based on customer requirements
   - (ii) Preparing the list of nodes as model facts, relationships as fine-grained or generic
   - (iii) Predicting the performance
   - (iv) Reviewing the executables
   - (v) Make a timeline tree
   - (vi) When graphs are updated, they are versioned
   - (vii) Iterative and incremental development

2. Application Architecture
   - (i) Embedded Architecture vs. Server Choice
   - (ii) Server Extensions
   - (iii) API Selection
   - (iv) Clustering
   - (v) Replication

   (vi)   Buffer writes: Global clusters
   (vii)   Load Balancing
   (viii)   Separate read and write traffic
   (ix)   Cache Sharding

3.   Testing
   (i)   Test driven Data Model Development
   (ii)   Testing server extensions
   (iii)   Performance testing
   (iv)   Query performance tests
   (v)   Performance evaluations of applications
   (vi)   Testing representative data items

4.   Capacity Planning
   (i)   Cost, performance, redundancy, and load performance are the optimiza-
         tion criteria
   (ii)   Calculate the cost of database performance [6]

5.   Importing and bulk loading data

Having glanced at the step-by-step process of graph-based data analytics, the application of the same in cyber security [8–10] is a major research area nowadays. Yet another discussion on enterprise indulgence with graph modeling has been given in [11]. In the process of exploration, the best graph databases are connected through the link for perusal. Therefore, the existing trends have been discussed in this section.

9.3   Various working techniques in graph database

Several techniques have been followed for generating the graph database model in this collective approach between the relational database models and whereas a simple RDBMS is incorporated into the graph database model with spin and the location of a foreign key, with relationships provided between entities generated by the graph database [12]. The first is a representation of a graph model, and the second is the north wind graph model. There are different techniques and the methods that have been followed for this model in the north wind data model are null values that are not defined or present in the database generated.

In a graph data model, the components are the node and relationship, which are represented as a graph model. In this model, the non-functional requirements are also specified separately by property key generation, which is obtained with the help of a csv file as shown in Figure 9.6.

9.4   Case study on the patient dataset to track Infections with Neo4j

In this database, the scheme is not concentrated; there is no scheme defined for each data entity in a given data model. The case study is on the healthcare system in which it is going to identify the infection spread inside the hospital.

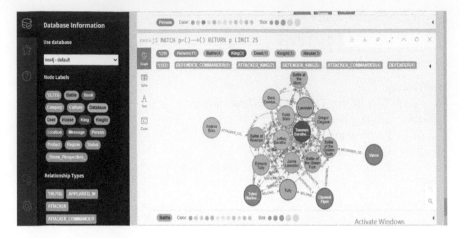

Figure 9.6   Graph data model with node labels and edges

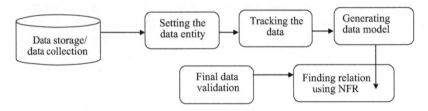

Figure 9.7   The data validation process using Neo4j

Tracking infections requires a lot of data that has to be combined with the patients who are going to visit the hospital from time to time. The system is to be developed in such a way that time-to-time update is possible. The feasibility of increasing the system capability is important to find out how the infection spreads inside the hospital. The graph space and the time complexity have been identified using neo4j. The collected information has been transferred to the data model that has been generated using neo4j, and visualizing each individual data model yields a massive amount of information that has been related to the relationship and should meet the goal of finding the connection inside the network. The event entity includes the non-functional requirements like space complexity and time complexity in the place where the duration and the timestamp are being generated from the start to the end event, which is identified by the data model flexibility.

The graph data set has been generated using the graph algorithm, which has been grouped into various specific perceptions and the validation of the entire dataset was collected using the default system as shown in Figure 9.7.

9.5   Case study on Neo4j graph data science sandbox using general connectivity of the network

Neo4j is a Framework for analyzing and visualizing the graph database. This is one of the popular graph databases to store and retrieve the information and finding out the connection between each node and the edge. The graph technology is used through graph query language which describes about data formation. Graph query language is going to be standardized query for the non-functional requirement and also functional requirement of a standard proposal defined using resource with formal process of getting collaborated through data set.

Figure 9.8 defines the neo4j associated with the projects by naming the graph data science and the launch of the project using the browser. While launching, the initializing of the database has been obtained as the first step in the neo4j framework. In Figure 9.9, each project comes with a predefined data set that has been obtained with a desktop application as a project, and it can have additional data through collaboration by inviting the people to do the project. The database information is provided on the left-hand side by defining the node labels, relationship type, and property keys. Each model is defined with the graph query language, which is provided on the right hand. Match provides the appropriate connectivity between each node and the edge. It provides about 26 notes with 35 relationships. The color variations are provided for the functional and nonfunctional requirements of a given data set as shown in Figure 9.10.

Figure 9.11 selects property key has been selected for the battle type in which the maximum battle type is generated in blue color and the nodes that are identified

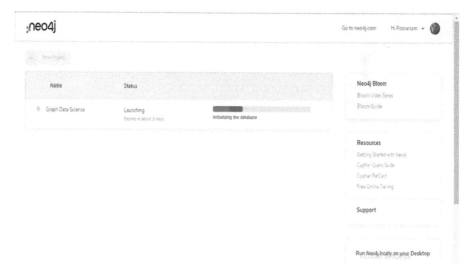

Figure 9.8   Starting Neo4j framework

Figure 9.9   Provides predefined dataset

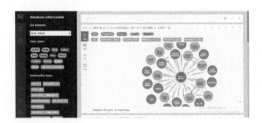

Figure 9.10   Describes about database information

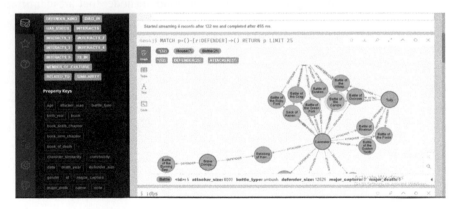

Figure 9.11   Detail description about the non-functional requirement of graph data

for this battle are represented using the non-functional requirements like ID, attacker size, battle type, defeater size, major capture, and major death.

Figure 9.12 defines the query that is provided at the top most right inside, which defines the entity and battle type so that a match is defined with an entity that returns the battle type with a limit value of 25.

Figure 9.12   Property key for battle_type entity

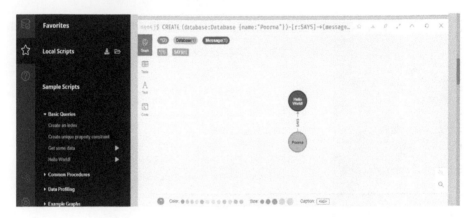

Figure 9.13   Creation of database

Figure 9.13 describes the creation of a database through the query language provided for the graph data structure, in which the name is provided with an entity and the message is captured through the edge. The match has been defined for generating the path through the pattern that is generated by the graph database that describes the structure of an entity with the limit value of 27 (Figure 9.14). A help manual is provided for identifying or getting information about a particular query, which helps the user identify the purpose of the particular query (Figure 9.15). A search button is provided for identifying the node and the entity. The pattern here is that the king and the battle are being combined to identify the relationship through the connectivity between each of the relationships (Figure 9.16).

The Python code is implemented using a PIP installation of the Neo4j driver, which installs all the people imported into the graph database. This particular coding defines the collection of information provided for the network connectivity between two nodes. This particular code is given and the report is generated on the

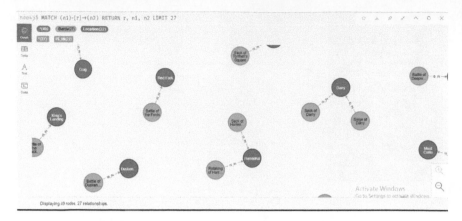

Figure 9.14   Pattern match with the limit value 27

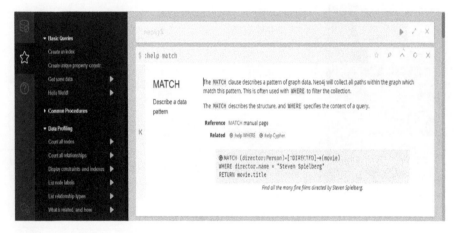

Figure 9.15   Help manual

Figure 9.16   Finding relationship model on data entity

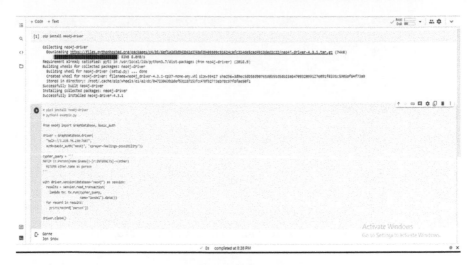

Figure 9.17   Implementing graph database using Pip Installation with neo4j drive

node called "person" and the driver provides the connectivity match between each node (Figure 9.17).

The output of the data report provided is based on the entity connection between each node provided during database generation. Though processing on each step of graph data is maintained, with a gradual increase in connectivity of the data model generated [13,14]. The first pip installation is done with pip install neo4j – driver syntax, which collects all the neo4j drivers by installing the graph database packages.

9.6   Case study on how to generate chart and data visualization using NEuler

NEuler is to define the graph algorithm using the neo4j environment, which provides a detailed description of the data library to analyze each data model. Here are two different frames that have been provided: one runs a single algorithm and the other is a run algorithm recipe. It is an encoded environment that provides an onboard facility to run the data science library [15,16] and support the graph algorithm (Figure 9.18).

This runs the various graph algorithms on different datasets [17]. The diagram depicts the chart representation of the note generated by the graph data entity, with each value generated in a single run. The second algorithm that is provided for running all the information by the graph database is the run algorithm with a specific entity (Figure 9.19).

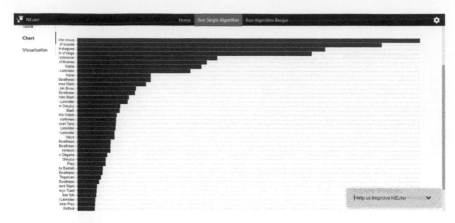

Figure 9.18   Chart representation on each node of graph data entity

*Figure 9.19   Provides data with relationship on each node through data
            visualization*

9.7   Conclusion

In this paper, it gives a detailed description of the working model of a graph
database in which two different models are being generated for analyzing the
functional requirements and also non-functional requirements. In this chapter, the
non-functional requirements have been comprised with the node and entity details.
The non-functional requirement specification defines the node ID, entity type, like

battle type, king, person, etc. The neo4j framework has been developed for implementing graph data mod in which a graph database is generated on each node which is capable of identifying property keys and values with limits. The relationship between each entity has also been identified using the package installed by the Python library and the NEuler Framework to identify the representation of a chart, and the data visualization is also carried out with the relationship between each entity. The data mode is highly efficient at retrieving information through scalability and flexible in adding all the data models into a single run algorithm.

9.8   Future direction

This builds a bridge between the researcher and trending technology for developing the open source innovative idea on graph database. There are several tools available for developing such kind of graph model in which it is easy for beginner to generate his or her Idea on the new applications. Further it can generate a scalable and flexible data model in each data requirement process.

References

[1]   https://blog.andric.name/2013/05/21/nosql-graph-databases-for-enterprises-aspects-and-requirements/
[2]   https://www.tutorialspoint.com/Types-of-databases
[3]   https://neo4j.com/blog/part-1-using-neo4j-in-business-process-modeling-scenarios/
[4]   H.M. Kienle and H.A. Müller, "Rigi—an environment for software reverse engineering, exploration, visualization, and redocumentation," *Science of Computer Programming*, 75(4), 2010, pp. 247–263, https://doi.org/10.1016/j.scico.2009.10.007.
[5]   H. Washizaki, Y.G. Guéhéneuc and F. Khomh, "ProMeTA: a taxonomy for program metamodels in program reverse engineering," *Empirical Software Engineering*, 23, 2018, pp. 2323–2358, https://doi.org/10.1007/s10664-017-9592-3.
[6]   https://www.perforce.com/blog/alm/what-are-non-functional-requirements-examples
[7]   https://rainbow-h2020.eu/methodologies-and-techniques-for-extracting-functional-and-non-functional-requirements-used-for-rainbow-project/
[8]   https://www.oreilly.com/library/view/graph-databases-2nd/9781491930885/ch04.html
[9]   https://www.oreilly.com/library/view/graph-databases-2nd/9781491930885/ch06.html#holy-grail
[10]   https://www.scylladb.com/2020/02/04/fireeye-providing-real-time-threat-analysis-using-a-graph-database/
[11]   https://blog.andric.name/2013/05/21/nosql-graph-databases-for-enterprises-aspects-and-requirements/

[12]   L.M. Cysneiros and J.C.S. do Prado Leite, "Nonfunctional requirements: from elicitation to conceptual models," *IEEE Transactions on Software Engineering*, 30(5), 2004, pp. 328–350.

[13]   https://neo4j.com/developer/data-modeling/

[14]   https://neo4j.com/product/bloom/?ref=sol-gds

[15]   J. Pokorný, "Functional querying in graph databases," *Vietnam Journal of Computer Science*, 5, 2018, pp. 95–105.

[16]   https://neo4j.com/product/graph-data-science-library/

[17]   https://dzone.com/refcardz/from-relational-to-graph-a-developers-guide

Chapter 10

Roadmap of integrated data analytics – practices, business strategies and approaches

*S. Thanga Ramya[1], V.P.G. Pushparathi[2], D. Praveena[3],
A. Sumaiya Begum[4], B. Kalpana[3] and Thangam Palani Swamy[5]*

Abstract

One part of productivity growth is creativity. Innovation can be used in processes as well as in goods. Innovation in the process helps a business to make the most effective use of its resources while innovation in products aims at creating new products or enhancing customer service. Innovative concepts have been derived from human naivety and imagination throughout history. But what if data and algorithms in some instances could help, boost or even substitute human ingenuity? Increasingly, data or analytical approaches are used to discover and develop hypotheses in vast quantities of various data. In fields including materials science, synthetic biology and life sciences, data and analysis will transform research and development. In addition, integrated data analytics helps to cleverly narrow the universe of possible combinations and leads to discoveries with the vast quantities of data to be sorted and almost limitless possible combinations of functions. With regard to this advent, this chapter provides a brief guide (i) to an era of integrated data analytics; (ii) to present a detailed roadmap of integrated, data analytics has been implemented in business strategies; (iii) to provide the approaches to construct integrated data analytics platform.

10.1   Introduction

In recent years, data and analytics have made a breakthrough. There was an exponential increase in the amount of available data, more advanced algorithms and continuous improvement in computing power and stowage. The convergence of these patterns drives rapid technological innovations and disruption of

[1]Department of Computer Science and Design, R.M.K. Engineering College, India
[2]Department of Computer Science and Engineering, Velammal Institute of Technology, India
[3]Department of Information Technology, R.M.D. Engineering College, India
[4]Department of Electronics and Communication Engineering, R.M.D. Engineering College, India
[5]Department of Faculty of Engineering, MCG, King Abdulaziz University, Kingdom of Saudi Arabia

companies. In most industries, data and analysis catch just a portion of the potential value. Location-based utilities and retail services with digital rivals have made the greatest progress. In comparison, development, the public sector and healthcare have achieved less than 30% of their potential value. Furthermore, since 2020, there have been new ways to expand the divide between leaders and laggards [1]. Companies face great hurdles in data extraction and analysis; many fail to integrate data-driven insights into daily business processes. The attraction and retention of the right talent is another challenge – not just data scientists but corporate trans-lators who add experience and skills to industry [2].

The basis of competition is changing for data and analysis. Leading companies not only improve their core businesses but also launch completely new business models. In certain markets, the network effects of digital platforms create the most dynamic winner taking. Data is a critical business asset now. They come from the web, billions of telephones, sensors, payment systems, cameras and a huge range of other sources – and their value is related to their end use. While data itself is becoming more and more commoditized, there is a risk that value will be gained by owners of scarce data, by players who aggregate data in a single way and in par-ticular by providers of valuable analytics. The introduction of new types of data sets ('orthodontic data') is able to disturb industry and massive capabilities to integrate data are able to break through organisation, technology and new insights and models [3].

Digital platforms hyper scale can match buyers and sellers in real-time and transform ineffective markets. Granular data may be used to customise products and services, especially healthcare intriguingly. New methods can fuel innovation and discovery. Data and analytics are especially capable of making decisions that are based on evidence faster and faster. Recent progress in machine learning can be used to address various problems, and deep learning pushes boundaries further. Machine learning systems can offer client support, manage logistics, analyse medical records or even write news. Even in industries that are slow to digitise, the value potential is everywhere. These technologies could produce productivity gains and better quality of life, as well as job losses and other disorders. Machine learning can be an automation technology for 80% of such activities. Natural language processing breakthroughs could further enhance this impact [22].

Multiple industries are already being shaken up by data and analysis and their influence only increases with acceptance hitting a critical mass. An even greater wave of shifting is emerging as deep learning matures, allowing machines to think, resolve and comprehend language unprecedentedly. Organisation that can effi-ciently leverage these capabilities can generate tremendous value and vary, whereas others are becoming more and more inconvenient [4]. Many business plans require access to information from other suppliers, business payers and other 'unowned' data sources. While this is an exciting objective, it takes time to resolve trust barriers. Legal and psychological trust will be generated slowly and externally focussed implementation activities may jeopardise launch timeframes, most of the data used for health, organisational and financial indicators were originally not produced with analytical considerations in mind. Although the majority of information management and analytical practitioners understand this, issues in interpretation are more common when the conventional statements and data sources are cross-linked. Likewise, the incentive for data entry (fill in, billing accuracy or simply screens to complete a fast registration process) has a significant impact on the consistency of the data [5].

10.1.1   Best practices

- Using an aggregation of data sources into analytic repositories that is analytically aware.
- Ensure data management and integration specialists understand the end purpose of the study correctly, so that effective transitions are accomplished during data loading and editing.
- When real-time analytics are implemented against unstructured data, ensure that dynamic ad hoc queries are carried out in collaboration with professionals that understand the source systems and their operative processes.

In the face of management influence of the resulting observations, this sense retains reputation.

To be deceptive at the fact that data population and coding are not consistent. Uneven administration, record management implementation, lack of standardization and other data gaps are typical for biometric data elements. The workflow and software will continue, but data capture will remain a reality beyond meaningful data packages and partial streams. Data analysts will work extremely hard with input experts, different device suppliers and the IT workers to ensure the completeness and accuracy of the information is achieved on an ongoing basis. Imputing patterns statistically based on best available data will seldom be completed over the entire care spectrum, to grasp the full data set denominators and full trend lines of data. Basically, we use analytical frameworks that provide a balance between analytical precision and the underlying data limitations, as far as possible. Ensure that the study given retains the comprehension at consumption point of these trade-offs [6,21].

A practical approach to machine and data mining starts by carefully thinking about what you actually want to calculate. Terminology mapping and standards should be used on data sets selectively which would be used intensively. Versatile data mining methods should be used for choosing data packs, which are broader and comparatively unstructured and less intensively used. Apply re-time and integrated data analysis of data stored at the receiving point and introduce large-scale retrospective analysis against standard measures and data subsets which are previously measured to improve their performance. Trust in data sources, research derivation and data presentation are of utmost importance. Analytics, for example, are being used increasingly to track actions and results, and to create compensation at the physician and management level. Finding goals and targets which affect shared savings and other risk-sharing contracts is responsive and accurate [7].

In particular, as scientists, physicians analyse data sets and underlying validity and precision methodologies. Stakeholder buy-in relies on an analysis-conscious implementation, knowledge of information sources and resources to take into an account of imperfect data. Failure to cover these foundations would jeopardise the integrity of the company and potentially restrict the use of decision making data. Ensure full knowledge of the analytical confidence chain from data collection, ad hoc consultation, vocabulary management and data manipulation. To appropriately curate and manage data properties, select confident and validated collaborators to provide benchmarking inputs and statistically sound methodologies tailored to new data sets and frameworks. Assess each connection in the chain's limitations. It is not easily restored once confidence is lost [8].

In designing the integrated data analytics strategy as shown in Figure 10.1, organisations should consider the unequal territory of data sets and terminology, the confidence mechanism for inter-organized data sharing, and the need for external benchmarking and analytical approaches tailored to the underlying data variability. The real-time, voluminous and unstructured existence of new data sets requires a versatile data collection and analysis approach. While integrated analytical solutions in business strategies are not all-round, they are gaining momentum to play a key role in helping providers and organisations improve the quality of care they provide [20]. With this detailed introduction of an era of integrated data analytics in Section 10.1, Section 10.2 briefs the roadmap of integrated data analytics that has been implemented in business strategies. Section 10.3 studies the driving analytic value with integrated data streams and predictive models and challenges. Section 10.4 describes the approaches to develop an integrated data analytics platform followed by a conclusion in Section 10.5.

10.2   Roadmap of integrated data analytics

10.2.1   Data integration

The incorporation of data includes the combination into a single, coherent view of the data from various sources. Integration starts with intake and involves steps including purification, ETL (extract, transform, and load) mapping and processing as shown in Figure 10.2. Finally, data integration allows no universal data integration solution exists. In general, however, data integration solutions include many common elements, such as a data source network, a master server and clients accessing master server information.

The client sends a request to the master server for data during a typical data integration process. The master server then receives the required data from both internally and externally. The data are collected from the sources and then aggregated into one, coherent collection of data. This is used by the customer to generate productive business intelligence by analytical methods [9].

Even if a company receives all the information it requires, the data is often collected in a number of different sources. For example, for a usual view case, data from customer relationship management (CRM) systems, web traffic, customer software, sales and customer success systems, even partners, may be combined for a typical customer 360 view case to name just a few. Knowledge from all these sources also needs to be integrated for analytical needs or operational steps, and data technicians or developers cannot have a small task in getting them all together.

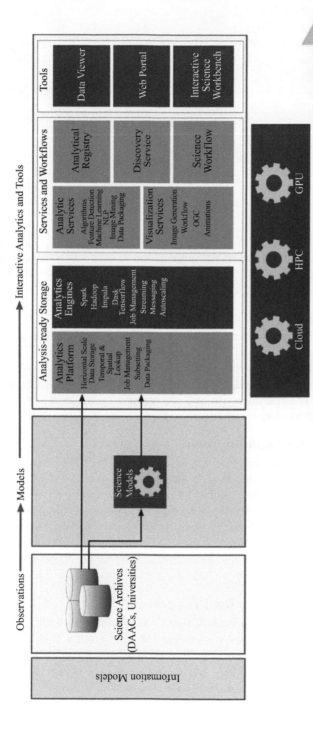

Figure 10.1 Integrated data analytics platform

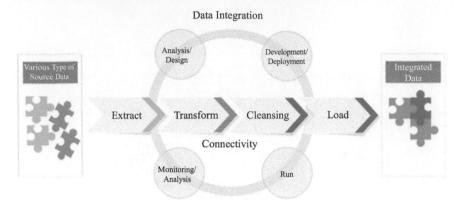

Figure 10.2   Data integration process

It highlights the importance of data integration to conduct all these operations as efficiently as possible [10]. It also demonstrates the main advantages of an extensive data integration approach.

10.2.1.1   Enhances system collaboration and unification

Increased access to company data is required for joint and individual projects by workers in every department – often in different physical locations. For IT to provide data through self-control, it needs a secure solution across all business lines. Furthermore, workers produce and develop data that the rest of the company needs in almost every department. In order to improve cooperation and unification across the organisation, data integration needs to be collaborative and unified.

10.2.1.2   Saving time and improving performance

When a firm takes steps to integrate the data correctly, the time taken to plan and analyse the data is greatly reduced. The automation of centralised views removes the need to collect data manually and employees do not have to create connections from scratch, whenever a report or an application is required. In comparison, the team returns even longer (and money overall) with the right tools rather than hand coding integration. The time saved for these activities can be used more efficiently by delivering hours of analyses and execution to increase the efficiency and competitiveness of the company.

10.2.1.3   Reduces mistakes (and rework)

When it comes to company data capital, there is a lot to keep up with. To manually collect data, workers have to know wherever and what account they may need to explore – to ensure their data sets are complete and correct – and have all appropriate software enabled before they begin. If a repository is introduced and the employee does not know, an incomplete data set would be added. Furthermore, the reports must be reported annually to account for any revisions without a data integration solution that synchronises data. However, reports can be easily executed in real time when they are needed with automatic updates.

10.2.1.4 Provides more precious details

In reality, data integration activities increase the value of data in the organisation over time. With data being integrated into a centralised framework, quality concerns are detected and required changes are made, which eventually lead to more reliable information – the basis for quality analysis.

10.2.2 Integrated data analytics in modern business

Data integration does not suit all; according to various business requirements, the right formula will differ [11, 12]. Such common cases for data integration software are as follows in the following sections.

10.2.2.1 Making use of big data

Data lakes can be incredibly complex and voluminous. For example, companies such as Facebook and Google process data from millions of users without interruption. Big data is commonly referred to as this degree of information consumption. More big data firms are coming up with more data for companies to leverage. That means many great organisations need sophisticated data integration efforts.

10.2.2.2 Data stores and data lakes are built

Initiatives for data integration, particularly in large organisations, are used frequently for the development of warehouses that combine many data sources into a relational database. Data storage helps users to scan, compile and review reports and retrieve data consistently. Many businesses, for example, rely on Microsoft Azure and AWS Redshift data warehouses to produce business information.

10.2.2.3 Simplifying business intelligence

Data integration simplifies business intelligence processes by offering a single view of data from various sources. The available data sets can be easily accessed and rapidly understood by companies to obtain operative information about the business status. With data integration, analysts can compile more data without being overwhelmed by large volumes to allow more accurate assessment. In comparison to business analytics, the emphasis is not on predictive analysis, but on explaining the current and past in support of strategic decision-making. This use of data integration is ideal for data storage where high-level summary information suits well in an easy-to-consume format as shown in Figure 10.3.

10.2.2.4 ETL and data integration

Extract, Convert, Load is a method that is typically called ETL and that brings data from the source system into the warehouse. Data is incorporated. This is the ongoing phase performed by data stockpiling to make various data sources useful and consistent knowledge for business intelligence and analysis.

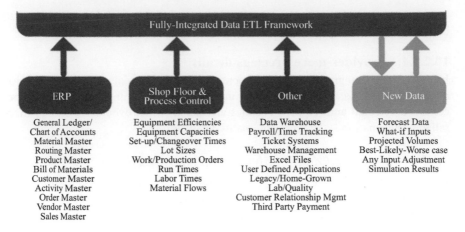

Figure 10.3   Business modelling and analytics platform

10.2.3   Integration strategies for business

There are many ways in which data can be combined depending on the size, requirements and available resources of the organisation.

- The integration of manual data is essentially the method by which an individual user directly accesses interfaces, manually gathers the appropriate data from different sources and purifies it as necessary and integrates it into a single store. This is extremely ineffective and contradictory, making no sense for anyone, with limited data capital, including the smallest organisations.
- The integration of middleware data is an integration method where the middleware programme serves as a mediator to normalise and carry data into the master data pool. Legacy applications are also not good for others. Middleware is used if a data integration device cannot access data on its own from one of those applications.
- Integrating software applications to locate, retrieve and integrate data is an approach for integration centred on applications. The programme must make data from various systems mutually compatible to transmit them from one source to another during integration.
- Uniform access integration is a data integration type designed to create a front end which allows data to appear consistent from various sources. However, the data is left in the source. This approach can be used to establish uniformity in the appearance of databases using object-based database management systems.
- Popular storage integration is the most common solution for data integration storage. The integrated system holds a copy of the data from the original source and processes them for one view. In comparison, the data is held in the source and not evenly accessed. The fundamental concept behind the conventional data storage solution is the common storage strategy.

10.2.4 Data integration tools

Data integration software can make the business process much easier [13]. The characteristics that companies in a data integration tool can look for are:

- There are many frameworks and software around the world. The larger the Data Integration tool has pre-built connectors, the more time the team saves.
- Usually, open source architectures offer more flexibility and helps to prevent vendors from locking in.
- It is critical for businesses to be able to create and operate their data integrations once, increasingly heading towards hybrid cloud models.
- Data integrated software with a GUI interface should be easy to understand and use to make the data pipelines easier to envision.
- The data integration tool provider should not be able to increase the number of connectors or data volumes in a straightforward pricing model.
- The data integration tool of cloud consistency can operate in a cloud, multi-cloud, or hybrid environment.

10.3 Driving analytic value with integrated data streams and predictive models

A visual platform is used in real time to quickly detect key features and to compute predictive models in order to help information extraction from data streams. In stream learning and visualisation, many state-of-the-art algorithms are adapted to this end. High-frequency data streams popular in different fields can extract useful information. In order to, for example, learn hot topics and predict patterns, textual data from social media such as Twitter and Facebook can be analysed. In another example, numerical data obtained by a network of climate sensors can be inspected to catch events like floods, storms or emission peaks that could precede possible catastrophes. Consequently, various data mining strategies to extract predictive models in the data streams have recently been proposed [14].

Traditional techniques of analytics can be implemented on streams with a certain observational pool (by using a sliding window, e.g.). On the other hand, such online/incremental approaches can be used to refresh results dynamically. A JAVA framework is used to inspect on-the-fly data streams and incorporate the leading predictive models to enhance stream analyses. Several specific third-party modules, such as Waikato Environment for Knowledge Analysis (WEKA) for static data mining or Massive Online Analysis (MOA) for some stream processing, can be incorporated into the programme.

The platform supports two types of data sources:

- Remote streams (i.e. web APIs): on-the-fly processed.
- Local streams (e.g. from potentially massive files): iteratively processed on a single pass without requiring access to previous values.

The user interface was designed to be reactive (by monitoring constant arrival values on-the-fly) and interactive (by giving the end user a real power, such as play/

break/shut down the data stream or by selecting the processing speed). In order to inspect the data streams in question continuously, different analytical modules were created.

10.3.1   Existing integrated data analytics market research for marketing

Incorporated data analysis gets more coverage like machine learning. While data analytics are more involved than machine learning (ML), there were two major challenges modern marketers face in the world of business and marketing:

- Creating more custom messages for more selective purchasers.
- Build tailored marketing strategies with a broader variety of key players and influencers in the purchase process earlier.

The statistics are present and advanced analytics tend to have the ability to double marketing performance measures in the B2B and B2C sectors, as well as customer participation and targeted sales [15]. The study of Forrester provided three main findings:

- The use of data collection correlates with improved market performance and measurements.
- Data marketing analyses allow marketers in their companies to play a leading role.
- In order to have a greater consumer life cycle effect, data marketers employ advanced strategies.

10.3.2   Five applications for marketing current data analysis

Although a complete list (and sublists) could extrapolate 20 or more individual uses, we have highlighted five current predictive analysis applications for which marketers today should know [16, 17].

10.3.2.1   Predictive modelling for customer behaviour

Customer actions and expectations are predictable in companies such as Amazon and eBay, but the technology is increasingly available and important for smaller companies as well. A full catalogue of predictive models would be a complex and complicated process, but relatively simple types of models apply in the marketing domain. AgilOne describe three major groups of predictive models based in Silicon Valley:

1. *Cluster*: Used for customer segmentation; target group algorithms focussed on several factors, from demographics to average total order. Popular cluster models include behavioural clustering, product-based clustering and branded clustering.
2. *Predictions*: Used to make 'true' consumer behaviour forecasts. Popular models include life-cycle predictive value; probability of engagement; vulnerability to unsubscription; convertibility; buyability; and churning tendency.
3. *Recommendations*: Using a number of factors, including past sales, to advise goods, service and advertising for consumers. Popular models (such as Amazon and Netflix) provide suggestions for up-selling, cross-selling and next-selling.

The primary method that companies use for the predictive analysis is regression analysis in their different forms. Simply defined, an analysis of the regression results shows how associations between specific client variables with the acquisition of a particular product can be formed and then utilises 'regression coefficients' (i.e. to what extent each variable affects the acquisition behaviour).

10.3.2.2   Leads certification and priority

In a study released recently by Forrester, three types of marketing cases with B2B have been established that represent early predictive performance.

1. *Predictive scoring*: Keeping in mind their possibility of taking action, the priority given to known perspectives, leading and studies.
2. *Identification models*: Identify and acquire opportunities with customer-like characteristics.
3. *Automated segmentation*: Customized messages segmenting leads.

All in this context is about qualification and prioritisation and prepares teams to adopt the following strategies. Salespeople who can prioritise will be in a stronger place to shut down more frequently (or take those next steps that will most likely move forward). Although predictive marketing capabilities are increasingly accessible for start-ups and small businesses, these techniques require a high volume of sales in order to effectively create and train a predictive model. While even small businesses can produce billions or millions of e-commerce items on low-ticket printing, data on face-to-face transactions with smaller or newer companies are harder to obtain. This could lead to larger businesses successfully returning on investment from sales data-containing techniques.

10.3.2.3   Right product and business services

The data visualisation is a powerful tool not just for the eye, but also for educating, encouraging and directing client-based behaviour (and other business information). For example, a brick and mortar marketing team can make data-based choices about which goods and services can best be brought to market with all available information about consumers. Using data visualisation to show the types of consumers in the neighbourhood of a shop, teams may answer key guiding issues:

*   Do they purchase more hard products or soft products?
*   Is the density of the age group indicating what should be stored?
*   Will the ideal composition of your product shift with or without you going towards competitors?

This type of knowledge may also be related to the overall management of the supply chain.

10.3.2.4   Target the right clients with the correct content at the right time

Customers with the best deal will return to consumer segmentation at the right time. This can be the most popular predictive analytical marketing application because it is one of the 'most' and straightforward ways of optimising a marketing offer and seeing a fast turnaround on better return on investments (ROIs). Predictive analytical users classify high-value consumers twice as likely and market the correct bid. Excellent approaches dictate the use of and the use for personal communications of historical data about the actions of current customers. A variety of predictive analytical models, including affinity analysis, response modelling and churn analysis, can be used in this application. Many vendors, such as salesforce, provide a cloud platform for marketing teams that allow audience profiles to be created by integrating data from multiple directions, from CRM to offline data. Feeding relevant data and monitoring actions in the system over time provides a conduct model that enables teams to make long-term, real-time, data-based decisions.

10.3.2.5   Marketing campaigns focused on predictive research

In addition to the above, more drilled-down applications for predictive marketing research include:

- Accessing internal structured data.
- Accessing social media data.
- Applying behaviour scoring to customer data.

Predictive analytic insights are an important method for 'channel proliferation and changing buyer behaviour'. All of the above applications can be used to assess if a social media marketing campaign can have a greater impact or whether a social media marketing campaign is more suitable for the target audience by mobile. Another example of gathering information that can be used to guide marketing campaigns and potential product development is text analysis and sentiment analysis applied to social media data.

10.3.3   Challenges to data integration

Integrated data analytics is a technological challenge for oneself to take multiple data sources and convert them into a united whole within a single framework. As more businesses develop solutions for data integration, it is the challenge of developing pre-built processes to continuously transfer data. While this brings a short-term saving in time and costs, multiple barriers will prevent implementation.

Here are some common challenges faced by companies to improve their data integration analytical systems:

- *How to get to the finish line*: Companies normally know what data integration they want – the answer to a particular problem. What they do not really think about is the direction that they are going to take. Anyone who is integrating data must consider what kinds of data should be collected and analysed, where the data originates, the processes using the data, what kinds of analyses should be carried out and how often data and reports should be modified.
- *Legacy systems data*: Attempts to consolidate data contained in legacy systems which need to be included. However, these data also lack markers such as times and dates for events that are typically more recent.

- *Data from emerging business needs*: Today, new systems produce different types of data from various sources, such as images, IoT devices, sensors and the cloud, such as un-structured and in real time. Figure out how to change the data integration system rapidly to fulfil the requirements for the integration of all these data becomes vital to your company but incredibly challenging, because the number, the speed and the latest data format present new challenges.
- *External data*: Data obtained from external sources cannot be presented with the same degree of detail and rigour as internal sources. In addition, contracts with external vendors can make it difficult for the entire organisation to exchange data.
- *Maintaining*: The mission is not completed until an integration system is running. The data team is responsible for keeping efforts to incorporate data consistent with best practises, together with the company and regulatory agencies' recent demands.

10.4 Approaches for an integrated data analytics environment construction

An integrated data analysis framework simplifies the development and automation of data pipelines and workflows to provide business users with knowledge. It breaks down data silos, increases protection and governance and removes redundancies in the system. It can also increase the performance of operations, minimise costs and speed up insights.

In an interconnected world there are two key ways:

1. Buy an all-in-one platform from a single provider that offers all essential functions for designing, enforcing and tracking workflows in data analytics.
2. Acquire a framework for orchestration that coordinates the inputs and outputs of countless standalone instruments, systems and applications.

The two methods are designed to achieve the same outcomes – an interconnected environment that accelerates the delivery for corporate users of stable, high-quality data analysis solutions, but each has distinct pros and cons. All-in-one platforms simplify the data set at the detriment of the provider. Orchestration tools offer the best options for raising, but do not reduce the software landscape's underlying complexity. The real question is how you can choose the best solution for your business or situation.

10.4.1 Unified data analytics platform (UDAPs)

As shown in Figure 10.4, UDAPs simplify and accelerate creation of data pipelines and research solutions while lowering costs by consolidating all data and analytics into a single platform. Many startups have designed these systems from scratch, like Domo or Incorta, and have built integrated platforms from current tools for existing software companies, such as, Microsoft and IBM. UDAPs provide all components essential for the provision of a data analysis solution, including data intake and integration, refinement of data, data analysis software, and management

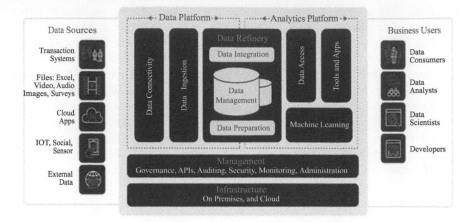

Figure 10.4   UDAP

and administrative tools. UDAPs create a single stop-shop for data analytics solutions to develop and consume. This consolidation simplifies distribution, management and use, reduces costs and speeds up insight.

The downside for UDAPs is that they are usually no masters of all trades. They provide a comprehensive range of functions, but may not support every function that an organisation needs or requires and their support functions may not be as rich as the functions provided by best-of-breed instruments. UDAPs are well suited for large and smaller businesses, which have no legacy software, to modern data analytics or divisions [18].

10.4.2   Orchestration tools

Just as an artist uses a wide range of paint for colour access and mix, a corporation uses a method of orchestration to access and merge many resources, systems and applications into a cohesive workflow as shown in Figure 10.5. These products

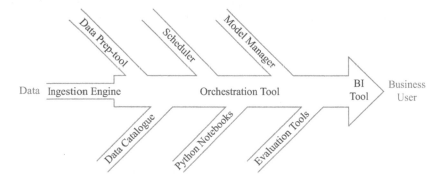

Figure 10.5   Integration-oriented orchestration tool

promote a best-of-breed approach because they attach any instruments already in place by an organisation. Orchestration tools are most suitable for organisations with many internal data and analytical tools. This suggests that the majority of large enterprises with current company data and analytical resources are successful orchestration candidates. These tools enable organisations to have and eat their own cake – best breeding tools and highly organised workflows [19].

10.5 Conclusion

Process innovation allows an organisation to make the most productive use of its resources, while product innovation tries to create new products or to enhance customer service. Throughout history, human naivety and creativity gave birth to revolutionary ideas. In the fields of materials science, synthetic biology and the life-sciences, data and analysis can transform R&D, and analytical techniques are used to discover and establish hypotheses in large amounts of diverse data. Additionally, integrated data processing leads to the intelligent restriction of the universe of potential combinations and results in discoveries with massive volumes of data and virtually infinite usable combinations. As far as this advent is concerned, this chapter offers a brief guidance on an age of integrated data analysis, along with a comprehensive map of integrated data analysis in business strategies. Finally, the section presents approaches for creating an integrated framework for data analysis.

References

[1] Wang, C.-S., Lin, S.-L., Chou, T.-H. and Li, B.-Y. (2018). An integrated data analytics process to optimize data governance of non-profit organizations. *Computers in Human Behavior*, 101, 495–505, doi:10.1016/j.chb.2018.10.015.

[2] Armstrong, E., Bourassa, M., Cram, T., *et al.* (2019). An integrated data analytics PlatformTable_1.DOCX. *Frontiers in Marine Science*, 6, 354, doi:10.3389/fmars.2019.00354.

[3] Mohan, R., Narayanan, R., Yazeedi, H. *et al.* (2018). Integrated data analytics and visualization for reservoir and production performance management. In: *Abu Dhabi International Petroleum Exhibition & Conference*, doi:10.2118/192987-MS.

[4] Begum, S. and George. (2017). An integrated data analytic framework with enhanced security using hybrid hardware and software based encryption/ decryption. In: *2017 International Conference on Intelligent Sustainable Systems (ICISS)*, 841–845, doi:10.1109/ISS1.2017.8389296.

[5] Saggi, M. and Jain, S. (2018). A survey towards an integration of big data analytics to big insights for value-creation. *Information Processing & Management*, 54, 5, 758–790, doi:10.1016/j.ipm.2018.01.010

[6]   Nguyen, A., Gardner, L. and Sheridan, D. (2020). Data analytics in higher education: an integrated view. *Journal of Information Systems Education*, 31, 1, 61–71.

[7]   Fatima, T. and Nausheen, S. (2020). Secure data analytics for cloud-integrated internet of things applications, *International Journal of Computer Engineering and Applications*, 9, 9, 16–27, doi:10.13140/RG.2.2.34809.90724

[8]   Memon, M., Soomro, S., Jumani, A. and Kartio, M. (2017). Big data analytics and its applications. *Annals of Emerging Technologies in Computing*, 1, 1, 45–54. doi:10.33166/AETiC.2017.01.006

[9]   Bergamaschi, S., Beneventano, D., Mandreoli, F., *et al.* (2018). From data integration to big data integration. In: *A Comprehensive Guide through the Italian Database Research over the Last 25 Years*, New York, NY: Springer, pp. 43–59, doi:10.1007/978-3-319-61893-7_3

[10] Wang, C. (2018). Integrating data analytics and knowledge management. In: *The 58th Conference of International Association for Computer Information Systems (IACIS)*, doi:10.13140/RG.2.2.35669.68328.

[11] Cui, Z., Henrickson, K., Biancardo, S.A., Pu, Z. and Wang, Y. (2020). Establishing multisource data-integration framework for transportation data analytics. *Journal of Transportation Engineering, Part A: Systems*, 146, 5, doi:10.1061/JTEPBS.0000331

[12] Salina, A. and Rao, Kalla (2016). A study on tools of big data analytics. *International Journal of Innovative Research in Computer and Communication Engineering*, 4, 10, doi: 10.15680/IJIRCCE.2016/0410149

[13] Purcell, B. (2012). Emergence of "Big Data" technology and analytics, *Journal of Technology Research*. 4, 1–6.

[14] Oesch, S., Gillen, R. and Karnowski, T. (2020). *An Integrated Platform for Collaborative Data Analytics. 2020 International Conferences on Internet of Things (iThings) and IEEE Green Computing and Communications (GreenCom) and IEEE Cyber, Physical and Social Computing (CPSCom) and IEEE Smart Data (SmartData) and IEEE Congress on Cybermatics (Cybermatics)*, pp. 648–653.

[15] Alshura, M., Zabadi, A. and Abughazaleh, M. (2018). Big data in marketing arena. Big opportunity, big challenge, and research trends: an integrated view. *Management and Economics Review*, 3, 1, 75–84, doi:10.24818/mer/2018.06-06

[16] Al-Gumaei, K., Schuba, K., Heymann, S., *et al.* (2018). A survey of the Internet of Things and Big Data integrated solutions for industrie 4.0. In: *2018 IEEE 23rd International Conference on Emerging Technologies and Factory Automation (ETFA)*, pp. 648–653, doi:10.1109/ETFA.2018.8502484

[17] Tashchian, A. and White, Dennis J. (2015). The application of exploratory data analysis in marketing: an introduction to selected methods. In: *Proceedings of the 1986 Academy of Marketing Science (AMS) Annual Conference*, pp. 407–411, doi:10.1007/978-3-319-11101-8_86

[18] Kim, S. and Kwon, Y. (2017). Unified platform for AI and Big Data analytics. *Journal of Computer and Communications*, 5, 8, 1–8, doi:10.4236/jcc.2017.58001

[19]   Garg, S., Wang, S. and Ranjan, Rajiv (2018). Orchestration tools for Big Data. In: *Encyclopedia of Big Data Technologies*, Cham: Springer, pp. 1–9, doi:10.1007/978-3-319-63962-8_43-1

[20]   Kościelniak, H. and Puto, A. (2015). Big data in decision making processes of enterprises. *Procedia Computer Science*, 65, 1052–1058, doi:10.1016/j. procs.2015.09.053

[21]   Naqishbandi, T. and Sheriff, I. (2015). An integrated analytics platform using big data, complex event processing and the Internet of Things. In: *International Conference on Electrical, Electronics & Computer Engineering-2016*.

[22]   Wang, Y., Kung, L., Wang, W. Yu C. and Cegielski, C. (2018). An integrated big data analytics-enabled transformation model: application to health care. *Information & Management*, 55, 1, 64–79, doi:10.1016/j. im.2017.04.001

Chapter 11

Introduction to graph analytics

Sajeev Ram Arumugam[1], Anusha Bamini[2], S. Oswalt Manoj[3], Rashmita Khilar[4] and V. Felshi Sheeba[5]

Abstract

Graph is considered to be the collection of the points or vertices or nodes and the lines between the points or the edges. The structural characteristics of a data can be plotted easily using graphical representation. In this chapter, we are going to deal about the introduction of graph analytics and about graph structure data. A detailed discussion about the graph algorithms and graph databases gives an additional advantage to read this chapter. Some of the latest graph analytics tools also explained. Data science plays a major role in today's computing world. The subdivision of data science that contracts with mining information from graphs by executing analysis on them is known as "Graph Analytics." These graph analytics are mainly supported in data science for handling huge datasets such as Google, Amazon, Facebook, e-Commerce, and Finance. It can also support use cases include cybersecurity, drug interaction, reference engines, contact tracing, social networks, and supply chains.

11.1 Introduction

Graphs are *n* the form of mathematical structures used to represent a wide range of interactions and methods in physical, biotic, communal, and statistics. A graph is a combination of nodes connected by edges, and it represents complex data dependencies. Graphs are used in road networks, social networks, communication networks, etc. [4]. Graph analytics determines the stability and path of interactions amongst elements in a graph. Graph analytics focuses on relationships between two

[1]Department of AI & DS, Sri Krishna College of Engineering and Technology, India
[2]Department of Computer Science and Engineering, Karunya Institute of Technology and Sciences, India
[3]Department of Computer Science and Business System, Sri Krishna College of Engineering and Technology, India
[4]Department of Information Technology, Saveetha School of Engineering, Saveetha Institute of Medical and Technical Sciences, Saveetha University, India
[5]Faculty of Computer Science, Universiti Teknologi Mara (UiTM), India

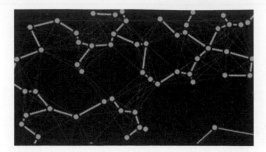

Figure 11.1   Structural representation of graph

items at a given time and the structural properties of a graph [1]. Graph analytics saves a lot of time since it takes less time to organize the data and requires less work to merge more data sources or points. It also allows for data analysis modeling, storage, and retrieval [7]. Graphs are also more visually appealing and understandable than most other data analytics tools and methods. Figure 11.1 explains the structure of a graph.

11.2   Graph-structured data

The graph-structured data is a widely used basic mathematical form. It is used in almost every facet of our lives, including pandemic outbreak reaction, information retrieval, circuit design, etc. Learning and inference from graphs have been among the most important study issues in machine learning and data science. As data grows in volume and complexity at an unprecedented rate in modern times, classical graph learning approaches are insufficient to model rising complexity and harness rich contextual information. With large-scale graphs, you can scale information as well. Deep learning's recent emergence and the representation learning field have drastically increased machine learning research, pushing the graph learning frontier. Graph representation learning is a potential new learning paradigm that tries to learn parametric mapping—low-dimensional embedding function for nodes, subgraphs, or the complete graph spaces with continuous vectors.

11.3   Graph algorithm

Graph algorithms tackle problems like portraying graphs as networks, such as airline flights, Internet connections, and Facebook social network connections. They are also used to build networks in NLP and machine learning. Here, we are explaining ten basic graph algorithms that are useful for analysis.

11.3.1   Breadth-first search (BFS)

One of the most basic operations that are performed on graphs is traversing or searching. It begins at a specific edge and investigates adjoining edges before going to the next level edges in BFS. Graphs contain cycles. We must track the vertices we have visited. We employ a queue data structure to implement BFS. Figure 11.2 explains the BFS algorithm. We begin traversal from vertex 2 in the graph below. When we get at vertex 0, we search for all of its nearby vertices. Besides being a neighboring vertex of 0, 2 is an edge of 0. The visited nodes are to be marked—else they keep on iterating without termination. The graph in Figure 11.2 has a Breadth-First Traversal of 2, 0, 3, 1.

11.3.2 Depth-first search

Depth-first search begins from a specific vertex and traverses each branch as far as possible prior to backtracking the steps in the depth first search. The visited edges are to be tracked. To allow backtracking, we employ a stack data structure for constructing DFS. Figure 11.3 shows an example for a depth first search. If the nodes allotted is four and the edges allotted is six, the depth first search from vertex one are: 1, 2, 0, 3.

11.3.3 Shortest path

The shortest path among two vertexes is where the total edges weight to be travelled is the smallest. The two shortest path algorithms are Dijkstra's shortest path algorithm and the Bellman–Ford algorithm. Dijkstra's algorithm discovers the

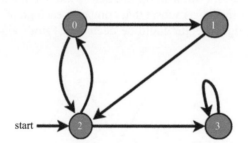

Figure 11.2   BFS algorithm

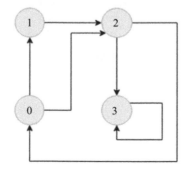

Figure 11.3   Depth-first search algorithm

direct path among nodes and uses the edges' weights to predict the path that reduces the overall distance amongst the origin node and the remaining nodes. The Bellman–Ford algorithm output the shortest distance from a particular node to all other nodes. Figure 11.4 shows the shortest path from vertex 1 to vertex 6.

11.3.4   Cycle detection

A cycle is a graph path that has the same starting and ending vertices. This path is a cycle if we start at one vertex, move down a path, then return to the initial vertex. The process of detecting these cycles is known as cycle detection. There are two cycle detection algorithms. Floyd's cycle-finding algorithm is a pointer algorithm with two pointers that move at different speeds through an order. It explains how this algorithm uses Linked Lists and what the results are. Brent's cycle detection algorithm employs a two-pointer approach as well. We keep one pointer stationary until the end of the loop and then relocate it to the other pointer at every power of two. The least power of two at which they come across determines the start of the cycle. By lowering the number of calls, improves Floyd's algorithm's constant factor. Figure 11.5 shows the formation of the graph in a cycle.

11.3.5   Minimum spanning tree

A minimum spanning tree links all the edges with the least totality of edge weights and not have any cycles. Prim's algorithm detects the minimum spanning tree from a graph. It identifies the edges subset that comprises each graph vertex such that the summation of the edges weight could be decreased. Prim's algorithm begins from

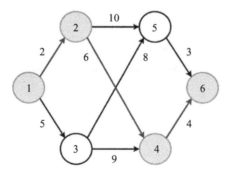

Figure 11.4   Shortest path algorithm

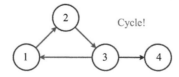

Figure 11.5   Cycle in a graph

the single node and examines all the nearby nodes with all the associated edges at each stage. The edges with the least weights do not create cycles in the graph. Kruskal's algorithm considers the graph as input and discovers the subset of the graph's edges to create a tree with each edge. It has the least amount of weights out of all the trees that are found in the graph. Figure 11.6 shows the working of minimum spanning tree.

11.3.6 Strongly connected components

If each edge in a graph can be reached from any edge, the graph is said to be strongly connected. The Kosaraju algorithm is used for locating strongly connected components (SCC) in a graph. It is founded on the premise that if one can reach a vertex v from vertex u, then one should go vertex u from vertex v and they are said as strongly connected are in a strongly connected sub-graph. To locate strongly connected components of a directed graph, Tarjan's Algorithm is utilized. This approach can be implemented using DFS traversal. Strongly connected components can be seen in the DFS tree. When the root of a subtree is discovered, the entire subtree can be viewed. That subtree is a single component with a lot of connections. Figure 11.7 shows the strongly connected components with edges red, green, and yellow.

11.3.7 Topical sorting

The vertices of a topological sorting are in linear order in which vertex x appears before vertex y for every directed vertex (x,y) in the order. Kahn's topological sort algorithm works by finding vertices with no incoming edges and removing all

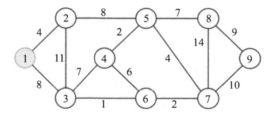

Figure 11.6. Minimum spanning tree

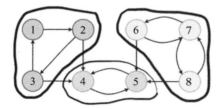

Figure 11.7 Strongly connected components

outgoing edges from these vertices. Figure 11.8 shows a topological ordering of edges. Here, edge 3 come after edges 1 and 2. Likewise, edge 8 come after edges 6 and 7.

11.3.8   Graph coloring

Graph coloring assigns colors to graph nodes while guaranteeing that specific constraints are met. The most frequent graph coloring approach is vertex coloring. Vertex coloring uses k colors to color the graph edges, with no two neighboring edges having the identical color. Edge coloring and facial coloring are two other coloring approaches. A chromatic number is the least quantity of colors required to color it.

The greedy coloring for a given vertex ordering can be computed by an algorithm that runs in linear time. The algorithm checks through the vertices in the given sequence, assigning a color to each as it goes. Numbers can represent colors, and each vertex is assigned the color with the lowest number that is not already in use by one of its neighbors. To find the smallest available color, count the number of neighbors of each color in an array, then scan the array for the index of its first zero. Figure 11.9 shows the edge coloring using four colors.

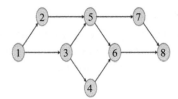

Figure 11.8   Topological ordering

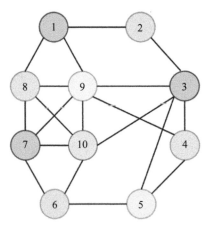

Figure 11.9   Graph coloring

11.3.9 Maximum flow

A graph can be represented as a flow network, with edge weights representing flow capacity. The maximum flow problem requires us to create a flow path that allows us to achieve the highest feasible flow rate. The Ford–Fulkerson algorithm is a solution to the problem of max-flow min-cut. That is, how much flow can a network process at a given time if it has vertices and edges between those vertices with specific weights. Flow can refer to anything, although it most commonly refers to data flowing over a computer network.

The Edmonds–Karp algorithm is simply a BFS-based version of the Ford–Fulkerson method for discovering augmenting pathways. The perception is that each time we observe an augmenting path, one of the vertex turn out to be saturated, and the interval between the vertex and s will be lengthier if it acts in another augmenting path later. The distance of a simple path is also constrained by V. Figure 11.10 shows the maximum flow of a network for finding the value of final flow.

11.3.10 Matching

Matching is several edges with no shared vertices in a graph. If a matching comprises the most feasible set of edges corresponding to as several vertices as possible, it is called a maximum matching. The Hopcroft–Karp algorithm takes a bipartite graph as input and returns a maximum cardinality matching – a set of as many edges as feasible with no two edges sharing an endpoint. The assignment problem can be solved using the Hungarian matching technique to identify maximum-weight matchings in bipartite graphs. An adjacency matrix, in which the weights of edges are the entries, can represent a bipartite graph.

The bloom technique can be used to create a maximum matching on any graph. By decreasing cycles in the graph to reveal augmenting pathways, it improves the Hungarian technique. Furthermore, the Hungarian technique is limited to weighted bipartite networks, but the blooming technique applies to any graph. The bloom algorithm is a maximum graph matching algorithm with polynomial time. Figure 11.11 shows a bipartite graph corresponding to two sets of vertices represented in pink and blue.

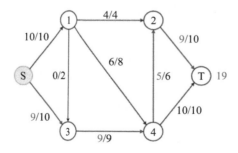

Figure 11.10   Maximum flow graph

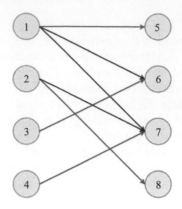

Figure 11.11   Matching graph

11.4   Basic concepts of graphs

Once a graph is generated some of the important things are degree, clustering coefficient, and distance.

- Degree: The degree of a node represents a number of connections of each node have.
- Clustering coefficient: It denotes the proportion of edges between each node divided by the edges possibly between them.
- Distance: It shows the number edges in the shortest path between nodes.

11.5   Importance of a node

Like graph, each node of a graph also has basic concepts. They are,

- *Centrality* is a vital thought used for graphs to find the foremost important nodes. For instance, one will determine the most influential actor within the social network that we have created beforehand victimization the centrality of that node. Let us take a glance at some social network analysis measures and see however they work and once they ought to be utilized in the network analysis applications.
- *Degree centrality* assigns an importance score to the nodes in keeping with the amount of incoming and outgoing relationships from that node. Usually, there exists two measures of degree centrality in directed graphs; indegree and out-degree wherever the previous one represents the amount of incoming edges to it node and also the latter one represents the number of outgoing edges from that node. If the perimeters represent positive relations like friendship, indegree are often taken as a sort of popularity. Thus, the upper the degree of a node, the a lot of vital it is in an exceedingly graph.

- *Eigen centrality* may be a live of the importance of a node supported its neighbors. In distinction to degree centrality, we will determine nodes with influence over the total network not simply the connected ones to that node. If a node is connected to extremely vital nodes, it will have a better Eigencentrality value.
- *Closeness position* measures every node supported its closeness to any or all the opposite nodes inside the network.
- *Betweenness centrality* quantifies the amount of times a node lies on the shortest path between other nodes. If the node has high betweenness centrality then it plays a big role within the network.

11.6 Applications of graph analytics

Due to the extreme predicted market increase, graph analytics is critical. A new graph analytics industry analysis reported that the graph analytics market was worth $600 million in 2019 and is predicted to develop to $2.5 billion by 2024. Several graph analytics algorithms comprising simple heuristics to demanding algorithms aim to find optimal solutions. Different algorithms might be used depending on the value of the solution.

- *Clustering*: Objects are grouped according to their characteristics. Machine learning, data mining, statistics, image processing, and various other physical and social scientific applications all use it.
- *Partitioning*: Identifying the smallest number of crossed edges. It is used to uncover flaws in data and communication networks and detect communities in social networks.
- *Shortest path:* Calculate the shortest path among two virtual nodes. It is utilized to solve problems like social network analysis, transportation logistics, and various other optimization issues.
- *Widest path*: A weighted graph predicts a path between two chosen vertices that maximize the path minimum edge weight. It is employed in IP traffic routing and traffic-sensitive path planning.
- *Connected components*: The sub-regions of a graph for which every sub-region is firmly associated are strongly connected components. It is a tool for analyzing social networks.
- *Page Rank*: This is a metric for how popular a website is. It is employed in social network analysis and recommendation systems, and natural science for new applications.

  Statistique, application programming, and management study is used in regular analytics to reveal insights. Graph analytics examines relationships between items using graph-specific methods. Graph analytics is the only place to find congregating, segregating, PageRank, and shortest path algorithms.
- Journalism

The International Consortium of Investigative Journalists investigation on the Panama Papers is an example of employing graph analytics to recognize links networks. This study revealed how authoritarian leaders and politicians exploited a complicated web of husk firms to hide their prosperity from the ordinary people eye. Reporters extract data from the documents on companies in administrations using graph analytics and document extraction tools and traverse through the data in the documents to identify the companies actual proprietors.

1. **Compliance**
   Graph analytics identify fraudsters and culprits and illegal activities such as concealing and payments to approved things. Analysts combine public network, chatting, toll call, and electronic mails to produce a graph. Administrators use that graph to discover hazards posed by non-obvious patterns of relationship.

2. **National security**
   National intelligence agencies employ graph analytics to detect illegal activities, even though it is contentious. The conversation of distrusted and confirmed persons is gathered and evaluated to discover non-obvious ties and probable crimes.

3. **Fraud detection**
   Graph analytics is employed in scam revealing in firms that operate with telecommunications, e-business platforms, and banking.

4. **Supply chain optimization**
   Graph analytics algorithms like shortest path and partitioning help air passenger carrier, carriage networks, and supply chain networks to improve their routes.

5. **Utility optimization**
   Companies that deliver services including aquatic, garbage, power, dams, and natural gas can use graph analysis to design the network.

6. **Social network analysis**
   Social networking platforms like Instagram, Spotify, and LinkedIn are based on relationships and connections. In social media networks, graph analytics aids in the identification of influencers and communities. Owing to the growing social network users and growing customer distrust of more traditional marketing, social network influencer marketing is becoming more popular.

11.6.1   Overview of graph analytics libraries

For academics and scientists working in a variety of fields, understanding massive graphs is critical. A variety of graph analytics libraries have been created over time. igraph, NetworkX, and the Stanford Network Analysis Project are all excellent examples.

- **igraph**
  igraph allows us to analyze graphs in various ways, from simple operations like adding and removing nodes to more advanced theoretical constructs like community discovery. We can plot with an igraph object using the plot() function, just like we can with the network package. igraph handles large networks efficiently. It is used in many open-source packages.

- **NetworkX**

  NetworkX is a graph and network analysis library written in Python. NetworkX is designed to work with big real-world graphs. It has the potential to draw small graphs with NetworkX. You can transfer network data and draw with other programs. It can construct random graphs. To make a graph object in networkx, use the edge and node lists. Add each edge and its accompanying characteristics to graph g by looping through the rows of the edge list. Similarly, you add these node properties by looping through the rows in the node list. One can easily install NetworkX by using the following commands:

  pip install networkx

- **SNAP**

  The Stanford Network Analysis Platform is a network analysis and graph mining framework is written in C++. It can handle networks with many nodes and edges with ease. It manages big graphs quickly, analyses structural features, produces regular and random graphs, and supports node and edge features. Aside from handling enormous graphs, another advantage of SNAP is that networks and their properties are entirely dynamic, meaning they may be changed at little cost during the computation.

11.7 Graph database

Graph database is a platform used for creating and manipulating the graphs. Graphs usually include Nodes, Axis, and Edges which help us in mentioning the properties of a data and stored in a spiralized manner not as in relational databases.

The process of analyzing the data with a help of graph is termed as graph analytics. It uses nodes to represent the datapoints and the relationship between the nodes are expressed in terms of edges. A database is highly required to support the formats and hence a dedicated database is usually assigned or a database which supports multiple formats including graphs are considered.

11.7.1 Graph database types

Graph databases are broadly classified into property graphs and resource description framework (RDF) graphs. Property graphs emphasizes on analytics and the data integration are carried over using RDF graphs. Both the classes of graphs consist of edges and vertices, where vertices are collection of points and edges are connection between those points.

11.7.2 Property graph model

Figure 11.12 explains about property graph well. These types of graphs are used model the relationship between points(nodes) which helps to make analytics based on the points and edges of the graph.

Labels are the names of the points and the edges. Relationships between the points could be identified with the help of the arrow heads of the connections. Being versatile in nature, property graphs are being used in wide range of industries including manufacturing, retail outlets, safety, and many more.

11.7.3   RDF graphs

RDF graphs are majorly used to represent information about the resources. RDF conform to a set of W3C (Worldwide Web Consortium) standards which are designed for representing statements or relations. These types of graphs are mostly used in knowledge graphs. They could easily represent a complex formation and the same point could be used to give multiple information as shown in Figure 11.13. It has many sentences clubbed together and one such sentences could be, Bob a person is interested in The Mona Lisa Painting which was drawn by

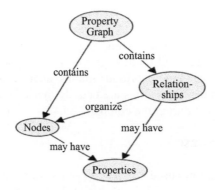

Figure 11.12   Property graph. Source: *http://graphdatamodeling.com/Graph%20Data%20Modeling/GraphDataModeling/page/PropertyGraphs.html*

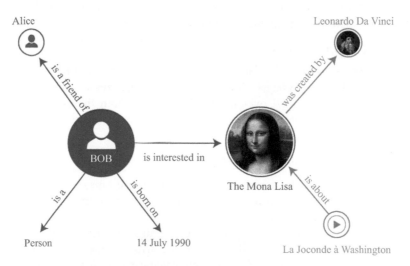

Figure 11.13   RDF graph

Leonardo Da Vinci. These RDF graphs could also be used to represent Rich semantic in a single graph.

RDF graphs are also called as RDF triple as it has three elements, the tow vertices which are connected and representing the subject and object of a sentence. All the vertices and the edges are identified using a unique resource identifier (URI). RDF are widely used in all government organizations and health care industries because of its multiples usability [8].

The major advantage of using graph databases is, reduced running time of queries which helps in identifying the relationship between points which takes hours or weeks in relational database models.

11.8   Popular graph databases

There are many graph databases which are NoSQL databases, which provides high-speed retravel. The query language used with graph databases are GraphQL, AQL, Gremlin, SPARQL, and Cypher. The top ten popularly used graph databases are the following: Neo4j, Microsoft Azure Cosmos DB, OrientDB, ArangoDB, Virtuoso, JanusGraph, Amazon Neptune, GraphDB, Giraph, and AllegroGraph.

1. **Neo4j**

   Neo4j, which is considered to be the most used graph database. This database is completely open source and are labeled graph database model. As like most of the graph databases, nodes, relationships and properties are the key elements of Neo4j. Neo4j can be used in both linux as well as Windows operating systems and it supports most of the high-level programming languages including .Net, Python, Ruby, Scala, Java, Go, and many more.

2. **Microsoft Azure CosmosDB**

   Microsoft owned Cosmos DB is a globally distributed graph database model service provider, which helps in managing planet scale [6]. It was launched in the year 2017. This DB is also classified as NoSQL database. In CosmosDB, the objects are automatically indexed. The performance of the DB is considered to be good. Cosmos DB have two types of indexes, range indexing and spatial indexing. Range indexing supports ORDER BY queries and on the other side Spatial indexing supports Spatial queries.

   Cosmos Db is hosted in the Azure platform and supports APIs in various languages including, Java, .Net, Nodejs, Go, and many more high-level languages. The Graph API and the supported languages of cosmos DB are shown in Figure 11.14.

3. **OrientDB**

   An open source, java-based NoSQL database management system, owned by Orient DB ltd which was initially released on 2010 and had a stable release on February 2021. This is a multi-model database which supports many models including document, graph, and object models. The relationships are

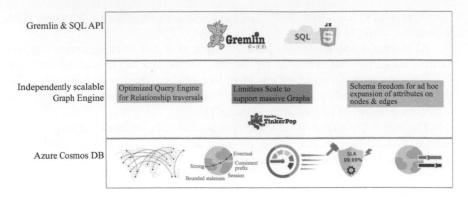

Figure 11.14   Azure Cosmos DB – graph API PaaS. Source*: https://docs.*
microsoft.com/en-us/azure/cosmos-db/graph-introduction

managed in graphs to make the query retravel more efficient. The indexing in OrientDB is performed using B-tree and hash indexing. One of the significance of OrientDB is that it can store up to 120,000 records each second and it also supports all high-level programming languages.

4. **ArangoDB**
   A multi-model database which supports graphs, document, and key/value data models, and have its owned Query language named as ArangoDB Query Language (AQL) which is used to create and manipulate data. Its free and also open sourced which works on all OS platforms. It allows the users to model their data in more flexible manner. This DB model is also distributed-based model enhancing the user experience and security of the data. ArangoDB has geoJSON support which enriches the search queries with geo-location.

5. **Virtuoso**
   A secure, cross platform, and high performing data server, which delivers data access, data integration, and multi-modal data management. Not only graph databases Virtuoso also supports other DB models including Native XML, relational models, and RDF store data models. It is owned by OpenLink Software and launched in the year 1998, it supports all major high-level languages. It has the ability to deliver the relationships between the nodes in many forms which makes the user to understand and retrieve the information.

6. **JanusGraph**
   Completely free and open sourced database developed by Linux Foundation and released in the year 2017. JanusGraph is developed using java and supports high-level languages such as Clojure, Java, and Python. Its highly durable which could even support thousands of users accessing complex graph traversals concurrently. It also supports various data sources and

includes advanced search capabilities. It also supports variety of visualization tools like Graphexp, and Key Lines.

7. **Amazon Neptune**

Neptune was designed and released in 2017 by Amazon. It works in cloud platform which is schema free and supports variety of high-level languages like C#, GO, java, and Python. It is a high-performance engine capable of storing billion of graphs and able to process and fetch the results in very short time. It supports all classes of graph database and allows the user to build the query in an easy way. It is encrypted using HTTPS client server connectivity which makes the connection more secured between the server and the client. It takes continuous backup to Amazon S3 and which helps the data to be more reliable and Secured.

8. **GraphDB**

Graph DB was developed by ontonext and launched in the year 2002. It is a high efficient RDF-based database which has external index synchronization support [11]. It was developed over Java platform and able to process languages such as .Net, C#, PHP, and Python. It allows the user to configure complex search and retrieve the information in a short span of time. It indexes the data automatically which helps information retrieval easier.

9. **Apache Giraph**

A high scalable graph processing system to perform graph processing in big data. It is developed over Java and ready of handling huge data simultaneously [2,3,9,10]. Currently it is being used by Facebook to analyze the users and the connections created by them. The entire system was developed in Google labs funded by Apache Foundation and are implemented since 2010.

10. **AllegroGraph**

AllegroGraph is a product of Franz Inc. which was released in 2004. It supports multiple models including Document, graph, and RDF models. It supports almost all the major languages including, C#, Java, and Python. It supports most of the query processing including, rollbacks, and check points which helps the user to go back to some points if needed. It also handles scheduled backup and point in time recovery system. It is a triple level secured system. The AllegroGraph RDF are scripted using the JavaScripts.

11.9 Graph analytic tool

Graph theory plays an major role in data science technology. In this data science, mathematics can be applied completely to know and get the relationship between each data. The major data sources called Google, Amazon, Facebook, and all eCommerce data bases are applying graph theory concepts only. Graph theory software converts the work easier for this databases. Tools used in this graph theory software are denoted as Graph Analytic Tool or Graph Analytics, which is used for determining the relationship between each and every graph as well as the strength of entire graph. The main objective of graph analytics is to analyze the pairwise relationship of nodes as well as structural characteristics. To simulate the graph

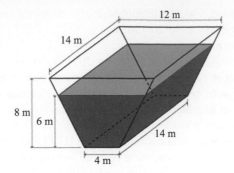

Figure 11.15   Plotting using Tikz

analytics, some of the tools are used. These tools can work on various operating systems such as Linux, Unix, MacOS, and Windows.

1. **Tikz and PGF**

   Tikz and progressive graphics file (PGF) are different software used as a same package. These two tools are working with the help of TeX language. Standard structures including the drawing of points, lines, arrows, paths, circles, ellipses, and polygons can be drawn. PGF is a lower-level language, while TikZ is a set of higher-level macros that use PGF vector-style graphics are created using this tools. Complex graph are generated using Tikz and visual diagrams are generated by PGF. The scientific area applied are Astronomy, Biology, Chemistry, Computer Science, Economics, Geography, Geometry, etc. (Figure 11.15).

2. **Gephi**

   Gephi tool is mainly supported to data analysis. It was an free downloadable software. This tool uses a 3D render engine to generate a complete graph. Coding of Gephi is written in Java on NetBeans platform. It provides only one force-directed layout. It has the capacity of 800K nodes or edges. It supports in the scientific area of network science, infovis, visualization, visual analytics, exploratory data analysis, graph, graph namely, graph theory, etc. (Figure 11.16).

3. **NetworkX**

   This tool is working with the help of Python Library. This supports graph and networks. It is used for conversion of graph from various formats. Structure, function, and dynamics of complex networks can be studied. Random graphs can be generated using NetworkX. It can support large real-world graph over than 10 million nodes and 100 million edges. It is mainly portable for social network analysis (Figure 11.17).

4. **LaTeXDraw**

   LaTeXDraw is a widely used tool for documentation and graphics editor. It is built using Java language. Set of macros in built in LaTeX is enabled and

Figure 11.16   Photo network visualization with Gephi

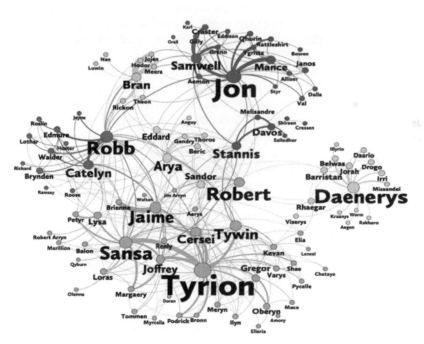

Figure 11.17   Social network analysis using NetworkX

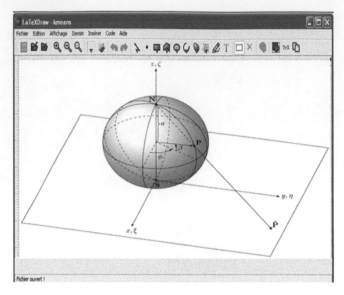

Figure 11.18   LaTexDraw image

different graphical shapes are also drawn. It was a markup language for high-quality typesetting. LaTeXDraw can be used to generate PSTricks code and directly create PDF or PS pictures. It can run on all platforms (Figure 11.18).

5. **Sage**

   Sage is a mathematics software as well as an open source tool to improve the functionality of mathematics. It is used for plotting graphs and hypergraphs. It can produce 2D, 3D graphs and animated plots. Visualization meant the activities that serve to review and gift in a very graphical type, and to use such graphical forms analytically. Nearly any reasonably information is pictured, and therefore there are a variety of visualizations such as pictures, maps, timelines, graphs, or tables, and therefore the like [5]. Relevant techniques embrace plotting and mapping (Figure 11.19).

6. **Inkscape**

   It was an vector style graphic generating tool. It is in scalable vector graphics format. It is used for generating graph, tree, and digraphs. This creates rectangles, ellipses, polygons, arcs, spirals, stars, and 3D boxes. These objects are filled with solid colors, patterns, radial, or linear color gradients and their borders may be stroked, both with adjustable transparency. Embedding and optional tracing of raster graphics is also supported, enabling the editor to create vector graphics from photos and other raster sources. Created shapes can be further manipulated with transformations, such as moving, rotating, scaling and skewing. Figure 11.20 represents the creation of car image using Inkscape tool.

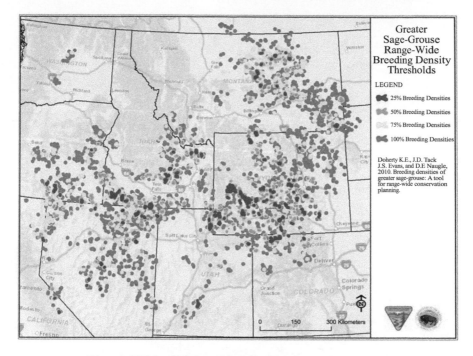

Figure 11.19   Substantial risk identifying using sage

Figure 11.20   Image created using Inkscape

7. **NodeXL**

NodeXl is an open source tool created based on Microsoft Excel, used for creating network graphs [12]. It creates an Excel environment for generating graph. While entering network edge in a list, graphs are created. It mainly supports social network analysis, automation of task, etc. Figure 11.21 shows the NodeXl output for social media.

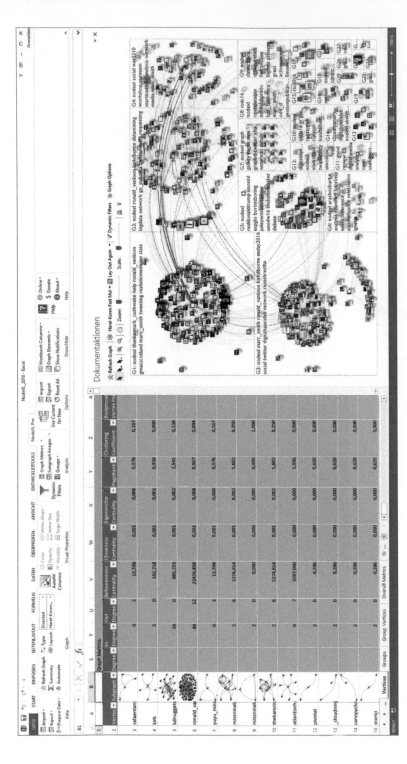

Figure 11.21   NodeXL output for social media

11.10 Conclusion

Graphs can be used to solve many complex problems like mapping, route finding, matching relationship. Networks graphs are rapidly growing nowadays because of the large set of data growth. An efficient processing of big data is necessary to gather and organize large volume of data. This can be handled by graph analytics concept. This chapter provides an overview of nodes, graphs, and graph analytics. The widely used graph databases and analytical tools are explained. The demonstration output of each tools are shown in the chapter.

References

[1] Nguyen D, Lenharth A and Pingali K. A lightweight infrastructure for graph analytics. In *Proceedings of the Twenty-Fourth ACM Symposium on Operating Systems Principles*, 2013 Nov 3, pp. 456–471.

[2] Ahmed NK, Duffield N, Neville J and Kompella R. Graph sample and hold: a framework for big-graph analytics. In *Proceedings of the 20th ACM SIGKDD International Conference on Knowledge Discovery and Data Mining*, 2014 Aug 24, pp. 1446–1455.

[3] Nisar MU, Fard A and Miller JA. Techniques for graph analytics on big data. In *2013 IEEE International Congress on Big Data*, 2013 Jun 27, IEEE, pp. 255–262.

[4] Lenharth A, Nguyen D and Pingali K. Parallel graph analytics. Communications of the ACM. 2016;59(5):78–87.

[5] Fu Z, Personick M and Thompson B. MapGraph: a high level API for fast development of high performance graph analytics on GPUs. In *Proceedings of Workshop on Graph Data Management Experiences and Systems* 2014 Jun 22, pp. 1–6.

[6] Hoque I and Gupta I. LFGraph: simple and fast distributed graph analytics. In *Proceedings of the First ACM SIGOPS Conference on Timely Results in Operating Systems* 2013 Nov 3, pp. 1–17.

[7] Xia Y, Tanase IG, Nai L, et al. Graph analytics and storage. In *2014 IEEE International Conference on Big Data (Big Data)*, 2014 Oct 27, IEEE, pp. 942–951.

[8] Wang F, Cui P, Pei J, Song Y and Zang C. Recent advances on graph analytics and its applications in healthcare. In *Proceedings of the 26th ACM SIGKDD International Conference on Knowledge Discovery & Data Mining*, 2020 Aug 23, pp. 3545–3546.

[9] Huang HH and Liu H. Big data machine learning and graph analytics: Current state and future challenges. In *2014 IEEE International Conference on Big Data (Big Data)*, 2014 Oct 27, IEEE, pp. 16–17.

[10] Miller JA, Ramaswamy L, Kochut KJ and Fard A. Research directions for big data graph analytics. In *2015 IEEE International Congress on Big Data*, 2015 Jun 27, IEEE, pp. 785–794.

[11] Ravindra P, Deshpande VV and Anyanwu K. Towards scalable RDF graph analytics on MapReduce. In *Proceedings of the 2010 Workshop on Massive Data Analytics on the Cloud*, 2010 Apr 26, pp. 1–6.

[12] https://www.smrfoundation.org/.

Chapter 12

A study of graph analytics for massive datasets

Neha Gupta[1] and Rashmi Agrawal[1]

Abstract

The analysis and research of data which can be altered into a comprehensive graph is referred to as "graph analytics." Graph-based data analytics is a budding field in both data mining and data visualization and is applied for a wide variety of applications such as network protection, banking, and healthcare, both multi-disciplinary and high impact applications [5]. Despite the fact that many methods have been developed in the past to analyze unstructured collections of multi-dimensional objects, graph analytic technologies are a recent trend that poses several challenges, not only in terms of the output of algorithms that are related to data mining that facilitate algorithmic computational data discovery [3]. Graph analytics primarily aimed to evaluate graph oriented structured data in order to uncover answers to queries (e.g. Identify the person who is the most prominent person in a community? What are the main technology nodes for better practice and decision-making on the internet and urban networks?)

Analysis of graphs has always attracted and has always been an important topic for researchers in the history of computing; however, the rise of the uses of advanced analytics for large amounts of semi-structured or unstructured data and the revolution of big data has lately picked up the interest of the information systems community [1]. The qualitative effect of data, as well as the impact of graph analytics technology on organizations, has affected the requirements for business outcomes. Graph analytics for big data can not only recognize but also visualize crucial insights in big data. Furthermore, graph analytics may assist in identifying associations between different types of data and determining their existence and meaning within the context [2].

In this chapter, we will present the fundamentals of graph analytics and how graphs are related to big data. The chapter will also show some of the most common graph databases and discuss various big data graph analytics approaches which use the massive datasets, as well as different frameworks for each approach. In the latter part of the chapter, various issues and challenges related to big graph analytics will be addressed. A case study for implementation of graph analytics using python will also be discussed.

[1]Faculty of Computer Applications, Manav Rachna International Institute of Research and Studies, India

12.1   Introduction to graph analytics

Graph analytics is one of the most fascinating and important topics in the community of visualization and analysis. In particular, the phrase "graph analytics" refers to the study and analysis of data represented in big graphs [2]. The analysis of the relationships between organizations, such as consumers, goods, operations, and devices, is also known as a network analysis. Organizations use graphical models to obtain insights for marketing or social networks analysis. With the help of graph analytics, companies can create relations between the different data points in order to build a context and provide insights into business decisions in a better informed way. An emerging form of data analytics, graph analytics refers to a combination of analytical methodology which shows the link between diverse entities such as people, places, and things [4].

The analysis of graphs provides a comprehensive solution for the resolution of complex relationships, distant connections between data and the analysis of relationship quality in an easy-to-digest format [6]. Graph analytics offers a broad variety of applications, such as social media analysis, fraud detection, management of resources, genome research, and much more! In order to accelerate data preparation and facilitate flexible data science, organizations increasingly utilize these technologies.

Graph analytics is based on the theory of graphs (a branch of Mathematics). Hands-on urban planning problem gave rise to theory graph. In Konigsberg, the problem began (old city in Russia) [9]. The city was linked by seven bridges with two big islands. Back in 1736, the problem was to build a walkway to cross all seven bridges only once from one part of town to another. A mathematician, Euler, mathematically demonstrated that because of the strange number of bridges this problem did not solve. He reformulated and resolved the issue by removing all characteristics except land masses (called vertex) and connecting bridges (termed as edge) [8]. It was considered a graph in the resulting mathematical structure. Different operations on a graph include adding/removal of a vertex, adding/removing an edge and/or finding closest neighbors (i.e. finding nodes linked to the vertex). The graph analytic models as a set of graphs contain massive and complex data issues. It expresses the pattern of relationships of objects using data's mathematical properties and statistical methods for providing effective algorithmic solutions and finding meaningful patterns [8]. Many organizations, by taking precise and expeditious decisions, compete with their market peers through graph analytics. Various methods are available for analytic charting such as path analysis, connectivity analysis, centrality analysis, and community analysis based on solutions to various types of problems. Each one employs distinct concepts and methodologies to answer distinct analytical issues.

12.2   Techniques used for graph analytics

Various techniques for graph analytic are the following.

12.2.1 Path analytic

Path analytics deals with the easiest way to locate two nodes. Specifying "best" may include optimizing certain functions, crossing some nodes/corners, avoiding nodes/corners, and satisfying certain preferences [7]. For example, on Google maps, weather, traffic, and road conditions will change the shortest path.

12.2.2 Connectivity analytic

The connectivity analysis examines the connection pattern and similarity of graph topologies based on several features [10]. It also determines resiliency, or which node should be the next victim of an intruder. In a social networking graph, for example, Listeners symbolize nodes with more edges of incidence than outgoing edges.

12.2.3 Community analytic

A community is a group of nodes that are more connected to each other than to the outside world. Community analytic is concerned with the detection and patterning of community behavior. For instance, who are the members of the community? Where do they come from? Is the neighborhood stable? Do you have a dominant member of the community? Is the community changing, expanding, dividing, or dying?

The inner degree of a subgraph is the sum of the edges of all vertices in the group. The total of all vertical borders outside the subgraph is called the external cluster degree [12]. Communities are determined by comparing the internal and exterior degrees of clusters.

12.2.4 Centrality analytic

In regard to a particular analysis problem, the central analytical approach finds relevant nodes (influencers) inside the network. The value of the node depends on the importance they play in a community. We are all aware that every node in inside a network cannot be important. Certain nodes are more essential in some respects than others. A central server in a computer network, for example, or a junction station in a transportation network, to name a few examples [11]. We need to find the nodes that are the most connected to other nodes and would cause the most disruption to other nodes' communication if they were removed. Network centrality possesses both centrality and centralization properties. The key is to measure the significance of a node (or edge) based on the position of the network. At the same time, centralization is the metric for a network (not just a single node). If more nodes begin to be larger, the central value of the network will be less variable. This results in a decrease in network centralization.

12.3 Graph databases

A graph database is a specialized platform to create and manipulate graphs. Graphs contain nodes, edges, and properties which are all used in a manner which relational databases are not equipped to do to represent and store data [14]. Graph analysis may be a dedicated graph database or a converged database that supports a range of data models, including graphs. Graph analytics may support a graph format.

12.3.1   There are two popular models of graph databases

Property graphs: The charts are analyzed and interviewed. Property charting is used to model relationships between data and enables the analysis of queries and data based on these connections. An image graph contains vertices which can contain detailed information on a subject and borders which indicate the relation between the vertices [13]. The vertices and edges are associated with characteristics known as properties. Due to their versatility, property graphs are used in various industries and sectors such as finance, production, public security, retail, and many more.

RDF graphs: The RDF diagram focuses on data inclusion. DF graphs (RDF stands for resource description framework) comply with all standards set for the representation of comprehensive metadata and master data by the W3C (Worldwide Web Consortium). Often they are used for data connections, data integration, and knowledge graphs [12]. They may represent complex concepts in a field or provide rich semantics and data inferences.

Three elements are represented in the RDF model: two vertices connected by the edge that reflect a subject, a prediction, and a sentence's object – this is called RDF threefold. An individual URI or Unique Resource Identifier is used to identify each vertex and edge. The RDF model provides a standard format for publishing data with a clear semantic that enables the exchange of information [13]. The RDF graphs were widely adopted by government agencies, pharmaceutical and health-care organizations.

Graphs and databases provide graph models for data relationships. They allow users to conduct 'cross-sectional queries' based on connections and use graph algorithms to detect patterns, pathways, communities, influencers, single failure points, and other relations that allow more effective analysis against mass data quantities [15]. The graphs have the authority to analyze them, their perspectives, and their ability to link different sources of information.

In the analysis of graphs, algorithms investigate the paths and distance between vertices, the significance of vertices, and the clustering of vertical lines. For example, algorithms are often concerned with incoming edges, the importance of nearby vertical areas and other indicators to determine their importance [14].

Since graphic databases specifically store relations, queries, and algorithms which use vertical connectivity can be executed in sub seconds instead of hours or days. Users do not have to run countless connections and the data can be used more easily to analyze the world around us and to learn about the machine. Important graph databases are as follows:

- *Neo4j* (*Neo Technology*): Neo4j, the world-leading graph database, is a scalable, powerful and resilient business-friendly database. Neo4j features high-speed cross-cutting, scale to triple nodes and relationships, declarative graph query language, etc. [12].

- *DEX*: DEX is an efficient system for the querying graphics graphs. DEX comprises the best honesty model for temporary graphs. In different networks, DEX enables graph query for social network analysis, pattern recognition, link analysis, and keyword search.
- *InfoGrid*: It is a web-based graph database which is open-source and built in Java. It contains many key components of software that make it easier to create web applications on a graph.
- *Titan*: Titan is an extremely scalable graph database with billions of vertices and trillions of edges for querying and storing graphs. Titan supports many concurrent users running the complicated graphical cross-sections in real time. It provides quick answers to extremely complex inquiries and moreover offers other significant characteristics such as global graph data analysis with the integration of Apache Graph.

12.4   Big data graph analytics

Google has demonstrated its superiority as a search engine by finding direct and indirect links between the huge volumes of data. Google has adopted a graph-centered approach and graphical analytics techniques to represent and model relations between documents in order to understand the semantics and contexts among the varied data and to find relevant details [8]. By examining the large and complex data accessible over the Internet, the most pertinent information can be collected. Devices, systems, individuals, and other organizations are more connected than ever in the world of today. As the number of sources evolves, the underlying interconnections between them need to be established. This exponential rise in global data coined the term "big data" as a description of vast datasets produced from many heterogeneous sources [10]. The collection and analysis of these data allows us to gain a deep understanding of the hidden values, which provide new ways to explore new values. With increasing data diversity and volume, more specialized methods are needed to discover the useful information that is hidden.

Though large data generated from a variety of sources may seem discrete on the surface, but all of them are nodes of a broader network connecting them through ways of complex relations. Modern big data have become more and more complex in the form of large graphs/networks. These include large and complex networks [12]. These graphs/networks are transient, bright, and complex in addition to their large sizes. Thus, these massive graph-structured data are considered as "big data graphs."

Graphical analytics have always been a fascinating topic for researchers in computational history, but the large-scale data revolution has drawn the attention of the computer science fraternity in recent years since the advanced analysis has been increasingly used in vast amounts of semi-structured or unstructured data [14]. The need for advanced graphic analytics to derive something from big data is all the more important as the sources, formats, and amount of information continue to expand in today's digital environment. In this context, it is necessary to explain the

qualitative effects of data and the impact of graph analytics technology on organizations seeking to identify the cause, effect, interconnections, and influence of
events on the business results. As a result, big data graph analytics would be able to
not only recognize but also visualize crucial insights in big data [15]. Furthermore,
they can identify patterns in the results and assess their nature and significance
within the context. New technologies and algorithms must be built on a regular
basis to assist company stakeholders in optimizing their main business processes
and opening up new opportunities.

12.4.1 Defining big data graph analytics

Big data graph analytics is a fascinating new field in data analytics. The big data
graph analysis is a modeling, storage, recovery, and analysis methodology used for
large data volumes. The processing of graph-structured data is done using a combination of graphics, theoretical and graphic database techniques. These techniques
help researchers to understand the nature of a large network and how it changes
under different circumstances, such as identify sub-graphs similar to one particular
pattern, identify interacting sub-groups within a graph, and find ways between pairs
of organizations that meet different limitations [13].

The big data graph analytics is fundamentally an essential and powerful
method for big data information exploration. The big data underlying graph analytics may be modeled or arranged as a sequence of graphs in a native manner.
Graph-structured data are used to visualize and understand linkages between
devices and network entities [11]. The pair of wise relations between objects,
people, or network nodes can be defined. Big data analysis shows insights into the
capabilities and orientation of hidden big data relationships.

Examples of strength of the relationship are the following:

(a)   How often does one interact with another individual or nodes?
(b)   Which other people or nodes are likely to join the conversation?

Some of the examples of directions of the relationship are the following:

(a)   Identify the node that has started the conversation?
(b)   Is that a two-way dialogue or any one node is leading the dialog?
(c)   Under what circumstances and how much is it sent to others?

Big graphic analysis describes and reinforces certain dynamic relationships
through the use of mathematical graph theory principles.

12.4.2 Relationship of graph analytics to big data

The fundamental concepts of links and relationships drive the OSNs (e.g.,
LinkedIn, Twitter, and Facebook). Facebook users may use services such as Graph
Search in order to locate friends who like or live in one cricket team, and the site
also suggests "people you should meet" because of the shared connections that
have been created by two or more unconnected people. LinkedIn focuses on
assisting professionals in expanding their social networks [11]. Furthermore, a key

factor driving the field of business analysis is the ability to evaluate and understand certain relationships. Leaders of business are still interested in who is the most influential social influencers are and who is able to exploit the views of others? Take a major question: How can two or more people are connected with social media? This question can seem straightforward at first glance, but upon closer inspection, it becomes more complicated. The simplest issue is to understand how two or more people can be linked on Facebook [10]. These relations may be between friends or between friends of friends. Often two people can only communicate by exchanging a few "Likes." This knowledge may be useful to the company. So, out of the trillion Facebook users, we want to identify those specific individuals so that we can reach out to them.

12.5   Big data graph analytics approaches

Big data graph analytics have been classified majorly into four broad categories.

12.5.1   In-memory big data graph analytics

In memory graph analytics, users can easily recognize patterns, analyze large quantities of fly big datasets, and perform operations in real time. Important performance and cost efficiency include the advantage of in-memory graph analysis. The following are some of the most popular large graph analytics systems that use this approach:

- *Pregel*: Pregel is a graph-parallel distributed analytics engine that is scalable, in-memory, and fault-tolerant. It concentrates on the synchronous bulk sync (BSP) model of Valiant. Pregel's C++ (API) programming application is a graph method that is suitable for "think as a vertex" researchers. The input graph is downloaded once at Pregel at the start of a program and each operation is done. By conducting calculation on locally stored data Pregel ensures the data location (to avoid overhead communication).
- *Apache Giraph*: Apache Giraph is an iterative graphical framework for big graphs. It is also used for social media data evaluation. Apache Giraph is used by companies such as Yahoo, Facebook, and Twitter. These businesses are changing Giraph to meet their needs. Pregel's open source equivalent, Apache Giraph, is being developed at Google. With several new functions, such as master computing, edge-oriented input, sharp aggregator, and out of core computation, Apache Giraph is extending a simple Pregel model. For coordination, checkpoint, and failure recovery systems, Apache Giraph uses the ZooKeeper Apache. Apache Giraph is a wide-ranging forum for the use of structured data potential.
- *GraphLab*: GraphLab is a big, distributed parallel graph analytics engine with asynchronous graph. GraphLab allows vertices to be asynchronously processed according to scheduler [15], as opposed to Pregel, which uses the BSP model. In contrast to Pregel that uses message-passing programming model, GraphLab

features include automated defect tolerance, customizable graph algorithms, and mutual memory abstraction. The common theory of memory is used by GraphLab to the distributed environment through the relaxation of the scheduling requirements, improvement of the execution model and implementation of a new distributed data graph, execution engines, and fault tolerance systems.

- *Ringo*: Ringo is an interactive graph analysis system that blends high efficiency with speedy and scalable performance analysis. It has a number of advantages:

1. The Python interface is simple to use.
2. Extensive array of more than 200 sophisticated graphic operations and algorithms, integrated table and graphics, and aiding effective graphics generation and transformations between graphs and tables.
3. Tracking the origin of objects facilitates the exploitation parallel and later replication of research by the data scientist of a number of data exploration routes.

- *Trinity*: Trinity is a distributed graph technology that is elastic and memory-based. Trinity's primary aim is to optimize memory and connectivity costs while keeping in mind that the entire graph is spread around the memory cloud. It is intended primarily to support quick graph scanning and simultaneous graph calculations. To support large-scale graphics, Trinity organizes the memory of several computers into the geographically dispersed virtual address area. In addition, graphic access patterns in both offline and online calculations are utilized to reduce memory and connectivity costs for better results. Trinity supports a language called Trinity Specification Language for bridging the data storage and graph model.
- *PowerGraph*: PowerGraph is coded in C++ and is a distributed computing system that is scalable and graph-parallel. PowerGraph can simulate both the computationally powerful asynchronous GraphLab model and the extremely parallel bulk synchronous Pregel model of computation. In order to break large hills, factor vertex programs over edges and expose more parallelism, PowerGraph uses the computer collection-appliance-scatter (GAS) model. In a distributed context, PowerGraph allows vertex splitting to efficiently place its large-scale graphs. PowerGraph reduces the communication and storage costs of large distributed power-law graphs by using vertex partitioning and fast-greedy heuristic arrays.
- *GraphX*: GraphX is a graph analytics engine that can be used with distributed data flow systems like Spark. GraphX provides a configurable graph interface to represent existing graph APIs. The API makes tabular and graph data composition easier with unstructured data and enables the same physical data as objects and graphs to be seen without the use of reproduction or movement of data. GraphX unifies parallel data structures and parallel graph systems.

12.5.2 *SSD-based big data graph analytics*

Analyzing massive-scale graphs necessitates the use of a cluster of computers. The average memory is also higher than that of the graph. The use of low cost commodity solid-state drives would solve this problem (SSDs). FlashGraph is a popular framework that adopts this method.

FlashGraph: FlashGraph is a scalable graphical processing engine that fixes SSDs with a user-space SSD file system for the vertex status of the storage and e-lists on SSDs. FlashGraph uses SAFS (set-associative file system), and a user-space file system to create both high IOPS and lightweight caching for non-uniform memory and I/O arrays. With the selective edge list access required by SSD graph algorithms, FlashGraph reduces data access. It increases the I/O requests conservatively to reduce the CPU consumption and increase the I/O efficiency. For a wide range of graphic algorithms and optimizations, FlashGraph provides a plain, scalable programming interface.

12.5.3 Disk-based big data graph analytics

Large graphs, including biological networks, social networks, and chemical compounds, can be extremely difficult to analyze. Many distributed engines analyze large graphs efficiently, but because of efficient graph partitioning and graph distribution on a cluster of computers, they are incurred in overhead costs. Cluster management and fault tolerance are also important for distributed graph processing. Many disk-based graph processing systems have been suggested as solutions to these problems.

Some of the following are mentioned:

GraphChi: GraphChi is a disk-based graph processing unit for computing large-scale graphs. GraphChi may use a number of advanced machine learning, data mining, and graphing algorithms to analyze graphs of billions of edges. GraphChi gathers neighbor data first by reading the edge values and then calculates the new vertices and then spreads the new values to neighbors across the edges. The new ones are then dispersed by the values. GraphChi can process large graphs in reasonable time if random I/O access by using Parallel Sliding Windows is reduced to a minimum (PSW).

X-Stream: X-Stream is a graphic edge-centric technology for large-scale graph analytics. X-Stream uses streaming partitions to use simultaneous storage media streaming bandwidth. X-Stream exposes the familiar scatter-gathering programming paradigm but works under the concept of storage streaming data. It is close to Pregel and PowerGraph systems.

GridGraph: GridGraph is an extensive graphics system using hierarchical two-tier partitioning on one monitor. In this graphics system, large graphs are divided into single, divided chunks of vertex and twin, partitioned edge blocks.

12.5.4 Shared memory and data flow-based big data graph analytics

Recently, the processing and analysis of large graphs received great interest in alternative dataflow-based approaches, shared memory, and multicore machines. Below are some popular big data graph analytics frameworks focused on data streaming and the concept of shared memory.

Pregelix: Pregelix is an accelerator for graph analysis based on data flow which can handle in- and out-of-core workloads. The Pregel architecture, which can manage multiple user workloads, is free and open source. Pregelix incorporates a PRECEL API to allow large-size graphical analysis with data-parallel query evaluation techniques. It results in more efficient and straightforward out-of-core support, higher throughput and scalability, as well as improved physical versatility and software simplicity.

Ligra: Ligra is a shared-memory programming model for parallel or multi-core computers. Ligra automatically switches between push-based and pull-based operators based on the user-specified threshold.

12.6   Issues and challenges of big data graph analytics

In parallel graphics processing, much progress remains to be done to solve broad graph problems. Many characteristics of graphic problems present significant parallel problems. Some of the major issues and challenges are listed below.

12.6.1   High-degree vertex

High-grade vertices are common in the charts; for example, a famous individual (such as the Indian Prime Minister Narendra Modi) has a connection with many others on OSNs. These graphs are difficult to partition in computational terms.

12.6.2   Sparseness

Most vertices have relatively few neighbors in real-world graphs, while some have many neighbors. For example, some people have more than 50,000 follower graphs on Twitter (for example, the United States President: Joe Biden), whereas ordinary users have just one hundred followers or even fewer. In addition, the sparse charts need more calculation, synchronization, and communication.

12.6.3   Data-driven computations

In most cases, data is fully driven on the graph calculation algorithms. If the structure of graphical computation is not known a priori in these algorithms, it may be difficult to express a parallelism based on partitioning the computation.

12.6.4   Unstructured problems

Data is generally unstructured and irregular in nature in graphical issues. Although graph problems are paralleled, it is difficult to remove parallelism by partitioning graph problem data by irregular structure of the graph problem data.

12.6.5   In-memory challenge

Natural graphics are huge, and they do not fit into a single memory. In order to decrease response time, the Graph Data should reside in the RAM rather than on the HTD or SSD.

12.6.6   Communication overhead

The high-quality vertices (like most individuals in Twitter) lead to general communication. At the moment, the high-grade vertices are thousands, but they will be trillions and more in the future.

12.6.7   Load balancing

Many of the natural graphs follow the rule of graduate distribution. This signifies that most vertices have little vertices, and additional vertices are linked with only those little vertices. If we analyze these graphs, the load balancing must be given extra attention.

12.7   Implementation of big data graph analytics using Python (case study)

A graph network can be created in python using NetworkX package.
    To install the package use:

pip install network
    if you are using it on the anaconda use:
conda install -c anaconda network
    To understand the graph analytics, first we will create a symmetric network. To create a symmetric network nx is imported from network.
import networkx as nx
G_symmetric = nx.Graph()

We can add various edges in this empty graph. It is known that for a symmetric relation if A is related to B, then B must be related to A. We added few edges in the graph and get the following symmetric network as in Figure 12.1.

We created another network where if A is related to B, then B is not related to A and thus obtaining asymmetric network as shown in Figure 12.2.

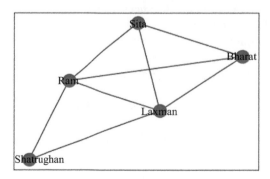

Figure 12.1   Symmetric network

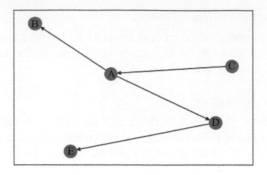

Figure 12.2   Asymmetric network

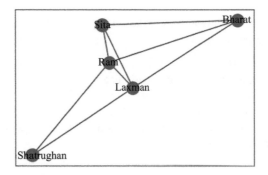

Figure 12.3   Weighted symmetric network

Figure 12.1 represents a symmetric network where all the edges are equal. We can assign weights to the edges and thus we can create the weighted graph by providing more weight to the important edges. Figure 12.3 represents the weighted version of Figure 12.1.

We will be able to locate the distance of a node from every single other node in the network applying breadth-first search algorithm, opening from that node. For example, in the graph mentioned in Figure 12.1, we want to calculate the distance of node "Ram" with every other node which is shown in Figure 12.4.

T = nx.bfs_tree(G_symmetric, 'Ram')

12.7.1   Graph analytics using Facebook data

To understand the graph analytics from the Facebook, we downloaded the Facebook data of ten individuals' Facebook friends list from the Stanford university website.

G_fb = nx.read_edgelist("facebook.txt", create_using = nx.Graph(), nodetype = int)

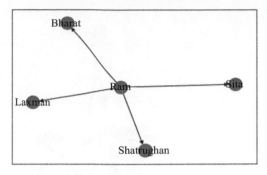

Figure 12.4   Distance of node "Ram" with other nodes

Figure 12.5   Facebook network

The details of the dataset are the following:

```
print(nx.info(G_fb))

Name:
Type: Graph
Number of nodes: 4039
Number of edges: 88234
Average degree:   43.6910
```

Network can be seen in Figure 12.5.

To visualize the network with varying colors as per degree of the network and betweenness Centrality, we plotted the network as shown in Figure 12.6. Betweenness centrality is the centrality of control.

Figure 12.6   Visualization of Facebook graph

Table 12.1   Highest centrality measures

Degree centrality	Betweenness centrality	Eigenvector centrality
107	107	1,912
1,684	1,684	2,266
1,912	3,437	2,206
3,437	1,912	2,233
0	1,085	2,464

We also evaluated the highest centrality measures (Degree centrality, Eigenvector centrality and betweenness centrality) for top five nodes which is shown in Table 12.1.

It can be seen from Table 12.1 that few nodes are having same value for degree centrality and betweenness centrality because it is inherent that nodes that are further connected likewise lie on shortest paths among other nodes.

12.8   Conclusion and future work

For researchers, graphical analysis has long been an important subject. In this chapter, we discussed various techniques of graph analytics and the relationship of graph analytics in context of big data. We also discussed various approaches in graph analytics for big data. We have also shown the implementation of graph analytics using python. We also analyzed the graph analytics using Facebook data and evaluated the highest centrality measures (degree centrality, Eigenvector centrality, and betweenness centrality). In future, we would like to extend our work by analyzing massive datasets of other social network and applying machine learning algorithms.

References

[1]   A. Gandomi and M. Haider, "Beyond the hype: Big data concepts, methods, and analytics", *International Journal of Information Management*, 35(2), pp. 137–144, 2015.

[2]   R. Angles, "A comparison of current graph database models", in *2012 IEEE 28th International Conference on Data Engineering Workshops* (*ICDEW*), IEEE, 2012, pp. 171–177.

[3]   Y. Lu, J. Cheng, D. Yan and H. Wu, "Large-scale distributed graph computing systems: an experimental evaluation", *Proceedings of the VLDB Endowment*, 8(3), pp. 281–292, 2014.

[4]   M. Han, K. Daudjee, K. Ammar, M. T. Ozsu, X. Wang and T. Jin, "An experimental comparison of pregel-like graph processing systems", *Proceedings of the VLDB Endowment*, 7(12), pp. 1047–1058, 2014.

[5]   A. Roy, I. Mihailovic and W. Zwaenepoel. "X-Stream: edge-centric graph processing using streaming partitions", in *24th ACM Symposium on Operating Systems Principles* (*SOSP '13*), New York, 2013.

[6]   W.-S. Han, S. Lee, K. Park, *et al.* "TurboGraph: a fast parallel graph engine handling billion-scale graphs in a single PC", in *19th ACM SIGKDD International Conference on Knowledge Discovery and Data Mining* (*KDD'13*), New York, NY, 2013.

[7]   A. Roy, L. Bindschaedler, J. Malicevic and W. Zwaenepoel. "Chaos: scale-out graph processing from secondary storage", in *25th Symposium on Operating Systems Principles* (*SOSP'15*), New York, NY, 2015.

[8]   X. Zhu, W. Han and W. Chen. "GridGraph: large-scale graph processing on a single machine using 2-level hierarchical partitioning", in *2015 USENIX Conference on Usenix Annual Technical Conference* (*USENIX ATC'15*), Berkeley, CA, 2015.

[9]   Y. Bu, V. Borkar, J. Jia, M. J. Carey and T. Condie. "Pregelix: Big(ger) graph analytics on a dataflow engine", *VLDB Endowment*, 8(2), pp. 161–172, 2014.

[10] J. E. Gonzalez, R. S. Xin, A. Dave, D. Crankshaw, M. J. Franklin and I. Stoica. "GraphX: graph processing in a distributed dataflow framework", in *11th USENIX Conference on Operating Systems Design and Implementation* (*OSDI'14*), Berkeley, CA, 2014.

[11] D. Zheng, D. Mhembere, R. Burns, J. Vogelstein, C. E. Priebe and A. S. Szalay. "FlashGraph: processing billion-node graphs on an array of

commodity SSDs", in *13th USENIX Conference on File and Storage Technologies (FAST'15)*, Berkeley, CA, 2015.

[12]   D. K. Singh and R. Patgiri. "Big Graph: tools, techniques, issues, challenges and future directions", in *Sixth International Conference on Advances in Computing and Information Technology (ACITY 2016)*, Chennai, India, 2016.

[13]   S. van den Elzen, D. Holten, J. Blaas and J. J. van Wijk, "Reducing snapshots to points: a visual analytics approach to dynamic network exploration", *IEEE Transactions on Visualization and Computer Graphics*, 22, pp. 1–10, 2016.

[14]   S. Papadopoulos, A. Drosou, N. Dimitriou, O. Abdelrahman, G. Gorbil and D. Tzovaras, "A BRPCA based approach for anomaly detection in mobile networks", in *30th International Symposium on Computer and Information Sciences (ISCIS)*, Lecture Notes in Electrical Engineering, vol. 363, 2015, pp. 115–125, 10.1007/978-3-319-22635-4_10

[15]   S. Papadopoulos, A. Drosou and D. Tzovaras, "A novel graph-based descriptor for the detection of billing-related anomalies in cellular mobile networks", *IEEE Transactions on Mobile Computing*, 15(11), pp. 2655–2668, 2016, 10.1109/TMC.2016.2518668

Chapter 13

Demystifying graph AI

Pethuru Raj[1] and Nachamai Muthuraman[2]

Abstract

Graphs are emerging as futuristic and flexible data structures that can fluently and fluidly model different relationships and processes over physical, biological, social, and information systems. Graph nodes or vertices represent the system's entities. Nodes are connected by edges/links, which represent relationships between those entities. Such an influencing representation helps to express and expose complex interdependencies in data.

The Artificial Intelligence (AI) domain fundamentally represents a collection of pioneering algorithms and approaches to uncover and emit out human-like intelligence from data volumes through an iterative and insightful process of building, evaluating, and optimizing AI models. As indicated above, another interesting facet gaining prominence in the recent past is the aspect of data representation through enigmatic graph structures. This transition has resulted in solving a myriad of complex business problems. Now by applying proven and potential AI procedures and processes on graph data, the task of knowledge discovery out of data mountains is becoming simpler and speedier. The prediction accuracy and performance of AI models when applied on graph data show a lot of perceptible improvements. This strategic and subtle convergence is being widely touted as the Graph AI paradigm. In this chapter, we are to discuss what, how, and why Graph AI is acquiring all the attention and how this new paradigm is bound to be a trend-setter for the ensuing era of knowledge.

13.1 Introduction

The field of Artificial Intelligence (AI) is showing a lot of promises these days for worldwide businesses and national governments. AI is being proclaimed as one of the most ambitious and adventurous visions for producing intelligent systems across industry verticals. Automation is now the new normal everywhere with the numerous noteworthy advancements in the AI domain, which is being bombarded with many powerful algorithms, predefined models, enabling frameworks,

[1]Edge AI Division, Reliance Jio Platforms Ltd., Bangalore, India
[2]Siemens Healthcare Pvt. Ltd., Bangalore, India

hardware accelerators, and software libraries to collect and crunch a massive quantity of multi-structured data to extract actionable insights. The knowledge thus discovered can be disseminated to the right and relevant business workloads, IoT devices, and IT services in time to exhibit the much-needed intelligent behavior. Thus, AI technologies and tools are to serve immensely and immeasurably for the ensuing knowledge era. Every institution, individual, and innovator is able to leverage the AI prowess in an exciting and elegant manner to bring in premium and path-breaking capabilities to their clients, customers, and consumers.

Data and its easy availability and accessibility help the AI domain to flourish. As the field of high-performance computing matures fast, data heaps in conjunction with high-end computational capabilities and storage capacities are to be subjected to a variety of deeper investigations to uncover hidden patterns, useful associations, etc. The world has been using tabular and Euclidean data for long. With the increasing availability of graph-represented data, there is a big twist in the domain of big data analytics. With big data, there is a craze for leveraging NoSQL databases for simplifying data analytics. A graph database is a kind of NoSQL databases. Thus, the faster maturity and stability of graph databases have brought in a bevy of strategically sound improvisations in the field of data analytics and science. This chapter is specially allocated and added to this book for explaining the nitty-gritty of analysing graph data through a host of advanced technologies and tools.

13.2   Reflecting graphs

Graphs are everywhere. In social sciences, graph networks are widely used to represent people's relationships, etc. Nowadays, a lot of information are being represented in graphs/networks. For example, we have social media networks, documentation citation networks, transportation networks, etc. In chemistry and material sciences, graphs are used to represent the molecular structure of a compound, protein interaction networks, as well as biological and biochemical associations. In a general sense, graphs are a powerful tool for representing rich and complex data. Formally, a network (or graph) is a representation of connections among a set of items. This representation is often written as G=(V,E) , where V={V1,...,Vn} is a set of nodes (also called vertices) and E={{Vk, Vw},...,{Vi, Vj}} is a set of two-sets (set of two elements) of edges (also called links), representing the connection between two nodes belonging to V. The diagram below shows about nodes/vertices and edges/links.

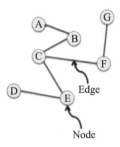

Thus, a graph is being seen as a structured data type that has nodes (entities that hold information) and edges (connections between nodes and edges also hold information). Therefore, graphs support a compositional nature as well as a relational nature. Graphs/networks can also take different structures and attributes, as exemplified below.

- Undirected graphs do not have direction, and they are useful for cases where relationships are symmetric.
- Directed graphs, on the other hand, have direction and they are primarily useful for asymmetrical relationships.
- In cyclic graphs, paths start and end at the same node.
- But in acyclic graphs, paths start and end at different nodes.
- In weighted graphs, not all relationships are equal. That is, relationships carry varying weights.
- In unweighted graphs, all relationships are equal.
- In sparse graphs, every node in the subset may not have a path to every other node.
- However, in dense graphs, every node in the subset has a path to every other node.
- In monopartite, bipartite, and k-partite graphs, nodes connect to only one other node (e.g., users like movies) or many other nodes (e.g., users like users who like movies).

Networks have some basic properties that advanced methods and techniques can build upon them.

- The order of a graph is the number of its vertices |V|. The size of a graph is the number of its edges |E|.
- The degree of a vertex is the number of edges that are adjacent to it. The neighbors of a vertex v in a graph G is a subset of vertex Vi induced by all vertices adjacent to v
- The neighborhood graph of a vertex v in a graph G is a subgraph of G, composed of the vertices adjacent to v and all edges connecting vertices adjacent to v.

Thus, graphs are data structures to describe relationships and interactions between entities in complex systems. In general, a graph contains a collection of entities called nodes and another collection of interactions between a pair of nodes called edges. Nodes represent entities, which can be of any object type that is relevant to our problem domain. By connecting nodes with edges, we will end up with a graph (network) of nodes. In addition, every node and edge may have attributes (properties/ features) that contain additional information about those instances.

For example, if we want to know how clients of a bank are related to each other based on their money transactions, then we can model this as a network of clients that transfer money to each other across the entire client data set. In this network, each node would be a client, and an edge between two clients represents that those two clients have once transferred money to each other. Node attributes could be bank account numbers and date of birth. Edge attributes could be the total amount of money, the number of transactions, and date of the first transaction. The graph below illustrates a directed and an undirected graph.

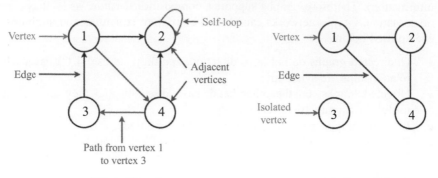

Directed Graph   **Undirected Graph**

In summary, graphs come in different kinds. There are directed and undirected graphs. Further on, there are multi and hypergraphs, graphs with or without self-edges.

Homogeneous vs. heterogeneous graphs: When all nodes in a graph are of the same type, then the graph is called a homogeneous graph. The above directed graph is a homogeneous graph because the nodes represent only persons. If in a graph, some nodes may be companies, whereas other nodes represent persons, then the graph nodes have different sets of features. These are being termed as heterogeneous graphs. Further on, if there are graphs with different types of edges (this means there are multiple ways in which nodes can interact), then these graphs are called multi-relational. The below diagram shows a network where the money is being transferred between companies and persons. This graph contains edge directions and heterogeneous nodes.

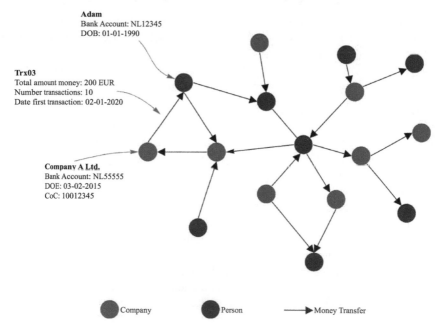

Why graphs? – Knowingly or unknowingly, graphs are everywhere. Essentially, a graph is an abstract data type with two central ingredients: nodes and edges. Vertices are mainly used to establish and express relationships between pairs of nodes. Such a structure comes handy in representing and modelling a variety of real-world things. The prime distinction with other prevalent data representation methods is that all kinds of relationships between people, products, transactions, happenings, etc. can be easily expressed and exposed through graphs. Social networks such as Facebook, LinkedIn, Twitter benefit greatly through graph representations. Other widely articulated examples include a virus spreading during a pandemic situation (this helps in predicting third and future waves of COVID-19), a highway system connecting many cities, airplanes flying across multiple airports spread across cities, counties, countries, continents, etc. That is, a graph of airports and flights connecting them, flights and connecting passengers, airlines forming alliances, etc. is facilitating automating and orchestrating several cumbersome activities. Ultimately, graphs contribute in envisaging, implementing, and providing a host of sophisticated, people-centric, and business services and applications.

The graph above shows a list of direct flights one could take from Madrid. Thus, graph-based data representation is being seen as a huge enabler and differentiator for many things. Not only humans but also software applications can easily make sense out of graph data. Graphs show flexibility and extensibility in representing complicated things. For example, look at the picture as follows.

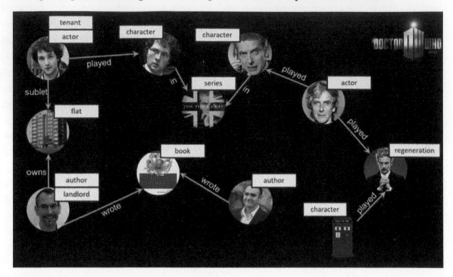

Representing, exchanging, and processing such complicated relationships and interactions through graphs are quite easy. Graphs help much more.

13.3   Describing the graph operations

Before diving into the widely used graph operations, let us discuss the fundamental precepts of graphs in this section.

Adjacency matrix (A): An adjacency matrix is a N × N matrix filled with either 0 or 1, where N is the total number of nodes. Adjacency matrices are able to represent the existence of edges that connect the node pairs through the value in the matrices. For example, if we have 5 nodes in our graph, then the shape of the matrix is [5, 5]. Matrix element A_{ij} is 1 if an edge exists between nodes i and j. A graph is a complete graph if all elements of adjacency matrix A are 1, except along the diagonal.

Node attributes matrix (X): Unlike adjacency matrices that models the relationship between nodes, this matrix represents the features or attributes of each node. If there are N nodes and the size of node attributes is F, then the shape of this matrix is N × F.

Edge attributes matrix (E): Edges also can have its own attributes, just like nodes. If the size of edge attributes is S and the number of edges available is n_edges, the shape of this matrix is n_edges × S.

Graph density: The maximum possible number of edges is $n*(n-1)/2$ as every node can be connected to exactly $n-1$ other nodes and the edges are undirected. It measures how close is the graph to a fully connected graph, or a clique. Most real-life networks are very sparse, thus the measure is, in most cases, not very informative.

Graph diameter: The shortest path between two nodes u and v is the minimum number of edges that need to be traversed in order to reach v after starting at u. The graph diameter is the maximum shortest path length between any two nodes in the graph. If the graph has more than one connected component, then its diameter is infinity. Graph diameter can be used to distinguish between different types of networks. For example, subway networks are likely to have a larger diameter than small social networks.

Closeness centrality: The farness is sum of its distances from all other nodes. The closeness is the reciprocal of the farness.

Betweenness centrality: The number of times a node acts on a bridge along the shortest path between two other nodes. This measure actually captures the influence nodes have in the graph. For each node u, we count how many shortest paths between node pairs go through u. Nodes with high betweenness centrality are considered more important in the network. The distribution of betweenness centrality scores provides us with further insights into the graph structure.

Network connectivity: A connected graph is a graph where every pair of nodes has a path between them. In a graph, there are multiple connection combinations as pictorially represented below.

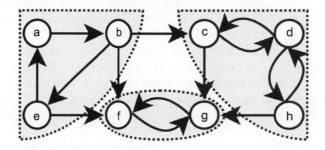

Network distance: Distance between two nodes is termed as the length of the shortest path between them. Typically, any path length is identified by the number of steps it contains from beginning to end. That is the number of steps for a node to reach other node. Finding this distance, especially in the case of large-scale graphs, can involve huge computational resources. To mitigate the complexity, there are two well-known algorithms.

Network clustering: Clustering is an important assessment of networks to start decomposing and understanding their complexity. Triadic closure in a graph is the tendency for nodes who share edges to become connected. This is commonly done in social network graphs when person A is friends with person B and person B is friends with person C, so a recommendation to person A may be to befriend person C.

Network degree distributions: The degree of a node in an undirected graph is the number of neighbours it is blessed with. The degree distribution of a graph is the probability distribution of the degrees over the entire network. In directed graphs, we get in-degree and out-degree distributions.

Network centrality: When networks become large, it is imperative to use the centrality measures in gaining a good understanding of graph data. Centrality comes handy in learning about the importance of nodes/edges in a graph. Some of the ways to appropriately quantify importance in a network include the amount of degree of connectivity, the average proximity to other nodes, the fraction of shortest paths that pass through a node, etc. There are applications that leverage the proven centrality measures.

- Finding influential nodes in a social network.
- Identifying nodes that disseminate information to many nodes or prevent epidemics.
- Hubs in a transportation network.
- Important pages on the web.
- Nodes that prevent the network from breaking up.

Degree centrality: The degree centrality values are commonly normalized by dividing by the maximum possible degree in a simple graph $n-1$, where n is the number of nodes in G. There are several other centrality types to simplify and streamline the process of graph understanding.

Graph visualization: Visualizing problems drastically simplifies problem resolution fast. For example, if we are presented with an increasing sequence of numbers, such as [0.234, 0.243, 0.249, 0.257, 0.263], we might find it a bit difficult to notice the trend. But if the sequence of numbers is plotted, then it is quite easy to recognize the trend. Moreover, any graph representation of data is visually appealing and easy to understand what is being conveyed. However, the power of visualization diminishes significantly when there are graphs comprising thousands of nodes/vertices and edges. Humans find it difficult to tackle huge graphs, but computers are capable of exploring and extracting useful information by analysing large-scale graphs.

Graphs provide the much-needed flexibility, accommodate heterogeneous data, easily integrate new data sources, and intrinsically enable data analytics. Dr Leskovec (https://towardsdatascience.com/graph-machine-learning-with-python-pt-1-basics-metrics-and-algorithms-cc40972de113) provides some critical insights into classic and cognitive applications of graphs.

- *Node classification*: Predict a property of a node. For an example, categorize online users/items.
- *Link prediction*: Predict whether there are missing links between two nodes. For an example, knowledge graph (KG) completion and recommender systems.
- *Graph classification*: Categorize different graphs. An example is molecule property prediction.
- *Clustering*: Detect if nodes form a community. Social circle detection is an example.
- *Graph generation*: Drug discovery is a prime example.
- *Graph evolution*: An example is physical simulation.

Graphs are a general language for describing and analysing entities along with their relations/interactions. Without an iota of doubt, graphs are prevalent all around us in the form of computer networks, social networks, and disease pathways. Representing data as a graph helps to express complex structural information as features. This is certainly useful in some domains, as relational databases are providing some unique advantages in certain domains. Besides providing stronger feature representation, graph-based methods leverage the technique of representation learning to automatically learn features and represent them as an embedding.

Graphs are doing an excellent service at empowering users to discover and learn about connections between different data items/points. These connections are definitely first-class citizens, guaranteeing a lot for businesses as well as individuals. The nodes generally represent the real-life objects, which we wish to try to model. The edge is the relationship between them. For example, we have many friends on Facebook. The tabular data model being followed by relational databases does not treat these intricate and interesting connections between items as first-class citizens. The data relationships have to be extracted through an expensive and time-consuming computation. But, through graph structures, this connection is materialized and made visible. This makes it possible to perform traversals across multiple such connections over huge scales of data at a performance that a tabular implementation cannot match.

13.4   Delineating graph algorithms

Graph models are gaining a lot of attention as it is insightfully capable of dealing with big data. Graph data has to be subjected to a variety of investigations to simplify and speed up the discovery of new business opportunities. There are three kinds of algorithms (graph traversal, centrality, and clustering). Graph traversal is the process of visiting each vertex in a graph. Centrality identifies the most important vertices within a graph. The graph cluster identifies a group of vertices which are connected in a particular way.

These algorithms do a lot more for lessening the workload associated with the operations and analytics of graph data. In this section, we are to discuss the popular graph algorithms that are able to uncover useful patterns, associations, tips, and insights out of data heaps. Data-driven insights are essential for businesses to draw plans to increase business capacities and capabilities (https://towardsdatascience. com/10-graph-algorithms-visually-explained-e57faa1336f3).

Breadth-first search (BFS): In BFS, we start at a particular vertex and explore all of its neighbours at the present depth before moving on to the vertices in the next level. Unlike trees, graphs can contain cycles. Hence, we have to keep track of the visited vertices. When implementing BFS, we use a queue data structure.

Depth-first search (DFS): In DFS, we start from a particular vertex and explore as far as possible along each branch before retracing back (backtracking). This visits nodes by traversing the graph from the root node all the way to its first leaf node before going down a different route in the graph. In DFS also, we have to keep track of the visited vertices. When implementing DFS, we use a stack data structure to support backtracking.

Shortest path: The shortest path from one vertex to another vertex is a path in the graph such that the sum of the weights of the edges that should be travelled is minimum. There are two popular shortest path algorithms (Dijkstra's shortest path and Bellman–Ford's algorithms).

Cycle detection: A cycle is a path in a graph where the first and last vertices are the same. If we start from one vertex, travel along a path, and end up at the starting vertex, then this path is a cycle. Cycle detection is the process of detecting these cycles. There are two well-known algorithms (Floyd's cycle detection and Brent's algorithms).

Minimum spanning tree: A minimum-spanning tree is a subset of the edges of a graph. The condition is that the edges have to connect all the vertices with the minimum sum of edge weights and consist of no cycles. The two popular algorithms are Prim's algorithm and Kruskal's algorithm.

Strongly connected components: A graph is said to be strongly connected if every vertex in the graph is reachable from every other vertex. The well-known algorithms are Kosaraju's algorithm and Tarjan's strongly connected components algorithm.

Topological sorting: Topological sorting of a graph is a linear ordering of its vertices so that for each directed edge (u, v) in the ordering, vertex u comes before V. Kahn's algorithm is one of the algorithms for topological sorting.

Graph coloring: Graph coloring assigns colors to elements of a graph while ensuring certain conditions. Vertex colouring is the most commonly used graph colouring technique. In vertex colouring, we try to colour the vertices of a graph using k colours and any two adjacent vertices should not have the same colour. Other coloring techniques include edge-coloring and face coloring. The chromatic number of a graph is the smallest number of colours needed to colour the graph. Greedy colouring is one of the widely used graph colouring algorithms.

Maximum flow: We can model a graph as a flow network with edge weights as flow capacities. In the maximum flow problem, we have to find a flow path that can obtain the maximum possible flow rate. There are several maximum flow algorithms including

- Ford–Fulkerson algorithm.
- Edmonds–Karp algorithm.
- Dinic's algorithm.

Matching: A matching in a graph is a set of edges that does not have common vertices. No two edges share a common vertex. A matching is called a maximum matching if it contains the largest possible number of edges matching as many vertices as possible. The matching algorithms are:

- Hopcroft–Karp algorithm.
- Hungarian algorithm.
- Blossom algorithm.

Graph algorithms are used to simplify and solve various business, scientific, and social problems. In addition, graph algorithms come handy in emitting out valuable insights out of data structured through graphs. Searching, sorting, traversal, shortest path finding, etc. are some of the graph problems, which can be easily tackled through a host of graph algorithms discussed above. With the consistent rise in adopting graph algorithms, coding experts and evangelists have come out with source codes (using different programming languages) for the above-mentioned algorithms, and you can find them at this site (https://www.javatpoint.com/graph-algorithms) and (https://www.tutorialspoint.com/parallel_algorithm/graph_algorithm.htm).

13.5 Graph models and databases

Graph data models: Database management systems (DBMSs) are being compared and conformed of various attributes including performance key indicators (PKIs), complexity, query style, data types, transactions, consistency, etc. In this section, we are to discuss about the recent graph database management systems and how they are able to meet up the distinct requirements of digital world. Let us start the discussion with an overview of two dominating graph data models. Predominantly there are two graph data models: Property graphs and *Resource description framework* (RDF) graphs.

Property graphs: A labeled-property graph model is represented by a set of nodes, relationships, properties, and labels. Both nodes and their relationships can store properties represented by key–value (K–V) pairs. Nodes can be labeled to be grouped. The edges representing the relationships have two qualities: they always have a start node and an end node, and are directed making the graph a directed graph. Relationships can also have properties. This is useful in providing additional metadata and semantics to the relationships between the nodes.

A property graph excels at showing connections among data scattered across diverse data architectures and data schemas. They provide a richer view on how data can be modelled over many different databases, as well as how different kinds of metadata relate. Property graphs also show data dependencies not seen in a relational database schema. Here is a pictorial representation of property graphs.

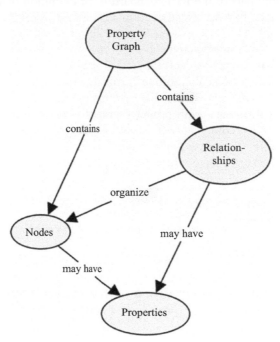

What makes a graph a "property graph" (also called as a "labeled property graph") is the ability to have values on the edges. Property graphs are closer to what programmers are used to. They are easy to get started and are blessed with attributes on the edges. They pragmatically simplify network analytics.

One of the primary use cases for attributes on the edges is adding weights. Such an addition enables network analytics. For instance, a network representation of how to get from one town to another might include a number of alternate subroutes through different towns or intersections. By putting weights on each edge that represented distance, a network algorithm could calculate the shortest path between two towns. By putting weights on the edges that represent average travel time, a network algorithm could calculate the route that would take the least time.

RDF graphs: The RDF graph data model basically consists of two elements.

- **Nodes** can be resources with unique identifiers, or they can be "literals" with values that are strings, integers, etc.
- **Edges** are also called predicates and/or properties. The "from node" of an edge is called the subject. The "to node" is called the object. Two nodes connected by an edge form a subject-predicate-object statement, also known as a Triple. While edges are directed, they can be navigated and queried in either direction.

Everything in an RDF graph is called a resource. Edges and Nodes are just the roles played by a resource in a given statement. Fundamentally, in RDF, there is no difference between resources playing an edge role and resources playing a node role. An edge in one statement can be a node in another. There is a standard query language for RDF graphs called SPARQL. It is a fully-featured query language and supports the HTTP protocol. Thus, it is possible to send query requests to endpoints over HTTP. A key part of the RDF standard is the definition of serializations and the most commonly used serialization format is called Turtle. There is also a JSON serialization called JSON-LD as well as an XML serialization. All RDF databases are able to export and import graph content in standard serializations making it easy and seamless to interchange data. The RDF data model provides a richer and semantically consistent foundation over property graphs. KGs fully comply with the RDF graph data model. That is, KGs are represented in RDF.

The singular difference with property graphs is the RDF KG standards were designed for interoperability at web scale. As such, all identifiers are globally unique and potentially discoverable and resolvable. It is easy to differentiate RDF graphs from property graphs on the following attributes.

- Schema.
- Globally unique identifiers.
- Resolvable identifiers.
- Federation.
- Constraint management.
- Inference.

Schema: Property graphs do not have a schema. In property graphs, the nearest equivalent to a schema is the "label" in "Labeled Property Graph." A label is essentially putting a tag on something. So you can label a node as "Person," but the issue here is that the label does not say anything more about the node. KGs have a very rich and standardized schema. They do not require all the schema to be present before any data can be persisted, unlike relational databases. However, when you are ready to add schema to your graph, you can do so with a high degree of rigor and go to as much or as little detail as necessary.

Globally unique identifiers: The identifiers in property graphs are strictly local. This is seen as a huge limitation when you are looking to integrate information across many systems. Especially, combining third-party data is a difficult proposition. KGs are based on URIs, which are a lot like URLs. The real difference is that a URI identifies a "thing." Every node in a KG is assigned a URI/IRI, including the schema or metadata. This makes discovering what something means as simple as "following your nose."

Resolvable identifiers: Clicking on a URI can redirect to a server in the domain name of the URI/IRI, we get the page that represents the resource. In the case of a schema/ metadata URI, the page might describe what the metadata means. This typically includes both the "informal" definition (comments and other annotations) as well as the "formal" definition. For a data URI, the resolution might display what is known about the item (the outgoing links). This style of exploring a body of data by clicking on links is a very effective way of learning a complex body of knowledge. Property graphs have no standard way of doing this.

Federation: It refers to the ability to query across multiple databases to get a single comprehensive result set. This is almost impossible to do with relational databases. The property graphs also have no mechanism for federation over more than a single in memory graph. Federation is built into SPARQL. You can point a SPARQL query at a number of databases (including relational databases that have been mapped to RDF through another W3C standard, R2RML).

Constraint management – One of the things needed in a transactional system is the ability to enforce constraints on incoming transactions. KGs have the W3C standard, SHACL (SHApes Constraint Language), to specify constraints in a model driven fashion. Property graphs have no transaction mechanism and no constraint management capability.

Inference: It is the creation of new information from existing information. A property graph creates a number of "insights" which are a form of inference. The challenge here is it is in the heads of the persons running the analytics and interpreting what the insight is. But KGs have several inference capabilities. What they all share is that the result of the inference is rendered as another triple. That is, the inferred information is another fact which can be expressed as a triple. Any fact that can be asserted in a KG can also be inferred if the right contextual information is provided.

Two of the prime creators of inferred knowledge are RDFS and OWL. RDFS provides the simple sort of inference that people familiar with object oriented programming (OOP). OWL (the Web Ontology Language) allows for much more complex schema definitions. OWL allows you to create class definitions from Booleans and allows the formal definition of classes by creating membership definitions based on what properties are attached to nodes.

RDF graphs fulfil the other points (provenance and convergence), but property graphs do not have them natively. Thus, the RDF graph data model is unique in several aspects and contributes immensely. A KG is a popular RDF graph and let us discuss how a KG is intrinsically powerful enough to bring forth a variety of advantages as described below.

13.6   The evolution of KGs

KGs represent a collection of interlinked facts about a domain. Actually, all kinds of entities and relations are methodically extracted from the unstructured data and are stored in the form of a triple: subject-predicate-object. For example, the statement "Captain Marvel is the strongest Avenger" can be broken into a subject (Captain Marvel), a predicate (is the strongest), and an object (Avenger) and stored as a triple along with other related entities in a KG of Avengers.

KGs come with these features: (1) they generally define real-world entities of a domain; (2) they provide relationships between them; (3) they define rules for possible classes of entities and relations via some schema; (4) they enable reasoning to infer new knowledge (https://venturebeat.com/2021/06/28/why-knowledge-graphs-are-key-to-working-with-data-efficiently-powerfully/).

Why KGs?: A KG is self-descriptive as it is being seen as a single place to find the data and to understand what is all about the data. The meaning of the data (semantics) is encoded alongside the data in the graph itself. KGs bring additional value by providing the following capabilities.

- *Context*: KGs provide context to algorithms by integrating various types of information into an ontology and also guarantee flexibility to add new derived knowledge on the go.
- *Efficiency*: KGs offer computational efficiencies for querying stored data and for generating insights.
- *Explainability*: Explainability/interpretability is a huge challenge for complex AI models. Large-scale networks comprising an enormous number of entities and relations solve the issue of understandability by integrating the meaning of entities available within the graph itself. AI's trustworthiness is elegantly solved through KGs.

KGs help in organizing unstructured data in a way that information can easily be extracted where explicit relations between multiple entities help in the process.

A   KG   (https://www.ontotext.com/knowledgehub/fundamentals/what-is-a-knowledge-graph) represents a collection of interlinked descriptions of entities (objects, events, or abstract concepts). KGs put data in context via linking and semantic metadata, and in this way, KGs provide a flexible framework for enabling data integration, unification, analytics, and sharing. Descriptions have formal semantics that allow both people and computers to process them in an efficient and unambiguous manner. Entity descriptions contribute to one another, forming a network where each entity represents part of the description of the entities related

to it and provides context for their interpretation. Some distinguished characteristics of KGs are given below.

- *KGs innately communicate context*: By storing information and its sources in a
  graph, the much-neglected context details are being made readily available.
  With context information at hand, any decision-making process is bound to be
  accurate and appropriate. The interconnectivity between information sources,
  aptly etched through graph structures, contributes for the solid enrichment of
  information with context details. Ultimately, KGs hence correct and cognitive
  decisions can be taken. KGs ultimately lead to have a human-like decision-
  making capability. Data stored in graphs mimics the intuitive way humans
  understand information. By integrating information, we can make general-
  isations and contextualize our information. As we learn new information, we
  relate it to the knowledge we already have gained.
- *KGs can span types of information:* Without an iota of doubt, human intelligence is non-linear and is able to take multiple perspectives before arriving at a
  decision. The schema-less nature of KGs supports flexibility by not being
  rigidly enforcing types on data. KGs are also able to represent data according
  to a schema.
- *KGs change*: New data is being continuously discovered. Even some existing
  data becomes irrelevant. Then the KG can grow or prune accordingly. There
  are business and technology changes, and even the relevance of the context
  may change. A KG has the wherewithal to accommodate any perceptible
  change. The KG will have a means via inference to make the connections for
  any newly added information.

Ontologies represent the backbone of the formal semantics of a KG. They can be
seen as the data schema of the graph. They serve as a formal contract between the
developers of the KG and its users regarding the meaning of the data in it. A user
could be another human being or a software application that wants to interpret the
data in a reliable and precise way. Ontologies ensure a shared understanding of
the data and its meanings. When formal semantics are used to express and interpret
the data of a KG, there are a number of representation and modelling instruments.

- *Classes*: An entity description contains a classification of the entity with
  respect to a class hierarchy. For instance, when dealing with business information, there could be classes such as person, organization and location.
  Persons and organizations can have a common superclass. The location usually
  has numerous sub-classes, e.g., country, populated place, city, etc.
- *Relationship types*: The relationships between entities are usually tagged with
  types, which provide information about the nature of the relationship, e.g.,
  friend, relative, competitor, etc. Relationship types can also have formal definitions, e.g., that parent-of is the inverse relation of child-of. They both are
  special cases of relative-of, which is a symmetric relationship.
- *Categories*: An entity can be associated with categories, which describe some
  aspect of its semantics, e.g., "Big four consultants" or "XIX century

composers." A book can belong simultaneously to all these categories: "Books about Africa," "Bestseller," "Books by Italian authors," "Books for kids," etc. The categories are described and ordered into a taxonomy.

• *Free text descriptions*: Often a 'human-friendly text' description is provided to further clarify design intentions for the entity and improve search.

Not every RDF graph is a KG: For instance, a set of statistical data (for example, the Gross Domestic Product (GDP) data for worldwide countries represented in RDF is not a KG). A graph representation of data is often useful, but it might be an overkill to capture the semantic knowledge of the data. It might be sufficient for an application to just have a string 'Italy' associated with the string 'GDP' and a number of '1.95 trillion'. There is no need to define what the 'GDP' of a country is. It's the connections and the graph that make the KG, not the language used to represent the data.

13.7   KG use cases

The KGs have laid down a stimulating and sparkling foundation for advanced and automated data analytics. For arriving at trustworthy, unbiased, fair, and transparent AI models, KGs play a very telling role. The domain of AI interpretability/ explainability/understandability is getting a strong boost with the pervasiveness of KGs. To have integrated systems, it is imperative to have the data virtualization capability in place. That is, multiple, heterogeneous, and geographically distributed data sources have to be integrated through technically competent solutions. First, data integration provides a lot of advantages for institutions and individuals to visualize and realize next-generation software packages. Second, connected data enriched with meaning (semantics) facilitates multiple and meaningful interpretations to be derived from the same data. This arrangement enables getting proper answers to complex queries and to derive actionable insights.

Fraud detection: Identifying fraudulent transactions is essential for financial service providers. KGs have all the wherewithal to detect any fraud and wastage, thereby banking and insurance services providers can survive and thrive in their core assignments. KGs in conjunction with transparent machine learning (ML) models are being portrayed as the way forward for proactive and pre-emptive fraud identification. ML models can pinpoint and predict fraudulent acts and patterns by purposefully traversing through interconnected entities in a large network in real-time.

Drug discovery: Drug discovery is another complicated and cost-intensive task, and hence there is a need for automation. KGs have shown considerable promise across drug repurposing, drug interactions, and target gene-disease prioritization. There are several open-source databases for publicly exposing drug details. Huge biomedical KGs are being formed by integrating these drug databases in conjunction with published research papers, survey articles, and case studies. These KGs ably assist medical scientists, scholars, and students in mining and understanding the intricacies between different entities such as genes, drugs, diseases, and medication. All kinds of medical information are being annotated through KGs, which, in turn, support knowledge discovery. Medical experts and common people can draw a fair and unbiased understanding of all the advancements that are happening in the medical field.

Semantic search: We are heading towards the much-discussed semantic web. The traditional searches are being regally replaced with semantic searches. As explained above, a KG stores entities and their meanings. Therefore, KGs are the base for fulfilling the semantic search vision. Semantic search is to improve the accuracy of search results significantly. The leading search engines, such as Google, will get empowered through KGs. Further on, text mining/analytics and breakthrough indexing techniques take us to experience the semantic web.

Recommendation systems: Recommendation is an active research area. In our everyday life, such systems play a very important role. There are several techniques and tools to build recommendation systems. However, they are found to be incomprehensive and inadequate. Also, the explainability is a big issue with them. KG-based recommendation systems are able to surmount the above-mentioned demerits. As users and their preferences are connected through multiple relationships, the recommendation being made is correct and cognitive.

KGs give data scientists the ability to not just extract interrelated facts and assumptions from massive quantities of data, but also help in forming contextual connections. A number of advanced applications squarely rely on KGs. Examples include data and information-heavy services such as AI models, context-aware services, knowledge-centric applications, expert and recommendation systems, KG-powered drug discovery, semantic search, investment decisions, market intelligence, information discovery in regulatory documents, advanced drug safety analytics, etc.

KGs help text analysis: A KG typically gives an illusion of the assemblage of interconnected descriptions/representations of real-world entities (objects, events, or concepts). Text mining or analytics is an important activity, and KGs help here tellingly.

- Big graphs typically provide background knowledge, human-like concept, and entity awareness. This enables a more accurate interpretation of the text.
- The results of the analysis are semantic tags (annotations) that link references in the text to specific concepts in the graph. These tags represent structured metadata that enables better search and further analytics.
- Facts extracted from the text can be added to enrich the KG, which makes it is much more valuable for analysis, visualization, and reporting.

Data Integration: There are many approaches and methods attempted to solve the disparate data problem. KGs are being presented as the most modern and best-in-class method to harmonize enterprise data. All kinds of data types, data sources, and databases can be represented and operationalized in a KG.

Cognitive computing: KGs can help companies move away from traditional databases and use the power of natural language processing (NLP), ML, and semantics to leverage data beneficially. Cognitive systems will be pervasive and persuasive too.

In short, KGs are inventive, revolutionary, and rewarding indeed.

13.8   Graph databases

Graph databases are being exclusively built and used to store and navigate relationships. As articulated above, relationships are the first-class citizens in graphs and their databases. In directed graphs, an edge always has a start node, an end node, type, and direction, and an edge can describe parent–child relationships, actions, ownership, etc. In graph databases, traversing the joins or relationships is very fast because the relationships between nodes are not calculated at query times but are persisted in the database. Graph databases have advantages for use cases such as social networking, recommendation engines, and fraud detection. The following graph shows an example of a social network graph. Given the people (nodes) and their relationships (edges), you can find out who the "friends of friends" of a particular person are.

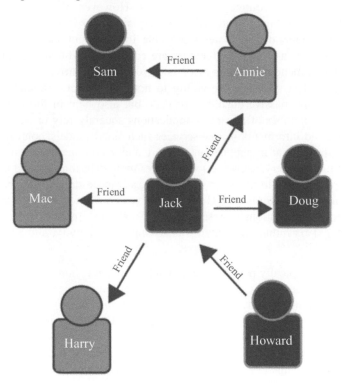

Graph databases are commonly referred to as a NoSQL database, implying that the approach to storing, querying, and describing these data structures differs significantly from a traditional relational database.

Amazon Neptune (https://aws.amazon.com/nosql/graph/) is a purpose-built and high-performance graph database engine optimized for storing billions of relationships and querying the graph with milliseconds of latency. Neptune supports the popular graph models (property graph and W3C's RDF). Neptune also supports their respective query languages (Apache TinkerPop Gremlin and SPARQL).

Graph databases use cases: Graph databases carry some specific advantages when compared with SQL and other NoSQL databases. Complex interdependent relationships between nodes can be added and removed in a graph database. Doing so in a traditional tabular database precipitates a few challenges. Similarly, in a NoSQL document database, it is tough to optimise join operations across documents.

Due to the unique flexibility of graph databases, the graph data model can be modified without having to perform costly schema changes. For example, if there is a need to incorporate a new property in a relation, it is quite easy in a graph database. Further on, a graph database abstracts join complexity and provides a query language. Such an arrangement makes it easy to pose relationship-based questions of data. Various graph algorithms make searching and sorting through all of the graph data easier. With these distinct advantages, there are several real-world use cases emerging to substantiate the surging popularity of graph databases.

Fraud detection: This is an indispensable use case for the banking sector. KGs help in fraud detection. Graph databases in association with ML models contribute favorably here. Customer banking data such as new accounts, loan applications, and credit card transactions can be accommodated in a graph in order to facilitate fraud detection. By looking for suspicious patterns of customer activity metadata and by cross-referencing with previously identified fraud, it is quite easy to flag up any currently running and predict any futuristic potential fraud. There are proven methods, such as entity link analysis, coming handy in pinpointing fraudulent activities.

With graph databases, it is possible to accommodate and analyse relationships to gain a deeper understanding of financial and purchase transactions in near-real time. With fast graph queries, it is easy to detect that, for example, a potential purchaser is using the same e-mail address and credit card as included in a known fraud case. Graph databases can also help you easily detect relationship patterns such as multiple people associated with a personal e-mail address, or multiple people sharing the same IP address but residing in different physical addresses.

With ML algorithms, this manually performed fraud detection can be automated. With more transaction data in place, any created and curated ML model can block or flag fraudulent transactions without any interpretation and involvement of humans.

360-Degree customer view: Customer and business information is typically spread across multiple systems/data stores. Therefore, it is mandatory to integrate different and distributed systems to arrive at a comprehensive view of the activities of businesses and customers. That is, a 360-degree customer view is vital to take correct decisions on time with all the clarity and confidence. By streaming data out of systems and services into a graph and by using a common data model, it is easy to provide integration, which, otherwise, is a difficult proposition. Having a live graph of all the information about a customer is the foundation to send queries on customers to accrue useful information. With more features getting added to customer data, the leverage of ML algorithms and models gains speed to do deeper and more decisive activities.

Infrastructure mapping: In cloud environments, there are physical and virtual systems in plenty. If infrastructure inventory data gets accommodated in a graph, then establishing mapping relationships between connected infrastructure components and their services goes a long way in fulfilling a variety of needs. Currently, enterprises use configuration management databases to keep up the inventory of their IT systems and business workloads.

Instead, a graph articulating and accentuating the relationships between infrastructure modules not only enables interactive visualisations of the network estate but also network tracing algorithms to traverse through the entire graph.

Dependency management: Dependencies are generally problematic. Graphs help to identify single points of failure and to simulate the impact of their failure on services. Such knowledge discovery helps to identify cascading failures before they happen.

Bottleneck identification: Networks, as usual play a very vital role in shaping up performance parameters of networked systems. Graph databases are inherently able to find weak links in network routing. Such insights extracted helps to pinpoint network bottlenecks. This leads to heightened utilization of network resources.

Latency evaluation: Latency is a huge blocker always. The business and IT worlds are pitching for low-latency systems and networks. Therefore, estimating latency across network paths and its impact on IT systems, which are being approached and accessed from geographic regions, is an important task. With clouds emerging as a one-stop IT solution for all kinds of business automation requirements, cloud IT infrastructure complexity is bound to go up remarkably. This makes assessing the impact of latency a bit more difficult. By using a graph database, metrics can be used to estimate impact before appropriate updates and upgrades can be initiated and implemented to surmount latency-induced limitations. Smart algorithms can identify bottlenecks and recommend routing changes or upgrade paths.

Asset management: Critical assets are being tagged and tracked closely. Additionally, assets are being monitored for where they are currently put up, who is using a particular asset, etc. Predictive maintenance of assets is also facilitated through assets data analytics. Graphs emerge as the viable and venerable structure for keeping up with asset details. Such a setup goes a long way in optimal utilization and upkeep of important assets.

With the continued rise of digitization and digitalization activities, there is a massive amount of multi-structured digital content getting generated and accumulated. Graph databases provide a flexible and scalable database model to precisely and perfectly keep track of digital assets, such as research publications, white papers, case studies, market research documents, evaluations, contracts, etc.

Context-aware services: Context information is very much needed to diligently develop and deploy context-aware services and solutions. Aggregating context details through traditional data engineering methods is found to be insufficient. With the emergence of graphs, capturing and leveraging context insights become an easy thing. For example, natural disaster warnings, traffic updates, or product recommendations for a given location are being elegantly accomplished through graph databases.

Recommendation engines: With graph databases, you can store varied relationships. For example, customer interests, friends, and purchase history are etched in a graph. Highly available graph databases fulfil real-time product recommendations to an user based on his or her previous purchases and preferences. Friendship recommendation also happens in a similar way. Real-time product and e-commerce recommendations substantially enhance user experiences while maximizing profitability for businesses. Netflix, Amazon, and other retail stores engage graphs to explore fresh avenues to increase revenue.

As depicted above, graph databases carry some specific capabilities, and hence distinct use cases are being derived out of graph databases, as explained above. There are web pages illustrating several practical use cases https://neo4j.com/use-cases/ and https://www.profium.com/en/blog/graph-database-use-cases/.

Graph databases have been evolving with the ready availability of high-performance computing. Data size, scope, structure, and speed are also varying fast. The proclaimed digital era is to produce big digital data. The graph database will become the primary database for stocking and investigating digital data and to unearth hidden patterns in data volumes. Businesses are keen to be customer-centric in their offerings, operations, and outputs. The role and responsibility of graph databases in extricating actionable insights out of data heaps are bound to go up drastically.

The point to be noted down here is that a graph structure leaks a bunch of useful information, which can be readily used to build, release, and run intelligent systems. Through a host of advancements in the form of graph algorithms and databases, more pioneering and pragmatic use cases across industry verticals can be fulfilled through graphs.

With the unprecedented growth of digitization and digitalization technologies and tools, a massive amount of multi-structured data gets accumulated. NoSQL databases are being presented as the best-in-class data stores for multi-structured data. Graph databases is one of the prime NoSQL databases. Certain classes of big data are more advantageous and adventurous when they get accommodated in graph databases. Social networks are obviously graphs. Molecules can be represented as graphs (atoms are nodes and bonds are edges). Any kind of interaction in physics can be modeled as a graph. Common tasks include graph classification/regression and node/edge classification/regression. The nodes in your graphs are tweets, and you want to regress the probability that a certain tweet is spreading fake news. Your model would associate a number between 0 and 1 to that node and that would be an example of a node regression task. The renowned use cases for graphs include massive-scale recommender systems, particle physics, computational pharmacology/chemistry/biology, traffic prediction, and fake news detection. With a broader and deeper understanding of graph structures, there will be more breakthrough real-world use cases for graphs.

13.9 Graph analytics

Data has become a new fuel for the business world to march ahead in their goals. As the data volume is growing rapidly with the huge increase in data-generating digital entities, we are extensively talking about ways and means of tackling big data beneficially. The process of transitioning data to information and to knowledge is being optimized and speeded up with a suite of automated tools. The new concepts of data-driven insights and insights-driven decisions and actions are becoming the new normal. Enterprises, in order to be ahead of their competitors in delivering premium services to their esteemed customers and clients, are meticulously collecting all kinds of internal as well as external data to crunch them to emit out useful insights on time.

As we know, there are big, fast, and streaming data analytics platforms. There are SQL, NoSQL, and distributed SQL databases to assist data analytics. The analytics process is being seen as the foremost method for squeezing out usable insights out of data mountains. That is, the fields of knowledge discovery and dissemination play a very fundamental and foundational role in shaping up worldwide enterprising businesses, governments, organizations, institutions, and establishments. The data-driven business value comes handy for business executives, strategists, and stakeholders to steer their business in the right direction towards the intended destination.

Graph analytics is a set of tools and methods for extracting knowledge from data modeled as a graph. As understood, the graph paradigm tends to be an ideal one to make the best out of linked data. The business value is mostly hidden in data relationships. But even with meticulously crafted graphs, extracting knowledge is beset with challenges. With large-scale graphs representing big data, data scientists and analysts need automated tools to accelerate knowledge discovery. Thus, the paradigm of graph analytics is gaining market and mind shares.

Graph analytics is being seen as the way forward to give a strong boost for business verticals. As told above, there is batch and real-time processing of data assets. Further on, there are integrated platform solutions for easing out big, real-time, and streaming data analytics. However, with the faster maturity and stability of ML and deep learning (DL) algorithms, the domain of analytics is to see a series of automations. That is, the long-pending automated analytics is being enabled through a host of highly efficient and explainable ML algorithms and models.

Before the full-fledged analytics process getting initiated and implemented, there are several critical activities to be performed. The need is to get the complex information from multiple internal and external sources. There are structured, semi-structured, and unstructured data emanating from different and distributed sources. Further on, applications from third-party service providers have to be integrated. Data by itself does not contribute much value. But data, when it gets connected with one another, has the intrinsic power to provide the much-needed context. That is, connected data generates a bigger value for businesses. Any context information captured through linked-up data greatly contributes for accurate business insights. Context contributes in making sense out of

In nutshell, graph analytics is all about analysing all kinds of useful relationships between graph database entries via a graph model in order to extract actionable business insights. This analysis uniquely combines various concepts and components, including graph theory, statistics, database technology, and data, to model, store, retrieve, and analyze graph-represented data. There are graphs/networks being formed and vetted in plenty across industry verticals. Business houses are meticulously strategizing and planning to make sense out of growing graph data to target specific business problems. Graph analytics is gaining the much-needed maturity with the arrival of competent tools, products, and platforms. Graph data and analytics help to resolve a variety of persisting problems and to produce real-world applications.

13.10   The types of graph analytics

As representing a variety of data-centric problems through graph structures is gaining the speed, seriousness, and scope, different kinds of graph analytics methods have emerged as articulated below.

1. *Path analysis*: This is all about analysing the relationship between nodes in a graph to determine the shortest distance between two nodes.
2. *Connectivity analysis*: This analysis helps to pinpoint which connectivity between two nodes is strong or weak. This determines how many edges are flowing into a node and how many are flowing out of that node.
3. *Centrality analysis:* As mentioned in the beginning, this specific analysis identifies the importance of a node in the network's connectivity. How influencing a node is being estimated through this analytics.
4. *Community analysis/network analysis*: This is a distance and density-based analysis of relationships between nodes. This helps to find the groups of people, who are frequently interacting with each other in a social network.

Enterprise, social, and network applications employ promising graph-centric algorithms that painstakingly traverse across and analyze graphs to bring out insights. Such a traversal may land in interesting patterns, which can open up possible solutions for currently unsolved problems and also can lead to fresh and long-term business opportunities. There are a set of proven graph analytic algorithms succulently empowering graph analytics.

- *Path analysis algorithm*: Path analysis algorithm helps to analyze the distances and shapes of the various paths that connect multiple entities designated within the graph. In money-laundering investigations, path analysis can help determine how money flows through a network of individuals, how it goes from company A to person B. The famous shortest path algorithm is facilitating path analysis
- *Clustering algorithm*: Clustering algorithm is to examine the various properties of the vertices and edges to identify the entities' characteristics. The knowledge acquired can be used to group the vertices accordingly. This is particularly helpful to find groups of people that might belong to a common criminal organization. The popular algorithm is the Louvain method, also known as the label propagation algorithm.

- *Pattern matching algorithms*: Pattern matching algorithms allow to identify one or several subgraphs with a given structure within a graph. For an example, a company node with a country property containing "Luxembourg" is connected to at least five officer nodes with a registered address in France.
- *Connectivity algorithms*: Connectivity algorithms find the minimum number of nodes or edges that need to be removed to disconnect the remaining nodes from each other. It is helpful to determine weaknesses in an IT network, for instance, and find out which infrastructure points are sensitive and can take it down. The Strongly Connected Components algorithm is one of the connectivity algorithms.
- *Densely connected subgraphs*: These are subgraphs in the original graph where almost all node pairs are connected by an edge. This is the basis of algorithms for community detection. But the number and the density of these dense components are also important statistics.
- *Centrality algorithms*: Centrality algorithms determine a node's relative importance within a graph by looking at how connected it is to other nodes. It is used, for instance, to identify key people within organizations. The popular centrality algorithm is the PageRank algorithm.

Probabilistic graphical models have use cases across various medical diagnoses, speech recognition, or default risk assessment for credit applications. The prime examples of such models are Bayesian networks and Markov networks. From detecting anomalies to understanding what are the key elements in a network, or highlighting communities, graph analytics reveals information that would otherwise remain hidden in your data.

KGs for graph analytics: We have already discussed KGs in detail. KGs are the most popular way to represent knowledge in the database. The NLP capability can provide the relevant answer to a query in natural language. Querying and answering are greatly simplified through KGs. KGs are the basis for useful analytics and business intelligence.

13.11   Graph analytics use-cases

With a greater understanding about the strategic benefits, graph analytics is gaining widespread usage across industry verticals.

Compliance: Graph analytics help to spot frauds and unlawful actions such as money laundering and illegal payments. Analysts use social media data to detect cybercriminals. Data scientists use texting, phone calls, and e-mails to create a graph that shows how these data are related to criminals' records. Government agencies can identify the threats from non-obvious patterns of relationships from those graphs.

Investigative journalism: Graph analytics is being used by researchers to quickly browse through thousands of interlinked documents to spot money swindling and stashing. How did authoritarian leaders and corrupt politicians used complex sets of shell companies to horde and hide their ill-gotten wealth from the public scrutiny? Using graph analytics and document extraction tools, it is easy to structure the data from thousands of documents on companies in off-shore jurisdictions. The companies' real owners can be easily identified.

Supply chain optimization: In transportation networks, supply chain networks and airline companies use graph analytics algorithms such as shortest path and partitioning as tools to optimize routes.

Social network analysis: Social media networks such as Instagram, Linked In, and Spotify are relationship and connection-driven applications. Graph analytics plays an important role in identifying influencers and communities on social media.

Typically, we need to initiate and implement analytics in order to extract workable insights from data volumes. But, through the already-discussed visualization of graphs, it is possible to acquire some useful intelligence straightaway. However, visualization is not sufficient.

The process of analytics on relational data is quite primitive in most cases. For example, take Amazon's recommendations. If I buy a pair of shoes through Amazon.in, a leading B2C e-commerce website in India, it will continue to recommend more shoes as days go by. But if the recommendation is approached through graph-based data representation, then I will get comprehensive and correct recommendations (that is, not only shoes but also the products that are closely related to shoes). Thus, graphs go a long way in extending a helping hand in envisaging hitherto unknown possibilities and opportunities. Businesses and people benefit with such technologically enabled transitions.

There are valid and verified examples for showcasing how simple queries could generate smart results through the leverage of graphs. Besides products and their properties, the unique relationships among products and their components come handy in obtaining deeper insights when compared with traditional data representation methods. Another noteworthy facet is graph that guarantees higher performance. Even if dataset is massive, any query emits out proper response quickly. Because in the graph world, the latency between your query and response is directly proportional to how much of the graph you want to traverse whatsoever may be the data size. It is written that Neo4j, one of the popular graph databases, could do 40 million traversals per second.

13.12 The emergence of graph AI

Graph AI is the strategic sound combination of graph data and AI techniques. By applying the breakthrough capabilities of AI tools on graph data, the IT industry and the business world are to experience game-changing applications. In this section, we are to discuss the various concepts such as ML on graph data and deep learning on graph data.

Briefing the power of AI: The field of AI is famous in facilitating the process of producing actionable insights out of data heaps. This is done by simplifying and streamlining the complex process of data to information and to knowledge. Thus, for the ensuing knowledge society, AI's distinct advantage of knowledge discovery and dissemination come handy. Knowledge extracted through the AI process is readily and rewardingly supplied to the right and relevant everyday devices, business workloads, and IT services. Such an empowerment makes business and IT systems to be intelligent in their decisions, deals, deeds, and deliveries. AI ultimately empowers enterprises and entrepreneurs to envisage scores of sophisticated and smarter applications for solving professional, social, and personal problems.

In short, with AI-driven knowledge at hand, software developers can build intelligent applications across business verticals. Such knowledge discovery is being facilitated through the power of the ML and deep learning (ML/DL) algorithms. Computer vision (CV) and NLP are the keys AI use cases. In short, AI is pioneering in solving some specific problems such as classification, regression, clustering, recognition, detection, translation, etc. Precisely speaking, AI is widely termed as automated analytics. Just a set of data, whether labeled or unlabeled, is enough for AI systems to make sense out of it quickly. Automatically learning from the input data, ML/DL algorithms help to craft AI models, which can do a long of things, including proposing new theories, patterns, associations, conclusions, inferences, and predictions.

The AI's history and journey is simply mesmerizing. The first generation of AI was predominantly anchored in deterministic rules for creating and deploying expert systems in specific business domains such as healthcare. Then came scores of statistical models such as ML/DL algorithms that can infer intelligence from correlations, anomalies, and causal relationships from a huge volume of complex data.

Now we are getting ready for another revolution in the AI space. For a long time, we have been fiddling with a variety of rigid data schemas. Now data is represented through graphical structures. Such graph-based data representation goes a long way in facilitating a variety of things for AI engineers. Graphs can optimally encode linked data, and such a graphical representation gives the much-needed contextual details to enrich intelligence. Graphs can illuminate the shifting relationships among nodes.

13.13   ML on graphs

As mentioned above, ML has become a key approach in the AI space to solve specific and hard problems by automatically learning from input data. The learning leads to finding patterns and predicting future events. There are supervised, semi-supervised, and unsupervised ML algorithms. Let us discuss how ML algorithms work with graph data. ML has to learn from connections between data points in a graph. The traditional ML learns from individual data points but graph ML learns from the relationships between data points. Learning from the properties or features of individual data points is bound to lose some useful details whereas the properties about relationships between data points provide valuable information to describe the data set.

With graphs, the data points are represented by nodes, and information about the relationships is captured on the edges of the network. In the traditional ML, data scientists have to manually pick that information and transition it into decision-enabling features during the feature engineering phase, which is an important phase in an ML model development lifecycle.

ML with graphs is semi-supervised learning: The second key difference is as follows. ML with graphs tries to solve the same problems that supervised and unsupervised ML models attempt to do. The difference is that the requirement of having labels or not during training is not strictly obligated. ML on graphs takes the full graph to train the model. This includes all the unlabeled nodes as well. The information about neighbourhood nodes and edges can contributes in enhancing the model's decision-making power. Therefore ML on graph data is often called semi-supervised.

Node embedding: Creating node embeddings is for aggregating information of a node's position in the graph and its local neighbors. This aggregation process results in an encoded feature vector, called node embedding. Node embedding summarizes the properties of a node and its relationships with its local neighbor nodes. Getting a node embedding is the first step towards implementing an ML model with graphs. A node embedding thus created will be passed into another downstream ML model during training as an additional feature.

For example, developing a random forest (RF) classifier to determine whether a person is a fraud or not is the assignment at hand. Conventionally, the ML development lifecycle would start with transforming raw data into structured data by using some established feature engineering techniques. The features, thus developed, are then passed into the RF model to predict the labels. But in ML with graphs, the node embedding is inputted into the RF model as a feature vector.

Node classification: In the previous case, we discussed how a node embedding gets created and fed into an ML classifier as an input feature vector. However, it is also possible to classify node labels directly from the graph structural data without relying on a downstream ML model. This is called node classification, which is to predict the label of each node based on its association with other neighborhood nodes. The true labels are only included on a subset of the entire graph. Thus, given a partially labeled graph, the aspect of node classification comes handy in predicting the labels of the nodes without labels.

For example, there is a need for building a wild-life trading network to pinpoint illegal trading activities and parties. In this graph, each node could be a buyer or seller, and an edge would represent a trade transaction between the buyers and sellers. Node attributes could include name, date of birth, and bank account number, while edge attributes could include product name, trade document number, and price. If a subset of the sellers are labeled as illegal traders based on reported data, then the task at hand is whether a trader who has not been labeled, should be labeled as illegal or not. Node classification helps here by looking into the trading behavior with others in its network. Nodes with similar features and edges to the ones that have been labeled as illegal are more likely to be illegal as well.

Link prediction: Given a node pair without having a link between them, we need to predict if they will get connected in the future based on their node features and neighborhood nodes. That is, to determine the probability of having a link between two nodes in a graph. Currently, heuristic methods are used to calculate similarity scores between two nodes based on heuristics such as graph distance, common neighbors, or Pagerank. These heuristics or properties can be calculated directly from the graph to obtain the similarity score for each node pair. By sorting the node pairs based on their similarity score, it can be predicted that an edge has to be there between the highest-scoring node pairs.

A drawback of heuristic methods is that it assumes when two nodes have common neighbors they are more likely to connect. This phenomenon works well for social networks and wild-life trading networks. But for a protein–protein interaction network, two proteins sharing many common neighbors are less likely to interact. There is a challenge of determining which heuristic method we should use to calculate the similarity score that makes sense for our use case. Researchers have proposed a workaround. For each edge, take the enclosing nodes and generate an embedding for those nodes, and then pass those two node embeddings into a function that concatenate (or sum, avg, distance, etc.) them into a new feature vector and pass that to a downstream binary classifier. For more details, refer this page (https://towardsdatascience.com/introduction-to-machine-learning-with-graphs-f3e73c38d4f8).

13.14   Deep learning on graphs

We have discussed how ML techniques can be applied on graph data to extract useful insights in time. In this section, we are to discuss how the deep learning (DL) algorithms can be applied on graph data. It is well known that DL algorithms are disruptive and transformative for Euclidean data such as images or text. But applying DL techniques on graph data is not straightforward. This gap has propelled AI researchers on tasks such as graph representation learning, graph generation, and graph classification. In this regard, there are a few buzzwords such as graph neural networks (GNNs), graph convolutional networks (GCNs), and graph recurrent networks (GRNs).

13.15   GNNs

Neural networks are pivotal and prominent for computer vision and language processing use cases. Convolutional neural networks (CNNs) are the classic and conventional method to perform image classification. CNNs can be used to make our everyday machines visualize things, and perform tasks like image classification, image recognition, object detection, etc. Recurrent neural networks (RNNs) are famous for speech recognition, text translation, etc. Images of digits are represented in pixels, and the CNN would run sliding kernels (or filters) across the images. And the CNN model subsequently learns important features by looking at the adjacent pixels.

ML and DL algorithms are efficient in simple data types such as images with the same structure and size. Such uniform representation can be thought as fixed-size grid graphs. Text and speech are sequences, so they can be considered as line graphs. But in the real-world scenarios, there are complex graphs without a fixed form. That is, there are graphs with a variable size of unordered nodes (nodes can have varying number of neighbours). Further on, ML algorithms have a core assumption that instances are independent of each other. For graph data, this assumption goes awry. Each node is related to others by links of various types.

GNNs are a class of deep learning methods designed to perform inference on graph data. GNNs are neural networks that can work on graphs, and they provide an easy way to do node-level, edge-level, and graph-level prediction tasks. In short, GNNs can do what the traditional CNNs could not perform.

Now, with graph representation gaining importance, images are also represented as a complete graph, where each node represents each pixel and the node feature represents the pixel value. Edge feature represents the Euclidean distance between each pixel. The closer two pixels are to each other, the larger the edge values. The figure below vividly tells everything.

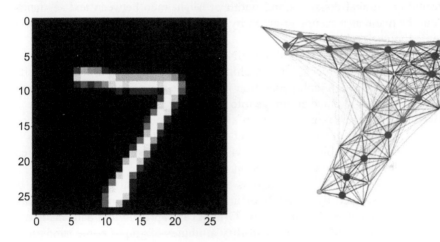

Actually, CNNs also see images as a graph, wherein each pixel (node) is connected to its adjacent pixels. These node connections are uniform among all pixels. However, where the node connections are dynamic, CNN has a problem. GNN can surmount this problem elegantly. That is, CNN works well on data with regular structure (Euclidean data). Also, CNN works with images (2-dimensional) and text (1-dimensional). GNN has the wherewithal to generalize CNN to work on data, which is not Euclidean.

GNN applications: Having understood the unique capabilities of GNNs, AI researchers and data scientists are exploring and experimenting to understand how GNNs can bring much-needed differentiation. One of the popular applications is information extraction tasks, especially information extraction from visually rich documents (VRDs). Another example is different useful entities getting extracted from receipts and invoices.

Normally, NLP is the way forward to accomplish information extraction. The famous technique is named entity recognition (NER). But, in the case of VRDs, NLP alone is not sufficient. Even for a human to recognize these entities, there is a need for other visual features such as the font size, the location of each text with respect to each other, etc. That means, any neural network (NN) model trained for VRDs has to be empowered to have both textual and visual features of the entities. Here, there is a role for GNNs. Here is a way to transform the data into a graph representation.

Each node represents an individual text segment (textbox). The node feature is the textual information of the text segment. This can be represented by a word embedding vector or encoding from sequence models such as recurrent neural network (RNN), gated recurrent unit (GRU), long short-term memory (LSTM), and so on. It is possible to enrich this representation by embedding more value-adding features, such as the text style (bold or italic) and Boolean features (e.g. isAlphabetic, isNumeric).

Now edge feature represents the linkage between two text segments, such as horizontal or vertical distances and width or height ratio between text segments. This can be made as a complete graph by defining all text segments (nodes) to be connected to each other.

GNNs in computer vision: With GNNs, machines can distinguish and identify objects in images and videos. GNN architectures can be applied to image classification problems. Scene graph generation is an image classification problem. Here, a GNN model aims to parse an image into a semantic graph that consists of objects and their semantic relationships. Given an image, scene graph generation models detect and recognize objects and predict semantic relationships between pairs of objects. The GNN-enabled computer vision applications include human-object interaction, few-shot image classification, etc.

GNNs in NLP: In NLP, the text is a type of sequential data which can be comfortably described by an RNN or an LSTM. However, graphs are increasingly used in various NLP tasks lately. Graphs can represent text data easily and elegantly. The flexibility and extensibility attributes of graphs come handy here in visualizing and realizing newer applications. Graphs are being leveraged for some of the renowned NLP problems like text classification, exploiting semantics in machine translation, user geolocation, relation extraction, and question answering.

GNNs in traffic management: Graphs are more appropriate for transport networks. Traffic congestion avoidance through traffic prediction is one key functionality in any smart transportation system. Spatial-temporal graph neural networks (STGNNs) can address the traffic prediction problem handsomely. The traffic network is typically a spatial–temporal graph in which the nodes are sensors installed on roads, the edges are measured by the distance between pairs of nodes, and each node has the average traffic speed within a window as dynamic input features. Spatial–temporal graphs utilize both spatial and temporal information to make predictions. By examining the spatial–temporal graph, we can predict traffic flow and driver maneuver anticipation.

GNNs in chemistry: As told above, GNNs are very efficient at expressing and exposing chemical interactions. Such a representation is for chemical experiments, which involve molecules. In these graphs, nodes are atoms, and edges are chemical bonds.

AI researchers are striving hard and stretching further to identify the potential areas and complicated problems wherein the smart leverage of GNNs is seen as a blessing. The application of GNNs is not limited to the above domains and tasks. There have been attempts to apply GNNs to a variety of problems such as program verification, program reasoning, social influence prediction, recommender systems, electrical health records modeling, brain networks, and adversarial attack prevention.

GNNs for text classification: GNNs utilize the inter-relations of documents or words to infer document labels. GCN and graph attention network (GAT) models are applied to solve this task. They convert text to graph-of-words and then use graph convolution operations to convolve the word graph. Researchers have shown that the graph-of-words representation of texts has the advantage of capturing non-consecutive and long-distance semantics. There are several other inspiring use cases for GNNs. Visit this page (https://neptune.ai/blog/graph-neural-network-and-some-of-gnn-applications).

13.16   Tending toward graph AI

There are a few critical issues with the current machine and deep learning approaches. The decisions and predictions being made by ML and DL models go wrong sometimes. Machines and deep learning have taken quite a bit of flak for being biased, unfair, and discriminative sometimes. Thus, there arose several hardcore research topics such as AI understandability, interpretability, explainability, transparency, and trustworthiness. This black-box problem is mainly caused by imbalanced sets of training data, or simply poor quality training data. That is easily fixed by employing more rigorous standards to the data before it is fed into the ML at the training stage. KGs are being touted as the best-in-class solution.

Another noteworthy problem is that the conventional ML and DL models tend to ignore context details. Any decision is going to be accurate when the context information is taken into consideration. That means ML can miss things that would be staggeringly obvious to a human. Without context details, AI models may be sabotaged to initiate cyberterrorism. Thus, when we move to deep automation through AI techniques and tools, there is a need for enhancing the AI model visibility. Deeper visibility enhances the confidence in the predictions of AI models.

By pivoting to graph modeling, the AI can look across a number of different datasets to infer context. The relationships between data points give more to AI models to arrive at correct and cognitive conclusions. That means when things change in one dataset, there is nothing to be bothered about. AI looks at corresponding anomalies in other relevant datasets to establish whether the problem is local or not.

With a large amount of digital data is being gathered from rapidly increasing data sources, data analytics is bound to be a complicated process. AI is being seen as a fabulous and futuristic paradigm for making sense out of digital data. There are transactional, social, biological, operational, application, service, device, and infrastructure data in plenty. Graph databases and KGs are being developed and deployed to leverage all kinds of internal and external data beneficially. Businesses and individuals are to benefit immensely out of data heaps if data gets changed methodically into knowledge.

There are manifold improvisations in data representations and schemas. SQL, NoSQL, distributed SQL, and in-memory databases are prevalent and paramount for enterprise automation. In the data engineering domain, there are a number of pioneering disruptions, innovations, and transformations. With the greater understanding of the power of graphs, there came a number of platform solutions for leveraging graphs for sophisticated data analytics. With high-performance computing technologies and tools are becoming pervasive and affordable, data analytics through graph representations of data is becoming the new normal. The positioning of clouds as the one-stop IT solution for business process automation requirements has led to the speedy implementation of graphs. Products capable of simplifying graph-based data analytics such as Microsoft Azure's Cosmos DB and AWS's Neptune have accelerated the adoption of graph analytics with all the confidence and alacrity. Graph neural networks are set to become a big and bright trend in enterprise IT.

13.17   Graph data platforms

Considering the strategic soundness and significance of graph databases in envisioning and implementing digital life applications, there came a number of graph data platforms for lessening the workload associated with graph data analytics. This section is allocated to write about a few prominent graph data platforms.

Neo4j (https://neo4j.com/product/) – The Neo4j graph data platform gives developers and data scientists a set of powerful tools to quickly build intelligent applications. This platform is powered by a native graph database. Neo4j stores and manages data in its more natural and connected state. It maintains data relationships for delivering lightning-fast answers, even for complicated queries. Further on, the platform supplies a deeper context for decisive insights. Analysts and data scientists can incorporate network structures to infer meaning, increase ML accuracy, and drive contextual AI. All these make better predictions. Neo4j is fuelled by a vast and production-ready algorithm library, and it is also blessed with advanced, ground-breaking ML workflows. Neo4j is an enterprise-strength graph database that combines native graph storage, advanced security, scalable speed-optimized architecture, and ACID compliance to ensure predictability and integrity of relationship-based queries.

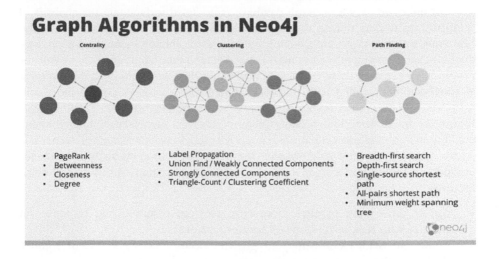

Graph data science (GDS) *library*: To predict and prescribe the best course of action, you need powerful data science created for connected systems. The Neo4j GDS library uses the relationships and network structures in data to help data scientists address complex questions about system dynamics and group behavior. Businesses use these insights to make valuable predictions, such as pinpointing interactions that indicate fraud, identifying similar entities or individuals, finding the most influential elements in patient or customer journeys, and how to minimize the impact of IT, phone, or other network outages.

Data scientists benefit from a repository of powerful, robust graph algorithms to quickly compute results over tens of billions of nodes. Graph algorithms provide unsupervised ML methods and heuristics that learn and describe the topology of your graph. The GDS library includes hardened graph algorithms with enterprise features like deterministic seeding for consistent results and reproducible ML workflows.

Cypher query language: Cypher is a powerful, intuitive, and graph-optimized query language that understands, and takes advantage of, data connections. When trying to find patterns or insights within data, cypher queries are much simpler and easier to write than massive SQL joins. Since Neo4j does not have tables, there are no joins to worry about. Neo4j supports GraphQL and drivers for .Net, Java, Node.js, Python, and more. There are drivers for PHP, Ruby, R, Erlang, and Clojure.

Neo4j AuraDB is Neo4j's fully managed cloud service – the zero-admin, always-on graph database for cloud developers. AuraDB is also on the Google cloud platform. AuraDB lets you focus on what's important – developing rich, graph-powered applications – without the hassle of managing infrastructure.

TigerGraph's graph platform enables users to connect, analyze, and learn from data (https://www.tigergraph.com/). Several unique use cases are being accomplished through this pioneering platform solution.

As inscribed above, a graph database is designed to facilitate the analysis of relationships in data points. A graph database stores data as entities and the relationships between those entities. Vertices represent entities such as a person, product, location, payment, order, and so on. On the other hand, edges represent the relationship between these entities. For example, this person initiated this payment to purchase this product with this order. Graph analytics is to explore these connections in data and to reveal insights about the connected data. These insights facilitates fraud detection, product recommendation, supply chain improvement, etc. TigerGraph architecture allows siloed data sets to be connected for deeper and wider analysis at scale. Additionally, the TigerGraph supports real-time in-place updates for operational analytics use cases. The graph database fulfils the following features.

- *Speed*: Massively parallel processing provides a sub-second response for queries with tens of millions of entities/relationships.
- *Scale-out*: Scales out with your growing needs (and stays fast, of course). Trillion-edge graphs are running real-time analytics in production.
- *Deep-link analytics*: Gain deeper insights through queries which can traverse 10 or more hops and perform complex analytics.
- *Graph query language*: The GSQL query language is the choice for high-performance graph operations and analytics. High-level syntax, Turing completeness, and built-in parallelism mean faster performance and development.
- *MultiGraph*: Multiple groups can share the same master database while retaining local control and security. This helps enterprises break down data silos, improving transparency and access to data.
- *Visual interface*: TigerGraph GraphStudio is a simple yet powerful graphical user interface. GraphStudio integrates all the phases of graph data analytics into one easy-to-use graphical user interface.

In short, graph data platforms are lessening the workload associated with the knowledge discovery of graph data. A number of platform and infrastructure services are being taken care of by such platform solutions. There are query languages for searching and retrieving information out of graphs. Product vendors are striving hard to build and release numerous automated toolkits for streamlining tasks associated with graph data analytics.

13.18   Conclusion

In the recent past, graphs are acquiring a surging popularity as they could easily and natively encode complex relationships between multiple objects in a domain, whereas other data representation methods are not found to be incompetent in accommodating product relationships and interactions. That means graph structures themselves could leak a lot of useful information to knowledge seekers. For deciphering any hidden insights, data scientists leverage a series of competent techniques and tools. There are a dazzling array of graph-specific algorithms for unearthing useful information out of graph structures. Then, there are graph databases, analytics methods, and platforms contributing immensely for enabling graph analytics. Thus, graph products and platforms in conjunction with established analytics methods are simplifying the complicated process of transitioning data into knowledge.

Now with the flourish of AI algorithms, libraries, frameworks, accelerators, and specialized engines, the task of producing accurate and high-performant AI models to predict a lot of things across industry verticals is being accelerated and automated. In this chapter, we have discussed and delineated how the power of AI can empower the prediction and prescription capabilities by leveraging graph data.

Chapter 14

Application of graph data science and graph databases in major industries

Yash Joshi[1] and Siddhesh Kapote[2]

Abstract

Graph data science can be used across several key industries such as Social Media Networks, Finance, Healthcare, Risk Management, Transportation, and Supply Chain. Using Graph databases, data can be presented in a new way which may open unlimited conceivable outcomes and help to tackle complex issues. In this chapter, we will see how these Graph Models help to resolve real-world problems in an unconventional and highly efficient way.

14.1   Introduction

14.1.1   Data science

Data science is the process of using data to find solutions or to predict outcomes for a problem statement to better understand data.

I am sure all of you have used Uber. What do you think makes Uber a multi-billion dollar company? Is it the availability of cabs or is it their service? Well, the answer is data. Data makes them very rich, but wait, is that enough to grow a business?

Of course, it is not. You must know how to use the data to draw useful insights and solve problems. This is where data science comes in.

Let us see how it affects our day-to-day activities. It is a Monday morning and I have to get to the office before my meeting starts. So I quickly open up Uber and look for cabs, but there is something unusual: the cab rates are comparatively higher at this hour of the day. Why does this happen? Well, obviously because Monday mornings are peak rush hours, cars and everyone is rushing off to work. The high demand for cabs leads to an increase in the cab fares. We all know this but how is all of this implemented?

Data science is at the heart of Uber's pricing algorithm. The Surge pricing algorithm ensures that their passengers always get a ride when they need one. Even

[1]Department of Computer Science Engineering, SRM Institute of Science and Technology, India
[2]Department of Electrical Engineering, Lokmanya Tilak College of Engineering, University of Mumbai, India

if it comes at the cost of inflated prices, Uber implements data science to find out which neighborhoods will be the busiest so that it can activate search pricing to get more drivers on the road in this manner. The number of rides it can provide and hence benefit from this Uber surge pricing algorithm uses data science. This is just one example of how data science affects our lives everyday.

14.2   Risk management

In the current online era, fraud has become a major issue for everyone who has an online presence. Risk is the effect of uncertainty on objectives. Risk management is one of the key components of an organization's overall governance framework.

Managing risk assists organizations in setting strategy, achieving objectives, and making informed decisions.

Taking risks is fundamental to an organization making profits and a non-for-profit delivering on its strategy innovation is risk. Growth is risk, an avoidance of risk poses a threat to the future of the organization, so doing nothing is probably the greatest risk.

This is where graph data science can come into the picture, as it provides advanced detection and analysis solutions.

With the help of graph data science, organizations can now take additional precautions to stay away from such frauds as the solution provides plotting relationships between data across various levels [1].

14.2.1   Fraud detection and analysis

These days, financial firms work toward passing on cash as quickly as possible to generous customers while also ensuring cash is not sent for unlawful purposes or covering the real beneficiary by getting sent in jumbled/hidden courses. This requires real-time fraud detection.

Graph data science discovers the association of individuals or typical patterns of deals/tracks in real-time to prevent ordinary frauds. To detect frauds, it is important to carefully look into the links between various verticals of business. This helps us in detecting which areas are more prone to threats and need to be fixed accordingly.

With this analysis, organizations can plan and implement measures to safeguard their operations. Graph analysis is also used by the police in tracking down the criminals by making optimum use of the available data such as phone records, previous history, date and time of places visited, location tracking, etc., and finding relationships between them.

A graph database enables associations to gather complex fraud detection details by separating the leads of various customers across a timeframe to recognize abnormalities that are by and large amazingly hard to see or encapsulate in hard-coded rules.

Property graphs are used as often as possible for fraud detection, especially in electronic banking and ATM region examination since customers can design the guidelines for perceiving fraud reliant upon datasets.

For instance, detection rules can be set up for:

- IPs who sign in with numerous cards enlisted in many places.
- Cards utilized in many places with extremely far distances.
- Records getting one-time inbound exchanges from different records enrolled in different spots.
- These guidelines can be applied in real-time since graph technologies can:
    - Keep graphs refreshed and synchronized to the first original table dataset
    - Run high-performance queries and algorithms

14.2.2   Anti-money laundering

Identifying the relationship or pattern of the people involved in fraudulent transactions from a mix of million other transactions is a major challenge. If you take the example of India, our country is densely populated and we have millions of customer accounts within the bank.

So how to identify patterns from within that huge data volume and how to make sure we identify or we consume it as a fraud pattern, since these are all customer account numbers which are all very sensitive information?

This information could be associated with real people or probably fake people trying to fake transactions under the name of real people, such information is very sensitive so you also have to look at the various regulations as well as the laws regarding the information technology practices.

We cannot just confirm a certain cycle is criminal in nature or fraud in nature. We have to find out different patterns from a mix of high-volume data landscapes and then try to identify and investigate further into the same transactions and that is exactly where graph analytics will empower an organization – by complementing the advantage of analyzing relationships between different people by using different attributes associated with the nature of the transaction.

By implementing such an innovative solution like graph analytics you are not just complimenting the organization you are also complimenting the government and the associated public entity that is related to the governance.

Information technology law practices now work to make sure crimes related to financial transactions are all regulated in a structured way.

Obviously with the graph what happens is that you will be able to analyze the relationship based on the vertex edges, different properties associated with the vertex, and add labels such that it gives a complete picture while trying to analyze the relationships.

Money laundering normally includes a very complex system and links through which it gets extremely difficult to find the fraud links as it gets merged in between the official transactions.

Various analytical and data science models can be applied to the data to analyze relations across various assets for more effective performance.

Illegal money generation has become extremely difficult to follow due to the extension of consistent mechanized moves and portions, complex overall laws, and an increase in advanced monetary forms.

The United Nations Office of Drug and Crime evaluates that money laundering is 2–5% of overall GDP.

Lately, money laundering is direct. Dirty money is passed around to blend it in with authentic resources and subsequently changed into hard assets.

Perceiving money laundering and financial deception requires going past solitary record leads, examining associations among get-togethers of records or substances as time goes on, often solidifying information from unexpected sources.

Traditional money laundering courses of action dependent on friendly informational collections are lacking.

Confirmation of money laundering issue [2]: Money launderers usually make complex transactions. This makes it a particularly difficult complex association of characters and records to channel the illegally earned profits.

Hence, it becomes very difficult and drawn-out to look for false alarms covered in someplace inside the store of authentic trades.

Think about the model where another entity is involved. This entity is categorized as an OK record under a standard scoring approach since no other attribute assessed by the typical evaluating technique like high-danger geography, trade aggregate, or several past alerts show basic money-related risk.

Regardless, the standard procedure fails to consider the pack of high-danger customers who have an undeclared relationship with the new customer.

The new customer shares a phone number with four other existing customers who have various SARs and are thus allocated as high risk.

Such concealed or undeclared associations through a phone number would have been exceptionally difficult to uncover using the human review or existing models and structures.

Graph data science reveals the mysterious relationship constantly and the new mindset of a high-risk alert.

Graph analytics used for creating queries to follow money:

Transaction data can also be represented by data in such way, hence making the queries:

- Intuitive
- Performant
- Better representing hidden relationships

For example, the queries which would once take a lot of time to write, for example queries for circular money, can be easily written. Moreover, they can be executed faster as well.

Queries such as traversal queries make it possible for the end user to find relationships that would be otherwise hidden, a good example would be the relationship between accounts and their owner, for example paradise paper.

Additionally, complex rules can also be written that can score suspicious accounts, i.e. give them a score of 0–100, and on the basis of that score we can have human experts to look into the matter more.

14.2.3 Identifying unexpected connections

With graph analytics, we can better understand and detect the relations that do or do not exist [3].

For companies, it is majorly about plotting down the right relationships. Suspicious activities are difficult to detect without understanding the proper links in the system.

Certain malicious software when found to have a presence at multiple places can be found to be suspicious. Identifying these relationships helps companies. Graph data science can be useful here.

Additionally graph visualization can be used to manually inspect suspicious accounts.

Users can expand the graphs to see particular information related to certain nodes.

Users can also run certain queries to find accounts that meet certain criteria, which helps the authorities examine the current criteria and create new criteria in the future as well.

One major issue that banks face is to find relationships in high volume data, i.e. financial cycles or identifying the criminal patterns by analyzing the relationships between the different customers. Customers are the prime focus of banks.

Individual customers: Individual transactions which are customers leveraging financial services from the banking applications including various frameworks like mobile web platforms.

They would be doing a lot of transactions over a period of time.

The relationship would obviously evolve or to multiple customers, multiple friends using the same bank accounts and trying to transfer the money between different people.

If we look at today's world, we have successfully tried recreating the relationships of a real world and between social network, what happens in this case is we would obviously try to capture information on the various transfers between different customers, map it to applications in the background and then try to identify the relationship and the bank would be having different challenges in relation to the high volume data landscape.

Let us take an example of a real company as they would obviously have different employees.

The company would at regular times send the salaries to the employees and there would be a loyalty factor between the company as well as the bank.

Based on the loyalty that they establish between the bank and the customer of the company the employees of that particular company would be eligible to leverage a lot of financial offers.

Such offers would be offered through credit cards, debit cards or even through the web platforms like applying for a loan and getting the same approved in very less amount of time or in an immediate way.

So they are all offers given to customers because they are part of a global company.

Now what happens when someone tries to create a fake company and then tries to register themselves as a sub company or a sub entity of the real company?

Such companies can associate different employees to the fake company just because they have registered or they have associated themselves with the real company in a fraudulent way.

At the end of the day they are employees of the fake sub company under this particular arrangement, they would also be eligible to avail the offers because of the loyalty factor between the original company and the bank.

This is a major issue where graph analytics can help identify unexpected connections.

14.2.4   Cyber security

Cyber security can be defined as the techniques and practices designed to protect data. And when we talk about data, we are talking about digital data.

Any network is a network of parts and cycles: the web is an interconnected plan of servers, routers, bridges, laptops, smartphones, and so forth – and measures are describing how these work together.

The interconnection between these entities can be immaculately tended to in a graph database. Any attack, either from outside an association or from inside it, can be shown using a graph database [4].

Graph is just a model of data where you care about how the data elements are connected to one another. Where those connections or those relationships between your data elements are as important as the data elements themselves.

Cyber security and cyber intelligence is a very broad domain and there are a number of different types of things where it can be useful to use graph data when you're collecting and looking at that kind of data such as IP communications, specifically all the way down to individual IP addresses and transport protocols between them can be modeled as a graph. So two IP addresses or devices are actually sending tcp/ip communications between them. That is the relationship looking at Network Devices internal to a LAN.

Graph propels get relationships between data entities, i.e., how PCs are related over an IT network.

They exploit additional signs from graphs for oddity distinguishing proof. They can overhaul digital risk recognizable proof by engaging interactive, visual examination of security data.

This sets up an ideal environment for digital risk pursuing.

Plus, graph databases are fit to recognizing and preventing dangers for reasons, including:

- Colossal data sizes – up to terabytes of log data made every day ought to be researched.
- Diverse data sources – information from different special sources, for instance, log archives, establishment data, and customer data, ought to be joined.
- Staggered structures – data set aside in organizations and microservices, regions and subdomains, legitimate reformist frameworks, ought to be addressed.

- Significant association with data science – requests need to cross different checks, regularly five and that is only the start.
- Fast response times – response ought to be given to queries within seconds.

14.2.5   Identity and access management

In the current on-premise and virtual era, it has become harder for organizations to manage access based on the identities of their employees.

Identity and access management is ensuring that the right individuals have access to the right resources at the right time and for the right reasons.

Graph database design takes into account real-time, cross-stage management of this data, including director data, end-user data, files, roles, and access rules for different employees. This will be looking specifically at the authorization rather than the authentication.

When it comes to important business work, dealing with such complex and huge amounts of data becomes of utmost importance and this is why graph databases are highly used. A graph database can help you solve some of those critical challenges that identity and access management faces.

From a high-level perspective, graphs are really good at complex queries. It is about the depth or the connectedness in the data, and the questions that you want to ask of the data.

Typically, those complex queries in a relational world, you would have to pre-calculate them. You would have to put them into some kind of a data warehouse, do some kind of modeling in it, and create a cue for a specific query, due to pre-calculation, and then you would expose it to an end user.

Here, essentially what you are doing is you are representing the data as a network, and then you can do all kinds of complex queries on it.

We model, we store, we manage the data as a graph, and represent that data in the forms of nodes and relationships, or they are called the vertices and edges.

Graphs can be really helpful with two things. The first is the high fidelity representation of complex real-world relationships. And the second thing is that the real-time queries that you are able to do to calculate, to assess, access controls in a live system, then you can do in a graph database, eliminate the need for integration and replication.

Using graph databases as our repository for these multi-dimensional views on access, also saves up on the integration work.

Graph database adoption today has been done in various verticals such as software financial services, retail media, social networks, telecommunication, healthcare, and then some other different verticals as well.

14.3   Marketing, product, and revenue

14.3.1   360-Degree customer view

One of the major reasons that organizations have started using Graph Data Science is to understand their customers better by getting access to all-around information.

Graph data science can estimate the expenses efficiently and quickly for organizations that have an extremely complex architecture involving various parameters.

A great use of graph databases is in consolidating a business' data from across its range of data storage facilities. This makes a complete view of the overall data architecture.

It is entirely expected for a business to have data about customers scattered across locations, and by explicit verticals of the association.

To make a 360-degree customer view, we stream data out of these locations into a graph, using a run-of-the-mill data model to give consolidation.

These datasets can be studied on graphs and the graph customers can fundamentally view the sum of the all-around data of on the customer.

With graphs, sponsors can procure a more extensive view of their customers – the associations, the customers, the associations between all of the purchased thing.

Having a live graph of all points of view contemplated by the customer leads to engagement of cutting-edge rich requests from customers.

Users can get significant information about explicit demographics or spaces of customers, gatherings of direct word on advancing events, and so on.

From the outset, data may be made open to promoters through rich visual query interfaces, with live views of customer snaps, coordinated efforts, and purchases, for example during an uncommon event.

As more arrangements are made of customer data, AI models can be lead to increased impact of organized, advanced development of customer data.

14.3.2   Recommendation engines

Data that is graph-structured very well represents the association among the data, hence it is used very frequently in the world of machine learning, specifically in recommendation engines.

People and song recommendations are some ordinary suggestions you hear these days on your online media profiles.

In graphs, you focus on the connections between data and you organize your data from entities and the relationships between them. So it is designed for working with highly connected, very complex data sets with a lot of relationships.

Graph data science helps with recognizing practically identical customers and engages tweaked recommendations while using filtering.

In development, consistent recommendations are ending up being a higher need than any time in ongoing memory [5].

The technology for collecting all of this data and outlining relationships to get a better understanding of customer needs and product trends and then to provide real-time recommendations is graph databases.

Graph databases are built so that the associations among customers and the things they like to buy are, which as of now spread out, it ends up being basic and speedy to run algorithms through the data to find recommendations.

By examining the simultaneous occurrences and amount of times such occurrences happen companies can use graph databases to make real-time recommendations based on.

And the great thing about it is often in an organization that is been around for quite a while we have a number of different data silos, different systems in which data lives. So our customer data could be in a customer relationship management (CRM) system. One might have third-party data, market data, and another system that holds our product data.

So being able to combine all that data, link all that data, and understand the relationships between it across all those systems gives you a really powerful view across your business you cannot really get when you approach your data in a structured way.

The machine learning technique of Collaborative Filtering also utilizes the same technique to get to know the comparative end-users and thus custom recommendations are possible.

Additionally, other companies which are not social media sites also use Collaborative Filtering, one example being – eBay, which uses the same to deliver the apt result as per the previous history of the user.

14.4 Social network – analysis and bot detection

14.4.1 Social network – analysis

LinkedIn, Facebook, and Apple Music are all social networks, hence they are driven by relations and connections. Graph data science recognizes key networks and influencers in such networks.

Such networks are a force to be reckoned with and advancing.

Social networking data analysis gives us tools to quantify those connections between individual points often in the visual format so that we can find patterns in the forces that connect us together as a society. It can generate graphical representations that reveal individuals in populations that bridge social groups.

By utilizing information from social networks in graph data science, associations can recognize forces to be reckoned with and pioneers [6].

The discussed technique is useful to screen preposterous encounters that can surge the unique cycle and associate with leading buyers more accurately progress them through the business pipeline.

Workforce data science is a technique that can similarly use the aforementioned technique to perceive pioneers and key social personalities who can affect the people to accept drives, make influence, and even assure shabby direct conditions.

Social network analysis is a very open field and there are lots of technical options to try out. Like adding geographic mapping data to understand how physical environments change network dynamics.

Ensuring buy-in and responsibility of these forces to be reckoned with can provoke a prevalent all-around laborer responsibility moreover [7].

14.4.2 Bot detection

Discovering bots in networks are important to companies. Data in such companies can be hugely affected because of the presence of bots.

In a case like this, graph data science can be used to find bots, which cause major problems.

Associations used in graph data science can be used to choose genuine accounts. Such accounts are chosen by looking at retweets and account activity with other accounts.

Accounts that are not normally advanced (bots) show characteristics that are varied from typically notable accounts for certain ordinary unnatural deviations.

Following are the methods used to distinguish a more critical number of bots that use graphs and associations in their working:

- Accounts having a high retweet count
- Inspecting the aforementioned by various accounts
- Recognizing those who get retweets from such bot

14.5   Compliance

14.5.1   Financial compliance

Companies in the finance ecosystem are expected to thwart transactions to a certain list of organizations and graph data science is used to identify such transactions.

Graph data science is used to spot cheats or lawbreakers and illegal exercises, for instance, tax avoidance and payments to approved components.

To recognize hooligans, specialists use the information of networks such as Facebook, Twitter, informing, calls, and messages to identify how the aforementioned are related to the violators. With that graph, government associations can perceive risks from non-clear instances of relationships [8].

Such structure can be taken as a part for compliance purposes. Financial organizations need to assure that their users are not connected to entities that are lawbreakers.

The main three applications of graphs in this industry are the following:

1. Following money frauds using graphs to follow edges on graph having bank accounts as nodes and transaction as edges graph queries can find the relationship between two account and also you can detect the specific patterns such as fraudulent activities.
2. The next application is that holding the data in the graph for visualization. Different types of data sets can be connected and visualized easily like in graph visualization applications that maintained not only the transaction data sets but also personal information such as family relationships withdrawal from ATMs and lobbying histories from the websites. So all this information for a particular account can be shown in one screen as a graph and this is useful for personalizing the services and manual investigation for suspicious accounts for protection.
3. The third application of graphs is to combine it with machine learning. Machine learning is the key method to enhance and automate fraud detection but its performance is limited by the training data set. So how we can generate

such features of the accounts from their relationship information is the key to train and improve the machine learning model.

Hence, we can conclude that important decisions in financial institutions can be made using graph data science.

14.5.2   Regulatory compliance

It is very important for organizations these days to comply with rules and regulations. It is essential to follow compliances, some important compliances include the following:

- Health Insurance Portability and Accountability Act
- Payment Card Industry Data Security Standard
- EU General Data Protection Regulation

It is mandated for companies to follow these compliance rules if they want to operate in a particular region.

Graph databases are essential to make sure that such compliance is followed as they can track essential information and give a birds-eye view of the data of the entire organization, hence providing a way to make sure that regulatory compliance is followed.

14.6   Healthcare

14.6.1   Critical node detection to find super-spreaders and contamination in a pandemic

Deriving insight from big data has quickly shown its ability to impact and enhance all aspects of our lives and health care is no exception where big data is revolutionizing medicine genomics research and disease management.

In its raw form, big data's value is limited. Unlocking its potential insight requires analysis. Graph analytics is a powerful new way to discover valuable hidden connections, relationships, and trends, where connections and relationships are realized through statistical analysis.

Using graph analytics users can visualize and identify meaningful relationships from large structured and unstructured data sets, this can enable life enhancing discoveries using large-scale biomedical graph analytics, healthcare genome sequencing, and healthcare genome analytics.

The 2019 novel coronavirus a new kind of coronavirus which have not seen among humans before was discovered. The theory is that it may have jumped from an animal species into the human population, and then begun spreading. So people were concerned, because we did not know exactly how severe the disease would be or how far it would spread.

When a new virus emerges, we often have to learn much more about it, and one of the things that we question is how it does transmit from person to person?

In graph structures, each node is different. For example, in a pandemic – a certain set of infected people and incidents are super-spreaders [9]. In such cases, graph data science can be used to find the aforementioned and hence avoid further spreading and ensure containment.

The world is going up against COVID-19. Since the disease is known as significantly difficult to track. Graph data science can help institutions prevent spreading and contain the spreading similar group nodes.

An association in China has manufactured an application using graph data science that grants Chinese authorities to verify if certain individuals were in touch with a known carrier of the virus.

14.7   Resource administration and optimization

14.7.1   Resource administration

Enhancing the utilization of organization resources and expanding usage in electronic and correspondence organizations requires changing burdens. By looking at the graph network, we can easily find out the resources which are burdened, and thereby we can reduce workload off those resources by changing the allocations.

Companies that provide fundamental resources can utilize graph data science to optimize their resource allocation and delivery, for example, organizations that are involved in:

• Electric supply to houses
• Water supply
• Gas and petrol supply
• Sewage services

Additionally, it can be used by companies in the supply chain and logistics industries to find routes that will help reduce the time and money involved.

14.7.2   Finding the shortest route and clustering

Graph data science enables to find the route between any two locations that are the following:

• Least in distance
• Least in cost

Traditional databases cannot be used for the same as they are not able to capture complicated relationships and cannot give a birds-eye view.

Data science can additionally be also used to group nodes that are similar.

While traditional databases can do low granularity groupings (clustering by Pin code), graph databases can help identify relations at a much higher granularity, for example – certain users which have the most time spent on a website may be the ones who purchase the most.

Additionally, we can cluster customers on the basis of their history of purchase and other variables including location, gender, time spent, etc.

14.7.3 Supply chain and utility optimization

In transportation associations, supply chain associations and delivery associations use graph analytics for calculating as the fastest path.

Supply and transport pipelines have dozens, if not hundreds, of stages, and an ability to analyze and appreciate the impact across many levels is essential. Graph data science powers advanced assessment and pattern recognition to separate item delays, shipment status, and other quality control and peril issues.

Companies can show their supply chain limits and business gauges logically, allowing the spread of interest and supply changes through the 10+ level significant worth chain to find out potential supply power outages and make the ideas for keeping an eye on those in an advantageous manner.

Graph data science also enables finding the path with the least distance, this can be used in industries such as aviation and transport and can be used in supply chain optimization.

14.7.4 Network mapping

Structure mapping and inventory are an ideal fit for depiction as a graph. Explicitly when mapping associations between related physical/virtual hardware and the organizations that they support.

They are used to screen parts, software versions, and the interdependencies between them.

Admins can similarly figure out which obligations are impacted on the plausible resource power outages and how to restrict the impact by moving the fundamental positions to other preparing or limiting laborers.

A graph of the associations between structure parts not just engages insightful visualizations of the network estate but furthermore networks follow algorithms to walk the graph.

14.8 Data science research

14.8.1 Graph neural networks

Various data scientists are starting to become motivated by graph neural networks, which can get a graph as a contribution of machine learning and neural networks.

Graphs are being widely adopted as they granularly represent the elements and their relationships which helps with modeling of the data in a more structured manner. This method uses the structural manner of representation of the graph and runs models on it for learning.

The graph may potentially hold a greater amount of data than standard tables because of the flexibility of the model.

Machine learning models with data obtained from graphs consistently give favored execution over machine learning reliant upon table shape input [10]. These models and graphs can be trained in a way that they help us with predicting the behavior of a user or a customer in a way that we understand the future activities of this user following a particular pattern.

Additionally graph analytics can be used to enhance machine learning models. These are majorly useful when the amount of labeled data is less than the amount of unlabeled data. Graph neural networks take input in the form of graphs and can be used for both to analyze a graph and to transform its type to something else.

Scores can be calculated using graph algorithms and these can be used as input features to enhance prediction models.

Some of the common examples of where graphs are commonly used with data science are:

- Recommendation system
- Search engine
- Maps
- Social media
- Web browsing

14.8.2   Feature engineering

Machine learning models rely on data. There is an entire development process to making a machine learning model, called feature engineering which includes working on the data.

Feature engineering is basically the making use of the raw data that is not processed or refined into creating features that your graph or machine learning model can use in order to provide you with better predictive results and decisions.

Endeavoring to do as such can require an extreme number of joins and be moderate and off-kilter to accomplish.

Features for machine learning models can be created through graphs by running graph algorithms on a dataset that has been stacked into a graph database and making upgraded dataset which would then have the option to be used for machine learning [10].

This movement of feature engineering outfits the machine learning model with more exhaustive, important data.

By including features obtained from graphs, machine learning models can end up being even greater and more definite.

Graph algorithms can be run on data to make new pieces of information, for instance, using clustering to find similar customers subject to the things they bought.

References

[1]   T. Pourhabibi, K.-L. Ong, B.H. Kam and Y.L. Boo, Fraud detection: a systematic literature review of graph-based anomaly detection approaches, *Decision Support Systems*, 133, 2020, 113303, ISSN 0167-9236, https://doi.org/10.1016/j.dss.2020.113303.

[2]   D. Salas, Combating Money Laundering: AML Compliance Program Design, https://neo4j.com/blog/combating-money-laundering-aml-compliance-program-design/

[3] C. Gaur, Overview of Graph Analytics Adoption and Business Use-Cases, https://www.xenonstack.com/blog/graph-analytics-use-cases

[4] F. Böhm, F. Menges and G. Pernul, Graph-based visual analytics for cyber threat intelligence. *Cybersecurity* 1, 2018, 16, https://doi.org/10.1186/s42400-018-0017-4

[5] M. Cimini, Graph-Based Real-Time Recommendation Systems, https://medium.com/quantyca/graph-based-real-time-recommendation-systems-8a6b39 09b603

[6] W.M. Campbell, C.K. Dagli and C.J. Weinstein, Social Network Analysis with Content and Graphs, http://pzs.dstu.dp.ua/DataMining/social/bibl/20_ 1_5_Campbell.pdf

[7] N. Mithili Devi and S. Rani Kasireddy, Graph Analysis and Visualization of Social Network Big Data, https://www.researchgate.net/publication/330004744_Graph_Analysis_and_Visualization_of_Social_Network_Big_Data

[8] A. Woodie, Graph Analytics Powers Insights in Financial Services, https://www.datanami.com/2021/04/26/graph-analytics-powers-insights-in-financial-services/

[9] L. Karl Branting, F. Reeder, J. Gold and T. Champney, Graph Analytics for Healthcare Fraud Risk Estimation, https://www.researchgate.net/publication/310809561_Graph_analytics_for_healthcare_fraud_risk_estimation

[10] A. Singh, Graph Analytics and Big Data, https://datascience.foundation/sciencewhitepaper/graph-analytics-and-big-data

Chapter 15

Graph data science for cybersecurity

Pethuru Raj[1] and Nachamai Muthuraman[2]

Abstract

Cybersecurity has turned out to be an important field of research and development. With the continuous rise of cyber-attacks on application data, business workloads, and IT services, there is a need for unearthing unbreakable and impenetrable security solutions. This chapter is to describe how data science methods come handy in producing and sustaining resilient and robust cybersecurity systems and services.

15.1 Introduction

A network (usually referred to as a graph) is a mathematical structure made up of nodes (or vertex or points) connected by edges (also called links). Nodes may represent different entities including customers, employees, or places like retail stores, airports, or represent things like assets, grids, bank accounts, URLs, and so on. Edges can stand for likes and dislikes, e-mails, payments, phone calls, and much more. Each node and edge can have some specific properties, which unambiguously describe its characteristics. For an appropriate example, let us take a social network. Herein the node can be a person, and the edges can represent the relationship between them (i.e., friendship). Each person node can be blessed with multiple properties like the person's name, occupation, address, etc. The friendship edge can have properties like the date on which they got hooked for the first time. All these are pictorially illustrated in the figure below.

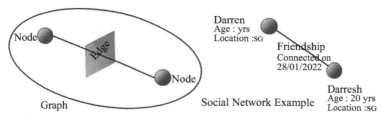

Graph

Social Network Example

[1]Edge AI Division, Reliance Jio Platforms Ltd., Bangalore, India
[2]Siemens Healthcare Pvt. Ltd, Bangalore, India

There are several types of graphs to accurately simulate different real-world networks:

- Undirected graph: In this graph, edges do not indicate any direction. As per the above-mentioned social network, the friendship relation is mutual between any two person nodes.
- Directed graph: Here edge(s) have orientations. This graph can be used to model non-mutual interactions between nodes. In the Research Gate professional site (https://www.researchgate.net/), A follows B but B might not follow A.
- Multi-edge directed graph: There can be multiple edge between two nodes with certain orientation(s). This graph can be used to model multiple transactions within a relationship like trips between station A and station B for public buses.
- Weighted graph: The edge of a graph can have weight. The links/connections between nodes carry some numerical attributes, like distance/cost/time taken for a trip from point A to point B.
- Self-loops: There are some nodes that are connected to themselves. In Facebook, one can like his own post. This is also called cyclic graph.

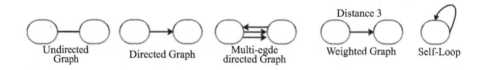

Undirected Graph   Directed Graph   Multi-egde directed Graph   Distance 3 — Weighted Graph   Self-Loop

Thus, datasets, their metadata, and relationships are being elegantly and explicitly represented through graph structures. Such an emphatic and enlightening representation helps immensely in simplifying and streamlining the act of knowledge discovery. Thus, the graph data structure plays a stellar role in succulently shaping up the process of insights generation out of data heaps.

15.2   Graph databases and platforms

A graph database is defined as a specialized and single-purpose platform for creating and manipulating graphs. As inscribed above, graphs generally contain nodes, edges, and properties. All of these entities are used to represent and store data in a way. Graph analytics requires a database that can support graph formats. There are two popular models of graph databases: property graphs and resource description framework (RDF) graphs. The property graph focuses on analytics and querying, while the RDF graph emphasizes data integration. Both types of graphs consist of a collection of points (vertices) and the connections between those points (edges). But there are differences as well.

Property graphs: These are used to model relationships among data and they enable query and data analytics based on these relationships. A property graph has vertices that can contain detailed information about a subject and edges that denote the relationship between the vertices. The vertices and edges can have attributes, called properties. In this example, a set of colleagues and their relationships are represented as a property graph.

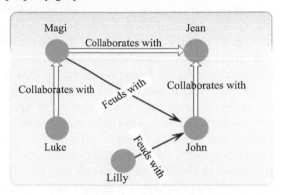

Property graphs are being applied across a broad range of industry verticals including finance, manufacturing, public safety, and retail.

RDF graphs are designed to represent statements and are best for representing complex metadata and master data. They can represent complex concepts in a domain or provide rich semantics and inferencing on data. In the RDF model, a statement is represented by three elements: two vertices connected by an edge reflecting the subject, predicate, and object of a sentence. This is known as an RDF triple. Every vertex and edge is identified by a unique resource identifier (URI). The RDF model provides a way to publish data in a standard format with well-defined semantics, enabling information exchange.

How graphs and graph databases work?: Graphs intuitively represent relationships in data. They allow users to perform "traversal queries" based on connections. Graph algorithms can be applied on graph connections to find useful patterns, outliers, optimal paths, and to form purpose-specific communities, and to identify influencers and fresh opportunities. Such an empowerment facilitates to do deeper and efficient analytics against massive amounts of data. In short, graphs not only link disparate data sources but simplify doing analytics on them to extract timely and trustworthy insights.

Graph algorithms explore the various paths between the vertices and understand the importance of the vertices. They can form clusters out of the vertices to solve specific problems. For example, graph algorithms can identify what individual or item is most connected to others in social networks or business processes. Graph algorithms can traverse through all connections between vertices quickly. That is, real-time exploration of graphs is fulfilled through advanced graph algorithms. There is no need for executing countless joins as we have been doing with the traditional databases.

Advantages of graph databases: The much-published graph format provides the flexibility for finding distant and deep connections. It can strengthen the aspect of data analytics based on multiple things especially the uniqueness of relationship. Graph structures help to pinpoint useful connections and patterns across a variety of networks such as social and professional networks, IoT devices meshes, transport networks, biological networks, etc. Such a capability accrued and captured through graphs goes a long way in helping out institutions, innovators, and individuals in their missions. Graph-based data processing on complex transaction data can result in several business cases including fraud detection. Data scientists are increasingly leveraging the unique competencies being offered by graph structures to exploit hidden insights in graph-represented data heaps. Any knowledge discovered is to assist varied and versatile business operations.

Because graph databases explicitly store the relationships, queries and algorithms utilizing the connectivity details between vertices can be accomplished in sub-seconds rather than hours or days. Users do not need to execute countless joins. Graph databases are turning out to be a powerful tool. Because of the graph format, complex relationships can be determined for deeper insights with much less effort. Graph databases generally run queries in languages such as property graph query language (PGQL). Any graph data can be used by graph analytics tools and machine learning (ML) models to intuitively discover more about the world around us.

15.3   Demystifying graph analytics

Generally speaking, data analytics is all about methodically leveraging statistical methods, enabling algorithms and frameworks, integrated analytics platforms, and scores of automated tools to collect, ingest, store, correlate, and crunch to extract actionable insights. The long-pending goal of data-driven insights and insights-driven decisions is being facilitated through a litany of data analytics methods. The process of transitioning raw data into information and into knowledge is being accelerated and accentuated through a bevy of digital technologies. There are data analytics techniques and tools in plenty. With the surge in the number of digitized entities, connected sensors and IoT devices, there is a massive amount of multi-structured data getting generated. It is a universal fact that there are a lot of useful information and insights hidden in data mountains. The perpetual challenge is how to make sense out of overflowing data volumes. Now with data gets represented through graphs, the aspect of data analytics becomes easier, deeper, and faster.

Graph/network analytics represents a set of integrated techniques to pinpoint and pick up useful relationships among actors. Not only enabling knowledge discovery and dissemination, graph analytics is also destined to interpret all kinds of decisions, conclusions, and inferences in an unambiguous manner. Graphs are becoming pervasive and persuasive too. There are social networks, transportation networks, biological networks, etc. They have a lot of intelligence hidden inside. Therefore, graph analytics has gained a lot of mind and market shares these days as it has the wherewithal to facilitate and fast track the extraction of usable and explainable insights in time from large-scale graph data. Interestingly, graphs simplify business and social problems as they carry the unique advantage of representing these new-generation problems in a flexible fashion. And then there are myriads of graph-centric tools, databases and platforms to deeply and decisively play around with graph data. Such an empowerment results in squeezing out actionable insights. Thus, graph analytics is being touted as the future of data analytics with the consistent contributions from worldwide tool and product vendors. With the greater awareness of graphs and their unique helps in data analytics, there are coordinated and concerted efforts being undertaken to make graph analytics a common and casual affair.

15.4 Graph analytics in the real-world applications

Graph analytics is primed for accurately modeling interactions between entities and subsequently to emit out viable insights out of the interactions. Graph analytics refers to the process of analyzing graph-represented data using data points as nodes and relationships as edges. Experts have pointed the following types of analytics.

- *Centrality analytics* – This analytics is mainly employed to identify the prominent nodes in a graph. It enables estimation of how important a node is for the connectivity of the graph. This is done by measuring the degree of centrality (the ratio of a total actual neighbor of a node compared to a total possible neighbor of a node) of each node and rank them. Such analytics is for finding key entities, like figuring out the influential people in a social network, key transportation hubs, etc.
- *Connectivity analytics* – This is to focus on the specific unique characteristics of the nodes' connections. This helps to determine how many edges are flowing into a node and how many are flowing out of the node. In a fraud detection case, this analytics method is to model user accounts and transactions, top in point users that are related to a known fraudulent user, and to put a limit to their transactions to prevent fraud. This determines how strongly or weakly connected two nodes are.
- *Community analytics* – Using graphs, it is possible to find several central nodes and discover groups/communities between them. This is a distance and density-based analysis of relationships used in groups of people, to find groups of people frequently interacting with each other. For example, in a social network like Instagram, besides their friends and relatives, people follow accounts with causes that spike their interests like photography, food, or fashion. Mapping these connections can be useful to make recommendations.
- *Path analytics* – This examines the relation between nodes in a graph. This is for determining the shortest distance between two nodes. This is mainly done on weighted graphs. This analytics method can be used to figure out the desired path to move between nodes of a graph. Path analytics can be implemented for transportation use cases like figuring out the shortest time to travel between cities, or in supply chain use cases like determining distribution center location.

In nutshell, graph analytics is the analysis of relations among entities such as products, solutions, services, devices, and consumers. Telecommunication operators operate fixed or mobile networks which can be modeled as graphs. Telecom customers talk to one another and these relationships form graphs.

We discussed the prominent graph analytics types and in the subsequent sections, we are to discuss how these are impacting various real-world use cases.

Social network analysis – There are several social networks gaining surging popularity these days. One main task being done as a part of social network analysis is to detect and identify influencers and decision-makers. By having the continued engagement with these influencers can lead to fresh possibilities and opportunities. Specific communities can be formed through such individuals. Product marketing and promotion campaign can be hugely simplified to reach out as many buyers as possible.

As we see, social web sites emerge as the next-generation platform product marketing and promotion campaign. Graph analytics can contribute intelligently in selecting the influencers. Using connectivity and community analytics, we can identify influencers and their followers easily. This leads to sell more items and helps to explore fresh avenues to increase revenues. The other implications of social media analytics include

- Identifying communities.
- Identifying users with the most influence.
- Finding connections between specific entities.
- Identifying malicious bots.

Fraud detection – Financial organizations are facing a number of challenges and concerns in their day-to-day operations and service delivery due to their richness and reach. There are brilliant cybercriminals, hackers, and other evildoers targeting financial services providers across the globe to steal customer, confidential, and corporate information. Advanced graph analytics comes handy in providing deeper insights. Such intelligence enables financial organizations to preemptively prevent any financial fraud while protecting customers.

Fraud detection involves identifying fraudulent transactions and bad actors in financial networks. This helps to look for already committed crimes and to analyze incoming transactions. Such an empowerment makes real-time decisions about their legitimacy.

Building recommendation system – Recommendation capability is an important one for a variety of service providers such as B2C e-commerce companies, video service providers such as Netflix. The above-discussed community analytics is the main contributor of this unique use case.

Transportation networks – There are many such networks like street networks, railway networks, river networks, and scores of pipeline networks (water, drainage, gas, electricity, etc.). Airports as nodes and edges connecting multiple airports across the world can be a prime example for the graph structure. Thus, several kinds of networks emerge and seek answers for a variety of analytical questions. Fortunately, these real-world networks can be modeled as graphs with edges connecting several points of presence (PoPs)/hubs/nodes. Graph analytics can bring a suite of verifiable and venerable insights in time out of these network datapoints. All kinds of transportation problems can be tackled through advanced graph analytics.

- Identifying the shortest path between two points in the network.
- Determining the most efficient route for a delivery vehicle to visit a series of stops.
- Defining the service area around a given location.
- Identifying an optimal store location to supply the largest number of potential customers effectively.

Thus, transportation networks facilitate newer use cases and applications through the careful usage of graph data analytics.

Supply chain management (SCM) – Previously SCM was easy and straightforward before as one producer supplies his fully developed products to his loyal and royal customers. However, with globalization, brands can source products from multiple providers across the globe. This makes inventory management a bit complicated. Having a tighter control on the sources and supplies along with all the connections turns out to be a tedious and time-consuming task. There is a need for a series of innovations to deal with such complications. Graph databases are being presented and pitched as the way forward to simplify SCM.

Chemical industry – In this cut-throat competitive environment, operational efficiency is being touted as the prime requirement for enterprising businesses. Especially chemical companies are consistently looking for viable strategies to improve the way they manage their production systems and resources in real time across manufacturing and supply chains. With the concept of digital transformation is all set to sweep the entire industry, chemical companies are plunging into digitization arena to empower their assets digitized. Also, they invest heavily in setting up and sustaining analytical systems and cloud infrastructures to face the challenges ahead. All kinds of digital data getting generated get meticulously captured and subjected to a variety of investigations to extract actionable intelligence in time. Any data-driven insights contribute handsomely for the industry sustenance. Data analytics is turning out to be a huge contributor for succulently achieving the intended success.

In short, graph analytics methods have cemented their place in the field of data science. While data becomes more complex and interconnected, the application of graph algorithms and graph query languages is essential for timely and trustworthy data processing and analysis.

15.5 Why graph analytics acquires special significance?

As articulated above, graph analytics is being flooded with a set of pioneering techniques and tools to enable data scientists to bring out useful connections among all of the nodes in a graph structure. The nodes may represent distributed places, things, systems, and events. The relationships among the nodes offer an enhanced business value to organizations as they guarantee improved customer understanding, service, logistics, and risk mitigation.

Graph creates context details – Context-awareness is important for visualizing and realizing smarter and sophisticated business workloads and IT services. Data scientists have to acquire context information. For that, they need to better understand the connections between seemingly disparate data from fragmented assets. Any decision based on context intelligence is bound to be right and strategically sound for worldwide enterprises to plan accurately and to execute the planned with all the clarity, confidence, and alacrity.

Graph is inherently superior in extracting and establishing context. Knowledge graphs (KGs) are primed for building deep contexts. KGs greatly contribute in bringing forth context intelligence. For creating interpretable AI, KGs play a very stellar role. The connections between nodes come handy in inferring new knowledge. AI systems are being substantially empowered through KGs.

Graph is critical for AI success – AI is for replicating human brain capabilities in our everyday machines including smartphones, consumer electronics, kitchen utilities, industrial machineries, robots, drones, gadgets, and gizmos. Knowledge has to be extracted from data emanating from multiple sources and has to be shared across. All kinds of data have to be meticulously collected, cleansed, and crunched in order to squeeze out actionable insights in time. The intelligence, thus acquired, can be supplied to various business workloads, IT services, connected equipment, machines, appliances, wares, instruments, etc. so that they can exhibit adaptive and adroit behavior to precisely reflect the change in situations and surroundings. There are powerful analytical methods to tackle structured data. But graph theory has laid down a stimulating foundation for the new era of graph analytics. With the faster maturity and stability of graph algorithms, databases, and platforms, the aspect of graph analytics has started to pick up. In other words, graph analytics is seen as an advanced analytical method to go deep into graph data to emit out actionable intelligence.

Especially with the advent of ML and deep learning (DL) algorithms, the much-adorned and adored graph analytics is bound to perform better in accurately recognizing hidden yet useful patterns and in bringing them out to be leveraged by devices, software products, solutions and services, and networks. AI-inspired graph analytics is to sagaciously empower data scientists in their everyday assignments. AI helps graph analytics to identify and inform context insights. With context, any decision and action are set to be right and relevant.

As indicated above, graph shines the light on deep neural networks (DNNs), which are typically termed as black-box models. Graphs help users to understand feature importance easily. Appropriate graphs can be created and used to explain the relationship between features. Such an empowerment can unambiguously explain why the AI model has arrived at such a conclusion/classification/recognition/detection/translation. Graph also provides information about AI models. That is, model metadata is being obtained from the graph structure directly.

Graph makes data science project management easier and effective – Data science projects typically involve data engineering steps such as data integration and virtualization, data ingestion, storage and preparation, etc. Then feature engineering is another important requirement. Model building, evaluation, optimization, and deployment are the subsequent tasks for data scientists. Graphs can play a significant role in accomplishing all these.

- *Accelerated data preparation* – Data integration and preparation are complicated, time-consuming yet essential tasks for AI model generation. The fast-emerging and evolving graph technology can augment and accelerate data preparation by harmonizing heterogeneous data formats and schema into a unified and useful model, which makes data transformation easy, fast, and automatable.
- *Data exploration through graph visualizations* – Graphs allows operations team, business executives and practitioners to find all that are needed (decision-enabling features/input predictor variables) intuitively and quickly to make accurate decisions.
- *Superior feature engineering* – Feature engineering is a manual process in making ML models. Extracting relevant features out of input training data is typically tedious and error-prone. Graphscan enrich training data with all the correct features. For example, in the centrality or influencer analysis, if another node is connected to the influencer, then it is used as an additional feature in the training dataset. Such contributions of graphs come handy in enhancing the predictive power of the ML model.
- *Improved communication and collaboration between data scientists and subject matter experts (SMEs)* – As discussed before, knowledge graphs are being proclaimed as the most significant derivative of the graph technology for the knowledge world. KGs, which emerge as a precise model of any knowledge domain, intrinsically provide common and communicable structures, taxonomies and ontologies. KGs are capable of providing relevant facts/clarifications and contextualized answers.

Thus, graphs are destined to greatly simplify data analytics and AI-driven data science activities. Graphs emerge as the foundation for achieving the ideals of composite AI, which is the combination of different AI techniques to achieve the best result. Proven and potential AI methods can be sophisticatedly combined to guarantee the best prediction every time.

How is graph analytics different from the rest? – Generally, the data analytics on relational data investigates relationships by comparing one-to-one or maybe even one-to-many relations. But data analytics on graph data can also compare many-to-many relations. The relational analytics works best on the structured and rigid data sorted in tables and columns. Graph analytics can play around with the unstructured and varying datasets. Graph analytics is extremely good at providing information and context about relationships in a graph. The insights being unearthed graph analytics is deep and decisive. Thereby the prediction accuracy is very high.

15.6   How graph databases and graph analytics work?

As articulated above, there are several business, technical, and user cases emerging and evolving with the combination of graph databases and analytics platforms is at work. With different professional, social, and personal problems are being stylishly represented as networks, the role and responsibility of graph databases and analytics are bound to go up sharply in the days to unfurl. The graph representation goes a long way in simplifying problem representation and speeding up the problem resolution. Several experts have come out with possible use cases when analytical techniques and tips are used on graph databases.

Money laundering – This is becoming a common yet grave issue. Money laundering (https://www.investopedia.com/terms/m/moneylaundering.asp) is all about illegally making large amounts of money through criminal activities such as drug trafficking, The challenge is that the money transaction appears to have come from a legitimate source. This money is termed as dirty and the process "launders" makes it look clean. Dirty money is passed around to blend it with legitimate funds and then turned into hard assets.

To detect this, users can create a graph from transactions between entities as well as entities that share some information, including the email addresses, passwords, addresses, and more. Once such a graph is created, running a simple query will find all customers with accounts who have similar information and reveal which accounts are sending money to each other.

Social media analysis – Social networks are hugely popular these days as they become a versatile platform for establishing and sustaining the societal relationship. Graph databases and analytics platforms play a very vital role in squeezing out useful information from social data. Who are active and dormant in a particular social web site? Who have gained much to be great influencers? Who command the greatest number of followings? There are several specific questions to be answered through graph analytics on social media data. However, a prickling challenge here is there is the extensive use of bots, which stealthily work in social application platforms. For example, bots automatically retweet, some tweets to spike up the popularity of a person or party. This is totally unacceptable. The recommended approach is to use graph analytics to identify a natural pattern versus a bot pattern. From there, it is a simple filtering out of those accounts.

Detecting credit card fraud – There are several anti-fraud technologies. Still credit card frauds are happening. To enable fraud detection, pattern identification is the way forward. Purchase patterns are typically based on location, frequency, types of stores, and other things that are compatible to the user profile. When something appears totally anomalous, pattern detection flags it as potentially fraudulent. Graph analytics excels at establishing patterns between different nodes such as cardholders, purchase locations, purchase category, transactions, and terminals. It is easy to identify natural behavior patterns for a person in a month. Graph analytics comes handy in delivering accurate and efficient predictions. Advanced graph analytics in conjunction with graph database tools helps to connect nodes (entities) and create relationships (edges) in graphs that users can query through a graph query language (GQL). The data and the relationship representation through graphs contribute in readily and rewardingly making sense out of data heaps.

The top tools for graph analytics – There are several tools to simplify graph analytics and for creating graph databases. Some popular graph analytics tools are

Neo4j (https://neo4j.com) – Neo4j gives developers and data scientists the most trusted and advanced tools to quickly build today's intelligent applications and ML workflows. This is available as a fully managed cloud service or self-hosted.

ArangoDB (https://www.arangodb.com/) – A scalable, fully managed graph database, document store and search engine in one place. ArangoDB Oasis is the cloud service for ArangoDB. It uses its own query language, AQL, similar to SQL, to retrieve and modify data. It also features ArangoML and a pipeline feature that makes transactions within the tool much simpler. It can also be used as an application server to fuse with databases, maximizing the output.

Amazon Neptune (https://aws.amazon.com/neptune/) – This is a fast, reliable, fully managed graph database service that makes it easy to build and run applications that work with highly connected data sets. The core of Amazon Neptune is a purpose-built, high-performance graph database engine optimized for storing billions of relationships and querying the graph with milliseconds latency. You can build KGs, fraud graphs, identity graphs, recommendation engines, master data management, and network security applications using Neptune.

Graph analytics saves much time since it takes less time in extracting insights out of data heaps and consumes fewer efforts while merging more data sources or points. The graph tool ecosystem is expanding fast. Graph data analytics, graph algorithms and databases, and scores of enabling and automated tools have laid down a stimulating foundation for simplifying and speeding up graph era. Graph analytics allows modeling, storage, and retrieval of data. Further, graphs are visually appealing and easier to understand. Besides direct relations, graph analytics can find indirect relations.

15.7   The emergence of graph data science

With the faster maturity and stability of digital technologies, businesses across the world are all set to be transformed decisively and profoundly. There are several innovative, disruptive, and transformative technologies emerging in the information and communication technology (ICT) space. It is, therefore, safe to expect the widely deliberated business transformation is to see the light soon. There are highly competitive and cognitive data analytics technologies and tools to facilitate the complex task of transitioning all kinds of data into information and into knowledge. In the recent past, we hear, read, and even talk about the mesmerizing advancements in the field of data science. Supported by a dazzling array of integrated platforms, toolkits, cloud infrastructures, ML and DL algorithms, data lakes, etc., the fledgling domain of data science is flourishing rapidly. The primary aim of data science is to play around with large-scale datasets with the unique intention of extracting hidden patterns, useful information, actionable insights, beneficial associations, impending risks, fresh opportunities and possibilities, etc. Without an iota of doubt, all kinds of improvisations in the data science paradigm are solidly empowering the goals of business transformation.

Now the fully matured paradigm of data science is being applied on graph data structure and hence the new field of graph data science is emerging steadily. The pace of graph data science adoption for business transformation is ceaselessly accelerating. Graph data science is emerging as a powerful and path-breaking subject of study and research. In association with graph algorithms, graph data science could bring the context details naturally for each piece of data. That is, graphs can bring out the information about the data with the help of graph algorithms. Data science methods through the distinct graph structure contribute immensely in making superior and richer predictions. ML algorithms are succulently and sagaciously contributing for the intended success of graph data science. Graph data science is revolutionizing how enterprises make predictions in diverse scenarios. Use cases such as fraud detection, disease prediction, drug discovery, etc. are being easily implemented through the connections existing between data points. In the drug discovery case, it is all about identifying all kinds of associations between genes, diseases, drugs, and proteins. Furthermore, the power of graph data science lies in extracting the much-needed context details to facilitate the understanding of the relevance or validity of any such discovery or decision. The capability to pinpoint predictive features from data will go to the next level through ML algorithms. The leverage of connected data to make accurate and explainable predictions is gaining the much-needed strength and sagacity. On the other side, there arise a number of new use cases for business houses to explore and expedite the graph data science methods.

Graph data science use cases – Corporates and governments across the world are keen on leveraging the distinctions of graph data science. For an example, the British government has embarked on a scintillating project. Data scientists are deploying their first ML model built on graphs. The resulting ML application automatically recommends appropriate content to users from the government online resource (GOV.UK) based upon the pages they are visiting. This recommendation system can be an enabler for many more advancements.

- *Supporting supply chains* – Graph data science is profoundly supporting the medical supply chain. Global medical device manufacturer Boston Scientific is using graph data science to identify the root causes of product failures. In its case, multiple teams, often in different countries, work on the same problems in parallel, but its engineers had to resort to analyzing their data in spreadsheets. This led to inconsistencies and difficulty in finding the root causes of defects. Boston Scientific says a switch to graph technology has delivered a more effective method for analyzing, coordinating, and improving its manufacturing processes across all its locations.

- *Enhancing search times* – Users can conduct meaningful and data science-enhanced searches. Analytical query times have dropped from two minutes to 10–55 sec. This is a huge boost increasing the overall efficiency of the entire analytical process. Organizations generate business value by using natural language processing (NLP) to analyze raw text detailing inspection failures. The NLP process can extract and correlate topics for investigation to infer the root causes of failures. Graph data science is making natural language processing of a large-scale repository of technical documents detailing repairs more effective.

Analytics is usually applied to multi-structured, numeric, or visual data to uncover decision-driving and deriving insights. Graph analytics is a special analysis on graph data and properties (attached with nodes and edges). Enterprising businesses around the world are beginning to implement graph analytics to help uncover impactful insights. Graph technologies are fast maturing and stabilizing and hence data representation through graphs and subsequently analytics though graph algorithms are gaining the momentum.

Graph data science algorithms – For manipulating graph data efficiently and purposefully, there are several popular algorithms. Prominent graph analytics platforms have implemented several standardized and proprietary algorithms in order to provide a variety of capabilities. Here is a list of algorithms provided with the Neo4j Graph Data Science Library:

- Community detection algorithms cluster a graph based on relationships to find communities where members have more significant interactions. The algorithm such as Connected Components and Louvain Modularity help to detecting communities that have some kinds of similarities. Such capability helps to predict to embark on something useful.
- Centrality algorithms reveal which nodes are important based on the graph topology. They identify influential nodes based on their position in the graph and this category of algorithms includes the famous PageRank algorithm. These algorithms are used to infer group dynamics such as credibility, rippling vulnerability, and bridges between groups.
- Node embedding algorithms transform the topology and features of any graph into fixed length vectors that uniquely represent each node. Such graph embeddings are beneficial because they preserve the key features while reducing the dimension of the graph. Embeddings capture the complexity and structure of a graph and transform it to be easily used by ML algorithms.
- Similarity algorithms employ set comparisons to score how individual nodes are similar based on their neighbors or properties. The properties and attributes of nodes are used to at the likeness score between nodes. This algorithm is for making personalized recommendations and developing categorical hierarchies.
- Pathfinding algorithms are to find the most efficient or shortest paths to traverse between nodes. The A* and Dijkstra's algorithms belong to the pathfinding category. These algorithms are to understand complex dependencies and to evaluate routes for efficient transportation.

15.8   AI-driven graph data science

We discussed about the uniqueness of graphs in data representation, presentation, and interchange. Having understood the fact that data analytics on graph data is able to achieve the much-needed efficiency and ease of use, the concept of graph data analytics is gaining the attention of business executives and IT professionals. Now with the noteworthy advancements in the form of powerful ML and DL algorithms, we see the days of automated and advanced analytics on graph-represented data.

ML with graphs helps to build highly accurate and trustworthy prediction models. This means there are two ways that ML with graphs can be deployed into the ML workflow. The first way is to create node embedding and to pass it into a downstream ML task. The second way is to apply ML algorithms on graph data by doing the label and link predictions directly on the graph data structure. A typical ML development workflow consists of the following phases.

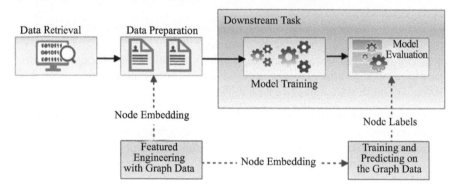

The ML development workflow always starts with data retrieval. This phase is typically termed as data engineering. A large amount of unstructured raw data is being captured from different and distributed sources. Then the data preparation step begins. The idea is to transform the raw data format into the easy-to-manipulate format so that the input data can be unambiguously used for model training. After the model is trained, the developed model can be evaluated for its various key performance indicators (KPIs). During the data preparation phase, feature engineering turns out to be a critical task. That is, the input data has to be transitioned into decision-enabling features /predictors/independent variables/parameters.

Efficient feature engineering simplifies and speeds up the creation of pioneering predictive and prescriptive models. All redundant and repetitive features have to be eliminated to derive optimal models. For arriving at highly optimized models, there are methods such as pruning and quantization. There are evaluation and optimization/compression mechanisms in plenty to arrive highly optimized and organized ML models, which consume less compute, storage, and network resources. Also, the electricity consumption goes down while the heat dissipation into our fragile environment is also bound to go down remarkably.

Feature engineering with graph data – Creating and choosing value-adding features are beset with a few practical and paramount challenges. Data scientists have to have a strong domain knowledge. The idea is to create the feature set automatically. That is, one can build a ML model that generates features based upon the relational properties between the data points (records) in the dataset. Those features are called node embeddings and every node there is a data point. Every node embedding is a precise representation of a structural relationship that it has with other nodes (data points) in the data set. Interactions between nodes with their neighborhood nodes are captured in the resulted node embedding. As discussed in the graph data science chapter, there are several methods emerging to create a node embedding. Thus, the complex feature engineering process gets accelerated and automated.

Training and predicting on the graph – The outcome from the feature engineering task is a node embedding that will be used as an input feature vector for the ML model. It is possible to do node classification and link prediction tasks directly from graphs. However, instead of hand-picking the relationship structure, which can make better predictions, the ML model can be trained to find the most important structural pattern and a set of node properties to assign labels to simplify relationship predictions.

In general, node classification is achieved by training a graph neural network (GNN) in a fully supervised manner. The loss function is defined on a node embedding. Thus, the model will be trained upon the node embedding and the output of the GNN will label each node. As each node is labeled, there is no need to pass the node embedding as a feature vector into a downstream task for classification or regression.

By applying the proven ML method on graphs, the feature selection task is automated during the feature engineering phase. ML with graphs trains a GNN to output a feature vector, which is called as node embedding, for every node in the graph. This node then can be passed into any downstream classifier. Second, it is also possible to do predictions directly on the graph data structure. Herein, a node embedding will be passed into a GNN to predict its label automatically.

ML is an important factor for empowering graph data analytics. With the combination of ML and graphs, several next-generation use cases are being unearthed and articulated by AI researchers. Let us go deep into how the cybersecurity needs are being accomplished by graph data science.

15.9 Graph data science for cybersecurity

Cybersecurity is one of the prime areas, which are hugely benefited out of the noteworthy advancements in graph data science. DNNs are being extensively explored and experimented for making numerous breakthroughs across a range of use cases. For ensuring the tightest security for digital infrastructures, platforms, services, and data, the field of cybersecurity gains greater momentum. Cyber assets ought to be secured in order to guarantee business continuity. Cyber resilience is the much-needed capability for the ensuing digital era. Cyber threat intelligence is turning out to be a proactive and pre-emptive security-enablement competency. In nutshell, cybersecurity is a growing collection of security techniques and tools for ensuring unbreakable and impenetrable security for information and communication technology (ICT) resources.

There are several security defense objectives, such as advanced persistent threat (APT) identification/tracking, attack attribution, the creation of competent threat model comprising threat hunting and response, and situational awareness. These features are more powerful than the traditional isolated detection systems. There are log analytics tools to make sense out of application, infrastructure and platform log files. There are security information and event management (SIEM) solutions for capturing security events for detecting any kind of impending security attacks. Further on, user and entity behavior analytics (UEBA) solutions are also gaining upper hand in securing digital systems. Endpoint detection and response (EDR) can detect threats in a networking environment and then respond to them accordingly. There are other innovations in cybersecurity products, solutions, and services. You can find more on these in this page (https://www.peterindia.net/Cybersecurity.html).

Graph technologies can help tackle big data – The cybersecurity teams are always under immense pressure from cyberattacks. They are obligated to understand and defend their organizations. With distributed architecture and applications, there is a wealth of security-related data. There are monitoring and observability tools to monitor business workloads and IT services. We have monitoring tools for microservices-centric cloud-native applications, containers, the Kubernetes platform, network solutions, storage appliances, compute machines, etc. There is a massive amount of multi-structured data getting generated by monitoring tools. It can go to the terabytes of data. The next course of actions is to cleanse all the captured data and to crunch it to extract actionable insights. Thus, security data analytics has become the new normal to guarantee thorough security for a variety of cyber systems. Not only logs but also system events play a very stellar role in proactively and pre-emptively pinpointing security attacks, loopholes, bugs, vulnerabilities, etc. Such a discovered knowledge gets disseminated to remediation services to embark on appropriate countermeasures in time to ward off any security mishap.

Large enterprises generally generate several billions of events per day. That sort of volume is a challenge for traditional SIEM tools. This is a classic big data problem as there is a need to capture and analyze disparate and distributed sources of SIEM/log management data. With much-celebrated graph intelligence, it is possible to cut through the noise to investigate a variety of cyberattacks in time to emit out useful insights, which comes handy in pondering and proceeding with the best-in-class countermeasures to weed out any kind of internal as well as external attack in an alacrity. The much-celebrated cybersecurity threat intelligence is being acquired through powerful graph analytics, which is evolving rapidly to cope up with the complexities of cyberattacks.

Take log management (LM) data, which can be acquired from Nginx, a renowned open-source web server with low-memory usage and high concurrency. SIEM with EventTracker using Syslog runs on the data to provide LM reports. With LM data that monitors, the security and operations of the server, it is possible to pinpoint any suspicious activity. More details are made available in this page (https://www.kineviz.com/allposts/2021/1/28/cybersecurity-threat-intelligence-empowered-by-graph-data-visualization).

Grapl is a next-gen SIEM that helps security teams better understand their environment and keep it safe. Grapl gives you limitless power to join your data across arbitrary data sources (cloud, endpoint, network, or in-house data sources). You can leverage Grapl to model complex relationships between various types of events in your environment like a process that is making network connections on an endpoint owned by a particular user in your environment. Grapl ships with built-in plugins so it is ready to use with common data sources like assets, people, etc. or you can write custom plugins for events specific to your environment. Detailed information about this SIEM product is available at its home page (https://www.graplsecurity.com/).

The intrinsic features of graphs can be leveraged artistically to achieve more with less. AI models can be created and compressed to arrive at competent models, which readily gain the competency to succulently automate the detection and prevention of cybersecurity attacks in time. Besides server machines, personal computers, network and security solutions, and smartphones, the future Internet is all set to comprise digitized entities (alternatively termed as the IoT sensors and actuators) and multi-faceted devices. In other words, with the larger participation of IoT edge devices in the fast-evolving Internet, the security scenario is going to be very complicated. The attack surface grows rapidly. Therefore, cybersecurity methods acquire special significance. Graph science is being presented and proclaimed as the most significant factor for confidently tackling growing incidences of cyberattacks.

Graphs have the inherent strength to detect cybersecurity threats. First, graphs can handle tremendous data volumes. Graphs can consume multi-structured data from multiple sources to enable knowledge discovery. Data engineering towards knowledge engineering gets hugely emboldened through the unique property of graph structures. Data variety, volume, viscosity, and velocity are being seen as a huge challenge to work with data. But graph representation of data comes as a solace and solution for data-related challenges and concerns. With the continuous contributions of product and tool vendors, the graph technology domain is experiencing numerous noteworthy advancements to facilitate efficient and real-time data analytics. The optimal representation and easy maneuver ability of disparate data through graphs come handy in quickly realizing the business value hidden in data. Therefore, graph data analytics through the leverage of pioneering AI algorithms is being pronounced as the future of data analytics.

15.10   Cybersecurity data science

We have already discussed how indispensable cybersecurity is for businesses across the globe to sustain their journey. Though there came a number of cybersecurity-enabling products, solutions and services, cyberterrorism is still on the rise in the extremely connected world. Enterprise-grade and web-scale applications are being accordingly modernized and migrated to cloud environments to reap all the originally expressed benefits of cloud computing. Also, slowly yet steadily customer, confidential and corporate information is being centrally stored. Cybercriminals are always zeroing down on expert moves to penetrate into connected systems to steal data.

Data science is being presented as a key method to tackle the nuisance of cyberterrorism. Especially, as already articulated, graph data science is being viewed as a futuristic and flexible way of detecting and nullifying cyberattacks well ahead of their occurrences. The primary goal of cyberattacks is to steal corporate data to embark on fraudulent activities. Cybersecurity uses the proven and potential graph data science to keep cyber infrastructures, systems, devices, applications, and services safe and secure.

Large amounts of data can be difficult to manage without the help of data scientists, who are well-versed in transitioning data to information and to knowledge. Especially security-related data gets collected and subjected to a variety of investigations to predict and prescribe the ways and means of stopping cybercriminals in their pursuits and purposes ahead of time. All kinds of financial risks are proactively identified through graph data science and saved from cyberattacks. The graph data science technologies and tools along with the education, expertise, and experience of data scientists are being seen as a strong deterrent for cybercriminals. There are graph databases and platforms in plenty to aid security experts and data scientists to strategize, plan, and execute the necessary things with all the alacrity and clarity. A predictive approach increases the efficacy of security measures surrounding sensitive data. Such a unique competency leads to systems that are exceedingly resistant to any infiltration.

The prediction process is as follows. Mission-critical organizations are collecting, processing, and storing highly sensitive consumer information. This has actually raised the quantity and quality of cyberthreats. Without an iota of doubt, data science has had an impressive impact on cybersecurity. Data science improves intrusion detection and prediction. It also enables data protection and behavioral analytics. Precisely speaking, data science becomes the eyes to cybersecurity's sword.

Cybersecurity data science (CSDS) offers a powerful approach for identifying hostile and heinous attacks on digital infrastructures, services, and data. In the recent past, AI algorithms (machine and deep learning) help the process of data-driven insights and insights-driven decisions. Threats can be ideally identified and stopped therein. Thus, any attempt to steal important information can be nullified through AI algorithms.

Anomaly detection is a prime use case of ML algorithms. Attacks are often committed by code that is different from the normal code. Such a deviation or anomalous code can be understood ML models and such a capability results in the tightest security for cyber systems. Thus, the goal of creating, evaluating, and optimizing ML models for ensuring cybersecurity attracts the attention of data scientists.

In short, data scientist empowers cybersecurity professionals in envisioning and eradicating cyberattacks in a precise and perfect manner. With the splurge of distributed systems in the cloud-native era, cyberattacks become bolder. Protecting distributed systems and data turn out to be a complicated task. There is a need for sophisticated approach to surmount cyberattacks on distributed applications.

AI models trained, retrained, and refined can be beneficial for identifying unusual patterns in large amounts of logs of data. Attack classification, outlier detection, etc. are the prominent use cases of AI models for cybersecurity. AI for cybersecurity enables the following three aspects: threat insights can be generated, appropriate countermeasures can be initiated and implemented automatically, correct recommendations can be made.

15.11 Conclusion

With the flourish of noteworthy digital innovations and disruptions in the digital era, the business world has gone for real business transformation initiatives with all the confidence. Digital technologies are forthwith in empowering legacy business workloads and IT services to be digitally enabled. All kinds of business and IT systems are digitally transformed to be benevolent for business behemoths and start-ups to fulfill the widely anticipated target of customer delight. Graph data science is one spectacular domain with the necessary wherewithal to fulfill the digital transformation requirements. Therefore, there is an insistence for the smart application of all the distinct advancements in the data science field on graphs. Such a transition facilitates an easy and fast knowledge discovery. Having understood the significant and strategic implications through the union of graphs and data science, academic professors and industry professions have coined and popularized the new term of graph data science. In this chapter, we have dealt with the topic of how graph data science fulfilling the cybersecurity needs.

Chapter 16

The machine learning algorithms for data science applications

*Pethuru Raj[1], D. Peter Augustine[2] and
P. Beaulah Soundarabai[2]*

Abstract

It is going to be data-driven insights and insights-driven decisions and actions for
the total humanity. Data is being recognized as the new fuel for any individual,
innovator, and institution to envisage and deliver smart and sophisticated services
to its clients and customers. Data is being touted as a strategic asset for any
enterprise to insightfully plan ahead and provide next-generation offerings and
premium services with clarity and confidence. Newer products and solutions can be
unearthed and deployed to assist humans in their everyday decisions, deals, and
deeds. However, for data to be overwhelmingly beneficial, data getting garnered
from multiple places have to be transitioned into information and knowledge. The
process for enacting this strategically sound transformation is being continuously
updated and upgraded for achieving the required optimization. That is, process
excellence is gaining the attention of professors and professionals. Further on, there
are scores of automated tools and enabling platforms for empowering this transition
activity. Data analytics is being touted as the prime method to extract actionable
insights out of data heaps.

In the recent past, with the flurry of artificial intelligence (AI) algorithms,
frameworks, libraries, platforms, accelerators, specialized engines, and high-
performance processing architectures, AI-enabled data analytics is seeing the reality. Data science is the fast-emerging and evolving domain of study and research
for finding viable ways and means that can simplify and streamline the activity of
emitting hidden and useful knowledge out of data volumes. In this chapter, we want
to dig deeper to spell out the strategic implications of data science technologies,
tools, platforms, and infrastructures. Especially how machine learning (ML) algorithms are influencing the futuristic field of data science.

[1]Edge AI Division, Reliance Jio Platforms Ltd., Bangalore, India
[2]Department of Computer Science, Christ University, India

16.1   Introduction

Data comes in several forms, formats, and factors. The number of data sources is increasing rapidly. Data sources are becoming distributed and disparate. Newer data sources such as IoT devices and sensors are emerging fast. The data generation, transmission, and receiving speed are also going through several changes. The data size has grown up significantly. The data structure, schema, and scope are also varying. In the midst of such data source multiplicity and data heterogeneity, the data complexity has gone up remarkably. Retrieving usable information and insights from increasing data volumes is not a simple task anymore. There is a need for technological solutions in the form of pioneering data analytics methods to simplify this complex job. Fortunately, there came a number of integrated analytics platforms for speeding up and streamlining the aspect of data analytics, which is becoming a hard nut to crack due to the massive quantities of multi-structured data. There are several types of analytical methods and mechanisms to do deeper and decisive analytics on big data to extract actionable insights in real-time. There are other challenges such as data integration, consolidation, curation, and preprocessing before subjecting data into well-intended analytics. Precise and concise analytics guarantee perfect decision-making and action.

On the infrastructure front, we need highly optimized compute, storage, and network infrastructure for persistently storing big data and for using data analytics platforms to perform analytics activity. With the availability of highly affordable, adaptive, and shared IT infrastructures, extracting data-driven insights is done with ease. Another noteworthy point is that there are methods such as batch, real-time, and interactive processing of data. Most of the personal, social, and professional applications need real-time insights in order to produce real-time applications, which tend to set up and sustain real-time intelligent enterprises. That is, real-time capture, processing, and decision-making are being insisted and hence the edge or fog computing concept has become very popular.

Thus, knowledge discovery and dissemination technologies and tools are indispensable for uncovering actionable insights in datasets.

16.2   The dawn of digital era

The digitization and edge technologies [1] have blossomed into a big and pulsating factor in transforming all kinds of cheap, casual, and concrete objects in our midst into digitized elements (alternatively referred to as smart objects, sentient materials, etc.). That is, all kinds of physical, mechanical, and electrical systems in our everyday environments get empowered to be digitized through one or more digitization technologies. Any digitized entity exhibits one or more special characteristics such as they are computational, communicative, sensitive, vision-enabled, perceiving, and responsive. They also collect a lot of data about themselves and their environments. The data collected then gets transmitted to data analytics platforms (locally to activate edge data analytics and remotely for comprehensive data analytics through cloud-based platforms and infrastructures). Such an intensive data analytics activity throws a lot of actionable insights, which, then, get fed back into digitized entities to exhibit intelligent behavior. Thus, digitized elements can take their own decisions and act upon them with all the clarity and alacrity. The leading market watchers and analysts have predicted that there will be trillions of such digitized objects in the year 2025 across the world. Precisely speaking, tangible things are peppered with and prepared for the future.

Mostly these are resource-constrained. Now with the fast spread of powerful connectivity technologies (wireline and wireless), digitized entities are being integrated not only with other digitized elements in the vicinity but also with cloud-hosted software services, applications, and databases. Thus, digitized entities talk to one another directly to share their unique capabilities and also with faraway digital services and applications indirectly through one or more intermediaries. As everyone knows, the Internet turns out to be an affordable, open, and public communication infrastructure. Digitized entities are being hooked to the Internet servers (web, app, and database). This unique phenomenon is called the Internet of Things (IoT). Today the Internet comprises only server machines, storage appliances, security solutions, etc. But the future Internet is to consist of not only server machines but also all kinds of digitized entities. When digitized objects get integrated with the Internet, a variety of newer capabilities can prop up digitized assets significantly.

The device ecosystem is on the rise. We are being bombarded with so many slim and sleek, handy, and trendy devices. We have consumer electronics, defense equipment, medical instruments, industrial machineries, robots, drones, kitchen utilities and wares, electronic gadgets and gizmos, etc. plentifully. In short, we have resource-intensive handhelds, portables, wearables, mobiles, implantable, fixed, and nomadic devices. With the Wi-Fi 6 and 5G communication facilities, all sorts of devices are being networked with the Internet, which has been expanding steadily. That is, we have a large number of networked embedded systems getting ready for visualizing and realizing context-aware and cognitive services. Popular market researchers have estimated that there will be billions of connected devices on the planet earth in the years to come.

Further on, a wider variety of gadgets and gizmos in our working, walking, and wandering locations are futuristically instrumented to be spontaneously interconnected and exceptionally intelligent in their behaviors. Once upon a time, all our personal computers were connected via networks (LAN and WAN) and nowadays our personal and professional devices are increasingly interconnected (BAN, PAN, CAN, LAN, MAN, and WAN) to exhibit a kind of intelligent behavior. This extreme connectivity and service-enablement of our everyday devices go to the level of getting seamlessly integrated with off-premise, online, and on-demand cloud-based business workloads, data sources, and stores. This cloud-enablement is capable of making ordinary devices into extraordinary ones. However, most of the well-known and widely used embedded devices individually do not have sufficient computation power, battery, storage, and I/O bandwidth to host and manage IoT applications and services. Hence, performing data analytics on individual devices is a bit difficult.

As we all know, smart sensors and actuators are being randomly deployed in mission-critical environments such as homes, hospitals, and hotels in order to minutely monitor, precisely measure, and insightfully manage the various parameters of the environments. Further on, powerful sensors are embedded and etched on different physical, mechanical, electrical, and electronics systems in our everyday environments in order to empower them to join in mainstream computing. Thus, not only environments but also all tangible things in those environments are smartly sensor-enabled with a tactic as well as the strategic goal of making them distinctly sensitive and responsive in their operations, offerings, and outputs. Sensors are sweetly turning out to be the inseparable eyes and ears of any important thing in the near future. This systematic sensor-enablement of ordinary things not only makes them extraordinary but also lays out a stimulating and sparkling foundation for generating a lot of usable and time-critical data. Typically, sensors and sensors-attached assets capture or generate and transmit all kinds of data to the faraway cloud environments (public, private, and hybrid) through a host of standards-compliant sensor gateway devices. Precisely speaking, clouds represent the dynamic combination of several powerful server machines, storage appliances, and network solutions and are capable of processing tremendous amounts of multi-structured data to spit out actionable insights.

However, there is another side to this remote integration and data processing. For certain requirements, the local or proximate processing of data is mandated. That is, instead of capturing sensor and device data and transmitting them to the faraway, cloud environments are not going to be beneficial for time-critical applications. Thereby, the concept of edge or fog computing has emerged and is evolving fast these days with the concerted efforts of academic as well as corporate people. The reasonably powerful devices such as smartphones, sensor and IoT gateways, consumer electronics, set-top boxes, smart TVs, Web-enabled refrigerators, and Wi-Fi routers are classified as fog or edge devices to form edge or fog clouds to do the much-needed local processing quickly and easily to arrive and articulate any hidden knowledge. Thus, fog or edge computing is termed and tuned as the serious subject of study and research for producing people-centric and real-time applications and services.

Besides digitization and edge technologies, we have so many promising digitalization technologies. The well-known digitalization technologies include AI, big, fast, and streaming data analytics methods, blockchain, microservices architecture (MSA), event-driven architecture (EDA), digital twins, cybersecurity, etc. The combination of digitization and digitalization technologies is termed as digital technologies, which have laid down a stimulating foundation for the digital era. Digital data is the first and foremost requirement for building next-generation digital applications and environments. In the recent past, we have a series of innovations and disruptions in the digital space. With the faster maturity and stability of digital technologies and tools, the much-expected digital transformation is to see the grandiose reality. Digitally transformed applications, services, systems, networks, and environments will become the new normal. Digitally transformed enterprises, governments, cities, hospitals, hotels, supply chains, etc. will be easily and elegantly implemented. Data science solutions are paramount and pertinent for attaining the originally expressed successes of the digital era.

16.3 The expanding data sources

As the digital era commences its long innings, the amount of digital data getting generated and stocked is astoundingly plentiful. There are fresh data sources emerging these days. Business, application, service, infrastructure, network, people, sensor, machine, and device data volumes are growing rapidly. In this section, we will throw more light on this.

16.3.1 Transactional, operational, and analytical systems

We have been fiddling with transactional systems extensively. The IT infrastructures, platforms, and applications are designed to be appropriate for efficiently handling transactions. However, with the faster penetration of devices and digitized entities into the IT landscape, there is a revisit and relook. That is, operational systems are becoming more prevalent and prominent. In the impending IoT era, a sensor or smart device that is monitoring temperature, humidity, vibration, acceleration, or numerous other variables could potentially generate data that needs to be handled by back-end systems every millisecond. For example, a typical Formula One car already carries 150–300 sensors. These cars are being continuously strengthened with additional sensors, actuators, beacons, controllers, stickers, and other edge technologies to derive deeper automation. These hundreds of sensors meticulously monitor, measure, capture, and release a lot of useful data every second. The racecars generate 100–200 KBs of data per second. This is bound to stack up to several terabytes in a racing season. Thus, with newer devices and machines, data volumes are to escalate drastically. The challenge is how backend systems are able to cope up with the continuously rising data volumes.

Not only the storage concern but also the real-time processing of data is also equally important. That is, missing a few seconds of sensor data or being unable to analyze it efficiently and rapidly can lead to risks and, in some cases, to disasters. Thus, we have highly sophisticated analytical systems to ease the process of data analytics to extract viable insights in time. These systems emerged as one of the leading data stores and suppliers. With the increased usage of enterprise-class, service-oriented, event-driven, cloud-hosted, knowledge-filled, process-aware, mission-critical, consumer, social, and business applications, the amount of data getting generated is simply phenomenal. These systems are being supplemented by scores of the above-mentioned transactional, analytical, and operational systems.

As IT is being presented as the greatest enabler of business operations, there arise a variety of business workloads and IT services continuously. With the faster proliferation of such software systems to automate various business operations, the amount of data getting realized and released is definitely tremendous. In short, the data volumes of digitized objects, electronic devices, business workloads, IT services, and people are seeing exponential growth these days. With the projection of trillions of networked embedded systems, billions of connected devices, and millions of microservices on the planet earth, the size of data is bound to increase tremendously in the years ahead.

16.3.2   Major IoT data types

There are a few major data types that will be common to most IoT projects.

16.3.2.1   Measurement data

Sensors monitor and measure the various parameters of the environment as well as the states of physical, mechanical, electrical, and electronic systems. Heterogeneous and multiple sensors read and transmit data very frequently, and hence, with a larger number of sensors and frequent readings, the total data size is bound to grow exponentially. This is the crux of the IoT era. A particular company in the oil and gas space is already dealing with more than 100 TB of such data per day.

16.3.2.2   Event data

Any status change, any break-in of the threshold value, any noteworthy incident or untoward accident, and any decision-enabling data are simply categorized as event data. With devices assisting people in their daily assignments and engagements, the number of events is likely to shoot up. We have powerful, simple, and complex event processing engines in order to discover and disseminate knowledge out of event data.

16.3.2.3   Interaction and transaction data

With the extreme and deeper connectivity among devices, the quality and quantity of purpose-specific interactions between devices are going to be greater. Several devices with unique functionality can connect and collaborate for achieving composite functions. The transaction operations are also enabled in devices. Not only inter-device communication but also human-device communication is fairly happening.

16.3.2.4   Diagnostics data

The delectable advancements in the IoT domain have led to millions of networked embedded devices, information, transactional, analytical and operational systems. There are a plenty of applications, data sources, and services available online, off-premise, on-premise, and on-demand. The application portfolio is consistently on the rise for worldwide enterprises. There are software infrastructure solutions, middleware, databases, data virtualization and knowledge visualization platforms, and scores of automation tools. The health of each of these systems is very important for the intended success of any business transaction. Diagnostics is the type of data that gives an insight into the overall health of a machine, system, or process. Diagnostic data might not only show the overall health of a system but also show whether the monitoring of that system is also working effectively.

Precisely speaking, the IoT data is going to be big and we have competent techniques and platforms for big data processing. However, the intriguing challenge is to do real-time processing of IoT big data. Researchers are on the job to unearth path-breaking algorithms to extract timely insights out of big data.

The IoT is turning out to be a primary enabler of the digital transformation of any kind of enterprising businesses. Companies are eagerly looking toward pioneering digital technologies to create and sustain their business competitiveness. The IoT and other digital technologies are helping companies to facilitate process enhancement, create newer business models, optimize the IT infrastructures, bring forth competent architectures, empower workforce efficiency and innovation, etc. The IoT closes down the gap between the physical and cyber worlds. It helps to connect the physical and digital environments. Data collected from connected devices are subjected to a variety of investigations to extract dependable insights.

Thus, the IoT data types are varying and enterprise and cloud IT environments have to be equipped with breakthrough storage, processing, and analytical systems to crunch IoT data quickly.

16.4   A brief on data types

In this section, we are to discuss structured and unstructured data, quantitative and qualitative data. Finally, we are to talk about the four levels of data. For data scientists, having a good grip on data types is essential to arrive at highly accurate models.

Structured or organized data can be thought of as observations and characteristics. It is usually organized using a table method (rows and columns). Scientific observations, as recorded by researchers and scientists, are kept in an organized or structured format to study further.

Unstructured or unorganized data exists as a free entity and does not follow any well-known organization hierarchy or structure. Data that exists in text form, including server logs, product reviews in B2C e-commerce portals, and posts on FB, is termed as unstructured. Images, videos, audios, and texts are typically referred to as unstructured data. A DNA sequence such as ACGTATTGCA is also referred to as unstructured data as we cannot form any descriptor of the sequence using a row/column format. Structured data is quite easy to work with. Statistical and probabilistic processing is being performed easily on structured data. Humans also make sense out of data in the row and column structure.

However, today around 85% of data being produced is unstructured. Social web applications such as Facebook, Instagram, Twitter, and WhatsApp, create a lot of unstructured data. Industrial machineries, handhelds, wearables, implantables, sensors, portables, and mobiles do generate a lot of unstructured data every day. We cannot discard such unstructured data as it contains a lot of useful and usable information and insights. During the exploratory data analysis (EDA) phase, we need to bring in a kind of structure on unstructured data. This simplifies for people to make sense out of data. Preprocessing is important for enabling the participation of unstructured or unorganized data toward comprehensive data analytics. Similarly cleaning or cleansing of data is essential to arrive at accurate results. Experts have come up with a few workable techniques to bring in a decent structure for unstructured data. For example, a tweet can be converted into a row and column structure by extracting some details out of it and adding them to arrive at a row and column format. That is, data gets converted into information because it informs something to data scientists and decision-makers.

There are quantitative and qualitative data. Quantitative data can be described using numbers, and basic mathematical procedures, including addition, can be done on quantitative data. On the other hand, qualitative data cannot be described using numbers and basic mathematics. This data is generally being described using natural categories and language. For an example, we can describe a coffee shop and its various data points: the name of the coffee shop, the revenue, the zip code, the average monthly customers, and the country of coffee origin. Each of these characteristics of a coffee shop can be classified as either quantitative or qualitative. The name of a coffee shop is qualitative as it cannot be expressed as a number and we cannot do any mathematical operations on the shop name. But the revenue is quantitative as it is described using a number. We can do mathematical operations on the revenue numbers. The zip code is a number. Still, it is being described as qualitative because, on this number, we cannot do any real-world mathematical operations. The average number of monthly customers is a number, and hence it is quantitative. The country of coffee's origin is qualitative.

Quantitative data can be broken down into discrete and continuous quantities. Discrete data describes data that is counted. It can only take on certain values. The number of customers in a coffee shop is discrete data because you cannot have a real range of people. On the other hand, continuous data describes data that is measured. It exists on an infinite range of values. The height of a person or building is a continuous number because an infinite scale of decimals is possible. Other good examples of continuous data would be time and temperature.

16.5   Describing the field of data science

The aspect of data science is gaining a lot of market and mind shares these days. There are many reasons and causes for this trend and transition to flourish in the days ahead. There are several noteworthy things happening simultaneously in the IT space. As illustrated above,

- The number of distinct data sources is increasing steadily, and hence the data volumes being generated grow exponentially. The data comes in multi-structured format (structured, semi-structured, and unstructured) and the velocity with which the data gets produced and processed also varies.
- The data storage capacity being offered by hyper-scale clouds has gone up significantly, and the data processing capability has grown rapidly with the assorted advancements in the processor architecture.

- There are different data processing methods (batch, real-time, and interactive) and open-source as well as commercial-grade integrated data analytics platforms for big, fast, and streaming data are emerging and evolving fast.
- In the recent past, path-breaking ML and deep learning (DL) algorithms, frameworks, libraries, accelerators, etc. are originating from worldwide research labs.

Precisely speaking, data analytics methods and platforms have stabilized and matured a lot. With ML and DL algorithms joining in, the aspect of data analytics gets speeded up and simplified. In other words, the ML and DL algorithms are capable of automating a few important parts of the data analytics process, which is becoming complicated due to rising data complexity. Data science is a new and popular phenomenon of making sense out of data heaps. Data analytics methods and the ML/DL algorithms are pronounced as the leading enabler of the data science idea. With the consistent and constant evolutions and revolutions in the landscape of implementation technologies and tools, the data science field is all set to get phenomenal advancements.

The above-mentioned technological advancements have speeded and spruced up the leverage of data science techniques and tools to play around with data with the sole aim of extracting actionable insights in time. Besides deterministic and diagnostic insights, the ML and DL algorithms have laid down a stimulating foundation for producing predictive, prescriptive, personalized, and prognostic insights. Such technologically inspired knowledge discovery and dissemination have led to the realization of a litany of good things for the entire world. Especially, producing and sustaining smarter and sophisticated software applications across industry verticals are possible now. When data science techniques are applied properly, we can easily and elegantly envisage intelligent devices, services, systems, networks, and environments (smart homes, hotels, hospitals, etc.). Predominantly, there are five essential steps to perform data science are as follows:

- Understanding the business expectation through a slew of questions and clarifications is the first and foremost step for data scientists to arrive at competent solutions for the business problems at hand. This will smoothen the path ahead for data scientists to steer the whole process in the right direction to reach the desired destination.
- *Obtaining the data*: Data is the prime requirement for any data science project to succeed. There are multiple sources to obtain the data to initiate the data science process.
- *Exploring the data*: This phase is termed as exploratory data analysis (EDA). Herein, data scientists spend their talent and time to have a detailed and deeper look into the data in order to preprocess and prepare the data obtained for the subsequent phases.
- *Modeling the data*: There are ML and DL algorithms emerging and evolving to bring forth a viable data model. In this phase, mathematical validation metrics are implanted in order to quantify the models and their effectiveness.
- *Visualizing knowledge*: There are solutions for displaying the results obtained in a preferred and digestible format.

These steps are being presented as prominent and paramount in the data science process. There are multiple people including data stewards, engineers, analysts, and scientists and administrators, for insightfully coordinating to complete enterprise-scale data science projects. There are a plenty of statistical and mathematical approaches to accurately extract quantifiable data. There are technical and algorithmic methods to enable working with big data. There are integrated data analytics platforms for facilitating knowledge discovery and dissemination.

16.6   Classification and regression techniques

There are certain problems wherein ML and DL algorithms excel. One of the problems is classification. In this section, we are to discuss the specific ML algorithms that can handle classification and regression needs in an exquisite manner. One typical task getting assigned to data scientists is to identify the category to which a particular data belongs. The data may be an image of handwriting, and a data scientist has to know what letter or number the image represents. Or the data represents loan applications, and a data scientist has to know if it should be in the "approved" or "declined" category. There are several other classical requirements such as an incoming e-mail is a real or spam or a tumor is malignant and normal.

In summary, a classification problem has a discrete value as its output. For example, "likes pineapple on pizza" and "does not like pineapple on pizza" are discrete. There is no middle ground. On the other hand, a regression problem has a real number (a number with a decimal point) as its output. For example, we could use the data in the table below to estimate someone's weight given their height.

Height (Inches)	Weight (Pounds)
65.78	112.99
71.52	136.49
69.40	153.03
68.22	142.34
67.79	144.30
68.70	123.30
69.80	141.49
70.01	136.46
67.90	112.37
66.78	120.67
66.49	127.45
67.62	114.14
68.30	125.61
67.12	122.46
68.28	116.09

We have an independent variable (or set of independent variables) and a dependent variable (the thing we are trying to guess given our independent variables). Also, each row is typically called an example, observation, or data point, while each column (not including the label/dependent variable) is often called a predictor, dimension, independent variable, or feature.

There are powerful ML and DL algorithms and methods for solving classification and regression problems. Based on different features, various objects can be discriminated using a ML model, namely a classifier. In this section, we are to discuss the renowned classifiers.

16.6.1   Decision trees (DTs)

A DT is a flowchart-like structure whereas each node will indicate the next course of action on an attribute, such as 0 or 1 probability in coin-flipping. The branch extending from the node will represent the outcome, and the decision arrived after computing all attributes will be represented by each leaf node (https://en.wikipedia.org/wiki/Decision_tree). The below diagram vividly illustrates the nitty-gritty of DTs. There are root, decision, and terminal nodes for simplifying and streamlining classification and regression.

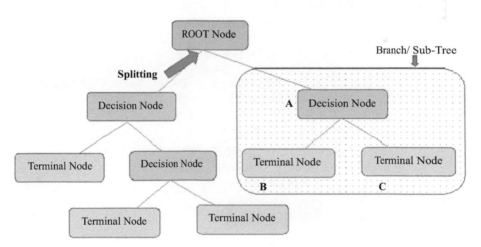

Note:- A is parent node of B and C.

A DT algorithm divides a training dataset into branches, which are further segregated into other branches. This sequence continues until a leaf node is attained. The leaf node cannot be segregated further. The nodes in the DT represent attributes that are used for predicting the outcome. Decision nodes provide a link to the leaves. Following are some of the assumptions we make while using the DT.

- In the beginning, the whole training set is considered as the root.
- Feature values are preferred to be categorical. If the values are continuous, then they are discretized before building the model.

The information theory can provide more information on how DTs work. Entropy and information gain are the building blocks of DTs. Entropy is a metric for calculating uncertainty. Information gain is a measure of how uncertainty in the target variable is reduced, given a set of independent variables.

The information gain concept involves using independent variables (features) to gain information about a target variable (class). The entropy of the target variable (Y) and the conditional entropy of Y (given X) are used to estimate the information gain. In this case, the conditional entropy is subtracted from the entropy of Y. Information gained is used in the training of DTs. It helps in reducing the uncertainty in these trees. A high information gain means that a high degree of uncertainty (information entropy) has been removed. Entropy and information gain are important in splitting branches, which is an important activity in the construction of DTs.

Let us take a simple example of how a DT works. Suppose we want to predict if a customer will purchase a mobile phone or not. The features of the phone form the basis of his decision. The root node and decision nodes of the decision represent the features of the phone mentioned above. The leaf node represents the final output, either buying or not buying. The main features that determine the choice include the price, the processing power, internal storage, and memory (RAM). The DT will appear as follows:

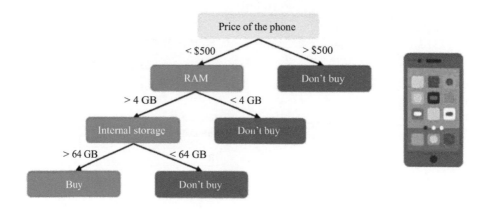

DTs are a supervised learning method used for classification and regression. The goal is to create a model that predicts the value of a target variable by learning simple decision rules inferred from the data features. This acts as a decision support tool that natively uses a tree-like structure for making decisions and their possible consequences, including chance event outcomes, resource costs, and utility. DCs are appropriate for exploratory knowledge discovery. DTs can handle high-dimensional data. In general, the decision tree (DT) classifier has good accuracy. DT induction is a typical inductive approach to learning classification knowledge.

16.6.2 Naive Bayes classifiers

A Naive Bayes classifier is a probabilistic ML model that is extensively used for classification tasks. The core of the classifier is based on the Bayes theorem:

$$P(A|B) = \frac{P(B|A)P(A)}{P(B)}$$

Using the Bayes theorem, we can find the probability of **A** happening, given that **B** has occurred. Here, **B** is the evidence, and **A** is the hypothesis. The assumption made here is that the predictors/features are independent. That is, the presence of one particular feature does not affect the other.

For example, a fruit may be considered to be an apple if it is red, round, and about 3 inches in diameter. Even if these features depend on each other or upon the existence of the other features, all of these properties contribute independently to the probability that this fruit is an apple. The Naive Bayes model is easy to build and particularly useful for very large data sets. Along with simplicity, Naive Bayes is known to outperform even highly sophisticated classification methods.

Applications of the Naive Bayes algorithm

- *Real-time prediction*: The Naive Bayes algorithm could be implemented for getting predictions in real-time scenario.
- *Multi-class prediction*: The Naive Bayes can also be used to foresee the chances of multiple classes of the variable of preference.
- *Natural language processing*: Naive Bayes classifiers are mostly used in text classification due to better results in multi-class problems and independence rule. Also, they have achieved higher success rate.

Therefore, this algorithm is widely used in spam filtering (identifying whether an e-mail is spam or not) and sentiment analysis (that is, to identify positive and negative sentiments of users of a product or an offering). Naive Bayes is mainly used in text classification that includes a high-dimensional training dataset. It is a probabilistic classifier, which means it predicts on the basis of the probability of an object. Some popular examples of the Naive Bayes algorithm are spam filtration, sentimental analysis, and classifying articles.

When the assumption of independence holds, a Naive Bayes classifier performs better compared to other models like logistic regression, and it requires less data for training purposes. Especially, when categorical input variables are given. The Naive Bayes gives better output related to numerical variable(s). There is a good description of the famous problem of playing golf in this web page (https://towardsdatascience.com/naive-bayes-classifier-81d512f50a7c). There is another page defining and delineating about this Naive Bayes algorithm for classification purposes (https://www.geeksforgeeks.org/naive-bayes-classifiers/).

16.6.3 Support vector machines (SVMs)

The SVM algorithm works intending to find a hyperplane in an N-dimensional space, whereas N is the number of features that classify explicitly the data points.

16.7   SVM can be of two types

- *Linear SVM*: It works with linearly separable data, and the classification of a dataset represents this characteristic into two classes using a single straight line. Then such data is termed linearly separable data, and the classifier is called a linear SVM classifier.
- *Non-linear SVM*: This SVM works with the dataset that cannot be classified by using a straight line. Such dataset is termed as non-linearly separated data. The classifier used is called a non-linear SVM classifier.

The table below describes a bit about hyperplanes and support vectors.

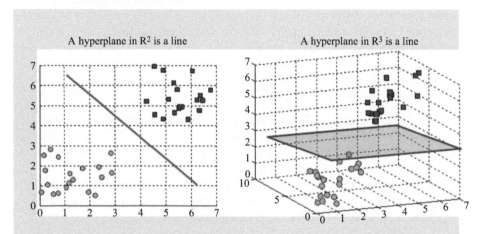

A hyperplane in R^2 is a line   A hyperplane in R^3 is a line

The data points are classified using the decision boundaries termed as hyperplanes. The two distinct classes are formed from the data points dropping on either side of the hyperplane. Depending upon the number of features, the dimension of the hyperplane is denoted. When the hyperplane is just a line, it is understood that the number of input features is 2. If the input features are 3, then the hyperplane becomes a two-dimensional plane. It becomes difficult to imagine when the number of features exceeds 3.

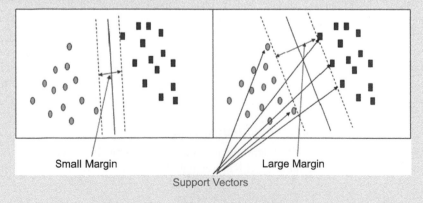

Small Margin   Large Margin

Support Vectors

Support vectors are data points that are closer to the hyperplane and have an influence on the hyperplane's position and orientation. We maximize the classifier's margin by using these support vectors. The hyperplane's position will be altered if the support vectors are deleted. These are the points that will assist us in constructing our SVM. This page has more information on the subject. More on this can be found on this page (https://towardsdatascience.com/support-vector-machine-introduction-to-machine-learning-algorithms-934a444fca47).

Let us proceed with an intuitive example. Let us imagine we have two tags: red and blue, and our data has two features: x and y. We want a classifier that, given a pair of (x, y) coordinates, has to output it is either red or blue. We plot the already labeled training data on a plane.

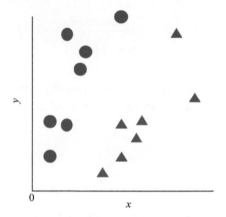

A SVM takes these data points and outputs the hyperplane (which, in two dimensions, is simply a line) that best separates the tags. This line is the decision boundary. Anything that falls to one side of it, we will classify as blue, and anything that falls to the other as red.

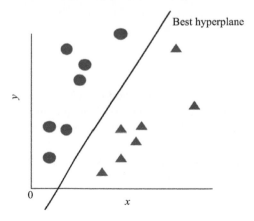

What exactly is the best hyperplane? For SVM, it is the one that maximizes the margins from both tags. In other words, the hyperplane (this is a line in this case) whose distance to the nearest element of each tag is the largest.

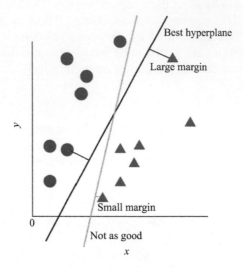

Non-linear data: This example is easy since the data is linearly separable. It is possible to draw a straight line to separate red and blue. Now consider the below figure:

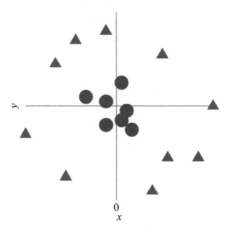

Here, there is no linear decision boundary. That is, drawing a single straight line that separates both tags is beset with challenges. However, the vectors are very clearly segregated, and it looks as though it should be easy to separate them.

How to proceed from here? In the last example, we have only two dimensions: x and y. In this example, we create a new z dimension, and we rule that it has to be calculated in a certain way that is convenient for us. This equation works well:

$z = x^2 + y^2$. This will give us a three-dimensional space. Taking a slice of that space, it looks as follows.

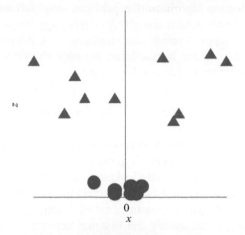

What can SVM do with this? Note that since we are in three dimensions now, the hyperplane is a plane parallel to the *x*-axis at a certain *z* (let us say $z = 1$). What's now left is mapping it back to two dimensions.

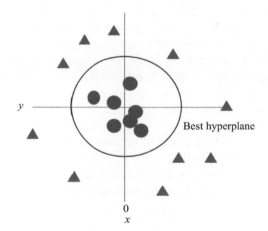

We are now back to our original view. Everything is now neatly separated. Our decision boundary is a circumference of radius 1, which separates both tags using SVM. Increasing the margin distance has several advantages, such as allowing subsequent data points to be categorized with absolute credibility and clarity. Hyperplanes are decision boundaries that aid in the classification process. Different classifications can be given to data points on either side of the hyperplane.

A SVM is a supervised ML model for two-group classification problems. Compared to newer and deeper algorithms like neural networks, they have two main advantages: higher speed and better performance with a limited number of samples (in the thousands). This makes the algorithm very suitable for text classification problems, where it is common to have access to a dataset of at most a couple of thousands of tagged samples. In other words, SVM is a fast and dependable classification algorithm that performs very well with a limited amount of data to analyze. More details are given on this page (https://monkeylearn.com/blog/introduction-to-support-vector-machines-svm/). A detailed tutorial on SVM with full source code is made available on this page (https://www.javatpoint.com/machine-learning-support-vector-machine-algorithm).

16.8   K-Nearest neighbor (K-NN) algorithm

The K-NN algorithm is a simple and easy-to-implement supervised ML algorithm that can be used to solve both classification and regression problems. Most of the time, similar data points are situated close to each other. The K-NN algorithm hinges on this assumption to be a hugely useful algorithm for classification. K-NN captures the idea of similarity (sometimes called distance, proximity, or closeness). There are methods for calculating the distance between points on a graph. The widely used one is the straight-line distance (also called the Euclidean distance).

K-NN is one of the supervised ML algorithms. The K-NN algorithm assumes the similarity between the new case/data and available cases and puts the new case into the most similar category to the available ones. The K-NN algorithm stores all the available data and classifies a new data point based on the similarity. This means when new data appears, using the K-NN method, it can be quickly sorted into a well-suited category. The K-NN algorithm can be used for regression as well as for classification. K-NN is a non-parametric algorithm. That is, it does not make any assumption on underlying data. The KNN algorithm at the training phase just stores the dataset and when it gets new data, then it classifies that data into a category that is much similar to the new data.

Let us say we have an image of a creature that looks like a cat or a dog, but we are not sure if it is a cat or a dog. So, because the KNN algorithm is based on a similarity measure, we may utilize it for this identification. The KNN model will compare the similarities between the new data set and the photos of cats and dogs and classify it as either a cat or a dog based on the most similar attributes.

KNN Classifier

Input value   Predicted output

Suppose there are two categories, i.e., Category A and Category B, and we have a new data point $x1$, so this data point will lie in which of these categories? To solve this type of problem, we need a K-NN algorithm. With this algorithm, we can easily identify the category or class of a particular dataset. How the K-NN algorithm works is enumerated as follows:

- **Step 1:** Select the number K of the neighbors
- **Step 2:** Calculate the Euclidean distance of **K** number of neighbors
- **Step 3:** Take the K nearest neighbors as per the calculated Euclidean distance.
- **Step 4:** Among these k neighbors, count the number of the data points in each category.
- **Step 5:** Assign the new data points to that category for which the number of the neighbor is maximum.

Suppose a new data point arrives in and we need to put it in the required category. Consider the diagram below.

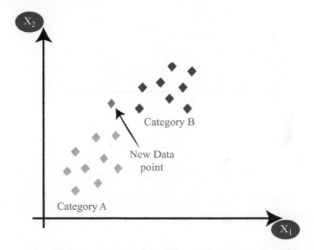

First, we will choose the number of neighbors, so we will choose *k*=5. Next, we will calculate the Euclidean distance between the data points. It can be calculated using the below formula

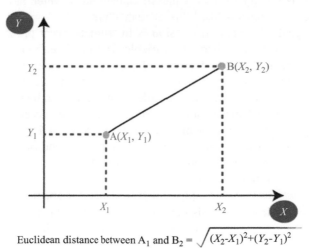

Euclidean distance between A_1 and $B_2 = \sqrt{(X_2-X_1)^2+(Y_2-Y_1)^2}$

By calculating the Euclidean distance, we got the nearest neighbors, as three nearest neighbors in category A and two nearest neighbors in category B. Consider the diagram below.

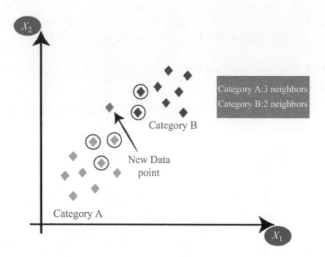

We can see the three nearest neighbors are from category A, and hence this new data point must belong to category A. Even with such simplicity, K-NN can give highly competitive results. The calculation time is also very less.

16.9   Logistic regression

Logistic regression is a statistical analysis method, and this ML model is used to forecast a data value based on previous data set observations. The system can get more helpful in predicting classifications among data sets as more relevant data comes in. This is mostly for binary classification issues, which have just two possible outcomes. Predictions like "this or that," "yes or no," and "A or B" will be possible. The goal of logistic regression is to estimate event probabilities, which includes establishing a link between variables and the likelihood of specific outcomes. A logistic regression, for example, could be used to predict whether a political candidate will win or lose an election or if a high school student would be accepted into a specific institution. Multiple input criteria can be taken into account by the analytical model that results. In the case of college acceptance, the model can take into account the student's GPA, SAT score, and a variety of extracurricular activities. It assesses new cases on their likelihood of falling into a particular outcome group based on the historical data regarding past outcomes involving the same input criteria.

In order to set the stage for efficient data analytics, logistic regression is bound to play a key role in data preprocessing by allowing data sets to be placed into predetermined buckets during the extract, transform, and load (ETL) process. The number of hours spent studying is supplied as a feature for predicting whether a student will pass or fail an assessment, and the dependent variable has two values: pass and fail.

Organizations can improve their business strategies by using recommendations from logistic regression results and decisions to achieve their business goals, such as expense rationalization and reduction. A B2C e-commerce company can understand whether a particular customer is likely to accept and respond to a discount offer. A credit card company can develop a model for determining whether or not to provide a bank card to a customer based on many decision-enabling characteristics such as monthly salary, and previous defaults. Logistic regression can also be used in:

- Healthcare to identify risk factors for diseases and to plan preventive measures.
- Predicting snowfall and weather conditions with weather forecasting applications.
- Voting applications to see if voters are likely to vote for a specific candidate.
- Insurance that estimates the likelihood that a policyholder will die before the policy's term expires based on factors such as gender, age, and a physical examination.
- Banking to estimate whether a loan application would default on a loan's annual income, previous defaults, and previous debts.

Thus, several use cases are emerging for the logistic regression algorithm.

16.10   Linear regression

This is used to find a linear relationship between one or more predictors and the goal. Linear regression can be divided into two types.

Simple linear regression: It is a technique for determining the association between two continuous variables. The predictor or independent variable is one, while the response or dependent variable is the other. To put it another way, simple linear regression is used when there is just one input variable (x).

Several linear regression is used when there are multiple input variables. Linear regression typically looks for a statistical relationship but not a deterministic relationship.

Statistical vs. Deterministic Relationship

If one variable can be precisely described by the other, the relationship between the two variables is said to be deterministic. The temperature in degrees Celsius, for example, may be used to reliably predict the temperature in degrees Fahrenheit. In determining the relationship between two variables, statistical relationships are not correct. The association between height and weight, for example, is statistical.

Because of its straightforward representation, linear regression is a popular model. The representation is a linear equation with a set of input values (x) and an output value. As a result, both the input (x) and output (y) values are numeric. Each input value or column is given one scale factor, which is referred to as a coefficient, by the linear equation. The intercept or bias coefficient is the name given to a third coefficient. For example, in a simple regression problem (with only one x and one y), the model would have the following form:

$$y = B0 + B1 * x$$

The line is called a plane or a hyperplane when there are several input values. The complexity of any regression model depends on the number of coefficients used in the model. When a coefficient becomes zero, it sharply reduces the influence of the input variable on the model ($0 * x = 0$). The computation becomes easy and fast. The importance of the input variable comes down remarkably.

16.11   An illustrative example

We have a dataset with data on the association between "number of hours studied" and "marks received." This is our training data. The job at hand is to create a model that can predict grades based on the amount of hours spent studying. A regression line can be obtained using the training data. This linear equation will give the minimum error and confidently be used with any fresh data.

The regression line representation is $Y(\text{pred}) = b0 + b1*x$

The variables $b0$ and $b1$ must be carefully chosen in order to minimize the mistake. If the sum of squared errors is used to evaluate the model, the aim of finding the line that reduces the error the most is met. The error calculation formula is given as follows:

$$\text{Error} = \sum_{i=1}^{n} (actual\_output - predicted\_output) * *2$$

If the error is not squared, the positive and negative points will cancel each other out. The intercept calculation formula for a model with one predictor is as follows.

$$b_0 = \bar{y} - b_1 \bar{x}$$

The co-efficient calculation formula is as follows:

$$b_1 = \frac{\sum_{i=1}^{n} (x_i - \bar{x})(y_i - \bar{y})}{\sum_{i=1}^{n} (x_i - \bar{x})^2}$$

- If $b1 > 0$, then x (predictor) and y (target) have a positive relationship. That is, any increase in x will increase y.
- If $b1 < 0$, then x (predictor) and y (target) have a negative relationship. That is, any increase in x will decrease y.

16.12   Coefficient estimation methods

Statistics method: For simple linear regression, to estimate the coefficients, we can apply statistics. That is, statistical properties such as means, standard deviations, correlations, and covariance can be calculated. To traverse and calculate statistics, all of the data must be available.

The ordinary least squares method: When there are multiple inputs, the ordinary least squares (OLS) approach can be used to estimate the coefficient values. The sum of the squared residuals is minimized using this strategy. Given a regression line across the data, we measure the distance between each data point and the regression line, square it, and add all of the squared errors together. This is the amount that the OLS method attempts to reduce. It implies that you must have access to all of the data and sufficient RAM to fit the data and perform matrix operations. The computation time for this approach is quite short.

Gradient descent: If there are one or more inputs, you can utilize an iterative method to optimize the coefficient values by reducing the model's error on the training data.

Gradient descent (GD) is a technique that works by starting with random values for each coefficient. The sum of squared errors is determined for each pair of input and output values. As a scale factor, a learning rate is utilized, and the coefficients are updated to minimize the error. The procedure is repeated until the sum squared error is reduced to a minimum or no further improvement is possible. It would be best if you chose a learning rate (alpha) parameter that sets the magnitude of the improvement step to take on each iteration of the procedure while utilizing this method. This method is useful when you have a very large dataset, either in the number of rows or the number of columns that may not fit into memory.

Regularization: These strategies aim to lower the model's complexity while minimizing the model's sum of squared errors on the training data (using ordinary least squares) (like the number or absolute size of the sum of all coefficients in the model). For linear regression, there are two normalization approaches.

- *Lasso regression*: The OLS technique is tweaked to reduce the absolute total of the coefficients as well (called L1 regularization).
- *Ridge regression*: The OLS technique is tweaked to reduce the squared absolute sum of the coefficients as well (called L2 regularization).

When your input values are collinear, and OLS will overfit the training examples, these strategies are useful. You can find more information on this page (https://machinelearningmastery.com/linear-regression-for-machine-learning/).

16.13   Making predictions with linear regression

If the representation is a linear equation, then making predictions is quite easy. Imagine we are predicting weight (y) from height (x). This problem's linear regression model is as follows:

$$y = B0 + B1 * x1$$

or

$$weight = B0 + B1 * height$$

where *B0* is the bias coefficient and *B1* is the coefficient for the height column. Let us use *B0* = 0.1 and *B1* = 0.5 and plug them in and calculate the weight (in kilograms) for a person with the height of 182 cm.

Weight = 0.1 + 0.5 * 182

Weight = 91.1

In two dimensions, the above equation might be drawn as a line. Regardless of our height, the *B0* is our starting point. We may enter a range of heights between 100 and 250 cm into the calculation to receive weight values. This creates a line, which is pictorially represented as follows:

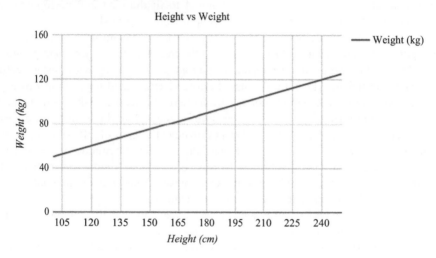

Logistic regression vs. linear regression

The major distinction between logistic and linear regression is that logistic regression produces a constant result, whereas linear regression produces a continuous output. The outcome of logistic regression, such as a dependent variable, has a finite number of potential values. The output of linear regression, on the other hand, is continuous, which means it may take on any of an unlimited number of values. Logistic regression is utilized when the answer variable is categorical, such as yes/no, true/false, or pass/fail. Linear regression is employed when the response variable is continuous, such as the number of hours, height, or weight.

For example, logistic regression and linear regression can predict various outcomes based on data on a student's study time and exam scores. Only particular values or categories are permitted in logistic regression predictions. As a result, logistic regression can forecast whether a student will pass or fail. Because linear regression predictions are continuous, such as numbers in a range, the student's test score on a scale of 0–100 may be predicted.

16.14 Linear regression use cases

Linear regression is to provide better insights by uncovering patterns and relationships that your business colleagues might have previously seen and thought they already understood. The linear regression algorithm is being widely used across industry verticals. Linear-regression models have become a way forward to scientifically and accurately predict the future.

Analyze pricing elasticity: Consumer behavior is typically influenced by price changes. For example, if the price of a product fluctuates, you may use regression analysis to check if consumption decreases as the price rises. What if, when prices rise, consumption does not fall significantly? When do customers quit buying a product because it is too expensive? Leaders in the retail industry would benefit greatly from this information.

Assess risk in an insurance company: Risks may be analyzed using linear regression methods. An insurance firm, for example, may have limited resources to investigate homeowners' insurance claims. The company's staff can use linear regression to create a model for estimating claim expenses. The research might aid corporate executives in making critical judgments about which risks they should accept. There are several exciting use cases for linear regression (https://www.ibm. com/topics/linear-regression).

Data analytics: Analyzing sales and purchase data might help you identify unique purchasing habits on specific days or at specific times. Regression analysis may provide business leaders with insights on when their company's products will be in high demand.

In conclusion, linear regression models are straightforward and give an easy-to-understand mathematical formula for generating predictions.

16.15 Random forest

A random forest (RF) is a ML technique to solve regression and classification problems. RF uses the ensemble learning method, which combines many classification algorithms for solving complex problems and for improving the accuracy of the prediction. (https://www.section.io/engineering-education/introduction-to-random-forest-in-machine-learning/). That is, a RF algorithm typically consists of several DTs. The RF algorithm is trained through bagging (bootstrap aggregating), which is an ensemble meta-algorithm.

The RF algorithm establishes the outcome based on the predictions of the DTs. It takes the mean value of the output from the participating DTs to arrive at the prediction. With more trees, the prediction precision is bound to go up. DTs are the building blocks of a RF algorithm.

The features of a RF algorithm are as follows:

- This gives more accurate results when compared with the DT algorithm.
- It does well in effectively handling missing data.
- It can produce a reasonably good prediction without hyper-parameter tuning.
- This answers the call to solve the overfitting issue in DTs.

In short, RF, an ensemble algorithm could easily eliminate the widely reported limitations of the DT algorithm, which is discussed in the beginning of this chapter.

The main difference between the DT algorithm and the RF algorithm is that the act of establishing root nodes and segregating nodes is done randomly in the RF algorithm. Bagging involves using different samples of data (training data) rather than just one sample. A training dataset comprises observations and features that are used for making predictions. The DTs produce different outputs, depending on the training data fed to the algorithm. These outputs will be ranked, and the highest will be selected as the final output.

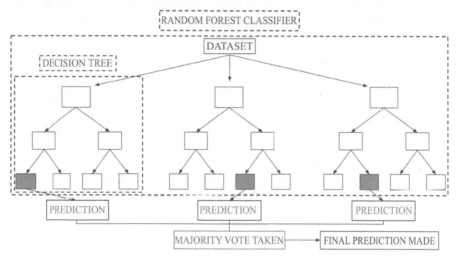

Let us assume we have only four DTs. In this case, the training data comprising the phone's observations and features will be divided into four root nodes. The root nodes could represent four features that could influence the customer's choice (price, internal storage, camera, and RAM). The RF will split the nodes by selecting features randomly. The final prediction will be selected based on the outcome of the four trees. The outcome chosen by most DTs will be the final choice. If three trees predict buying, and one tree predicts not buying, then the final prediction will be buying. In this case, it is predicted that the customer will buy the phone.

Let us take another example of a training dataset consisting of various fruits, such as bananas, apples, pineapples, and mangoes. The RF classifier divides this dataset into subsets. These subsets are given to every DT in the RF system. Each DT produces its specific output. For example, trees 1 and 2 are predicted to produce an apple. Another DT (n) has predicted banana as the outcome. The RF classifier collects the majority voting to provide the final prediction. The majority of the DTs have chosen apple as their prediction. This makes the classifier choose apple as the final prediction.

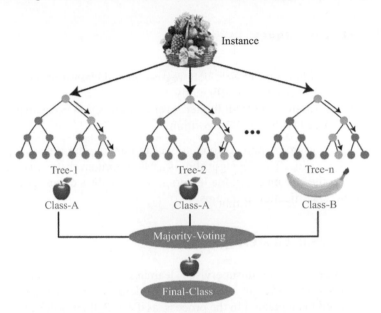

Regression in RFs: Regression is the other task being accomplished through the RF algorithm. The RF regression follows the concept of simple regression. Values of dependent (features) and independent variables are passed in the RF model.

There are simplifying frameworks to run RF regressions. In a RF regression, each tree produces a specific prediction. The mean prediction of the individual trees is the output of the regression. This is quite contrary to RF classification, whose output is determined by the mode of the DTs' class. Although RF regression and linear regression follow the same concept, they differ in terms of functions. The function of linear regression is $y = bx + c$, where y is the dependent variable, x is the independent variable, b is the estimation parameter, and c is a constant. The function of a complex RF regression is like a black box.

16.16   RF applications

- Banking: RF is used in banking to predict the creditworthiness of a loan applicant. This helps the lending institution make a good decision on whether to give the customer the loan or not. Banks also use the RF algorithm to detect fraudsters.
- *Health care*: Health professionals use RF systems to diagnose patients. Patients are diagnosed by assessing their previous medical history. Past medical records are reviewed to establish the right dosage for the patients.

- *Stock market*: Financial analysts use this algorithm to identify potential markets for stocks. It also enables them to identify the behavior of stocks.
- *E-commerce*: Through RF algorithms, e-commerce vendors can predict the preference of customers based on past consumption behavior.

16.17   RF advantages

- The RF algorithm can perform both regression and classification tasks.
- It can handle large datasets efficiently.
- The RF algorithm provides a higher level of accuracy in predicting outcomes when compared with the DT algorithm.

Typically, RF consumes more computational resources. The time complexity is also on the higher side. The RF algorithm is a ML algorithm that is easy to use and flexible. It uses the proven ensemble learning, which enables organizations to solve regression and classification problems.

16.18   K-Means clustering

K-Means clustering is an unsupervised learning algorithm, which groups the unlabeled dataset into different clusters. Here, K defines the number of pre-defined clusters that need to be created in the process, as if $K = 2$, there will be two clusters, and for $K = 3$, there will be three clusters, and so on. It is an iterative algorithm that divides the unlabeled dataset into k different clusters in such a way that each dataset belongs to only one group that has similar properties (https://www.javatpoint.com/k-means-clustering-algorithm-in-machine-learning).

It allows us to cluster the data into different groups and provides a convenient way to discover the categories of groups in the unlabeled dataset on its own without the need for any training. It is a centroid-based algorithm, where each cluster is associated with a centroid. The main aim of this algorithm is to minimize the sum of distances between the data points and their corresponding clusters.

22.3M
381
Hello Java Program for Beginners

The algorithm takes the unlabeled dataset as input, divides the dataset into k-number of clusters, and repeats the process until it does not find the best clusters. The value of k should be predetermined in this algorithm. The k-means clustering algorithm mainly performs two tasks:

- Determines the best value for k-center points or centroids by an iterative process.
- Assigns each data point to its closest k-center. Those data points which are near to the particular k-center create a cluster.

Hence, each cluster has data points with some commonalities, and it is away from other clusters.

The following diagram explains the working of the K-means clustering algorithm:

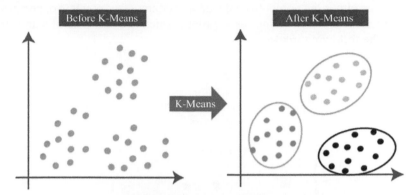

The working of the K-Means algorithm is explained in the below steps:

- **Step 1:** Select the number K to decide the number of clusters.
- **Step 2:** Select random K points or centroids.
- **Step 3:** Assign each data point to their closest centroid, which will form the predefined K clusters.
- **Step 4:** Calculate the variance and place a new centroid of each cluster.
- **Step 5:** Repeat the third step, which means reassign each data point to the new closest centroid for each cluster.
- **Step 6:** If any reassignment occurs, then go to step 4 else go to FINISH.
- **Step 7:** The model is ready.
- Suppose we have two variables, M1 and M2. The x–y-axis scatter plot of these two variables is given below:

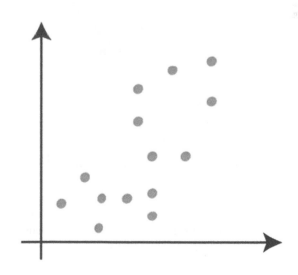

Let us take the number k of clusters, i.e., *K*=2, to identify the dataset and to put them into different clusters. It means here we will try to group these datasets into two different clusters.

We need to choose some random k points or centroid to form the cluster. These points can be either the points from the dataset or any other points. So, here we are selecting the below two points as *k* points, which are not part of our dataset. Consider the following image:

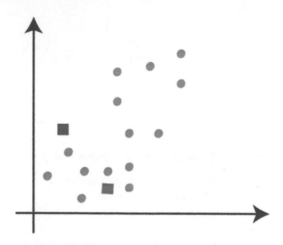

Now we will assign each data point of the scatter plot to its closest K-point or centroid. So, we will draw a median between both the centroids. Consider the below image:

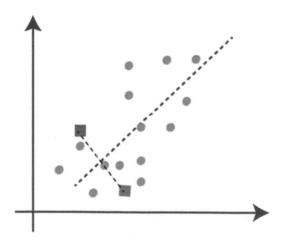

It is clear that points on the left side of the line are near to the K1 or blue centroid, and points to the right of the line are close to the yellow centroid. Let us color them as blue and yellow for clear visualization.

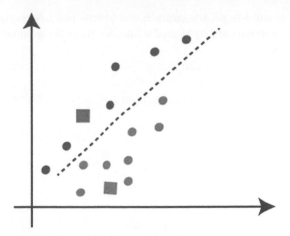

As we need to find the closest cluster, so we will repeat the process by choosing a new centroid. To choose the new centroids, we will compute the center of gravity of these centroids and will find new centroids as shown below:

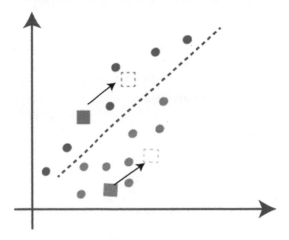

Next, we will reassign each data point to the new centroid. For this, we will repeat the same process of finding a median line. The median will be like below image:

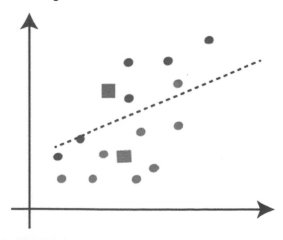

From the above image, we can see one yellow point is on the left side of the line, and two blue points are right on the line. So, these three points will be assigned to new centroids.

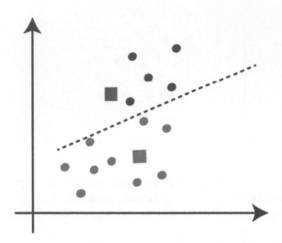

As reassignment has taken place, so we will again go to the step 4, which is finding new centroids or *K*-points.

We will repeat the process by finding the center of gravity of centroids, so the new centroids will be as shown in image.

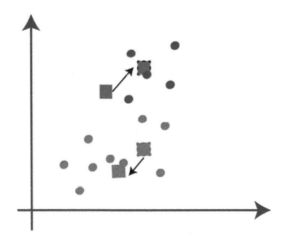

As we got the new centroids, so again we will draw the median line and reassign the data points. So, the image will be as below:

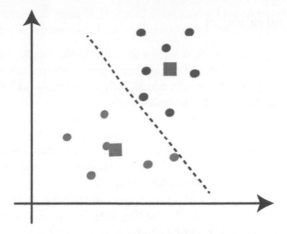

We can see in the above image; there are no dissimilar data points on either side of the line, which means our model is formed. Consider the below image.

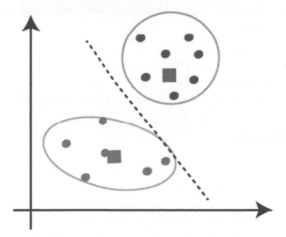

As our model is ready, so we can now remove the assumed centroids, and the two final clusters will be as shown in the below image.

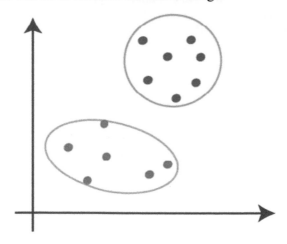

16.19   The advantages

- *Customer segmentation*: Let us assume the bank simply wants to segment based on income and debt. They gathered client information and visualized it using a scatter plot. This works across industry verticals, including telecom, e-commerce, sports, advertising, sales, etc.

   (https://www.analyticsvidhya.com/blog/2019/08/comprehensive-guide-k-means-clustering/)
- *Document clustering*: Let us imagine we have many papers and want to group them together. Clustering allows us to organize these papers such that comparable documents are grouped together.
- *Image segmentation*: In this case, we are attempting to group pixels in the image that are comparable. Clustering may be used to form clusters with comparable pixels in the same group.
- *Recommendation engines*: Let us suppose we wish to provide our pals' song recommendations. We may look at that person's favorite songs, then use clustering to discover songs that are similar, and lastly propose the most comparable music.

In summary, *K*-means is a centroid-based or distance-based technique in which the distances between points are calculated to allocate a point to a cluster. Each cluster in K-Means is paired with a centroid. The *K*-Means algorithm's primary goal is to reduce the sum of distances between points and their corresponding cluster centroid.

16.20   Conclusion

It is not an exaggeration to state that the contributions of ML algorithms, frameworks, accelerators, and platforms in replicating human brain functions into all sorts of IT products, solutions, and services are gleefully immense. Besides, all kinds of everyday personal, professional, and social devices, gadgets, handhelds, wearables, portables, mobiles, etc., are being embedded with tiny ML libraries to expose and exhibit intelligent actions and reactions. Thus, ML plays a vital role in shaping up the AI domain. This chapter is planned and produced to clearly articulate and accentuate the popular ML algorithms and how they come in handy in accomplishing automated data analytics. ML algorithms are skilled in automatically learning from data heaps and, hence, the field of ML is highly significant and sensible for the data science domain.

Reference

[1]   Norman, M. *Statistical Regression and Classification: From Linear Models to Machine Learning*, London: Chapman and Hall/CRC Press, 2017.

Index